SLINGIN'
SAM

SLINGIN'

THE LIFE AND TIMES

OF THE GREATEST

QUARTERBACK EVER

TO PLAY THE GAME

SAM

BY JOE HOLLEY

FOREWORD BY
Peyton Manning

UNIVERSITY OF TEXAS PRESS ⤜⤏ AUSTIN

Publication of this book was aided by the generous support of Cathy and Dwight Thompson.

Requests for permission to reproduce material from this work should be sent to:
    Permissions
    University of Texas Press
    P.O. Box 7819
    Austin, TX 78713-7819
    www.utexas.edu/utpress/about/bpermission.html

♾ The paper used in this book meets the minimum requirements of ANSI/NISO Z39.48-1992 (R1997) (Permanence of Paper).

LIBRARY OF CONGRESS CATALOGING-IN-PUBLICATION DATA

Holley, Joe.
    Slingin' Sam : the life and times of the greatest quarterback ever to play the game / by Joe Holley ; foreword by Peyton Manning.
      p.   cm.
    Includes bibliographical references and index.
    ISBN 978-0-292-71985-9 (hardback) — ISBN 978-0-292-74213-0 (e-book)
    1. Baugh, Sam, 1914–2008   2. Football players—United States—Biography.
    3. Quarterbacks (Football)—United States—Biography.   I. Title.
    GV939.B39H65   2012
    796.332092—dc23
    [B]
                                                2012013003

In memory of my dad, H. M. Holley, who introduced my brothers and me to Slingin' Sam

CONTENTS

FOREWORD

I n a small workout room in the basement of our Indianapolis home is what I call my quarterbacks wall. Hanging on it are nearly thirty photos I've collected over the years of me standing beside the game's best signal-callers, including several I've been privileged to play against.

Scanning the collection, you'll find many of the great ones: Troy Aikman, Brett Favre, Dan Marino, Steve Young, John Elway, Phil Simms, Jim Kelly, Warren Moon, Bart Starr, Roger Staubach, Terry Bradshaw, George Blanda. I like to glance at those guys while I'm working out.

You'll also find photos of my two all-time favorite quarterbacks—my dad Archie Manning and my brother Eli—as well as one of my all-time non-family favorites: Johnny Unitas of the Baltimore Colts.

I knew about Johnny Unitas from stories my dad told me, and every time I look at the photo, I think of the opportunity I had a few years back to let Johnny know in person how much I admired and respected him. In 1997 I was the recipient of the Johnny Unitas Golden Arm Award, and at the banquet that year I presented the Hall of Famer with a pair of black high-top football shoes. Anyone who had the privilege of watching number 19 play will know exactly what those shoes symbolize.

Now, take a closer look at the wall. Focus in on a place of honor near the center of my quarterback collection. You'll see a photo of an elderly man in a baseball cap and sweatpants sitting on a bench outside on a bright, sunny day; at his side is a barefoot young man in shorts and a golf shirt. The two men are laughing, obviously enjoying each other's company. That picture holds a special place in my heart.

The young man is me; the older is Slingin' Sammy Baugh, arguably the greatest quarterback ever to play the game. Even more important to me, he was a man I was proud to call a friend. As you'll come to know in the pages that follow, Sam Baugh was not only a great athlete but also one of the finest guys you'd ever want to meet.

Let me tell you how I came to know him. In the late summer of 2000, shortly before training camp opened for my third NFL season, I got a call from *Sports Illustrated*. The magazine was planning to run a story that would spotlight two NFL players at each position—the player they felt had defined the position during the twentieth century and the player who would lead it into the twenty-first. Sam and I were their picks at quarterback.

I was honored to be chosen, of course, but one of the stipulations was that the new player had to visit the home of the old, which presented a bit of a challenge. We had to do it quickly because of the magazine's deadline and because teams were about to go to training camp. I ended up going to see Sam in a hearse. (More about that later.)

I had heard of Slingin' Sammy Baugh. I knew he had played for the Redskins, knew he had been a great passer and was in the NFL Hall of Fame, but I didn't know much more than that. I called my dad and told him how excited I was about being chosen and how I was looking forward to meeting a bona fide football legend.

I asked him what he knew about Sam, and he reminded me that not only had Sam been an All-American at TCU and a Redskins star for many years, he also had been a magnificent punter and had played defensive back. Needless to say, times have changed.

I was familiar with Horned Frog football from an earlier era, having won the Davey O'Brien Award as a senior at the University of Tennessee. O'Brien, of course, was Sam's Heisman-winning successor at TCU. I've been back to the annual banquet several times since and have gotten to know the O'Brien family, but I was eager to learn more about Sam.

Dad said we also had almost a family connection to Slingin' Sam. One of the great influences on my dad's life was Johnny Vaught, the legendary coach at Ole Miss during my dad's playing days. Coach Vaught had been Sam's teammate at TCU in the 1930s.

Dad said that Coach Vaught thought highly of Sammy Baugh and used to tell stories about his exploits. Dad said he also had heard about how, when

Sam himself became a coach—at Hardin-Simmons—he would come out at halftime during games and hold punting and passing clinics. Fans were almost as eager to see the old Redskins quarterback's pinpoint passing and precision punting as they were to see the game itself. Not something you see every day, right?

Anyway, *Sports Illustrated* told me I would have to get to Rotan, Texas, for the photo shoot. I had no idea where Rotan was, but the magazine told me I could hitch a ride on the private plane that was ferrying the film crew to West Texas. They would pick me up in New Orleans, and then we would fly together to Snyder, not far from Sam's ranch near Rotan.

The plan worked perfectly until we got to Snyder and couldn't find a vehicle big enough to transport the six-person film and photo crew, all the equipment, and myself. That's how we ended up piling into the biggest car in town, a long, black hearse, to get to Sam's Double Mountain Ranch. I made sure I didn't sit in the back.

I'll never forget that day at the ranch. It was just a very, very special day for me.

Throughout the day, while the film crews were setting up, Sam and I got to visit with each other, just the two of us. I got to ask him about O'Brien, about Coach Vaught. I asked what it was like playing in Washington during the '40s. I remember I asked him whether he had met any presidents during his playing days.

He told me he didn't give much thought to Washington, D.C., or politics, or presidents. He was there to play football, to do the best he could. Once the season was over, he would pack his bags and head home to Rotan to ride horses and rope and be a cowboy. Life on the ranch was his passion, that and football.

Here's what else I remember: Sam Baugh was a world champion cusser and tobacco-chewer. He usually had his spitter right beside him. Fortunately, he could hit that coffee can as accurately as he could hit a receiver during his playing days.

I also learned that he was a man who knew his own mind and wasn't afraid to express it. At one point during the day, one of the photographers came over to us with an idea. "Sammy," he said, "I'd like to get the two of y'all pitching horseshoes together."

That was fine with me but not with Sam. "I don't pitch horseshoes," Sammy told him.

"Well, you know, Sammy, just kind of for the picture, we thought it would be kind of neat having two quarterbacks throwing horseshoes," the photographer said, all the while getting his camera ready for the shoot.

Sammy aimed a stream of tobacco at the grass (not at the photographer) and looked up at the man. "I don't know if you couldn't hear me the first time," he said. "I don't pitch horseshoes."

That was the end of that.

In the photo that ran in the magazine, Sam is chewing tobacco and I'm sitting beside him drinking iced tea. The "Mail Pouch" chewing tobacco thermometer on the wall of the shed behind us registers 105 degrees. We're just sort of sitting there shooting the bull about football and whatever else came to mind. It was, to me, a more appropriate picture than us pitching horseshoes would have been.

A friend of Sam's, Bob O'Day, told me that the Cotton Bowl people had been after Sam for years to come back to Dallas for a ceremony. (He and his fellow Horned Frogs played in the inaugural Cotton Bowl game.) Sam would always tell them, "Just move that Cotton Bowl to Rotan, and I'll be there in a heartbeat."

Once again, it kind of told you who he was. He was a man who, as long as it didn't hurt anybody, was going to do things his way.

Sam told me that day at the ranch that he still enjoyed football and especially liked watching Troy Aikman, the superb quarterback of the Dallas Cowboys. He also told me he enjoyed watching me play. From that day on, he said, he would follow my career even more closely. That made me feel good.

I left the ranch that day—in the hearse—with great respect for Sam Baugh. I never saw him again, but we stayed in touch.

Sam died eight years later, on December 17, 2008. That next Sunday we played Jacksonville, and on my wristband I wrote "SB," in tribute to my friend. As it turned out, I had a Sammy Baugh–quality day against the Jaguars: 17 straight completions to open the game, 29 of 34 completions overall for 364 yards, three touchdowns in a game that clinched a playoff spot for us.

"I was slinging it tonight," I remember telling reporters. "We were slinging it tonight."

Who knows, maybe somewhere up above that evening, Sammy Baugh was smiling—and, I'm guessing, slingin' a couple of affectionate cuss words my way as well. Sammy Baugh was quite a guy.

Peyton Manning
Indianapolis, Indiana

ACKNOWLEDGMENTS

When I think of all the people who have helped me get to know Sammy Baugh, I think immediately of Jeanne O'Neill. She was eighty-six when I met her in the parking lot of FedEx Field, where she and friends enjoyed tailgating at almost every Washington Redskins home game. Both elegant and fun-loving, the retired U.S. Postal Service executive had seen Sammy play, and when I mentioned his name, she smiled—as did almost everyone else who talked to me about the old football player turned Texas cowboy. Like Jeanne O'Neill, they were happy to share their stories. I thank them.

I am grateful to my friends at the *Washington Post* who encouraged me to tell Sammy's story, including Emilio Garcia-Ruiz, Lynn Medford, Matt Vita, Matt Schudel, Pat Sullivan, and Adam Bernstein. Although this is not an authorized biography, the Baugh family was a huge help, particularly David and Jean Baugh, who sat down over David's daily ham sandwiches at the kitchen table and talked candidly about the man who had meant so much to them. I am grateful to Sam's old friends Bob O'Day, Sonny Nichols, Pete Hart, and many others who were willing to share their reminiscences.

Thanks to my brother Ken, who made the long drive with me to Rotan and the Double Mountain Ranch and who offered suggestions and ideas throughout the writing of this book. Thanks also to my children—Heather, Rachel, Pete, and Kate—for their love and encouragement.

At the University of Texas Press, my old friend David Hamrick was quick to see the need for a biography of Sammy Baugh, and my editor, Allison Faust, was a sure and steady guide throughout the long process. Kip Keller, an old football player himself, copyedited the manuscript with care and precision. Thanks also to Lynne Chapman.

I owe a debt of gratitude to Bill Miller, who works his magic around the Capitol in Austin almost daily, and who came through for me in a big way. And thanks to Peyton Manning, who was willing to share his memories of Sam, despite a trying time for himself and his Indianapolis Colts.

And finally, Laura. She was good-natured and patient (sort of) when I was chained to the computer, ever encouraging when I got bogged down, and always willing to talk about the book when that was what I needed. She had so many great ideas, it almost became a joke between us. I am grateful.

PROLOGUE

C hicago. A dreary December afternoon so cold that anyone who dares to venture out runs the risk of frostbite, or worse. A punishing wind off frozen Lake Michigan only adds to the misery. The city is shut down, closed up, as Chicagoans seek warmth behind closed doors and boarded-up windows.

On the North Side, though, home to Wrigley Field, some 15,000 football fans have braved the dangerous conditions to watch a game, a National Football League championship game between the fearsome Chicago Bears and the upstart Washington Redskins. Swaddled in layered coats and mufflers, wearing gloves, hats pulled down over their ears, these fans are fanatics in every sense of the word. Some caught the elevated train and rode it through a desolate downtown, the train winding its way through the canyon of tall buildings blocking out a pallid sun. Others rode streetcars past mounds of snow shoved out of roadways. Still others maneuvered Model Ts, slowly and carefully, through the icy streets.

The locals have come to see their Bears, the "Monsters of the Midway," a team of hard-nosed, big-shouldered brawlers who not only defeat their opponents almost every Sunday but also punish them in the process. Chicagoans like to think that the Bears of George Halas and Bronko Nagurski and George Musso truly embody their big, tough, hog-butcher-to-the-world metropolis.

Several thousand fans are there from out of town. They boarded a special train in Washington's Union Station and headed west. Disembarking at Chicago's LaSalle Street Station, fortified against the cold by flasks of alcohol stashed away in their overcoats, they hailed cabs to take them to the tidy brick ballpark that baseball's Chicago Cubs have made famous. Their Redskins are completing their first season in Washington, but already the capital city has taken them to its heart.

Years later, the NFL championship game will be called the Super Bowl. Years later, millions of football fans around the world will gather in front of their televisions to witness the spectacle. Advertisers will pay millions for a few minutes of viewing-audience time. On this cold day in Chicago, fewer than 20,000 football fans, their very sanity in question, are on hand to witness one of the pivotal games in NFL history.

Shortly after noon, the two teams take the field for the kickoff, the Bears in their dark blue jerseys trimmed in orange, the Redskins wearing their trademark burgundy and gold. Both teams wear tennis shoes, hoping to get whatever purchase they can on the ice-encrusted field. Mist from their breathing is visible in the frigid air.

The tall, spindly-legged Texan who ambles onto the frozen turf of Wrigley Field on that dreary Sunday afternoon has played in miserable weather before. The pride of Sweetwater, Texas, he has known northers that barrel across the plains with little warning, straight from the Canadian Arctic. As a high school senior four years earlier, he played in a blizzard, with driving snow and sleet pelting players and fans alike. But he has never played in temperatures so frigid that it hurts to breathe, so cold that hands and fingers ache and barely move, so cold that it is actually dangerous to be outdoors. He has never played on turf so hard and brittle that it rips bare skin like a cheese grater whenever someone hits the ground.

Backed up against his own goal line the first time the Redskins get the ball, young Sam Baugh looks around the huddle, ten men snorting steam in the punishing cold. He glances over the helmeted heads of his teammates, sees the mob of blue-shirted Bears waiting impatiently at the line of scrimmage to tear him apart. Literally. That is their game plan—hurt him any way they can, send him to the sidelines, knock him out of the game.

The Bears know he is special; so do his Redskin teammates. From the moment he rifled a bullet pass to a teammate in the team's first scrimmage—"Which eye, Coach?"—the Redskins knew they had something. And now, four months later, their confidence has been confirmed.

Although he is barely out of college, he has gained his teammates' respect during the long season, a season that has culminated in this moment, this championship game. They wait for his instructions. He glances over at Riley Smith, the Redskins' signal caller. (Sam is actually the tailback in the Redskins' single-wing formation.) Smith hears him out.

"Let's trick 'em," he suggests in his Texas drawl. "I'll drop into punt formation. But I won't punt." He glances at stellar running back Cliff Battles. "See that chunk of ice right over there?" he says, nodding toward a white spot on the yellowed grass. "Run straight to it, cut to the sideline and look for the ball."

The Redskins break their huddle and line up in punt formation. The Bears aren't surprised, since punting on first down is standard strategy when a team finds itself bottled up in its own end of the field. The Bears know that Sam is also one of the best punters in the game, possibly the best.

Smith calls the signals and Sam waits for the snap, his face beneath the leather helmet red and raw. His cold hands received the ball, but instead of stepping into it with his strong right leg, he wraps his long fingers around it, feeling for the laces as he rolls to the right behind the goal line and looks downfield for Battles. The Redskin running back, running as fast as he can on the frozen field, carefully sets his pivot foot and cuts in front of a Bear safety, Gene Ronzani. As Ronzani slips on the ice, the Redskin halfback gathers in the Baugh toss over his right shoulder and motors up the sideline for a forty-two-yard gain.

Although the Bears hold shortly afterward, the pass from the end zone delivers a message: the Redskins' brilliant young passer isn't going to allow the elements to dictate strategy. Neither the weather nor the fearsome Bears can scare him.

SLINGIN' SAM

Sammy happens to be just about the most valuable football player of all time, according to most pro coaches I've talked to.

—SPORTSWRITER
GRANTLAND RICE, 1942

I still think he was the greatest quarterback who ever lived, college or pro.

—SPORTSWRITER
DAN JENKINS, 2006

In two hours, Sammy Baugh gave me the finishing touches for Augustus McCrae [in Lonesome Dove], and he didn't even know it.

—ACTOR ROBERT
DUVALL, 2006

INTRODUCTION

S am was his name. Sam Baugh. Not Sammy and certainly not Slingin'
Sammy. It isn't that he spurned the inspired appellation—coined by
the longtime *Fort Worth Star-Telegram* sportswriter Amos Melton—
but "Sam Baugh," a good, simple, common name, reflected how he saw
himself. To his friends, to his family, to himself, he was just plain "Sam."
(That was also how he signed his autographs; "Slingin' Sammy Baugh" took
too long.)

He was a man easy to like. Throughout his life—in college, as a big-time
pro football player, as a West Texas rancher—people gravitated to him.

Recalling Sam Baugh years later, a fellow TCU student named Ed Prich-
ard told the sportswriter Whit Canning: "He was our idol—our hero—but
we were never in awe of him, because he was also our good friend. He got
along with people very well—with everybody—and on the field he was a
good leader."

Joe Tereshinksi, an end on Washington Redskin teams of the late 1940s,
echoed that assessment. "He was our leader," Tereshinski told me in 2008.
"We all looked up to Sam."

"I loved Sam Baugh, not because he was a superstar, but because he was
a super person," Bob O'Day told me one hot July afternoon as we sat in his
living room in Snyder, Texas. O'Day, the retired golf coach at Western Texas

College in Snyder, was Sam's regular golfing partner for nearly twenty years. Tears welled up and his voice grew husky when he recalled his old friend.

O'Day told me one Sam Baugh story after another, including stories about his friend's salty language. Sam was one of the most gloriously profane men who ever lived. He couldn't utter a sentence—whatever the time, whatever the circumstance—without punctuating it with a cuss word or two, or three. He was never obscene, never malicious, his niece Ellen Stevenson was quick to remind me. "That's just Sam," Stevenson said, a phrase I heard time after time from friends and family.

He was a masterly storyteller, and when he got wound up, his hands were in perpetual motion, sometimes slapping his thigh for emphasis, and he would laugh now and then at the freshness of his memories. He always had a chaw of tobacco in his cheek (Red Man, not Skoal, even though his old friend Walt Garrison once sent him a case of Skoal).

Sam's son David recalled a summer Sunday morning years ago when Sam accompanied his wife, Edmonia, and the five Baugh kids to services at the First United Methodist Church in Rotan, Texas, the town nearest the Baugh family ranch. As the service droned on toward the end, Sam's mind began to drift to thoughts of horses and calves and the roping scheduled for after lunch. He felt a sharp poke in the ribs from Edmonia (Sam called her "Mona").

"The preacher just asked you to give the benediction," she whispered.

Sam stared down the row at the five younger Baughs, all leaning forward, all staring at him—and all wondering not only whether he was awake but also whether he could go to the Lord in prayer without uttering a cuss word. As David recalled, his dad, as usual, came through in the clutch.

"That's just Sam," Bob O'Day said, laughing, as he recounted the same story. O'Day, a deeply religious man and a member of the Gideon Society (the people who supply Bibles to hotel rooms) was willing to give his friend a pass when it came to taking the name of the Lord in vain. "His assets certainly outweighed his liabilities," O'Day said, his mind drifting to the happy times they spent together for nearly thirty years.

I saw Sam Baugh twice, the first time when I was a kid. On a Saturday morning in the mid-1950s, Dad woke my two younger brothers and me earlier than usual. Mom fixed us breakfast, and we drove to Holt's Sporting Goods across Fifth Street from the courthouse in downtown Waco. Holt's was where we bought our baseball gloves and bats every spring, our football equipment in the fall. All three of us were too young to play on school teams, but like most Texas youngsters, we played in the backyard every afternoon and during recess at school, so we had to have equipment. We enjoyed our trips to Holt's, enjoyed pawing over the brightly colored jerseys hanging on racks, enjoyed breathing in the new-leather smell of baseball gloves, footballs, basketballs.

On this morning, though, we weren't going to Holt's to buy. We were going to pay homage, although Kenny and Steve and I didn't know that was what we were doing. In the football section, toward the back of the store, surrounded by brand-new jerseys, helmets, and shoulder pads, we were ushered into the presence of a tall dark-haired man in a tan sport coat and slacks who, as I remember, was standing around talking football with some of the Holt's salesmen.

"Boys, meet Slingin' Sammy Baugh," Dad said, giving us a gentle shove forward.

What Sammy Baugh was doing in Waco on that Saturday morning, I don't know, although I suspect his Hardin-Simmons University Cowboys— he was head coach—were playing the Baylor Bears at Baylor Stadium that night, and he had dropped by Holt's for a personal appearance. Maybe Dad had read about his being there in the *Waco Times-Herald*.

His lean face crinkling into a smile, the tall man leaned down and shook our hands and signed an autograph for us. Unlike the treasured Mickey Mantle autograph we got in Dallas a few years later, we promptly lost Sammy Baugh's.

Although we were big sports fans, we had no idea who he was. We didn't know that he had been the quarterback of the Washington Redskins for sixteen seasons, that he was arguably the greatest passer ever to play the game.

Soon, though, as I got a little older and started going to high school football games, I began hearing the name. I began to understand who Sammy Baugh was and what he stood for.

What Babe Ruth's home runs did for Major League Baseball in the 1920s, Sam Baugh's passing did for the National Football League a decade or so later. "Ruth was more Bunyanesque," the sportswriter Tom Boswell once wrote, "more outside the parameters of previous imagination. But Baugh wasn't too far behind."

Like Ruth, he remained, for decades, the epitome of excellence for his particular sport. It is 1955, say, and a kid on the playground rears back and heaves a long pass downfield. Regardless of whether he completes it, his teammates chide his audacity. "Hey, who do you think you are, Sammy Baugh?" they'll say.

Sportswriters every fall assess the latest crop of Texas schoolboy passers, and the standard they used for decades was Sammy Baugh—Slingin' Sammy Baugh. For years, he remained an icon, to be gradually superseded in the fans' imaginations only when a young Johnny Unitas led the Baltimore Colts to victory over the New York Giants in the 1958 championship game in what would come to be called "the greatest game ever played." Or maybe when, nearly a decade later, a brash young quarterback named "Broadway" Joe Namath led his New York Jets to an improbable Super Bowl victory over the Colts.

The name and the memories began to fade, of course, as the years went by, as the game evolved, as new faces captured public attention, and as television magnified their fame in ways Sammy himself could never have imagined when he was playing. But Sammy's accomplishments on the football field didn't fade. They remain as astounding today as they were three-quarters of a century ago when he was a tall, gangly quarterback with a whiplike arm and a limber right leg that could kick a ball a mile.

In his sixteen seasons in the NFL—a long career by pro football standards—Sammy led the Washington Redskins to five title games and two NFL championships. He led the league in passing six times, in punting four times, and in interceptions once. (From his defensive safety position, he was the intercepter, not the interceptee.) His career punting average was more than 45 yards, but from 1940 through 1942, it was close to 50 yards (49.5). Before Sam, only one man had passed for 1,000 yards in a season. In 1947, Sam completed 210 passes for 2,938 yards—both marks that simply obliterated old records. Like Ruth, who changed the very perception of the game of baseball and how it was played, Sam transformed the notion of offense and how much yardage could be gained through the air.

In a game against the Detroit Lions in 1943, he threw four touchdown passes—and caught four interceptions. (That was the year he led the league in interceptions, with eleven.) During several seasons early in his career, he played every minute of every game.

"He really had a rifle for an arm," the sportswriter Dan Jenkins told me in 2006. "He could throw sidearm and underhanded along with it. He was tough and wiry, probably the greatest punter who ever lived as well. Plus, he liked to jaw around and kid with the zebras [referees], even in college, and certainly he was a leader."

Before Sam, professional football was at the periphery of American sports. With a limited fan base drawn exclusively from the Northeast and upper Midwest, and with few economically viable franchises, the pros were overshadowed by the Saturday-afternoon heroics of college teams. Football fans wanted to read about Harvard-Yale, Army-Navy, Notre Dame—or, in the Southwest, SMU-TCU—not the Boston Redskins or the Portsmouth Spartans. The former collegians who continued to play the game at the professional level didn't make enough money to make football their full-time job.

Sam was the bridge between the leather-helmet era and the modern. Not only was he professional football's most popular player, but he also was a superb athlete who revolutionized how the game was played.

Before Sam Baugh, football closely resembled rugby, with tightly packed linemen trying to open holes for ball carriers running primarily between tackles on a tighter field without hash marks. Confident enough to throw the ball from any spot on the field, on any down, Sam wrenched football free from its sclerotic past and made it a hell of a lot more fun to watch.

By the thousands, football fans in the nation's capital, in New York, in Chicago, wherever the pros played the game, saw what the tall slender Texan could do with a football—on offense and on defense, with his arm and his leg—and they decided they liked what they saw. They liked the way the rawboned young athlete from the wide-open spaces of West Texas opened up the playing field and made the forward pass a strategic weapon, not a desperation heave. They liked his gambler's instincts. They thrilled in delicious anticipation of multiple possibilities when the ball was in his hands.

The TCU all-American, a product of Sweetwater, Texas, changed the game almost instantaneously, beginning with his rookie season in 1937, when the twenty-two-year-old Texan took the Redskins to the NFL title, beating the Chicago Bears, the Monsters of the Midway, on their home field.

If football fans around the country weren't aware of Slingin' Sammy Baugh before, they were that day. On the first play of the game, he dared to throw from his own end zone to all-pro halfback Cliff Battles for forty-two yards. Down 21–14 in the fourth quarter, he looked one way and threw the other to his end, Wayne Millner, for seventy-seven yards and a score, then got the winning touchdown on a thirty-five-yarder to Ed Justice. Earlier in the half, he threw a fifty-five-yard touchdown to Millner. All this on his one healthy leg; the other had been almost broken in two by ruthless, rampaging Bears.

In 1937, when Sam Baugh entered the league as a rookie, a 47.4 percent completion percentage was good for tops in the league. He was that 47.4 percent passer, incidentally. And indeed, for nine of his sixteen seasons, he was the most accurate passer in the NFL; in two other seasons he was second. In 1945, he completed more than 70 percent of his passes, then a first for the NFL. His feat went unmatched for some thirty-seven years until Ken Anderson of the Cincinnati Bengals finally broke Sam's record in 1982.

He also led the league in punting for four straight years, and in another championship game against the Bears, he got off a punt that traveled eighty-five yards. In 1940, he averaged an NFL record 51.4 yards on his punts and was the master of the third-down quick kick, a tactical tool no longer used.

Sam still holds or is tied for six Redskin records: most touchdown passes in a career, 187; best punting average in a career, 45.1 yards; most passing yards in a game, 446; most touchdown passes in a game, 6; best punting average in a season, 51.4 yards; and most passes intercepted in a game, 4.

In a game against the New York Giants in 1943, he threw two touchdown passes, ran seventy-one yards with an intercepted pass, batted down two Giants passes in the end zone, and made seven tackles. A pretty good afternoon's work.

Almost from the day he entered the National Football League, the big number 33 on Sam's back was the biggest gate attraction in professional football. He made quarterback the glamour position, which means that Unitas, Namath, Brett Favre, Donovan McNabb, the Manning brothers, and all the other football field generals since Sam are in his debt (as are the fans, of course). During the 1940s, he was on a par in the public mind with Joltin' Joe DiMaggio, Bill Tilden, and Joe Louis.

The longtime political columnist David Broder, my esteemed colleague at the *Washington Post*, recalled a midwestern senator of another era who, some time in his third term, was heard to ask a colleague, "Who is this man Sammy Baugh that people keep talking about?" The story got around town and eventually back to the unnamed senator's home state, and in Broder's words, "the fellow was deservedly defeated the next time he was up for reelection."

Through it all, Sam Baugh kept a steady head on his shoulders, kept his accomplishments in perspective. Beyond the gridiron exploits as a Hall of Fame quarterback, all-pro safety, and record-setting punter, beyond the glamour that came with being the biggest name in the game, he fashioned another life, one he found even more satisfying than his football career. Like a movie cowboy riding off into the sunset, he decided to chuck it all in the early 1960s. Retiring as a player and coach, he left behind the gridiron glory, a possible movie career, and the money. He never looked back.

Nearly thirty years after the Redskin impresario George Preston Marshall sold Washington fans on the notion that the tall, lean Texan was a rootin'-tootin' cowboy—never mind that he had grown up in town, gone to college in Fort Worth, and was more preppy than pastoral—he became a genuine Texas cowboy. For nearly fifty years, until his body wore out, he lived in far West Texas on his Double Mountain Ranch near Rotan. On a flat

sea of scrub brush beneath two great rock peaks, where the only hardy vegetation is mesquite trees and prickly pear, he raised his cattle and horses,
made himself a champion roper, and reveled in the wide-open spaces.

That was where I found him, a half century or so after that long-ago
Saturday morning when he signed an autograph for my brothers and me
in Waco. As a staff writer for the *Post*, I was writing "Redskins Journal," a
weekly column during football season that took me to varied Washington-
area venues during Redskin games—a bar, a restaurant, the Walter Reed
Army Medical Center, a firehouse. I watched the game with fans and wrote
their particular stories.

One cold Sunday morning, I was wandering around the vast parking lot
of FedEx Field, the Redskins' home stadium, where two hours before game
time, thousands of fans were tailgating, sitting in lawn chairs or on pickup
tailgates, barbecuing ribs or charcoaling burgers and maybe tossing back
a brew or two, or three. Youngsters were flinging footballs back and forth
between lines of parked cars until it was time to troop into the stadium and
cheer for the burgundy and gold.

Notebook and pen at the ready, my "Redskins Journal" question for the
day was what Washington player of yore would fans love to see still with
the team. Many of the answers were predictable—Hall of Fame quarterback
Sonny Jurgensen was still immensely popular, as were Hall of Fame wide
receiver Charley Taylor and defensive back Darrell Green. I was astounded,
though, at how often a fan would answer with the name of a player who
hadn't taken the field in more than half a century—Slingin' Sammy Baugh.

The older ones, invariably, had a story to tell about being in the stands
when he intercepted four passes or got off a mind-boggling punt. One tail-
gater, seventy-seven-year-old Ray Augsterfer, wore a throwback leather
helmet in homage to his favorite player. Augsterfer, who lived in nearby
Annapolis, had been a thirteen-year-old in the stands for Baugh's very first
Redskin game in 1937, and he was there in '41 for his record-setting eighty-
five-yard punt.

"He was so much fun to watch," Jeanne McNeill told me that day. The
smartly dressed woman sitting on a lawn chair and nursing a gin and tonic
with friends was eighty-six, a retired U.S. Postal Service executive. She had
been a regular at Redskin home games since 1947, when the team played in
Griffith Stadium, the old Washington Senators baseball park. "He could do
everything—run, pass, kick," McNeill told me. "And he was a good guy too."

McNeill and Augsterfer and the other fans who recalled Sam that
morning would have seconded the view of the legendary *Washington Post*
sportswriter Shirley Povich, who wrote in 1994 in response to an official

announcement from the NFL that Sammy Baugh was one of four quarter-backs being acclaimed as the league's all-time, all-stars at that position: "No disrespect here to Johnny Unitas, Joe Montana and Otto Graham, who were bracketed with him in gross oversight of Baugh's patently superior credentials. They too were great quarterbacks, deserving of loud cheers. They evoked memories of Samuel Baugh, but not the reality of him. Simply put, they lacked his measure in so many skills."

But what had become of him? Was he still alive? None of the fans I talked to knew, and neither did any of the *Post* sportswriters. I persuaded my editors that we ought to find out, so one weekend in January, I flew back to Texas from my home in Washington, rented a car in Austin, and, with my brother Ken along for the ride, made the 300-mile drive to Sam's Double Mountain Ranch.

We filled up with gas in Abilene and then headed toward Rotan, eighty miles northwest. Not far from the Double Mountain Fork of the Brazos River, flat pastureland began to rumple up. The rocky, hard-packed ground was filigreed by canyons, ravines, and dry washes. Stubbled grass and mottes of dry mesquite were almost the only vegetation.

Sam's West Texas wasn't much to look at—at first glance, anyway—but like the coyotes, deer, jackrabbits, and wild turkeys that populate the vast area, the old football star took to it. For more than six decades, it had been home. The daily routines of the ranch, hard work outdoors, peace and quiet, even the extremes of West Texas weather—he found all of it deeply satisfying.

The ranch was still there, but Sam wasn't. His son David told us he had been moved to Jayton, thirty miles away. In a nursing home in the dusty little ranching town, where there seemed to be as many tumbleweeds as people, Kenny and I wandered into a simple room decorated with a child's drawing of a football player in the burgundy and gold uniform of the Washington Redskins.

Lying on his back, half-asleep on a single bed, was a gaunt gray-haired man who had been a resident for the past five years, since Alzheimer's disease had begun to erase the memories of nearly a century. Sam Baugh had no idea who we were, of course, but this time Kenny and I were certainly aware of who he was.

And people still remembered. He still got requests for autographs, still got cards and letters, including one from a Nebraska businessman, who dropped Sam a line not long after Kenny and I visited.

"Dear Sammy," he wrote.

When Dudley DeGroot was coaching the Redskins more than 60 years ago, I was sort of an assistant water boy for two Redskins games. This came about because my older sister was dating Dudley, Jr. and I made such a pest of myself that they decided to buy me off by letting me sit on the Redskins' bench. Then my sister broke up with Dudley and my career ended.

But I still remember the thrills of watching you play, not just for the passing but also for the punting and defensive interceptions.

Calling himself "a huge fan in Omaha" and wishing Sam the best, the letter writer signed his name: "Warren E. Buffett."

SAM BAUGH

⊰ THE BEGINNING ⊱

On a hot summer afternoon in 1933, on a hard-packed baseball field in West Texas, Dutch Meyer was watching his Texas Christian University Horned Frogs play a couple of practice games against a semi-pro town team in Abilene. Every summer the TCU coach would pick twelve Horned Frog players and barnstorm for part of the summer, driving around the Southwest in two cars the TCU team used for road trips, a Cadillac and a jump-seat Chevrolet. On this particular day, the team they were playing was the Mose Sims Oilers.

The Abilene team was made up mostly of guys in their twenties and thirties who had knocked around baseball for some years at various levels. Meyer, who also was an assistant football coach at TCU, couldn't take his eyes off a younger player, a tall, gangly high school kid playing third base for the Oilers.

"He had two great days against us," Meyer recalled years later. "He was quick as a cat, and the way he could throw that baseball—whew! And he could hit. I wanted him bad, but the trouble was I didn't have any baseball scholarships to offer him."

The kid's name was Baugh—Sam Baugh—and he had graduated from high school a few weeks earlier in Sweetwater, a town fifty miles northwest of Abilene. Meyer, the future Frog legend, may have wanted him for TCU, but the youngster wasn't even sure he was going to college. The Depression had hit West Texas hard, and jobs were hard to come by. Baugh's dad, who worked for the railroad in Sweetwater, thought he might be able to get his son a railroad job too if he was lucky.

The Baugh family was relatively new to Sweetwater—they had moved from the Central Texas town of Temple only three years earlier—but Baughs had been in Texas for three generations. Like many Texans, they were descended from southerners who had migrated to the Lone Star State.

The Baugh family originally settled in South Carolina in the 1760s. Sam's great-great-great-great-grandfather, John Baugh, with his wife Darcus Mitchell Baugh and nine children, moved to Georgia in the 1790s, where the couple farmed and were stalwart members of the Grove Level Baptist Church in Grove County, Georgia. Church records indicate that in 1822, two years after John Baugh's death, his wife was excluded from the congregation "for cursing, swearing and striking Mr. Savelle." Records don't say what caused the disagreement, but she was restored to fellowship five years later. (Perhaps Sam's penchant for cussing was genetic.)

William Baugh, the firstborn of John Baugh and Darcus Mitchell, fathered fifteen children and was married twice. A veteran of the War of 1812, he lived his whole life in Georgia and was known as an upright man and a successful, hardworking farmer, despite a war wound that left him with a disabled right hand.

A profile of William Baugh, found in "The History of Gwinnett County, Georgia," described him as "stern, solid and courageous even to his oddities. He was cool, not at all excitable, but calm and determined in all his purposes, and would resent an insult coming from whatever source it might."

William Baugh's anonymous profiler recalled that Baugh had a brother who was a bully "and had whipped every man with whom he had fought." Baugh and his brother had some kind of disagreement, and the brother told him

> that if it were not a disgrace for brothers to fight he would give him a whipping. Mr. Baugh replied: "You have got your name by whipping drunk men and boys. Pull off your coat and try a man." It was no sooner said than done. At it they went and the bully got a terrible licking. This occurred before he came to Gwinnett County, but after he had joined the church.

The author of the county history recalled that William Baugh was a deadly enemy to whiskies and to masculine long hair. He used to say: "I am always uneasy about my gimlets, augers, pocket knife and hen roost when the whiskered gentry come about my house."

A minister named Allen Turner, a friend of William Baugh's, was passing through the county on his way to a gospel meeting and was accompanied by Mr. Richard Whittick, "a gentleman of culture, of fine sense, good morals, a churchman and gentleman." Unfortunately for the fellow, he wore a long beard. According to the anonymous archivist:

> Upon their arrival and after an introduction to the strange brother and cordial greetings of old friends, Mr. Baugh brought out his razor with a basin of water and a towel and invited Brother Whittick to shave. He declined saying: "I do not wish to shave." Mr. Baugh insisted and still Mr. Whittick declined.

Finally, William Baugh told the visitor he was not welcome to stay the night unless he shaved. As a result: "Mr. Whittick, a little huffy, left and went over to the home of Mr. Flowers, who did not object to his beard, and there he spent the night."

More than a century and a half later, long after he had quit coaching, William's Baugh's descendant Sam Baugh told an oral historian that long-haired football players didn't bother him a bit; he didn't believe the length of their hair had a whole lot to do with how tough they were or how well they could play the game. "I wouldn't put in a rule I couldn't live with," he said. "I don't believe in making trouble for yourself."

Several of William Baugh's children moved to Texas. When annexed by the United States in 1845, Texas retained control of its public lands. The state used its bountiful natural resource to pay off debts, reward war veterans, finance public education, and build its grand capitol in Austin. It also used land grants to entice settlers, including the Baughs of Georgia, who were dividing up 300-acre farms among family members while Texas was giving away the same amount of land per head of household.

William Lovic Baugh, the firstborn son of William Baugh and his second wife, Elizabeth Lindsay, settled in Rusk County, in Deep East Texas, with his wife, Lucille Harris Purcell Baugh, in the 1840s. In 1854, they moved into Coryell County, in Central Texas, not far from the future town of Temple, in Bell County.

Establishing himself as a farmer and rancher, William Baugh—who favored a long beard—built a large rock house in the Leon River valley. A local historian described the house as a mansion with eight large rooms, each with its own fireplace, and thirty-two large windows. Because Indian raids on area homesteads were still a danger, William Baugh built his house with an escape tunnel in a downstairs room. It started in the side of the fireplace and ran 150 yards underground to the west, where it exited in a brushy area. Rocked on all sides, the tunnel was three feet wide and three feet high.

William Lovic Baugh died in 1914 at age ninety-three. Most of his children and their families settled in Central Texas, including John Pascal Baugh, the fourth child born to William Lovic and Lucille Harris Baugh. John Pascal Baugh married Geneva A. Medlin in 1874, and the couple had fourteen children, five girls and nine boys.

The couple's ninth was James Valentine Baugh, known as Jim, born on March 25, 1889. At age twenty-one, he married Katherine Lucinda Ray, known as Lucy, in 1910, and the couple's first child, Bobby Blake Baugh, was born in 1912. Their second son, Sam Adrian Baugh, was born two years later, on March 14, 1914, in a farmhouse outside Temple. A daughter, Nell Merwyn Baugh, was born in 1916.

A family genealogist noted that Jim Baugh's World War I draft card listed him as a farmer working in Falls County, near Temple, between the villages of Rogers and Heidenheimer.

"We lived out there on that farm when I was little—six miles out of town—and I really loved that life," Sam Baugh told a reporter years later. "We had a few dairy cows, and living out there in the country—just doin' the chores and not worrying much about anything else, seemed like the perfect way to go through life."

Growing up, young Sam may not have been worried about much, but farm life in the years before the Depression was hard and unpredictable. When he was about five, his father got on with the Santa Fe Railroad in nearby Temple. And in fact there was a bit more to it than that, whether young Sam realized it at the time. Jim Baugh was a gambling man, and the family farm was actually a front for a gaming house—complete with a pool table and card tables, and with cockfights and greyhound races out back.

"Everything you could gamble on ... they had," Sam recalled in later years. "My daddy played poker all the time, too. When he got older, he couldn't see, and I'm sure they cheated the living hell out of him."

The 1930 census shows the family living in Temple at 108 North 23rd Street; the house was valued at $2,700, and the family did not own a radio, the census noted. Seventeen-year-old Bob, sixteen-year-old Sam, and thirteen-year-old Nell attended school. Jim Baugh is listed as a weigh master at Temple's rail yards.

Temple, sixty-seven miles north of Austin, owed its origins to the railroads. It started out in the 1880s as a construction camp for the Gulf, Colorado and Santa Fe Railway. The railway company called it Temple Junction, while locals called it Mud Town or Tanglefoot. It remained a railroad interchange, and after three major hospitals were built in the early years of the twentieth century, it became one of the largest medical centers in the Southwest. By the time young Sam was a student at Temple High School in the late 1920s, the town had a population of about 15,000.

Nell Baugh Kendrick, the youngest child, remembered growing up in Temple. Both her brothers were good to her, she recalled nearly a century later. "If he had a dollar," she said, speaking of Sam, "he'd give me half of it, and dollars weren't easy to come by in those days." She remembered him being a paperboy for the *Temple Daily Telegram*.

Sam, known as "Buddy" growing up, remembered trying to pick cotton on the Blackland Prairie around Temple when the Baughs lived in the country. "It would take me all day to pick a sack of cotton when I was little," he recalled years later.

> But I remember dragging that dang sack full and how it hurt my shoulders. Later on, when I was playing football and practicing football, it was hot and we were tired, and you'd think, "Dang, this is tough." And then you'd think about dragging that sack and then you'd jump up and you're ready to go again. So I always promised myself that if I ever had an acre of land I'd never plant a stalk of cotton.

Sam's grandparents still lived out in the country, so he had at least a passing familiarity with farm life—and the drudgery of dragging a heavy sack down endless cotton rows—but basically he was a town boy. Life on a ranch would come much later.

One other thing happened in the country, something that would stay with Sam the rest of his life, although he rarely talked about it. He was maybe twelve, and a buddy of his had gotten a .410 shotgun for Christmas. Sam, the kid with the shotgun, and one other boy were ambling through a pasture looking for rabbits on Christmas Day when they came to a barbedwire fence. As they were climbing through the fence, the gun went off, killing the youngster who had gotten it for Christmas.

Years later, Sam would take his boys out hunting for jackrabbits, but he would never handle a gun himself.

Once the Baughs moved into town, Buddy always had a ball of some kind in his hand. The family lived behind Temple's Westside Baptist Church, and the youngster got in the habit of tossing a baseball over the tall roof and running around to catch it on the other side. And for hours at a time he tossed a baseball at the church building's concrete steps. The steps formed a semicircle, so young Sam had to be ready for the ball to carom off at odd angles. "I just played just by myself," he recalled. "My daddy used to play catch with me."

He once recalled that it was when he was in the third grade, maybe eight years old, that he first started tossing a football around, an imitation-leather ball somebody had bought for him at a drugstore. He first played football in elementary school, during recess, where his first coach, of sorts, was his third-grade teacher. She was "really, really interested in football," he recalled. "I've often tried to think of that woman's name, but I can't remember it. But she was the first football coach I had."

Like most Texas boys growing up in the 1920s and '30s, he played whatever sport was in season—football in the fall, basketball in winter, baseball in the spring. He first played organized sports in junior high school, when he came out for football. Because he was tall, his coach made him an end. The team won most of its games.

"The coach, after the season was over, was talking to three of us boys," Sam recalled years later, "and he said, 'You know,' he said, 'we had a pretty good year.' He said, 'If you three boys were back next year, we'd probably be the best junior high team in Texas.'"

The coach, wittingly or not, had planted the germ of an idea, and Sam and his two buddies liked how it sounded. They purposely failed eighth grade. Years later, Sam remembered how disappointed his mother was when he had to tell her that he had flunked English, but he didn't regret his decision. "We stayed there that extra year in junior high, which really helped me, because I wasn't very big anyway," he recalled.

Sam's junior high football coach turned out to be prescient. With his three ringers leading the way, the team beat every other junior high in Temple as well as every other team they played in Central Texas. They finished the season undefeated, as did a team from Cisco, an oil-boom town 200 miles to the west. The Cisco coach called his Temple counterpart to see whether he would be interested in a championship game of sorts to determine the unofficial state junior high champion. The Temple coach agreed.

Sam and his teammates traveled the 200 miles to Cisco by bus, stayed with host families, and played the junior high version of the Cisco Big Dam Lobos (named for a large hollow dam across Sandy Creek, creating Lake

Cisco). The Big Dam Lobos won the game, but Sam enjoyed the experience. Over the years, he would run into Cisco boys he had played against, who were proud to remind the football star that they had once played against him. "A lot of times," he recalled, "they'd come see a game and look me up and tell me about when we played that game in Cisco."

Sam's winning ways ended abruptly when he arrived—a year late—at Temple High School. Although the Temple Wildcats basketball team was one of the best in the state—winning state championships in 1928 and 1932—the football team was, in Sam's words, "the sorriest team Temple ever had, I guarantee you." The team had only two seniors. "And I was playing end, and we played Waco the first ballgame," Sam recalled. "Waco beat us 60 to nothing. Just ran over us, you know. Then we played Corsicana, and they beat us 55 to 0."

When the dismal season was about half over, Sam, weighing all of 155 pounds, was still playing end, but one day during practice, his coaches noticed in a passing drill that their string-bean end was throwing the ball back to the passers better than the passers themselves. They noticed that he had a natural, easy way of throwing, perfected through years of practicing at home. He had found an old tire, tied a rope around it, and hung it from a tree limb. He would get the rope to swinging and practice throwing a football through the tire at twenty paces and beyond. He had a strong arm, big hands for a kid, and—thanks to the tire—an understanding of how to lead a receiver. He was accurate.

He could also be obsessive about striving for perfection. His son David would recall years later that it didn't matter whether it was passing, calf roping, or dominoes, Sam Baugh would work at it incessantly until he was the best he could be.

Coach Henderson had an idea in the middle of the Wildcats' woeful season. "He called me in his office," Sam recalled, "and told me, he said, 'What would you think if I moved you from end to the backfield?' I said, 'Well, I've already played end. If you want me to move, I'll move.' He said, 'Well, I've been watching you since practice started,' and he said, 'You kick the ball better than anybody we've got. You throw the ball better than anybody we've got, so we haven't got another player in the backfield who can throw the ball.' He said, 'Maybe you could throw it a little bit and it might help us a little.' I said to him, 'If you want me to, I'll do it.' So I spent half a year in the backfield at Temple."

In a Hollywood version of the Sammy Baugh story—which Sam's life later resembled—the skinny young quarterback in Temple blue and white ambles onto the field the next Friday afternoon and starts flinging touchdown missiles before a surprised and delighted crowd. The Wildcats season is rescued. A star is born. For sophomore Sam, however, it didn't happen that way. "Didn't make a damn bit of difference that I could tell," he recalled. "We just kept on losin'."

"I don't recall what happened on the first pass he ever threw in a game, but he didn't do too well, I know, because we got beat," Henderson himself recalled three decades later. "I think [Austin High School] intercepted two or three of his passes."

Henderson lost more than games. He lost his job. He would eventually become the head basketball coach at Baylor University, thirty miles up the road in Waco. He took the Bears to the NCAA finals in 1948 and retired in 1961 with more wins than any coach in school history.

"Bill was a hell of a basketball coach when he was coaching at Baylor, but he wasn't much of a football coach," Sam recalled. "I would always tell him, 'See how lucky you are we had a damn bad team at Temple, which got you fired, and here you are coaching at Baylor.' He was a fine man."

Young Sam Baugh left Temple as well. With the Depression causing calamity throughout the country, and with the struggling Santa Fe Railroad laying off men, Jim Baugh suddenly found himself out of work. Union rules allowed anyone who lost his job to claim the job of the next person below him in seniority. The elder Baugh got caught in a railroad version of musical chairs, which meant he would have to leave Temple to find work.

"My daddy got bumped by someone with more seniority and lost his job in Temple, so he bumped somebody in Somerville and the family moved over there," he recalled. (The children stayed with their grandparents.) "Then he bumped somebody else in Sweetwater, and we moved out there. Nobody had any money, and if you just had a job you were ahead of a lot of people. So you went wherever the jobs were."

Rumors arose over the years, particularly after Sam Baugh became Slingin' Sam of nationwide renown, that football boosters in Sweetwater somehow had lured the elder Baugh because they wanted his son throwing the football for Sweetwater's Newman High School Mustangs. Although recruiting high school football players (or their parents) was forbidden by the state's newly established University Interscholastic League rules, it certainly went on, particularly in football-mad West Texas. No one has ever offered proof, though, that Sam was recruited, and since he was merely a promising athlete on a lousy team, not a star, when he left Temple, it is unlikely that it happened.

The Temple Wildcats had a sense of what they were losing. As Sam recalled years later, he was elected captain of the football team, the baseball team, and the basketball team. "I could understand the baseball, being elected the captain of the baseball team, but basketball—I knew damn well something was wrong, because we had four or five boys there better than I was at the time, and they ranked me captain of the damn team. And I wasn't smart enough to figure out they were trying to get me to where I'd stay at Temple with my grandmother and graduate from Temple. I never thought of that until later on."

Before Sam Baugh, Sweetwater's most famous resident—or infamous resident, depending on your point of view—was a young English scholar named Dorothy Scarborough, who wrote a novel called *The Wind* (1925). Set in the Sweetwater area in the late 1880s, the book depicts "a straggling collection of small houses of the rudest, simplest structure, some not even painted, some without fences . . . little bare box-like houses, naked and unbeautiful!—set down in a waste of sand." Scarborough's main character, a young woman from genteel Virginia, is so unnerved by the isolation, numbing emptiness, and incessant wind that she takes her own life.

The real Sweetwater got its start in 1877 when a trader named Bill Knight, following the buffalo hunters and government surveyors, opened a store in a dugout on the banks of Sweetwater Creek. The first house constructed of lumber was used for a saloon, and later two saloonkeepers acted as bankers for area stockmen.

A century later, Sweetwater would play on its frontier image by staging an annual Rattlesnake Roundup, but the Sweetwater the Baugh family discovered was a tidy town of about 10,000 people, with paved streets, multistory downtown buildings, and an economy that was thriving until the Depression set in. The West Texas wind still blew and sandstorms blanketed the town almost every spring, but residents had planted trees to act as windbreaks. It was still a market town for area sheep and cattle ranches, as well as cotton and grain farmers. In addition to the railroad shops where the elder Baugh worked, the local economy relied on the development of gypsum deposits in the area.

Sam attended high school in a distinguished-looking two-story redbrick building with white columns. It was known as Newman High School in Sam's day.

Sweetwater, like every West Texas town, was fanatical about high school football. The Mustangs were the talk of the barbershop during the week and the topic of conversation after church on Sundays (once members got past the preacher at the door and had complimented him on his sermon).

A Mustang who scored the winning touchdown was a hero for a week; a kid who dropped a potentially game-winning pass knew folks would remember for years.

On Friday afternoons, the town shut down to follow the Mustangs to away games in Big Spring, Roscoe, Colorado City—in auto caravans following the school bus if the game was relatively close by, on special trains when the team made the playoffs and traveled to Amarillo.

In Sweetwater, football gave Sam an opportunity to escape a home life that was becoming increasingly difficult. His father had added bootlegging to his repertoire. He was still promoting gambling and chicken fighting. Sam recalled the time his father took his wife's yard rooster and attached gaffs to him and used the bird to train one of his fighting cocks. As the story goes, the yard rooster inflicted a broken wing on the trained killer.

The elder Baugh eventually left the family and took up with a red-haired floozy named Ruby. Sam's mother, Lucy, was left with the three kids, no visible means of support during hard times, and a flood of resentment that the children shared. She took in sewing, and the children had part-time jobs to make ends meet. "I grew up knowing I wouldn't bet on the sun coming up," Sam once said. "You read a lot now about kids not having a shot because of their family life and things. You learn from your family, good or bad. I got enough bad to know I never wanted to live that way."

Years later, Sam's niece, then Ellen Kendrick, was sitting in the car with her mother on a downtown street in Sweetwater, where the family lived. Her mother gestured toward a man and woman walking along the sidewalk. The woman had flaming-red hair. "Do you know who that is?" Nell Kendrick asked her daughter. Ellen said she didn't. "That's your grandfather," Nell said. "And I want nothing to do with him."

Years after the three children were grown and living on their own, Jim Baugh tried to reconcile with them. David Baugh, Sam's son, remembered a man and woman coming out to the Baugh ranch and sitting on the front porch. He was a flashy dresser, Sam recalled, and the red-haired woman was pretty. "He was just as friendly to us boys as he could be," David Baugh recalled, "but Mom [Sam's mother] wouldn't come out of the house."

Sam was willing to reconcile, but not Nell. He couldn't persuade his sister that they ought to let their father back into their lives. Jim Baugh died in 1968.

D espite his unsettled home life, Sam had a good two years in Sweetwater. He helped his mother, who cooked and sewed for people in town and sold butter and eggs. It wasn't easy being a single mother.

Sam was a good student and popular at school. He also had two good years on the football field with the Mustangs, but nothing spectacular. Wearing number 21 for the red-and-white-clad Ponies, he played safety on defense—as he would throughout his long career—and blocking back or halfback on offense. (The school retired his number in 2006.)

In the single- and double-wing formations that most teams used in those days, the tailback and fullback carried the ball on most plays and did most of the passing. The halfback was primarily a blocker, although now and then he got to carry the ball.

"There's been some stuff written from time to time about how when I was in high school I led the Sweetwater Mustangs to the state playoffs," he recalled. "But it just ain't true. Hell, I was a long way from being the guy who led us to the playoffs." The real star of the team was a running back named Ney "Red" Sheridan. ""He was a good quarterback, a good baseball player; he was just a good athlete," Sam recalled. "He was a running back, could run like a deer. Weighed about 230 pounds."

At the end of the season, the Sweetwater newspaper called Sheridan "the finest running back and the smartest quarterback in the Texas interscholastic league." The paper also lauded Jack Dodson, "stellar Pony wingman," who "stopped everything coming his way through the season just past." There was no mention of Sam.

Behind the running of Sheridan, the Mustangs were one of three undefeated teams in the state in Sam's senior year, 1932. (Amarillo High and the Masonic Home of Fort Worth were the other two.) As district champs, they qualified for the state playoffs.

"Our big game that year was against Big Spring, which was averaging about 40 points a game and was probably the best high school team I ever saw," Baugh recalled. "They were real big and real fast, and nobody thought we could beat 'em, and I have to admit, it looked pretty darn near impossible. But Red [Sheridan] had a great game, and we won the district championship."

That set up a big bi-district game the next week against the Amarillo Golden Sandstorm, and all of Sweetwater was excited. A committee of local businessmen launched a campaign to sign up at least 400 fans to charter a special train to the Panhandle city. Twenty-five businessmen posted from $25 to $100, the high school band $90, and the athletic association $390 to pay the team's way, along with the 130 girls in the pep squad. Fans paid $3 for a round-trip ticket.

"Twenty-four husky Sweetwater lads mushed off for the northland Thursday and in the frozen Panhandle country Saturday they will prospect for that rich vein of pay dirt which may yield for them the nugget of a state quarter-final victory," reported a poetically inclined *Sweetwater Reporter* sportswriter. He noted that Sweetwater had never played in Amarillo and had never advanced so far in Texas high school football competition. He also noted that the Mustangs had been battling another foe all week. "The squad, after a hard game against the Flu Midgets—who play dirty football considering their size—had almost whipped down the germs' attack and were in some semblance of regular form as they pulled out at noon for the Panhandle city."

Playing in a blizzard that Saturday and perhaps still weakened by the flu, the Mustangs lost to the bigger, stronger Amarillo team 7–0.

Coach Ed Hennig, speaking to the Sweetwater Club at noon the next Thursday, declared that he was proud of his team. "The way those boys fought in the last few minutes of that Amarillo game, the way they stayed in there and battled when they were almost hopelessly whipped, numb and freezing, and finally came out with tears in their eyes—well that's what makes a season a success in my estimation," he said.

And so it was over for young Sam Baugh—the end of the season, perhaps the end of his football career. If he had any athletic future at all, he—and most everyone else—assumed, it would be on the baseball diamond.

"I had played baseball all my life, and that's what I wanted to be in the beginning—a professional baseball player," he recalled. "A fellow I played semipro ball with was going to get me a baseball scholarship to Washington State University, but I hurt my knee about a month before I was supposed to go. I was sliding into second base and caught a spike and tore up the cartilage. Well, if it'd happened today, they'd operate, but back in those days they didn't know much about knees. The doctor told me to use a mudpack. I put a mudpack with vinegar on my knee. But I couldn't straighten it out, and the scholarship to Washington State fell through."

The summer after he graduated, with no firm plans about work or college, he caught on with Mose Sims's amateur Oilers in Abilene. For the rest of his life, he had a cache of stories about Sims, who called his all-star third baseman "High Schooler."

When Mose drove the Oilers to diamonds around West Texas, Sam liked to sprawl out in the equipment trailer hitched to the car. He could stretch out his long legs back there. On one of their trips, with Mose behind the wheel, Sam and a teammate were in the trailer as the car sped down the highway. The trailer came unhitched. As the car slowed on a downhill grade, a teammate in the front seat commented, "Hey, Mose, there goes Sam," and Mose looked up to see the wayward trailer passing their car. As Sam's teammates watched, the trailer bounded over a ditch, sailed through a barbed-wife fence, and finally came to a stop, still upright, in a West Texas pasture. Mose stopped the car on the shoulder and watched Sam and Red climb out of the trailer, none the worse for wear.

Mose put his players up every summer in an old house he owned in Abilene. Each player was assigned a chore to do; Sam's was cooking. One day Mose barged in the door with a sack over his shoulder. "Boys, I found y'all something to eat," he announced. The sack was full of fresh corn. "I know he stole it," Sam always said.

"Mose, I need a quarter for a haircut," Sam told Mose as the coach was headed out the door. "Hell, High Schooler," Sims told him, "I don't have any money. I paid my last quarter for that corn."

Sam was holding down third base that summer, the summer Dutch Meyer saw him play. Saw him and wanted him at TCU. "I told him I didn't have any money, that I'd have to have a little help," Sam recalled.

Without a baseball scholarship to offer and knowing that Sam couldn't afford to go to college without financial aid, Meyer, who also coached the TCU basketball team, tried to work a deal with Francis Schmidt, TCU's head football coach. Schmidt controlled the scholarships.

"So I went back and told Coach Schmidt that I had found a kid named Baugh out in West Texas who was a real fine basketball player, was also a baseball player and maybe could play a little football, too. Schmidt had heard of him; Sammy had been blocking back on Sweetwater's single-wing football team, but the kid Schmidt really wanted from Sweetwater was Red Sheridan, the tailback."

"Baugh is just another blocking back," Schmidt told Meyer. "I've seen Baugh. No thanks."

John Knowles was the student manager on the TCU teams of the midthirties. Whether Schmidt would ever have noticed Sam and his abilities is hard to say, Knowles recalled years later. Schmidt, he said, was set in his ways. "He was a character, one of a kind," Knowles said. "He would be concentrating on football and didn't know anything else was going on in the world."

Regardless, Sheridan got away, opting to become a Texas Longhorn. And so did his teammate Sam Baugh.

"I was going to TCU right up until the last week," Sam recalled in 1981. "In about the last 10 days before we had to go to school old Billy Disch, who was the baseball coach at Texas, got in touch with me and told me he'd send me through Texas on a baseball scholarship if I'd come down there. Well, I also wanted to play football, but he talked me into coming down there with this promise—if I didn't like it he would send me to TCU on the bus. I thought, 'Well, I can't lose anything that way,' so I went and stayed about four days."

Coach Disch—William John Disch officially—already was on his way to becoming a legend. Nearly sixty years old when Sam met him, he had been coaching baseball in Austin since 1900—at St. Edward's University from 1900 to 1910, and then at the University of Texas from 1911 until he retired in 1940. Known as the "Grand Old Man" of Texas baseball, a strict disciplinarian who always sought perfection from players, he coached his Longhorn teams to twenty-one out of a possible twenty-six Southwest Conference championships. He sent several of his players, including Bibb Falk and Oscar Eckhardt, to the majors.

The tall young man from Sweetwater was impressed. He was pretty sure he wanted to be a Longhorn, even more so when white-haired Uncle Billy reminded him that the University of Texas would be a superb showcase for a baseball player with major league aspirations. There was only one hitch: "But when I asked Uncle Billy about playing football, he told me that if I came to Texas, it would have to be for baseball only."

He wasn't cowed by the big-name coach. He told Disch he would have to think about his offer. He worked out with the Longhorn baseball team every morning, and in the afternoon strolled around the Forty Acres, as the campus is known, gawking at the impressive buildings, lingering under the stately live oaks. And then he would wander over to the stadium where the Longhorn football team was working out under the watchful eye of Dana Xenophon Bible, another legendary coach.

Sam made up his mind one afternoon with the sights and sounds of colliding bodies, shouting coaches, and kicked pigskins echoing through the empty seats. "I finally decided, hell, I wanted to go to TCU, because I couldn't play football at Texas," he recalled.

Before he left Austin, he called Dutch Meyer and told him he was coming to TCU. Then he walked back to Disch's office and told him what he had decided. The Longhorn coach said he understood. As agreed, he gave the young man money for the 200-mile bus trip to Cowtown.

Sam enrolled in time to go out for freshman football.

....

DUTCH MEYER

SHORT, SAFE, SURE

Maybe the best thing that ever happened to Sam Baugh was meeting Dutch Meyer, the TCU coach who discovered the rangy young third baseman on a hardscrabble baseball diamond in Abilene and the first football coach in America to build an offense around the forward pass. Sam himself often said that he learned more about football from Dutch Meyer than anybody else he ever met. But Dutch was more than just his coach. He was a mentor, adviser, and perhaps even a surrogate father. "I think he was one of the greatest men I've ever known," Sam said. "He was hard, but he was fair. He treated everybody the same."

That was how John Knowles remembered him too. Knowles, the team's student manager during Sam's playing days, said Meyer was approachable. "You could relate to him more than you could Schmidt," Knowles recalled.

He was born Leo Robert Meyer in Waco, Texas, to German parents in a German neighborhood (thus "Dutch," a common nickname for immigrants from Deutschland). He didn't learn English until he started school.

TCU (known as Add-Ran College until 1902) was then located in Waco, and as a second grader young Dutch hung around a campus gathering place called the TCU Drugstore. He loved sports, and by third grade he was water boy and mascot for the Texas Christian University football team.

Years later he loved to recount the crosstown rivalry between TCU and

Baylor, which often resulted in citywide fights. In 1908, the two schools played each other three times. The Christians beat the Bears the first two games, and Baylor could not bear the thought that it might happen a third time. Trailing 8–6 at halftime, the Bears resorted to a bit of un-Baptist skullduggery by dressing its talented right end, John Fouts, in TCU purple. TCU howled, but Babe Grant, the Baylor captain, argued there was no rule against it. He was right. TCU was so befuddled and upset that Baylor rallied for a 23–8 win.

As Dutch recalled, windows were smashed in Waco that night, and trolley cars were derailed. It would be years before TCU acknowledged the Baylor "victory" in its record books.

Young Meyer couldn't wait until he was a Horned Frog himself. In 1911, fire destroyed the TCU campus, and Fort Worth's city fathers offered land and transportation connections if the small Disciples of Christ–affiliated school would relocate.

Dutch vowed to make the same move just as soon as he was old enough. At Waco High School, he played football for Paul Tyson, one of the most innovative coaches in the game. Tyson's Waco High Tigers won five straight state championships, lost only twice during that span, and in nine games scored more than a hundred points. Tyson also concocted an offensive scheme he called the "spinner series," and he was so successful with it that such big-name college coaches as Pop Warner at Stanford and Knute Rockne at Notre Dame made it their own.

Meyer, short and stocky, was a guard in football, a pitcher on the baseball team, and a hot-shooting guard on the Waco Tigers' basketball team. He graduated from high school in 1917—the class prophecy was that he would be a missionary in Africa—and enrolled at TCU.

Perhaps—or perhaps not—he recalled his father's parting dictum: "Don't you go out for football!" Once he got to Fort Worth, he immediately went out for the Horned Frogs' football team. He also played baseball and basketball.

TCU football was barely two decades old when Dutch donned the purple and white in the fall of 1917. In 1896, Addison Clark, the son of the university president when the school was at Thorp Spring, Texas (in its pre-Waco days), was just back from the University of Michigan, where, according to an early history of TCU, he had been "bitten by the Football bug." On Thanksgiving Day, "Little Addie" Clark and a professor named A. C. Easley, "lover of all sports and expert in the military drill," divided the boys on campus into two squads—the "black stockings" and the "brown stockings"—and had them play a game of football.

The Add-Ran boys had no idea what they were doing. They knew rugby, so the professors tried to explain to them that football was a variation on the old British game, although the way the TCU boys played it that afternoon, it was more a friendly brawl. The final score was 4–4. "It was a delightful shin-kicking affair with little rules and no skill, but it began an era," the official university history notes.

TCU's young men must have learned fast. They played their first intercollegiate contest that same year, against Toby's Business College. TCU won 8–6.

They became the Horned Frogs in 1898, in honor of the little horned creatures—they are actually lizards—that were in abundance on the TCU campus. (Today they are nearly extinct.) TCU had hired its first football coach, Joe J. Field, in 1897. He laid down four rules: "1. Abstain from all intoxicants, also coffee and tobacco. 2. Go to bed at ten. 3. Eat no sweets or pastry. 4. Indulge in no kinds of dissipation."

Whether Dutch was following similar rules then or later is not known, but the stocky kid with the lopsided grin was successful at the shin-kicking affair that quickly evolved into college football. He was undersized and knew it, so he relied on relentless aggression to survive among bigger, faster players. "I hunted them up and cut them down," he recalled years later, "and the bigger they were, the worse it hurt them."

He left TCU during World War I, serving as an ROTC instructor at Transylvania College in Kentucky. He also played end on a Transylvania team he described as the worst college football team of all time.

Back at TCU in 1918, he earned eleven varsity letters in three sports, and in 1920 played end on the team that won the championship of the Texas Intercollegiate Athletic Association. (TCU didn't join the Southwest Conference until 1923.) He didn't play football his senior year, because of some kind of dispute with his coach, Billy Driver, but he did play basketball, also coached by Driver. He and Driver later became good friends, perhaps because the coach needed Dutch's set-shooting skills.

He was forced to drop out of school a second time, briefly, because of his participation in a hazing incident against TCU ministerial students. Once he got back in school, a milk cow was found in the dean's office, and suspicion centered on Dutch, but nothing was ever proved.

When his nephew, Lambert D. Meyer, enrolled at TCU some years later, Dutch took him aside and told him: "I've been at TCU many years and have a spotless reputation here. So I don't want you to neglect your studies or get into any mischief, because that would reflect on my perfect reputation."

That "spotless reputation" must have relied on a lot of willful ignorance on the part of the TCU administration. A Houston-area coach attending a coaching school in 1939 recalled being in a Houston hotel room where

Dutch was staying and where a group of college coaches was shooting craps inside a larger ring of their colleagues. "Dutch was dressed in some long-handled drawers," the coach recalled, and when he got down on his knees to take a turn "that flap would come wide open and show his bare ass."

Dutch graduated in 1922 with a degree in geology and immediately signed with the Cleveland Indians baseball team on the strength of his 30-4 pitching record as a Horned Frog. Baseball was his best sport, but he had more brains than talent, scouts said. "He had perfect control but no speed," one of them recalled. "And when Dutch threw a curve, the third baseman had to duck to keep Dutch's thumb from hitting him in the eye."

As a sophomore at TCU, he had strained a ligament in his pitching arm, and it still bothered him as he bounced around the minor leagues during the 1922 season. He decided to give up baseball and return to Fort Worth to coach at Polytechnic High School. After a year at Poly, he was back at his beloved alma mater as coach of all freshman sports. He would stay for forty years, the last eleven as athletic director.

He was a bantam rooster of a man who loved to chest up to the big boys and beat them. He pulled off so many upsets that he acquired the nickname "the Saturday Fox." Dutch would scratch and claw until the last second to eke out a victory, whatever the sport. "Fight 'em till hell freezes over," the coach liked to say, "and then fight 'em on the ice."

Coaching the freshman football team—the freshman teams were known as the Polliwogs—in a game against Terrell Prep one year, his team was so banged up that Meyer had only ten able-bodied men who weren't limping, lame, or otherwise incapacitated. When the referee told him he would have to produce an eleventh or forfeit the game, he laid one of his injured players on a stretcher and positioned it just inside the out-of-bounds line. The wounded warrior lay quietly while his fellow Wogs finished the game.

Dutch's teams down through the years were always fun to watch—especially with Sam Baugh and his successor, Davey O'Brien, throwing passes—but Meyer was a sideline show himself. Always on the move, always talking, he would light one cigarette after another, and sometimes shove the lighted end into his mouth. He was constantly plucking and nibbling grass blades and would jam his expensive Stetson down over his ears until, as one observer put it, "he resembled a cat with its head halfway in a salmon can."

"He would tumble off the end of the bench like a drunken troll. And all the time, he'd ad-lib on the ebb and flow: 'Stop that drop-the-handkerchief and let's play some football. . . . What luck! Who put the hat on the bed! . . . Receivers as open as a butcher with a butcher knife! . . . They're blowing us out of the tub! . . . Judas H. Priest! We can't hit nobody!'"

By the end of the game he was an emotional basket case and would often break into tears—win, lose or draw. After one victory over traditional rival SMU, he wept unashamedly as the team physician wrenched his hat from around his ears, applied hot and cold towels, and sponged his face.

Gordon Brown, a legendary high school coach, recalled watching Dutch give a lecture to Texas high school coaches on his famous spread formation. "There was no air conditioning, so he pulled off his shirt, and here's this chubby little guy with his belly hanging over his belt, and he must have drawn two hundred plays on the chalkboard that morning." Brown recalled walking away and "thinking I must be the dumbest coach in Texas," adding, "I learned afterward that it is not the system that makes you successful, but the perfection of the system."

As Sam would soon learn, Dutch Meyer was nothing if not a perfectionist.

Dutch was a keen judge of athletic talent, but he didn't initially realize what he had when Sam Baugh showed up at TCU as a 170-pound freshman. He had promised the rangy West Texan a part-time job—it turned out to be sweeping out a campus music room—if he decided to enroll at TCU, and he promised him he could play all three sports. Unlike the University of Texas, TCU was too small to be picky about who played what.

Meyer wasn't really expecting much from Sam the football player. He had recruited him as a baseball player, and Sam considered himself primarily a baseball player who happened to play football. The first time the Frogs' trainer saw Sam in a football uniform, he hurried over to Meyer and told him he better get the puny kid off the field before somebody hurt him. Meyer just laughed.

Freshmen weren't eligible for varsity football, so Sam was tailback for the Wogs. "Hell, we only played a couple of games," he recalled years later, "and I can't even remember if we won any."

In fact, they played three at LaGrave Field, Fort Worth's minor-league baseball park, which was situated on the Trinity River bottoms between downtown and the stockyards. The Wogs won all three, including a matchup against the John Tarleton College Plowboys, a small college in Stephenville, Texas. "Undoubtedly he can throw a football farther and with more accuracy than anyone seen on Tarleton Field in recent times," a Stephenville sportswriter noted.

Meyer knew, of course, that Sam had played football in high school, but if he knew anything at all about his abilities, it was his punting skill. That was probably what he told Francis Schmidt, the football coach and athletic director. Meyer was counting on Baugh to play third base, but if he came out for football, maybe did a little punting, then that was just an added bonus for TCU athletics. After all, the Frogs needed everybody they could get. That was how things stood until about halfway through the fall semester.

Not unlike what happened at Temple during Sam's freshman year in high school, Meyer and his fellow coaches couldn't help but notice that the kid who could throw a clothesline strike from third base to first on a baseball diamond could do similar things with a football. "By that time, all the coaches realized that the best passing arm in school belonged to some freshman who had been a blocking back in high school," Meyer's nephew L. D. Meyer recalled.

The *Washington Post* sportswriter Shirley Povich talked to Dutch Meyer a few years after the coach's protégé had become an NFL star. "Anybody can throw a forward pass, there's no trick in that," Dutch told Povich. "The trick is to turn the pass loose at the right time. That's how forward passes are completed, and that's why Sammy Baugh is the best passer football ever saw." Sam had raw talent, of course, but Dutch refined it. "But he'd have been a fine passer under any coach," Meyer told Povich, "He has certain traits that makes a good football player. At any other school he'd have been just as successful. But when he came to me at TCU he was just a tall skinny kid who could throw the ball."

The nickname Slingin' Sam referred to the way he blazed a baseball from third to first, but the whiplike right arm made him Slingin' Sam on the football field as well. He often threw sidearm, like a third baseman scooping a hard grounder off the infield grass and throwing before he got set. He could throw a football from any position or angle, a skill that would come in handy years later when he often had to throw on the run behind weak protection from his Washington Redskin linemen. Unlike technically proficient passers of the modern era, Sam would throw off his back foot, off his front foot, or even with both feet off the ground. Today's coaches would no doubt try to change him—until they saw what he could do with his unorthodox style.

"He was like hundreds of other Texas kids—forward-pass conscious," Dutch said. "He had a nice pair of hands, and he could make that ball travel, but he was crude as college passers go. No deception, no finesse, and he didn't know exactly when to turn the ball loose. But he learned plenty fast. He didn't like to quit throwing those long passes, but we forced him to. When he began having some luck with those short flips, he was satisfied. But he became a great forward passer because he had kind of a sixth sense. He was a good passer instinctively."

MEYER, BAUGH, AND THE PLAN FOR TCU FOOTBALL

Dutch got his chance to work with Sam when Coach Schmidt parlayed his success at TCU into the head-coaching job at a midwestern power-house, Ohio State University. Twenty-five years after carrying water for his Horned Frog heroes, Dutch took over as head coach. He immediately began designing an offense that would make the forward pass a tactical weapon, not a mere desperation heave on third down. He would not only confound the Horned Frogs' opponents, but also rely on the skinny West Texan with a golden arm.

In those days most teams ran the single-wing formation on offense and the six-man line on defense. In the single wing, all four backs were usually tightly bunched behind the line (which is how Sam ended up as a blocking back in high school, his passing prowess unused and unappreciated). Tight ends, typically, were just that, lined up within a shoe's width of the tackles. The compact formation was tailored to the running game.

At TCU, Dutch didn't have an abundance of big linemen who could bunch together and blast out holes for powerful backs to trundle through. He had to be more devious, more daring. Like minutemen in the American Revolution relying on guerrilla tactics against the tightly bunched redcoats, Dutch had to fight his football battles unconventionally. That meant throwing the ball.

Nobody threw the ball in the early days of football; in fact, it wasn't even legal until 1906. In 1913, a small Catholic school in Indiana named Notre Dame, playing against a bigger, faster Army team, relied on the forward pass and upset the highly touted visitors from the East. Playing end for Notre Dame that day was a young man named Knute Rockne, who later became Notre Dame's coach. Rockne, Pop Warner, Jim Thorpe at Carlisle, Alonso Stagg at the University of Chicago, and John Heisman at Georgia Tech began to experiment with passing's possibilities.

The so-called Meyer Spread resembled the modern shotgun formation. "They said I had my ends sitting in the stands, spread out so wide they would sell soda water between plays," Dutch recalled. "The truth of the matter is, they were hardly spread at all by more than three to five yards, so spaced that any of them could make the two-way move to block, in or out. The formation wasn't conceived so much as a spread for the sake of spraying boys all over the field; it was set up for the purpose of 'anglization.' We always had a blocking angle in mind."

The man in the backfield who received the direct snap from center was the tailback, not the quarterback. In the old single wing, there was a quarterback, and it was he, not the coach, who called the plays. The rules at the time prohibited coaching from the sideline, and until 1941, a substitute was forbidden from communicating with teammates until he had been in for one play (unless he was substituting for the quarterback).

So the single-wing quarterback was indeed a "field general." But unlike today's quarterbacks, he seldom handled the ball. After calling the play and calling the signals, his main job was to block, and so he was commonly known as the "blocking back."

Dutch didn't have a blocking back in his spread offense, because his scheme derived from Pop Warner's double-wing formation, which didn't have a blocking back either. He didn't have a position named "quarterback." Instead, his tailback called the plays—and handled the ball on nearly every play.

In addition to his tailback, Dutch had a fullback and two halfbacks, deployed most of the time in such a way that with both of his ends split, he had three slot receivers.

Years after Sam's introduction to the Meyer Spread, he recalled sitting in a classroom and trying to make sense out of three words written on a blackboard: "Short. Safe. Sure." Sam recalled, "Dutch comes in and says, 'We're going to be playing teams that can score on us every time they have the ball. The only way we can match them is to keep the ball away from them. And we're going to do it with short passing.'" Dutch told his raw protégé that the Frogs would be "playing teams that were better than us, teams that would have us outmanned. And if we tried to play the same game they were playing, they would just run over us."

On the practice field, the new coach and his young passer worked on patterns—down-and-outs, hooks, curls, crossovers, slants, comebacks. Sam worked primarily with a receiver named Walter Roach, who had good speed and good hands and who knew how to run good patterns. He was all–Southwest Conference three straight years.

"Back in those days, nobody knew anything about the passing game," Sam recalled.

> Most teams—even in the pros—would try to pound at you with the running game and then, in desperation, throw on third and long. Then they would just try to throw it as far as they could.
>
> Dutch taught us the short passing game, and it was a revolutionary thing for that day and time. We would just move the ball right down the field hitting short passes—with little risk of an interception—and nobody could figure out how to stop it.

L. D. Meyer—also known as Little Dutch—became a favorite Baugh receiver as well. "In those days," Meyer said,

> he was the greatest passer I ever saw. And in all the years since, I don't remember ever seeing anyone better. In all my life, I never saw another passer like Sam Baugh.
>
> Sam could throw any kind of ball—off balance or whatever—and he could throw long, short or medium. But he threw a very light ball. Most of Sam's passes, you could catch 'em with one hand.

As good as he was at throwing the ball, he was just as good kicking it. Years after he quit playing, teammates and fans told stories about how he could punt the ball and make it land just about anywhere he wanted it to. In the days before passes became a potent weapon, teams relied on punters to keep their opponents backed up in their own end of the field.

Dutch taught his punters to kick away from the deep man in order to avoid punt returns. During baseball season, Sam would devote a day to punting practice, maybe with another punter on the team or by himself. If he had a partner, Sam would station the man at different spots on the field—the twenty, the ten, the five. He would practice punting the ball out of bounds within five yards of his man. "I could kick it, and the biggest part of the time kick it somewhere from the 20-yard line on in," he recalled many years later, "and every now and then you'd hit a great one and you'd get them on the one-yard line. If you've got a punter who can do that time and time again, shit, he can save you a lot of worry. You know that son of a gun will go out somewhere inside that perimeter—around the 10- or five-yard line—and he can do it consistently, you've got a good weapon. Nobody likes to start on their own five-yard line, I guarantee you."

FORT WORTH AND TCU IN THE 1930S

Off the playing field and on, TCU was a good fit for Sam. With its compact campus of handsome, blond-brick buildings and tree-lined walkways on a gentle hill south of downtown, the school was small, friendly, and oriented toward West Texas. On summer days, the prehistoric-looking little lizards that provided the school its nickname could be spotted taking in the sun.

Many of TCU's students were just like Sam, small-town youngsters who had little experience with the big city. Fort Worth, population 163,000 in 1930, was a big town to be sure, the fourth-largest in the state, but it was

Cowtown, "as thoroughly representative of the Southwest as a longhorned steer," the *WPA Guide to Texas* noted in 1940. Fort Worth became Cowtown in 1876, when the railroad linked the city's sprawling stockyards and its packinghouses to Chicago, a thousand miles to the north. For decades, cows were herded off the train by the thousands each day—a quarter million every year—and sold to the highest bidder. Many of the city's residents, the *Guide* noted, were descendants of the wiry pioneers of the plains.

"Boasting itself the Southwest's No. 1 grain and livestock market," *Time* magazine reported in 1936, "Fort Worth likes the virile stench of its stockyards, hates cultured Dallas, of late years has found the excitement of its annual rodeo surpassed by the excitement of watching its fast, rangy Texas Christian University football team play Dallas' fast, rangy Southern Methodists."

A few years earlier, Cowtown also had taken full advantage of the West Texas oil boom that overnight had transformed Ranger, Cisco, Desdemona, and other small, sleepy settlements into roaring, raucous boomtowns. Fort Worth was where the drillers, financiers, fortune hunters and farmers who owned the land came to spend their money.

The *WPA Guide* described Fort Worth as "one of the state's most hospitable cities.

> There is still time for a cordial "Howdy, stranger," and a nice disregard of the city's uproar in the easy pause for conversation that is definitely reminiscent of the top rail of a corral fence, with boot heels hooked for balance and plenty of time for talk.

By the time Sam got off the bus in downtown Fort Worth and headed out to the TCU campus in 1933, much of the conversation, no doubt, concerned the abrupt change of fortune the city had experienced a couple of years earlier. After the stock market crash, after the run on the banks and the collapse of the job market, Fort Worth, like most American cities, was in real trouble. Cattle prices had plummeted, soup lines lengthened, and city hall had to lock its doors during the day to keep the homeless from camping out in the hallways. In January 1932, Texas National Bank, one of the city's largest financial institutions, went under; First National Bank, with $24 million in assets, was on the brink.

TCU was not immune. Because of the Depression, most of the school's students were lucky to be in college at all. Almost all of them had to work, even athletes on scholarship. "Nobody had any money except one boy on our freshman team," Sam recalled. "He was a banker's son named Drew Ellis. Every time he would go down to the malt shop he would take a bunch of us with him. He was a good player and became my captain his senior year. I've thought about it a lot of times, how he would load up that old car with everybody. No one in our group grew up with any money. If you got a job, you worked for 10 cents an hour, all day for a dollar. Now Drew Ellis, he was such a sweet guy, a nice guy. He just wouldn't go anywhere by himself; he always took some of us with him. You don't forget things like that."

The Athletics Department tried to arrange on-campus jobs for the athletes. "What they'd do, they'd let you sign the note [for tuition, books, etc.], you'd pay them when you got out and got a job," Sam recalled. "That's how most of our kids went through school. They'd sign a note, they'd pay when they got out of school. And I know that the first year I played in the pros, when the season was over, I came back through Fort Worth and paid TCU what I owed them and went on to Sweetwater."

Enrollment at TCU was dwindling in the early 1930s—from 1,498 in 1929–1930 to a low of 907 in 1933–1934. Two weeks before the opening of the 1933 fall term, faculty members agreed to a 10 percent reduction in pay.

"It seemed to me that dang near all situations back in those days were kind of touch and go," Sam recalled. "We didn't know whether we were going to finish school or not. I can remember one night at a bull session and someone said, 'What if a guy comes up to you and offers you a job for $150 per month? Would you take it and leave school?"

As John Knowles recalled, the football players were just like everyone else. They lived in Goode Hall, one of the two men's dorms, and had to take the same classes all the other students took.

Knowles, whose duties as student manager included taking care of the equipment and logging in the number of minutes each player was on the field for lettering purposes, recalled being in Bible class with running back Jimmy "Squarehead" Lawrence. "He put up his hand one day," Knowles recalled, "and he said, 'Professor, who is this guy Verily they keep talking about?' as in, verily I say unto you."

Knowles enjoyed TCU, and so did Sam. "Despite those tough times in college, if I had it to do over again, I wouldn't change a thing," he said. "It was a good place to go to school."

The hundred-year history of the university, published in 1974, quotes a 1930s-era recruiting publication that reminded potential students that Fort Worth was a hub of passenger railways in the Southwest and had interurban lines to nearby Cleburne and Dallas. Students often chartered interurban cars to athletic events as well as for "class entertainments in which quartets, orators and readers can all be on the program and you will enjoy an evening of real pleasure—something different from the time-worn custom of banquets."

"It was mostly girls and preacher boys," L. D. Meyer recalled years later. Chapel attendance was required twice weekly for freshmen and sophomores, once a week for upperclassmen. In September 1934, the school's board of trustees approved student dances. "The problem was that our students were dancing not on campus but on the outskirts of the city," a letter from the president of the student council noted in 1933.

Tall, dark-haired, and handsome, Sam was well known on campus, and well liked. The 1934 edition of the *Horned Frog* included the underclassman from Sweetwater in a playful list of "Things These People Never Say." According to the yearbook, Sam would never be heard to say, "Teacher, what's a ladies man?"

T hough small and financially struggling, TCU was athletically ambitious. The Frogs' football team won the Southwest Conference championship in 1929—and again in 1932, with a 10-0-1 record—and the school's Athletic Committee recommended to the executive committee of the board of regents that it support a "quiet campaign" headed by the Fort Worth booster and newspaper publisher Amon G. Carter and members of the Athletic Committee to raise approximately $150,000 for a stadium designed to seat about 30,000 people. The Frogs had been playing on a field with two wooden bleachers of about twenty-five tiers, the field enclosed by a wooden fence. After TCU was admitted to the Southwest Conference in 1922, portable stands in the end zones accommodated larger crowds. The suggestion was opportune, the Athletic Committee noted, because

> TCU has won the conference championship this year and the citizens of Fort Worth are clamoring for the erection of a new stadium and a movement was started some two weeks ago by the *Star-Telegram* and the *Record-Telegram* to build such a stadium for TCU. Mr. Amon G. Carter was the instigator of the matter and feels that such a stadium could be built.

The new concrete-and-steel Frog Stadium—seating capacity 19,500; cost $350,000—opened on October 11, 1930. On that Saturday, 15,000 spectators saw the Horned Frogs pound the Arkansas Razorbacks, 40–0.

The largest attendance that season was a capacity crowd of 20,000 at the TCU homecoming game, which turned out to be a bitter loss to the University of Texas, 7–0. Five years later, thanks to Sam Baugh—Slingin' Sammy Baugh by then—20,000 seats wouldn't be nearly enough to accommodate TCU's rabid fans.

....

1934

THE BAUGH ERA AT TCU BEGINS

T
he year 1934 was one of pain, fear, and deep frustration for the United States. On the Great Plains, families abandoned farms to banks and dunes of dust as they headed to California in search of not just a better future but sheer survival. Businesses closed. Young men, and some women, rode the rails in search of a job, any job. President Franklin D. Roosevelt's New Deal programs had not been in effect long enough to put money in the pockets of the workingman or food on the table of the average family.

In Texas, a couple of outlaw lovers from West Dallas named Bonnie Parker and Clyde Barrow reached the end of the road. It was the year that 90 percent of voters in Germany approved the ascension to the presidency of a man named Adolf Hitler, the year that Huey Long became the virtual dictator of Louisiana.

Texans, like most Americans in 1934, had more immediate concerns: they were looking for work, trying to put food on the table, trying to get by as the Depression settled in over the nation. More than thirteen million people were jobless. Many who still had jobs were working either at lower wages or for fewer hours, or sometimes both.

They had their distractions, of course. Radio and the movies thrived during the Depression, precisely because Americans hungered for distraction, comfort, entertainment. Hollywood supplied those distractions, and so did sports.

It was also the year that Southwest Conference football came of age. It started on the afternoon of October 6 in an unlikely place—the state of Indiana, in fact. At almost the same moment and within a hundred miles of each other, the Texas Longhorns and the Rice Owls pulled off stunning upsets of two traditional football powers, and because big-city sportswriters and wire-service reporters were in the press boxes that day, the rest of the country took notice.

It was a great story because Texas teams in the early 1930s rarely played the big boys—the Ivy League, the Big 10, the two service academies, and, of course, Notre Dame. When they did, the results were disastrous: Notre Dame, for example, walloped Texas 36–7 and Rice 55–2 during a three-day swing through Texas in 1915.

At Lafayette, Indiana, on that October afternoon, the Purdue Boilermakers, potential national champions, were expected to have an easy time with the visiting Owls from the tiny Rice Institute in Houston. The Boilermakers had lost only four games in four years, while winning twenty-eight and tying two.

The game was scoreless until the final quarter, when the Owls' left-handed right halfback, Bill Wallace, dropped back from his own forty-three-yard line to pass and was hit by two Purdue linemen. As he was falling, he got off a low pass of about fifteen yards toward the sideline. His receiver, John McCauley, had broken deep and then drifted back when he saw Wallace in trouble. He made a shoestring grab of the ball, straightened up, and fell in behind his blockers, who convoyed him forty-two yards into the Boilermaker end zone. The extra point made it 7–0.

Late in the game, Purdue's quarterback, desperately looking for a receiver as he backpedaled into his own end zone, was hit hard by a Rice guard named Red Bale and fumbled. Frank Steen, a Rice end, fell on the ball for the touchdown, and the game ended before a stunned and disbelieving Boilermaker crowd—Rice 14, Purdue 0.

At South Bend, meanwhile, the contest between the Longhorns and the Fighting Irish featured opposing head coaches who were Notre Dame alumni. Elmer Layden, the fullback of the famed Four Horsemen, was in his first year as head coach of his alma mater, while Jack Chevigny, another Notre Dame backfield star and Notre Dame's backfield coach the year before, was in his first year as the Longhorns' head coach. It was Chevigny who reportedly uttered those immortal words in 1928 when he scored a last-second game-winning touchdown against powerful Army: "Here's one for the Gipper."

Notre Dame was opening its season with Texas. The Irish had not lost a season opener in forty years. The Longhorns were playing their second game of the year. In his Texas debut, a 12–6 victory over Texas Tech, Chevigny reportedly told his star running back, Bohn Hilliard, to fake a limp after scoring on a ninety-four-yard run, the idea being to fool Notre Dame scouts.

In South Bend a week later, Chevigny stoked the Longhorns to a fever pitch with a pregame speech worthy of his old coach, the legendary Knute Rockne. He also took advantage of his familiarity with Irish personnel. He knew that the Irish halfback George Melinkovich was prone to fumble in the opening minutes, so Chevigny had his kicker aim the ball at the jittery deep man. Sure enough, Melinkovich bobbled the ball at his own five and lost it for good to the swarming Longhorns at the eighteen.

On first and goal from the eight, a miraculously recovered Hilliard followed guard Joe Smartt through a hole over right tackle for a touchdown before the game was two minutes old. Hilliard then kicked the extra point, which turned out to be one of the biggest in Longhorn history.

Notre Dame got its chance for redemption shortly afterward when Texas fumbled on its own ten-yard line and the Irish recovered. Three plays later, Melinkovich scored, but somehow Notre Dame kicker Wayne Millner—a future Washington Redskins star—missed the extra point. Final score: Texas 7, Notre Dame 6.

On October 14, 1934, the Associated Press, in its roundup of college football games for Sunday newspapers, said of the day's events: "The football experts had better retire to their bomb-proof shelters. In as great a succession of early-season upsets as the game ever has known, Notre Dame's Ramblers, Purdue, Michigan, Cornell and Pennsylvania all went down to stunning and unexpected defeats yesterday. Two of these form reversals were credited to invading outfits from the Southwest Conference, the Texas Longhorns and Rice Owls."

Rice would go on to beat the Longhorns in Houston, 20–9, on the way to its first Southwest Conference championship. The game was so widely anticipated that Humble Oil and Refining set up a network of clear-channel radio stations in Dallas, Houston, and San Antonio. Although Southwest Conference football fans may not have realized it at the time, the golden age had begun.

"It would be hard to exaggerate the excitement that the first kiss of autumn generated at all levels of society," the *Texas Monthly* writer Gary

Cartwright recalled years later. "As early as 1934, the air was literally filled with Southwest Conference football, thanks to the Humble Radio Network, the nation's first broadcast network. You couldn't visit a drugstore or barbershop or even walk along a sidewalk without hearing the roar of the crowd and the boom of the marching bands at Kyle Field or the Cotton Bowl—or the voice of Humble's master of word pictures, Kern Tips."

The rest of the country also was learning to keep its eye on the Southwest Conference and its growing reputation for wide-open, crowd-pleasing football. Once the Owls and the Longhorns captured the nation's attention with their Indiana derring-do, two other Southwest Conference teams held it. At SMU, Coach Ray Morrison installed what came to be called the "aerial circus," with footballs flying all over the field. Thirty miles to the west, Dutch Meyer unveiled not only his disciplined short-pass offense but also the best passing quarterback the Southwest Conference had ever seen.

───

Young Sam Baugh began his TCU career on the bench. The Horned Frogs opened the 1934 season in Brownwood, Texas, against tiny Daniel Baker College. Dutch started Joe Coleman, a Waco product who was his senior quarterback, field-goal kicker, and co-captain. Sam got into the game after the Frogs had built a 10–0 lead. In a preview of what Frog fans could expect during the next three seasons, the Sweetwater sophomore scored once and threw three touchdown passes in a 33–7 victory over the outmatched Hillbillies. The banner headline in the *Star-Telegram* the next day put the spotlight on the newcomer: "Sam Baugh Lives Up to Expectations and Leads Frogs to Win Over Billies."

Dutch alternated his quarterbacks the next Saturday as well, as the Frogs defeated North Texas State 27–0 before a crowd of 5,000, reported to be "the largest crowd ever to witness a TCU home opener." (A year later, TCU would be desperately adding seats to accommodate a crowd of 40,000 for the SMU game.)

Sam's debut against a Southwest Conference foe was something less than auspicious. Playing Arkansas, the Frogs jumped out to a 10–0 lead behind Coleman. Late in the first half, Meyer sent in the sophomore.

He played like a sophomore. Not long after going in, he tried to catch a punt on the Frogs' own one-yard line and fumbled it to the Razorbacks. Arkansas scored an easy touchdown to make it 10–7. Early in the second half, Sam tried to throw from his own five and got intercepted. Arkansas ran it in for a touchdown to make it 14–10.

"I knew what he could do," Dutch would say in years to come.

Now, when you're in your own end of the field, you can fumble and get kicks blocked, and that's bad, but if you can pass well from there, you can get yourself out of trouble. Sure, sometimes a passer has to peel it and eat it, and we got a reputation for passing in the shadow of our own goal—but Sam could make it work for us. You have to remember that Sam could also kick that ball—and that also made him a great passer in the shadow of his own goal line with his kicking threat.

However much confidence Dutch Meyer had in his young quarterback, both he and the pass-oriented offense were still works in progress on that October afternoon against the Razorbacks. After costing the Frogs fourteen points with his mistakes, Sam got the team backed up deep into its own territory yet again and threw yet another interception. Arkansas scored to make it 21–10.

"So here he had cost us 21 points in pretty quick succession—and lost the game, as it turned out—but there was an interesting reaction," recalled Julius "Judy" Truelson, a senior tackle in 1934. "It never shook him at all. He never lost confidence, and took us on a couple of drives late in the game, although we didn't score."

The loss to Arkansas was costly, and yet Meyer and his fellow coaches saw something that day that gave them hope. Sam, they realized, possessed that rare quality of believing in himself and inspiring those around him to believe as well. It was the mark of a leader.

"He was kind of a quiet guy," John Knowles recalled. "There was not a lot of hurraw about him."

On the field, he never yelled at his teammates, never tried to be the big dog, even though he would eventually be the biggest of the big dogs. He hated reprimanding people or showing them up. His style was to lead by doing, and each week the team's confidence in their leader grew.

Over the two weekends following the Arkansas loss, the Frogs beat Tulsa and then Texas A&M, which set up an early-November clash with perhaps their bitterest rivals, the Baylor Bears. On the day before the game, some 1,200 fans boarded a train in Waco for the ninety-mile ride to Fort Worth. The Baylor band marched down Fort Worth's Main Street on the way to the game, held a pep rally at the Texas Hotel, and showed off its live bear mascot.

There was no marching when the afternoon was over. The Bears were limping. Sam not only threw three touchdown passes in a 34–12 TCU win, but also caught two interceptions that resulted in TCU touchdowns.

Playing both offense and defense, Sam was beginning to feel the rhythm of the game, learning to get to where he could survey the field, almost as if everything were happening in slow motion. And he was getting used to his receivers.

The high-flying Frogs traveled to Austin two weeks later for a crucial date with the Longhorns. Sam had another superb day, throwing for 206 yards and two touchdowns, but it wasn't enough. Longhorn running back Bohn Hilliard, the hero of the Notre Dame game, led Texas to a 20–19 victory in a game in which the Longhorns rushed for 320 yards and passed for exactly one. The Frogs lost when fullback Taldon "Tillie" Manton, playing with an injury, missed two extra-point attempts.

Up next were the Rice Owls, whose only blemish in nine games was an early-season tie with Louisiana State University. TCU would have been the clear underdog even if the team wasn't bruised and battered after the Texas game, but Dutch Meyer—the "Saturday Fox"—traveled to Houston with a trick tucked away in his game plan. Forsaking the passing game that had gotten more potent every week, he kept the Frogs on the ground almost exclusively. They scored on an eighty-yard opening drive and then relied on a clawing, snarling defense to keep the high-flying Owls out of the end zone. Sam's punting kept the Owls in a hole all day.

Years later, Judy Truelson remembered the touchdown: "When we took the ball on our first possession, Joe Coleman was at quarterback, and we just kept running Jimmy Lawrence at 'em until we were down on about their six-yard-line. Then Joe called 32X—which was a reverse to Lawrence on which he was supposed to throw to Harold McClure. But he was covered, and Rice was swarming back there, and it looked like Jimmy was trapped for a big loss when suddenly he threw back across the field to Coleman, who ran it in for the touchdown."

Late in the game, the Frogs gave the Owls a safety so that they could try to establish good field position with a free kick. Just a few plays later, the strategy appeared to backfire when Rice pushed to TCU's nine-yard line, thanks to a thirty-one-yard pass-interference call. They got to the five on the next play.

On the next play, the Frogs smothered the Rice ball carrier for an eight-yard loss. On the play after that, they lost fifteen, and on fourth down, they lost fifteen more. TCU took over on about the forty, and the clock ran out.

The hero of the day, aside from the Frog defensive unit, was "Little Joe" Coleman, the senior captain who had lost his job on offense to the preternaturally gifted underclassman.

"Joe was a great guy and a very unselfish football player," Sam recalled. "We always got along real well, and he tried to help me in any way he could. It made me feel good that he scored that touchdown against Rice."

Grantland Rice was in the stands that day. He didn't get to see much of Sam Baugh, although in a postgame column he proclaimed the Southwest Conference "the roughest and toughest in the country."

The Frogs were anything but rough and tough the week after the Rice victory. They lost to SMU 19–0.

Rice would go on to win its first Southwest Conference championship in 1934, while TCU would end the season on a high note as well. The University of Santa Clara, a college football power in the '30s, came into Fort Worth with only one loss on its record. The Broncos had beaten the California Golden Bears and tied Rose Bowl–bound Stanford. TCU squeaked by, 9–7, on the strength of a game-winning field goal late in the fourth quarter by Tillie Manton, the Frog turned goat against the Longhorns a few weeks earlier.

The Frogs finished Dutch Meyer's inaugural season with an 8-4 record and with fans vowing, "Wait'll next year." "Baugh appears to be the best passer TCU has had in several years," the 1934 *Horned Frog*, the school yearbook, noted. "He is an elusive runner and excellent punter also."

Meanwhile, Sam came out for basketball, playing guard, and then baseball in the spring. Playing third base in practice one day, he caught the eye of Amos Melton, a former TCU football player who had become a sportswriter for the *Fort Worth Star-Telegram*. Searching for a way to describe how the Frog third baseman rifled the ball across the diamond to first base, Melton bestowed upon Sam Adrian Baugh one of the most memorable nicknames in all of American sports—"Slingin' Sammy Baugh."

....

1935

THAT CHAMPIONSHIP SEASON

T he 1934 season set the stage for the true opening of the golden era of the Southwest Conference, 1935. Thanks to what had happened the season before, the rest of the nation was watching.

TCU, cofavorite along with SMU to win the Southwest Conference championship, sold 2,200 season-ticket packages at a cost of $5.50 for five home games. The Frogs' promising young passer sold a lot of those tickets.

Forty-seven players showed up for preseason practice in August, a bit fewer than the ninety competing for a spot on Jack Chevigny's Texas Longhorn team 200 miles to the south.

The Frogs would have to get by the Mustangs of SMU, who relied on fullback Harry Shuford and 147-pound halfback Bobby Wilson, described by one overwrought sportswriter as "a lizard-legged little bundle of mobile murder." Broadcaster Kern Tips described Wilson as "SMU's broken-field kid with the bulbous shoulders, the calves of a guard, the slim hips of a ballet dancer."

In Houston, defending champion Rice still had its two fine running backs, Bill Wallace and John McCauley.

TCU, with Sam starting at tailback, opened the season at home on a Saturday afternoon against Howard Payne, from Brownwood, Texas, which was coming off an undefeated season. Sam scored the first touchdown on a ten-yard run, and the Frogs went on to maul the Yellow Jackets, 41–0. SMU blanked North Texas State 38–0 that Saturday, and Rice beat St. Mary's 38–0.

The next weekend, the "Saturday Fox" almost outfoxed himself when he decided to start his second-string backfield against lightly regarded North Texas State. The Eagles put up a stiff fight before falling to the Frogs 28–21. SMU had an easy time with tiny Austin College, 61–0, while Rice took on LSU in Baton Rouge and defeated the Southeastern Conference power-house 10–7.

In mid-October, in the first matchup between the three top contend-ers, SMU caught Rice with running back Wallace out with an injury and defeated the Owls 10–0.

Also in mid-October, Flem Hall, a *Star-Telegram* columnist, reached a conclusion about the future of college football. "Night football," he wrote, "has probably passed its peak as a vehicle for major college competition. From all quarters, where it has been tried, are coming strong unqualified condemnations. Neither the players, coaches, officials nor close-observing spectators like the after-dark conditions. The only stanch friend of night play is the business manager—early-season games do bring in more money than those played in the afternoon."

Almost unnoticed as fall afternoons began to shorten were the Baylor Bears, who had won six straight games when they hosted TCU in Waco on November 2. The Frogs also were 6–0. Playing in front of a boisterous homecoming crowd at Waco's Carroll Field and boasting a successful pass-ing attack of their own, the Bears were set to waylay the visiting Frogs.

It was not to be. Sam completed ten of sixteen passes—three for touch-downs—ran for forty yards on eight carries and intercepted a pass in the 28–0 victory. He also did all the punting. The TCU defense held the Bears to six first downs and 124 total yards while intercepting three Baylor passes. TCU gained 324 yards, 204 in the air.

The Baylor game was big for TCU, but Sam and his boys were flat the next weekend in New Orleans against the Wolves of Loyola University. Playing in a Gulf Coast fog, Sam had trouble throwing the wet ball. Fortu-nately, running back Jimmy Lawrence scored twice, the defense shut down the Wolves, and the Frogs escaped the Crescent City with a 14–0 victory.

SMU was also mowing down opponents. Traveling to Los Angeles on November 11 for a rare Monday-night game, the Mustangs invaded Memo-rial Coliseum to take on UCLA. "Fifty thousand spectators marveled at the forward passing magic of the Texans, who threw the ball with abandon from first to last," the Associated Press reported. Halfback Bobby Wilson "ran and passed until the California players tired of the sight of him." He averaged six yards per carry as his Mustangs crushed the vaunted West Coast team 21–0.

The next Saturday, the Frogs boarded the train for Austin, where they expected to avenge their '34 defeat. TCU's president granted the students a holiday; most would make the trip to Austin by either car or train, the *Star-Telegram* reported.

Texas was always the team to beat, Sam recalled years later, the team that everybody else in the Southwest Conference geared up to beat. "Everybody wanted to beat Texas University, because they've already got the best boys," he said.

On a rainy afternoon in Memorial Stadium, the temperature 50 degrees, the lanky tailback the Longhorns had allowed to get away three years earlier passed for three touchdowns, and the Frogs ran in a blocked punt for a fourth. The Frogs intercepted four Longhorn passes, outgained their opponent 359 yards to 79, and, with reserves playing the whole fourth quarter, won going away, 28–0.

Writing in the *Star-Telegram*, Flem Hall couldn't get over Sam's punting. "Baugh was standing on the rear end of his own end zone the first time he was called upon to punt," he reported the Monday after the game. "The ball came down on the Texas 34-yard line—just 75 yards from where it took off of Baugh's foot. His next punt was across the Texas goal line 73 yards from where he punted." Hall noted that Sam was averaging better than forty yards a punt for the season, "and he boots a lot of them out of bounds with rare accuracy."

The Frogs beat the Longhorns twice during the years the spurned Teasipper was TCU's signal caller. Texas beat TCU and Sam once.

That same week, the *Star-Telegram* columnist reprinted a letter from Shelly Powers, a reader from Justin, Texas: "I am interested in some Southwest team playing in the 'Bowl' game in Dallas Jan. 1. I have always thought of such a game being called the Cotton (Boll) Bowl. Maybe then the Southwest could step out into the limelight and pick some strong Midwest team—I mean really 'pick' 'em in more than one way for and in our Cotton (Boll) Bowl."

A week after the Texas victory, the Rice Institute came to town to engage the Frogs—"the flaming and furious Frogs of Texas Christian University," Flem Hall called them, "as audacious and clever a football battalion as ever stepped on a gridiron."

As the Associated Press reported in Sunday's paper, "There was never a doubt concerning the outcome today from the time George Kline, Christian halfback, thrilled the 22,000 spectators by returning the opening kickoff 69 yards until Coach 'Dutch' Meyer removed his first-stringers and sent in reserves in the fourth period."

Sam completed eleven of nineteen passes, three for touchdowns, and gained more than 200 yards in the air in the 27–6 win. He had become a true believer in Dutch Meyer's "short, safe, sure" system.

"Sam wasn't merely a thrower but an artist with the pigskin who could shoot the leather direct to the mark and have it fall easily in the intended receiver's hands," the Associated Press reported. "There was no stopping his overhead thrusts. At least, Rice had no concrete defense against them. If one man was covered, Sammy usually had at least a couple of other mates waiting to be found and he overlooked few. The Owls intercepted only one of his throws, batted down two, and the others went aground chiefly because the intended receivers failed to reach their zones or had swung the opposite way from which they were expected to be traveling."

The Frogs' victory over "the obstreperous Owls of Rice Institute" (Flem Hall again) set the stage for a battle of the unbeatens.

Two cities only thirty-four miles apart were "in the grip of a football frenzy unprecedented in this section," the *New York Times* reported from Fort Worth. Both TCU and SMU were undefeated. The Mustangs had out-scored their opponents 244 to 18, while TCU had scored 244 points while giving up 45. SMU's opponents had scored only three touchdowns all sea-son, TCU's only five.

The game was the topic of conversation in offices around town, in church the Sunday before. Both the *Morning News* and the *Star-Telegram* offered a raft of game-related stories every day of the week. On both cam-puses, professors found it almost impossible to hold their students' atten-tion. On Friday night, a bonfire in a field near the TCU stadium drew at least 20,000 people.

For Sam and his teammates, the attention was more focused. The Frogs had to figure out a way to stop Wilson, the speedy halfback who had run almost at will against UCLA three weeks earlier. But "the Mustangs have an even larger problem to solve," the *Times* noted. "They must checkmate Sam Baugh, TCU quarterback, who has completed 71 out of 158 passes thrown, and at the same time guard against the thrusts by Jimmy Lawrence, jarring Frog halfback and All-Conference selection last year."

TCU was a slight favorite, in part because of the Frogs' convincing vic-tory over Rice a week earlier and SMU's less than convincing victory over Baylor, a team the Frogs had handled easily. SMU also would be play-ing without its stellar fullback Harry Shuford and guard J. C. "Iron Man"

Wetzel, both out with injuries. John Knowles recalled many years later that even the Ponies acknowledged that TCU was the better team.

"Texas, which has for many years clamored for national recognition for its Southwest Conference, is reveling in the attention centred [sic] on tomorrow's game," the *Times* noted.

TCU officials anticipated the largest crowd in Southwest Conference history. Reserve seats had been at a premium for weeks, and end zone seats were snapped up as soon as they went on sale. Standing room tickets were expected to push total attendance to at least 40,000.

Billy Sansing grew up in Dallas next door to O. J. Lawrence, whose brother Jimmy, nicknamed "Squarehead," was a TCU running back. Sansing, who was twelve, got invited to the biggest football game in Southwest Conference history. O. J. Lawrence had a ticket. Nearly three-quarters of a century later, Sansing remembered how desperate fans nudged their cars up against the wire fence around the stadium, climbed up on the roofs of their cars, and scrambled over. Halfback Wilson recalled years later that people threw blankets and overcoats over the cyclone fence. "They looked like sheep going over the top," he said. Eventually, the surging crowd broke the fence down, and officials gave up trying to keep them out. An extra 4,000 spilled into the stadium, and the standing-room-only crowd spilled over into the end zone during the game. Other fans perched on light poles.

Fans had started lining up outside Frog Stadium before sunrise, and the streets of Fort Worth were jammed with cars throughout the morning. The crowd of 40,000 or so who made it into the stadium was said to be the second largest ever to see a sporting event in Texas.

Wayne Connor was a kid growing up in Cleburne, thirty miles south of Fort Worth. He and a buddy rode their bicycles all the way into town, even though they didn't have tickets. Young Wayne tore a new pair of pants scaling a fence to get inside. To his chagrin, the cops opened the gates to all comers shortly after he had torn his new pants.

"Big-time scalping, formerly unheard of here, is rife, with 50-yard tickets commanding as much as $60," the *Times* reported. Some fans reported paying $100, Depression be damned. There were more people outside the stadium than inside, Billy Sansing recalled. (A $100 ticket would be the equivalent of $5,000 today.)

Also on the line was Fort Worth's civic pride. Cowtown always had felt a bit inferior to its bigger neighbor to the east, and was certainly disdained by Big D's aspiring sophisticates. Fort Worth's pride had been punctured yet again when it was announced that Dallas would be the official site for the upcoming Texas Centennial Celebration of 1936; it had been chosen

primarily because the city's business leaders simply outhustled their coun-
terparts from Texas towns with a more compelling historic claim—including San Antonio, Houston, maybe even Fort Worth.

In retaliation, Amon Carter, civic booster nonpareil, announced that the
Fort Worth Frontier Centennial would open the same time as the Dallas
centennial exposition and that the legendary showman Billy Rose would
arrange the entertainment. The *Washington Post* reported that Rose "took
in hand entertainment features of Fort Worth's frontier fiesta and transported a bit of Broadway out to where the West begins in a manner that
strongly appealed to natives of the State where men are men and a woman
was once Governor."

Meanwhile, the spotlight shown brightly on the pride of Cowtown,
TCU's fabulous football team. The nation's big-time sportswriters had
made the pilgrimage to Fort Worth for the biggest game since—well, since
football was invented, Grantland Rice proclaimed. On hand in their fedoras
and overcoats, pens and notebooks at the ready were Bill Cunningham of
the *Boston Globe*, Joe Williams of the *New York Herald Tribune*, Paul Gallico
of the *New York Journal-American*, Arch Ward of the *Chicago Tribune*, and,
of course, Rice of the *New York Sun*.

Big-time coaches showed up as well, including Bernie Bierman of the
University of Minnesota, Fritz Crisler of Princeton, and Pappy Waldorf
of Northwestern. Bill Stern broadcast the game for Mutual, Kern Tips for
NBC. It was the first coast-to-coast radio network broadcast of a game in
the Southwest.

SMU wore red helmets, pants that were red in back and canvas in front,
and red jerseys with blue numerals. Although a slight underdog, the Ponies
jumped out to a 14–0 lead, on drives of seventy-three and eighty yards, with
Wilson, the Corsicana comet, scoring the second touchdown. Fans in tem-
porary seats—men in dark suits, women in hats and Sunday dresses—sat
within inches of the end-zone line, and the two SMU extra points sailed into
the crowd.

The Frogs were careful to kick the ball away from the little man from
Corsicana, but he ended up with it often enough. "It was Wilson's day, and
he smiled nearly every time he came up with the ball after a long jaunt," the
New York Times reported.

The favored Frogs, wearing white jerseys with purple numerals, black
leather helmets, and khaki-colored pants that glowed golden in the sun,
finally got something going in the second quarter. Sam's punt went out of
bounds on the Mustang four, TCU held, and SMU's return punt was short.
The Frogs scored on the ground to trail 14–7.

At halftime, the TCU band played "Taps," and, in the midst of the Depression, fans donated $1,400 for a memorial to the humorist Will Rogers, who had died a few days earlier in an airplane crash with the famed pilot Wiley Post. In the SMU locker room, the normally low-key Matty Bell offered his boys something to think about. Quoting his old high school coach, he said, "You've got thirty minutes to play and a lifetime to think about it."

Sam's receivers were having trouble holding on to his passes, but he finally threw a touchdown strike to Jimmy Lawrence in the fourth quarter with twelve minutes left to play. Lawrence injured his ankle on the play, and since the rules dictated that an injured player had to sit out a quarter, he was through for the day. The injury would prove crucial to the outcome.

SMU took the kickoff and relied on Wilson and Bob Finley, Shuford's replacement, to move the ball into TCU territory. The Mustangs tried three running plays but netted only six yards.

Facing fourth and four, the Mustangs lined up in punt formation. TCU fans couldn't wait for Sam to get his hands on the ball, and the TCU passer felt the same way. Surely, with the game on the line, there would be no way to stop him. Knowles remembered that he had been calm, confident the whole day.

Pony fullback Finley, who was averaging forty-seven yards a punt that Saturday, stepped into the kick—only he held the ball at his hip as he followed through on what looked like a punt, his right leg thrust high into the air. Both feet back on the ground, he began backpedaling, the ball now high above his shoulder in his right hand as he looked downfield for a receiver. Suddenly, he let the ball go in the general direction of the fleet Bobby Wilson, who had slipped behind Harold McClure, subbing for the injured Lawrence. Finley was hit just as he threw; lying on his back, he couldn't see what happened after he had let the ball go in the general direction of the Corsicana comet, who was scurrying down the right sideline.

Kern Tips, the announcer, saw it all from the press box. "Now while that long ball was in the air," he recalled three decades later, "some will tell you that Wilson stopped, turned and came back for it; some that he looked over his shoulder anywhere from the ten, to the six, to the four-yard line trying to find the ball. . . . I'm going to say that Wilson never swerved from a straight sideline path, and that on the TCU three-yard line he looked back, leaped high in the air, tipped down the football into control, and hugged onto it as he scrambled into the TCU end zone, glad to be alive and part of a passing miracle."

Judging from the grainy black-and-white film of the game, Tips's memory would seem to be accurate. It was a magnificent pass, settling in over

Wilson's shoulder at about the five, with Sam and McClure right with him. His momentum carried him into the end zone. Many years later, Wilson recalled that SMU had designed the play to take advantage of Lawrence's tendency to close fast on punt coverage, which would allow the speedy Wilson to blow by him, but he wasn't on the field when Finley threw the pass. "The two guys closest to me when I caught the ball were Baugh and the kid who replaced Lawrence," Wilson recalled.

He said he had one regret about the catch: "Whether I'd have gotten behind Lawrence, I don't know. But I've always felt flat guilty about getting behind the guy who substituted for Lawrence. The poor boy couldn't help it."

In all the excitement following Wilson's miracle catch, the Mustangs missed the extra point, leaving the Frogs with a ray of hope. As long as the ball was in Sam Baugh's hand, they knew—as did the Mustangs—that they still had a chance.

As afternoon shadows lengthened across the playing field, with 40,000 spectators on their feet and shouting themselves hoarse, with countless thousands gathered around radios across the country, Sam drove his desperate Frogs down to the SMU thirty. The Mustangs held, but as time ticked away, Sam brought the surging Frogs back yet again: short, safe, sure. "Baugh was eating up ground at the SMU 25 when the final whistle blew, and SMU's supporters were almost in a panic from Baugh's deathly machine-gun fire," Grantland Rice wrote.

The tall kid from Sweetwater, the picture of calm and confidence, completed passes of fourteen yards, then eight yards, then ten yards. And then he found L. D. Meyer open for twenty more yards to the SMU twenty-two, but with the ball in Meyer's hands, the goal line just twenty yards away, the luck of the Frogs ran out. The receiver couldn't scramble out of bounds in time to stop the clock and give Slingin' Sam one last shot. A shell-shocked SMU hung on for the win, 20–14, and with it, a Southwest Conference team's first-ever trip to the Rose Bowl. Reporters called Finley's winning touchdown the $85,000 pass, the Rose Bowl payout.

Rice described the contest as "one of the greatest football games ever played in the 60-year history of the nation's finest college sport."

People, including Sam Baugh, were still talking about the game years later. "What I really remember is that SMU defensed us better than any damn team we played," Sam recalled.

They did some things I hadn't seen before. They'd throw up a six-man line with two linebackers, so they had eight guys close to the front. If they all came, they had a pretty good pass rush, but you had to call your blocking for six men coming. Sometimes the linebackers would come, but someone else would drop back. They usually had four men protecting that short, eight- or nine-yard area. But we never knew which ones.

"But give 'em credit. They made it tough."

Sam threw an incredible forty-four passes that day, completing seventeen for 180 yards. TCU receivers dropped eight passes. He also averaged forty-eight yards a punt.

Bill Cunningham of the *Boston Post* calculated that Sam found his receivers on all but two passes out of the forty-four he threw (an unheard-of number of passes for that era). "He merely lifted his arm, cracked his wrist like a whip and there through the sunlight went the shining, spinning spheroid," Cunningham rhapsodized.

"Mr. Slingin' Sammy Baugh can chunk that cabbage," Rice wrote. "He could murder a fly on a fence with the snout of that missile at any distance from a yard to at least 50."

The football writer Wilton Hazzard wrote that Sam's uncanny accuracy "smacked of witchcraft," while George White of the *Dallas Morning News* wrote, "Visitors sat back and marveled at his accurate throws, but his overanxious receivers could not hold his bullet throws."

Although Sam blamed himself for tossing bullet throws that were uncatchable, L. D. Meyer never believed Baugh was at fault. "He was throwing those balls right in there on the money," he told Canning, "and if you're a receiver, it's your job to catch those balls, no matter how hard they're thrown." The younger Meyer pointed an accusatory finger at his uncle. "I think the real problem was the pep talk Dutch gave us before the game," he said. "He normally didn't do a lot of that, but this time he was really trying to get us fired up, and he told us the winner would go to the Rose Bowl. We were mostly just a bunch of country boys, and this was the biggest thing that had ever happened in our lives. By the time we were out there, we are all tied up in knots, and Dutch always admitted that he thought he made a big mistake."

"I learned a good coaching lesson," Dutch said afterward. "You don't have to tell your kids it's a big game. They know it. Matty brought the Ponies out loose and laughing. I brought my team out stiff and tense with tears in their eyes. We dropped enough of Sam's passes in the first half to win two dang football games."

TCU should have been ready for the fake punt, Sam believed. "The thing that galled us," he recalled years later, "is that they won on a play we were expecting; we just didn't stop it. It was reported as a daring gamble, but it was actually a routine play for that era." In that era, if a team threw an incomplete pass into the end zone on fourth down, it was a touchback and the ball came out to the 20. "So if you were close enough," he said, "you might as well try it, 'cause you might score. And that's all they were doing."

SMU finished its 12–0 season the next weekend with a victory over Texas A&M and officially accepted a bid to the Rose Bowl. But the New Year's Day Mustangs barely resembled the inspired Pony Express that had rolled over UCLA on their earlier westward adventure. The Ponies lost to the Stanford Indians 7–0, although the team's $85,000 Rose Bowl cut allowed SMU to pay off bank bonds on its new football field, a handsome redbrick structure on campus called Ownby Stadium.

TCU had headed west nearly a month earlier, finishing its regular season on December 7 against the University of Santa Clara in San Francisco's Kezar Stadium. The *Fort Worth Star-Telegram* sponsored a special train to the game, and on the Tuesday following the SMU game, the train pulled out of Fort Worth's Union Station carrying the team, the TCU band, and several hundred fans who had paid $108.70 for an upper Pullman berth and all expenses, or $56.05 for those who took care of their own meals and expenses.

The train first stopped in Denver, where Dutch Meyer put his players through a light workout and the Horned Frog band paraded downtown. The team then headed to Salt Lake City, where the Frogs took in the Mormon Tabernacle and Brigham Young's home. In San Francisco for two days and nights, the Fort Worth entourage took in the exotic sights of Chinatown, marveled at the magical greenery of Golden Gate Park, enjoyed the view from Telegraph Hill, and sampled fresh shrimp on Fisherman's Wharf. Sam and his fellow Texans were a long way from Cowtown.

On Saturday, the TCU Horned Frogs tended to business, defeating the Santa Clara Broncos 10–6. Sam completed fourteen passes, one a touchdown strike to Lawrence; Tilly Manton kicked a field goal for TCU's other points. "After the game," Flem Hall reported, "hundreds of fans swarmed on the field and mobbed the slinger from Sweetwater with congratulations and for his autograph."

The Texas entourage then headed to Los Angeles for more sightseeing. Sam and Darrell Lester were photographed with the actress Maureen O'Sullivan.

Meanwhile, West Coast sportswriters sang the Frogs' praises. The

Associated Press described the Santa Clara victory as "a thrill-a-minute display that once again demonstrated the superiority of Southwest football over the Pacific Coast variety, as the Horned Frogs passed their rivals dizzy."

Looking back many years later on that glorious season and the West Coast trip, the sportswriter Dan Jenkins waxed nostalgic: "It must have been fun to have been a grownup back then, I've always felt. Ride the special trains to the out-of-town games, Stetson squared away, flask handy, dinner in the diner. What a giddy time for the fans who could afford to travel with the Frogs in '35 and '38, the national championship seasons."

The '35 Frogs still had a game to play—against Southeastern Conference champion LSU in the Sugar Bowl. The Tigers were 9–1, their only loss coming early in the season to Rice.

Frog boosters collected "bonus" checks for TCU coaches totaling $1,550 and organized another special train—three trains, in fact, with interest growing as New Year's Day approached. A round-trip ticket could be had for $4 (upper berth, Tourist Pullman), while the coach rate was $11.26. Those who could afford to go in style paid $30 for a drawing room. Eventually, more than 4,000 Frog fans made the journey from Fort Worth, most of them decked out in a white sombrero festooned with a purple Horned Frog.

"The whole thing was just amazing," L. D. Meyer told Whit Canning many years later.

> It was all orchestrated by Amon Carter, I'm sure. You can't imagine the extent to which he ran this town back then. He could do anything he wanted.
>
> He was a great supporter of TCU, and in a situation like that one, anything we needed we got. If we had to take a long road trip somewhere for a big game—poof—he got us a special train. He was a tireless supporter of anything he thought would promote Fort Worth.

Meyer's assessment of Amon G. Carter—born Giles Amon Carter—was, if anything, an understatement. A one-man chamber of commerce and a tireless booster, Carter had made millions in the oil business, and he spread the wealth in his adopted town. It was Carter who enticed early oil companies to make Fort Worth their headquarters. The W. T. Waggoner Building, the Sinclair Building, the Life of America Building, and several other downtown skyscrapers were the direct result of Carter's blandishments. His philanthropic efforts were as larger than life as he was.

He helped found the *Fort Worth Star-Telegram* in 1909, and by 1923 had become the newspaper's publisher. It was Carter who coined the phrase that adorned the paper's masthead: "Fort Worth is Where the West Begins."

In 1911, he headed a committee that brought the first airplane to Fort Worth. By 1928, he was director and part owner of American Airways, the forerunner of American Airlines. In 1922, he established WBAP, Fort Worth's first radio station.

A beefy, broad-faced man, he loved to drink, loved to womanize, and loved to gamble, particularly on football games, and was known to drink and play poker for forty-eight hours at a stretch in Suite 10G of the Fort Worth Club. He also loved to hate Dallas, the bigger, snootier city that anchored the eastern end of what, in decades to come, would come to be called the Metroplex. Carter—who would play a major role in Sam Baugh's ascension to the NFL—hated Dallas so much he always carried a sack lunch whenever he was forced to visit the place. He refused to spend a dime in Dallas, even for lunch.

A few days after Christmas, Carter and thousands of other Frog boosters boarded the special trains in Fort Worth for the ten-hour ride to the Crescent City. The Horned Frog band paraded up Canal Street, despite cold, gray skies and a steady rain. The *Fort Worth-Star Telegram* ran a photo of Sam, Dutch Meyer, Bear Wolf, and all-American center Darrell Lester in suits and ties and ten-gallon hats. The *New Orleans Picayune* reported that crowds were pouring into the city by car, train, and plane. Special trains were coming in from Pensacola, Montgomery, Atlanta, Mobile, and Memphis. Three special trains were coming from Dallas–Fort Worth.

The only damper on the festivities was the incessant rain, three straight days of cold, wintry drizzle. Oddsmakers installed LSU as the favorite, since their ground game was considered less susceptible to the elements than TCU's passing attack.

Although the field was not a sea of mud when the two teams took the field before 37,000 fans, the turf was heavy and treacherous, and the rain resumed shortly after kickoff. "I've never seen a rain like that in my life," Knowles recalled more than three-quarters of a century later.

The field soon became a quagmire, and it wasn't long before the Frogs in their purple jerseys and the Tigers in gold pants and white jerseys were virtually indistinguishable. A cold wind out of the northeast only added to the miserable conditions. "There was standing water over your shoe tops," Dutch Meyer recalled years later. "After every play, when they put the ball down, an official had to stand there with his foot on it to keep it from floating away."

In the second quarter, TCU lost Lester, its all-American center, when he broke his shoulder stopping an LSU drive at the goal line. Squarehead Lawrence also left the field with an injury.

The game was a defensive battle for three quarters. Although Sam had trouble with the slippery, waterlogged ball—footballs weren't changed out in those days—he kept the Tigers on their heels with his punting.

All the players on the field, including Sam, also were waterlogged themselves. Equipment in those days added about fifteen pounds to a player's weight. When the leather helmets, woolen jerseys, and ill-fitting equipment got soaked, a player could hardly move around.

An old friend also gave him trouble. Ernie "Son" Seago, LSU's "signal caller and brilliant blocker," had lived across the street from the Baughs in Temple. "Throughout the game," the *New Orleans Morning Tribune* reported, "the two kidded each other continually, with Ernie teasing Sammy to throw him a pass." Flem Hall of the *Star-Telegram* reported:

> Sam played a good part of the game without knowing what he was doing. A blow on the head from the knee of "Son" Seago knocked Baugh loose from clear thinking, but he went right on by instinct.
>
> "I kinda knew what was what, but I couldn't get things connected up," he said after the game.

Twice Sam passed from his own end zone, despite the slippery ball and the treacherous condition of the field. The second time he tried it, he retreated deep into the end zone, desperately looking for a man downfield, and when he could retreat no farther without falling back into the bleacher seats, he let the ball fly. The pass was incomplete, but unfortunately, Sam had stepped over the end-zone line, giving LSU a safety.

As the "Cowtown Christians" lined up at their own twenty to kick off to the Tigers, both teams were well aware that a 2–0 lead could hold up, given the trouble both offenses were having moving the ball. LSU fielded the kickoff at its own 40. On the first play from scrimmage, LSU's big fullback, Bill Crass, fumbled, and Will Walls, TCU's 190-pound end, fell on the ball. The Frogs drove to the LSU nineteen, where Manton kicked a thirty-six-yard field goal that gave TCU a 3–2 win.

"I'll never forget that," L. D. Meyer recalled, "because under those playing conditions, I was amazed that Tillie got the kick off. And from the time it left his foot, the whole way, it never rose more than two feet above the cross bar. We won that game on a line drive."

On the last play of the game, Sam ran through the LSU defense for a forty-three-yard gain, the longest run of the day. He was pulled down at the one-yard line as time ran out.

Afterward, young Meyer's irrepressible uncle was ecstatic. "Boy! Boy! Give me five!" he shouted, shaking Bear Wolf's hand in the dressing room. The coach called the Sugar Bowl victory "the greatest game I ever saw in the rain."

Addled or not, Sam had a superb day, especially with his kicking. He punted the heavy, waterlogged ball an amazing fourteen times, averaging more than forty yards a kick, often spiraling the ball out of bounds inside LSU's five-yard line, the old "coffin corner." His long run put the game out of danger.

"Texas may run dry of oil, the cows may die of old age or the butcher's knife and the Alamo might crumble like fresh Graham crackers," wrote columnist Charlie Dufour of the *New Orleans Item*, "but as long as Texas has Sam Baugh the Lone Star Staters are home on the range, footloose and fancy free."

After the bowl game results, the Williamson Rating Service, the only reputable poll of the day, declared TCU the top team in the nation. The little school from Fort Worth, a school few outside the Southwest had ever heard of a few years earlier, was now the national champion.

"Back then," Sam recalled, "we really didn't make a big deal out of it. I don't remember even being aware of the fact there was a national ranking until we were told after the season that we'd been voted the No. 1 team. What excited us most was the fact it provided some recognition for TCU outside the state of Texas."

The nation was getting to know Slingin' Sam, but as he recalled years later, he learned during his days at TCU not to take it too seriously.

"A Fort Worth sports writer came out and talked to me one time," he remembered. "He told me what they were going to do. He said they were going to try to get me some publicity."

The writer said, "We're going to try to get the news back East where people can hear about you. We've got to start early if we're going to do anything."

The writer also offered a bit of advice: "Now don't you get too damn wrapped up in this stuff and believe a lot of it. We'll embellish a little bit. You have to learn not to pay too much attention to the publicity."

It was a lesson he took to heart. Modesty served him well throughout his long career in the public eye.

Meanwhile, a News Orleans paper had some news about Sam Baugh the day after his team's Sugar Bowl victory. "Sammy is taking physical education at TCU and will not play pro football when he finishes school," the *New Orleans Morning Tribune* reported. "He is a junior and intends to try pro baseball. He is a third baseman. After a few years of baseball, he will try his hand at coaching football."

Unbeknown to the *New Orleans Morning Tribune*—and to Sam Baugh himself—a Washington, D.C., laundryman had other plans in store for him.

GEORGE PRESTON MARSHALL

FOOTBALL IMPRESARIO

George Preston Marshall was not happy. And when George Preston Marshall wasn't happy, no one around him was happy either. He made sure of that.

A big ruddy-faced fellow with slicked-back hair, a beaked nose, and bushy eyebrows, a showman with a flair for fancy dress (including full-length raccoon-skin coats) and a blusterer, even a bully, Marshall was used to having his way, used to people paying attention. He had made his debut on the burlesque stage at age sixteen and had been onstage in one way or another ever since.

Jack Walsh of the *Washington Post* once observed: "Whether having a shampoo in the Statler-Hilton barbershop, dining at Duke Zeibert's or holding court on the Shoreham [Hotel] terrace, Marshall considered it a lost opportunity were he not the center of attention."

Writing about him in 1935, the Associated Press noted that Marshall didn't drive but had a chauffer and an automobile "with a trick back seat that slides into a bunk and a small bar." The rest of his lifestyle was likewise a combination of the elegant and the odd: "He lives in a hotel with a valet-butler, never plays golf, has never been in an airplane and has traveled all over the world."

In the mid-1930s, though, the Washington laundry magnate, the flashy dresser who liked to think of himself as a bigger-than-life impresario, was not having his way with Boston sports fans. They didn't care that he had brought professional football to Beantown. They didn't care that in five short years he had built his Boston Braves (later Redskins) into a league powerhouse.

Certain habits of Bostonians upset Marshall to no end. First was their habit of finding other things to do—reading the Sunday papers, going for a drive, taking a nap—when the Braves were playing on Sunday afternoons. Second was the low priority the local newspapers gave his team. Editors laying out their pages invariably allotted more space and blaring headlines to traditional Boston favorites—to Harvard and Boston College football or to the city's two big-league baseball teams, the storied Red Sox and the less loved Braves.

The absolute nadir for the proud football impresario was when the *Boston Globe* gave more space to the Radcliffe College girls' field hockey team than to Marshall's gridiron minions. He stomped, shouted, and cursed—and redoubled his efforts to woo the Boston fans, even if not the Boston newspapers.

He had a legitimate beef. He may not have been Boston born and bred, and he was certainly no Brahmin, but he was no callow newcomer to professional sports. Although he wasn't present at professional football's creation, he has to be considered one of its pioneers and certainly one of its primary innovators. Right before their very eyes—the relatively few eyes of Boston fans—he was changing the game for the better. Boston didn't care.

George Preston Marshall had always been a go-getter. He was born on October 11, 1896, in Charleston, West Virginia, and grew up in Grafton, a small railroad town near the Pennsylvania border (and the town that bequeathed Mother's Day to the nation). His father, T. Hill Marshall, a descendant of Confederate officers, and his mother, Blanche Preston Marshall, were publishers of the local newspaper, the *Grafton Leader*.

Young George first displayed his lifelong flair for promotion when he went into the rabbit-breeding business. Unfortunately, he wasn't the only rabbit breeder around town, and he was having trouble moving his stock, even at the bargain-basement rate of fifty cents apiece. The fledgling entrepreneur (and born promoter) had an idea, either his own or someone else's suggestion. He took out an ad in the family newspaper touting "Rare Jacksonville Hares" that were going for only a dollar and a quarter apiece. He cornered the Grafton-area rabbit market.

He got into football at an early age as well. At fourteen, he organized a local team that traveled all the way to the Washington suburbs for games.

When George was in his teens, the Marshall family left the hills of West Virginia and moved to the nation's capital, where his father had acquired the Palace Laundry by way of a bad debt. George attended Friends Select School in Washington—now the prestigious Sidwell Friends School—and Randolph-Macon College. By age sixteen, he had resolved to become the next Douglas Elton Ullman, better known as the iconic star of stage and screen Douglas Fairbanks.

Young Marshall, tall and athletic-looking, with glistening black hair and a commanding presence, was cast in a few bit parts at Poli's Theater in Washington and at the old Morosco Stock Company in Los Angeles, and he occasionally landed a few roles in New York. Still, it soon became obvious—to casting directors first and then to Marshall himself—that his acting career was unlikely to measure up to his outsized ambitions, probably because he had trouble imagining himself as anyone but George Preston Marshall. He liked to be called the Magnificent Marshall.

Although he grudgingly conceded he wasn't much of an actor, he did like to tell about how he once brought down the house by delivering just a single line. "It was at the Walker Theater in Winnipeg, Canada, in 1917," he recalled. "The stage manager asked me to go out at intermission and make an announcement. I stepped out in front of the curtain and said: 'The United States has just declared war on Germany.' And those Canadians went crazy."

Marshall turned to managing theaters in the Baltimore-Washington area and produced a few theatrical shows in Washington, included a musical called *Getting Gertie's Garter*. His first wife was a Ziegfeld Follies girl; his second was a silent screen goddess, Corinne Griffith, known as the "Orchid of the Screen" because of her delicate features.

Discovering that he had a flair for the business end of entertainment, he invested big money in Broadway and Hollywood productions. He might have stayed with it had World War I not intervened. His father died during the year and a half George was in the army, and when the doughboys came marching home again, George returned to a widowed mother who needed his support and to a sadly neglected laundry business that was only a few laundry loads short of going broke.

Still only twenty-two, he plunged into the family enterprise with characteristic vigor and verve. He saw an opportunity to, in his words, "apply theatrical principles to merchandising." He would promote his area-wide laundry chain the way you would promote the latest Mary Pickford flick.

He painted his laundry storefronts around the Washington area—eventually, fifty-seven in all—blue and gold. He commanded his managers to strip away slapdash ads in the display windows touting "specials." He painted his delivery trucks blue and gold too, and outfitted his drivers in blue and gold uniforms. For the Palace Laundry's trademark, he chose a chrysanthemum in a simple blue vase. The message was cleanliness and professionalism; the company's slogan, "Long Live Linen."

He spent a hefty portion of his budget on paid advertising. Often he wrote the copy himself, which frequently was witty, humorous, and offbeat. He once took out a full-page newspaper ad that was completely devoid of print except for a line in small type at the bottom: "This space was cleaned by the Palace Laundry."

Soon, Marshall's laundry business was making him lots of money, and in 1926, he found a way to combine his business acumen, his promotional flair, and his love of sports. He took over a semiprofessional basketball outfit, and in exchange for paying team expenses and a token fee to the players, he had a ready-made advertising venue. He outfitted the team in blue and gold uniforms, "PALACE LAUNDRY" emblazoned on the jerseys.

On the basketball circuit, Marshall met Joe Carr, a Columbus native and former sportswriter for the *Ohio State Journal* who founded one of the first professional football teams, the Columbus Panhandles. In 1920, at a time when the nation was returning to "normalcy" under the leadership of Carr's fellow Ohioan, President Warren G. Harding, the Panhandles' owner sent out an invitation to other team owners around the East and Midwest to get together and organize a league. Ralph Hay, a sports fan and the owner of the Hupmobile agency in Canton, Ohio, offered his showroom as a meeting place.

On September 17, 1920, Jim Thorpe, player-coach of the Canton Bulldogs; George Halas, owner of the Decatur Staleys; and hardworking owners, coaches, and managers from tough midwestern industrial towns trooped into the downtown dealership. Carr himself chaired the meeting. Hay had forgotten to provide any chairs of the sitting variety, so the owners leaned against shiny new cars or found seats on running boards. Hay also provided buckets of beer that hung over the fenders. Apparently no one was concerned about violating Prohibition laws.

The minutes of that fateful meeting are imprecise. The recording secretary, Art Rooney, a little man with a big cigar, somehow wrote down that twelve cities were represented instead of the actual ten. The stated purpose of the meeting was "to raise professional football to the highest level," whatever that meant. The group formed the American Professional

Football Association that historic day in Canton and decided on a franchise fee of $100 for each of the ten teams, although it seems that no money ever changed hands.

They weren't rich men. Hay owned a Hupmobile dealership. Another man owned a cigar store. Halas was merely the manager of his team, which was owned by the Staley Starch Company of Decatur, Illinois. Thorpe was elected president because he had the highest public profile of any in the group, but not much happened under his leadership. Carr replaced the Carlisle legend as president in 1921 and served until his death, eighteen years later.

Halas was the most important man in the Hupmobile showroom that day, the most important man in the newly formed league. A former athlete himself, Halas had been a second-team all-American end and halfback at Illinois and a pro for eleven seasons. He had captained the Illini basketball team as well and was good enough on the baseball diamond to sign a contract with the New York Yankees in 1919. He played in twelve games for the Yankees, batted .091, and injured his hip sliding into third base one day. The Yankees replaced him with a youngster named Ruth, and Halas went back to football.

He became the player-coach, trainer, ticket seller, and pitchman for the Decatur Staleys, which became the Chicago Staleys, which became the Chicago Bears. As Halas morphed into Papa Bear over the years, he and Marshall would butt heads countless times as old friends and heated rivals.

It was Halas who suggested in 1922 that the football association change its name to the National Football League. The change was adopted. Three seasons later he pulled off the biggest coup in the fledgling league's history when he signed Harold "Red" Grange, the "Galloping Ghost" from Illinois and the greatest college football player of his time. His signing—for $3,000 a game plus 50 percent of the gate receipts—gave the pro game much-needed legitimacy. From them on, it was harder to make the argument that professional football was nothing but a haven for plodding has-beens slugging it out—usually on a borrowed baseball field—simply for the dollar.

Grange attracted huge crowds, and Halas took advantage of it. He led his team on a barnstorming tour that took the Bears from the Midwest to the East Coast, down to Florida, cross-country to California, and up the West Coast to Washington. During the first part of the whirlwind tour, the Bears played an incredible eight games in eleven days in eight different cities.

During Grange's first year, the Bears played a seventeen-game schedule—twelve was the norm—and when the team pulled into New York to play the Giants, more than 73,000 people packed the Polo Grounds. The game not only broke a newly set attendance record—it doubled the record. The Grange-led Bears drew 75,000 in Los Angeles.

Baseball—whether it was the Gashouse Gang out "west" in St. Louis, or Babe Ruth, Lou Gehrig, and their fellow New York Yankees—was still the national pastime, but professional football was beginning to catch on. No longer would teams take the fields on Sunday afternoons to crowds as small as two or three thousand, and press accounts were gradually migrating from back pages to the front of the nation's sports pages.

The Galloping Ghost played nine seasons for the Bears and served five more years as an assistant coach. His success drew not only fans to the pro game but players as well. Other college stars reasoned that if professional football could attract the likes of Red Grange, maybe the pro game had a future.

Maybe. Twenty-two teams took the field in the fall of 1926, even though Grange had helped start up a rival American Football League. The Galloping Ghost signed with the AFL New York Yankees. But the AFL was such a financial disaster that it folded before the season ended. The Yankees and Grange entered the NFL fold in 1927.

Red Grange or no, the NFL was struggling, and clubs in smaller towns— Canton, Akron, Dayton, Hammond (Indiana), Massillon (Ohio), Rock Island (Illinois)—couldn't draw enough paying customers to make a go of it. By 1927, the NFL's twenty-two teams had dwindled to twelve. Carr and Halas realized that the league had to establish beachheads in big cities; otherwise, it would fold completely.

They had their eye on Boston, where they placed a franchise in 1929. Beantown sports fans barely noticed. The Boston Braves in their first incarnation folded at the end of their inaugural season. By 1931, with the Depression taking hold around the country, only ten teams were left. Three of the ten—the Cleveland Indians, the Frankford (Pennsylvania) Yellow Jackets, and the Providence Steamrollers—packed it in at season's end.

Desperate to find sportsmen with the financial heft to take over some of the inactive franchises—particularly Boston—Carr and Halas set their sights on young George Preston Marshall. They knew him through basketball. Carr also was president of the fledgling American Basketball League, and Halas owned the ABL Chicago Bruins. In 1926, Marshall ventured into the big time when he signed a squad of journeymen pros, including "Horse" Haggerty, a star of the original Boston Celtics, and entered the ABL. He called his team the "Palace Big Five." The franchise turned out to be a financial disaster, so he sold it during the ABL's third season, in 1928.

Halas and Carr still had their eye on Marshall as a potential football owner, and in 1932 they recruited him to buy the bankrupt Duluth Eskimos. The price was right—$100—but the laundry magnate was leery, and with good reason. Professional football, particularly in Boston, was something far down the ladder of respectability.

Less than a decade earlier, the legendary Amos Alonzo Stagg, the football coach at the University of Chicago, had condemned pro football as an insidious enterprise on a par with gambling. And while Boston was a great baseball town, its football affections were reserved for hometown college teams—Harvard, Boston University, Boston College. And, of course, the nation was seeking to struggle out of the quicksand of the worst economic depression in history. It was not an auspicious time to launch a football franchise in a skeptical city.

Still, Marshall agreed to think about it, so he traveled to New York to watch a game between the two strongest franchises in the league, the Giants and the Bears. What he saw intrigued him. The inveterate showman recognized that football could benefit from the razzle-dazzle promotion approach that came naturally to him.

At a postgame party, he talked over the idea of ownership with three friends: Jay O'Brien, a New York investment banker; Vincent Bendix, an auto supplier from South Bend, Indiana; and M. Dorland "Larry" Doyle, a New York stockbroker. Before the evening was over, the four would agree to form a syndicate, buy the Eskimos, and move the team to a city big enough to support an NFL franchise. Marshall's own city was ruled out because it was considered too southern. Cities in the Northeast and the Midwest, with their large blue-collar ethnic communities, were more likely to be football towns. Or so the conventional thinking went.

Marshall, of course, would head the syndicate; there was no question about that. But the question lingered about where the franchise would be located. Carr was pushing Boston, and Jay O'Brien was a friend of Emil Fuchs, who owned the baseball Braves and presumably would give the football owners a good deal on a stadium lease. The four owners agreed to reactivate the Boston franchise and advised Carr they would field a team for the 1932 season.

More than three decades later, on the occasion of Marshall's induction into the NFL Hall of Fame, the Redskins owner was asked how much he had paid for the Boston franchise. What he had paid, he said, was nothing. Zero. The going rate for most franchises at the time was about $2,500, but with the league down to seven active teams after the 1931 season, league officials were in no position to insist.

He and his three partners each put up $7,500 for an initial working capital of $30,000 and hoped that amount would carry them until the team built a fan base. Marshall signed a one-year lease on Braves Field, built in 1915 and located about three miles west of downtown Boston and a mile west of Fenway Park, home of the Red Sox. The new owners decided to retain the Boston Braves name, hoping to build on the baseball fan base.

He hired a coach, Ludlow Wray, a former University of Pennsylvania standout who had played for the Buffalo All-Americans and the Rochester Jeffersons shortly after World War I. Wray had also been head coach at his alma mater.

Marshall put together a pretty good team. Anchoring the line was a 255-pound tackle, Glen "Turk" Edwards, an all-American from Washington State University and a future NFL Hall of Famer who played both offense and defense. He would go on to be named all-pro four times. A veritable iron man, he was on the field for all but ten minutes of play during one fifteen-game season in Boston. Signing Edwards was a coup for Marshall. Other teams coveted the giant lineman, but Marshall prevailed with the highest bid, $1,500 for the season.

In the backfield were two stars from the University of Southern California, a 225-pound fullback named Jim Musick and a superb blocking back named Erny Pinckert.

The undisputed star of the team was a shifty running back from West Virginia Wesleyan named Cliff "Gip" Battles. Also a future Hall of Famer, the six foot one inch, 190-pound Battles was fast and elusive, with a long stride and a deceptive change of pace. Marshall liked to say that he himself discovered his fellow West Virginian when Battles played in Washington in 1931 in a game against Georgetown University. A couple of other teams offered contracts, but Battles signed with the Braves because they were the only team that had sent a representative to see him play in West Virginia.

The *Boston Globe* announced the team's arrival on September 7, 1932, with a short item near the bottom of one of its sport pages: "Members of the Braves professional football team arrived in Boston yesterday, and, with Coach Lud Wray in command, will have their first practice session today at Lynn Stadium. More than forty men will take the field to condition themselves and perfect team play."

After three exhibition games against area semipro teams—including a loss to the Providence Steam Rollers—the new team opened its inaugural season on October 2 at Braves Field against the Brooklyn Dodgers. Marshall took out newspaper ads touting "Big League Football," with the game to be played "rain or shine." He also advertised that the Braves would keep the crowd updated on the World Series game between the New York Yankees and the Chicago Cubs. And he held a dinner for local sportswriters and Boston dignitaries.

Only 6,000 die-hard football fans ventured into the stadium to see the new team. There might have been more, but Marshall, for some reason, raised ticket prices shortly before game day. Boston sportswriters jeered, and a pattern was set. The Dodgers, behind the passing wizardry of Benny Friedman, beat the Braves that day 14–0. Marshall watched from his box, although he couldn't restrain himself from occasionally dispatching coaching tips to Wray on the field.

The next week, the Braves bounced back for their first regular-season victory, 14–6 over the New York Giants. Defensive back Algy Clark scored one of the Braves' two touchdowns when he intercepted a lateral and returned it fifty-five yards.

After losing to the Chicago Cardinals and tying the Giants in a rematch at the rain-soaked Polo Grounds, the Braves had to get ready for what promised to be the biggest game of the year, at home against Halas's Bears. Marshall could not imagine losing to the Bears. The prospect of falling to his good friend and arch foe was simply unthinkable.

He didn't lose, but he didn't win either. The game ended in a 7–7 tie. Even though a famous college coach years later would describe a tie as being like kissing your sister, Marshall was happy to settle for football's version of sibling affection against the heavily favored Bears.

The Braves ended the year with a 7–0 victory over the Dodgers to finish the season at 4-4-2. The team wound up in fourth place behind the Bears, Packers, and Portsmouth Spartans, and ahead of the Giants, Dodgers, Cardinals, and the Staten Island Stapletons. Battles led the league in rushing, with 576 yards on 148 carries, gaining more yards than Bronko Nagurski of the Bears, Ken Strong of the Stapletons, or any other backfield star.

With the Depression taking its toll on all professional sports, the Braves ended the season with a loss of about $46,000. Marshall's partners pulled out, but the Braves' owner announced he was sticking with football and with Boston. He told reporters he was determined to make the team "not only a treat for the people of Boston but also a profitable venture, without stinting on hiring the best players money can buy."

MARSHALL'S REDSKINS

▶ BOSTON BORN BUT D.C. BOUND ◀

"I wouldn't marry George Marshall, if he were the last man on earth."

That is the first line of *My Life with the Redskins,* an occasionally delightful, too-cute-by-half memoir by Corinne Griffith, star of stage and silent screen, recounting a phone conversation with Dorothy Kelleher. The dialogue went on, starting again with Griffith:

"It is impossible for me to marry George. He spends twenty-four hours a day in nightclubs."

"That isn't true, night clubs close in the day.... Besides, he has to work for a living. There's his laundry in Washington, he's president of it. He's trying to buy the Boston Transcript, he'll be president of that. He's president of the Roosevelt Raceway, and he's president of the Boston Redskins . . ."

"Sounds like he's president of everything but the United States.... How did he happen to overlook a little old presidency like that? And right there in his own home town!"

Corinne Griffith was smart, beautiful, and perhaps as ambitious as her Washington suitor. She did, in fact, marry the ambitious sports impresario—he was the third of her four husbands—and, despite her self-professed "little ol' me" sports ignorance, she immediately became an active and influential partner in her husband's efforts to make a success of his NFL venture, on the field and at the box office. The Boston Redskins became the Washington Redskins in large part because of her; a Texan named Sam Baugh became a Washington Redskin star in large part because of her.

Griffith herself seems to have been a Texan. According to a 1952 United Press biographical story, she was born in Texarkana, Arkansas, although she maintained that her place of birth was Waco, Texas, and *The Handbook of Texas*, a definitive historical resource published by the Texas Historical Association, puts her birthplace in Hill County, north of Waco, probably in 1895, not 1899, as she claimed. Her father was a Methodist minister from Virginia, her mother a Texan of Italian descent. Her first marriage, to the actor-director Webster Campbell, ended in divorce, as did her marriage to the movie producer Walter Morosco.

She married the recently divorced Marshall in 1936, during the same week he was in Philadelphia attending the Democratic National Convention. "George was a delegate, and on the Rules Committee," she recalled in her memoir. "It was very important for him to be there, otherwise Roosevelt might not have been nominated. In fact he practically nominated Roosevelt all by himself, or at least that's what he led me to believe."

Marshall was indeed a major Roosevelt backer, and FDR, despite the turmoil of the Depression, had been arguably more successful during the previous four years than the owner of the Boston Braves/Redskins.

After the so-so success of the Braves on the field in their inaugural year, and their failure at the box office, Marshall made wholesale changes. He abandoned Braves Field and moved to Fenway Park. He also abandoned the "Braves" nickname, but since he liked the Native American motif, he came up with a synonym—the Redskins. For his newly christened Redskins, he discarded the old blue jerseys and introduced burgundy and gold uniforms with an Indian insignia on the chest. He even had his players wear red and white war paint on their faces, until they complained that the paint clogged their pores. (Political sensitivity was decades away.) He also had an Indian medicine man sprinkle powder in front of the Redskins kickoff man. "The whole thing was so overdone it was embarrassing," Redskins running back Cliff Battles recalled years later.

Marshall knew showbiz, even if he didn't know football, but he gradually grew more confident about exerting influence on his fellow owners, particularly as he came to recognize the confluence between the two.

In the spring of 1933, the owners were about to adjourn from their annual meeting in Atlantic City when the young owner of the Redskins stood and asked for permission to speak. "Gentlemen, you know far more about the game of football than me," he said. "But, gentlemen, the game you are play-ing is not entertaining. It is dull, uninteresting and boring. This is how I look at it. We are in show business. And when the show gets dull, you throw it out. You put another one in its place. I want to give the public what it wants. I want to change the show."

He had in mind, basically, striking the set and replacing it with a show designed with the audience in mind. He suggested returning the goalposts to the goal line, permitting a passer to throw from anywhere behind the line of scrimmage instead of five yards back, spotting the ball on hash marks fif-teen yards in from the sidelines for greater offensive maneuverability, and relaxing substitution rules to allow what would eventually become two-pla-toon football.

Halas was the first to see merit in the suggestions of the brash Boston owner. With the Depression squeezing families across the country, spend-ing on entertainment was not a high priority. A sports franchise had to entertain if it were to stay in business. With Halas's encouragement, the other owners came around to seeing things Marshall's way.

The owners also eliminated the five-yard-penalty rule for an incomplete pass, as well as the change-of-possession rule for an incomplete pass in the end zone. They reduced the fat, rugby-style ball from fifteen inches in cir-cumference to eleven inches, making it much easier to grip and throw.

Marshall's best idea was to divide the cumbersome one-division league into two conferences, eastern and western, and staging a playoff for the world championship every year. More teams would be involved in the championship race, and more fans would have a reason to follow their team in its quest.

They were good ideas all, but one more suggestion he made would stain his reputation for the rest of his life. After the rules were passed, this owner who would claim the South as his team's bailiwick in a few years insisted that African Americans be banned from the league. "They are bad for busi-ness," he said. "They are bad for our image. What are out-of-work white people supposed to think when they look out on the field and see a bunch of damned Negroes?"

Black players had played pro football from the beginning, and there had been few problems. Still, the measure passed with ease. In later years, Mar-shall was fond of saying he would sign a black player when the Harlem Glo-betrotters signed a white one. A man who had opinions about everything, he rarely had anything to say about his refusal to sign a black player, although he bristled when the *Washington Post* columnist Shirley Povich mentioned in print that "the Redskins colors are burgundy, gold and Caucasian." His team would be the last in the NFL to sign a black player—Bobby Mitchell, in 1961—and that only under pressure from the Kennedy White House.

"Marshall was a loud, dynamic, forceful and arrogant man who many people thought was unpleasant," recalled Bernie Nordlinger, his longtime attorney. "I would say he was an intensely loyal man, which kept people close to him. And very few people who stayed around Marshall left him, because he was so darned interesting. He was a volatile, wild man, in that sense. There were so many times I wanted to quit because he made me so angry. But there were so many other times when he made up for that."

Marshall lost his coach in the summer of 1933 when Lud Wray signed on to lead a new team, the Philadelphia Eagles. The promoter nonpareil tracked down a real Indian to coach his Redskins.

The remarkable William Henry "Lone Star" Dietz was born in either 1884 or 1885 near Cut Meat, South Dakota, right outside the Sioux Indian reservation. His father was a German railroad engineer captured by the Sioux chief Red Cloud while working with a surveying party. He somehow ingratiated himself with the chief and ended up marrying a young Indian woman.

Their son, Wicarhpi Isnala (Lone Star), enrolled at the Carlisle Indian School in 1907, where he played for Pop Warner and blocked for Jim Thorpe. He was credited with inventing the "Indian block," later known as the cross-body block. Dietz unveiled the technique in 1911 against heavily favored Harvard, a game in which Thorpe ran wild and the Indians upset the Crimson 18–15.

An accomplished artist, singer, Hollywood actor, and dog breeder, he coached at Washington State and the Haskell Institute, the famous Indian school in Kansas, and was a consultant to Knute Rockne at Notre Dame (where the writer Damon Runyon called him "the coach's coach").

While coaching Haskell in a game against Duquesne, he was accused by the Dukes' coach, Elmer Layden, of using his cigar to send smoke signals to his players. At Washington State, he strolled the sideline in full tuxedo, stovepipe hat, and cane. How could Marshall resist such a colorful character, particularly after Dietz acceded to the owner's request to wear buckskin and an Indian war bonnet now and then?

With Boston, as with Washington State, Dietz indulged his penchant for trick plays, including the "squirrel cage" on kickoffs. After the deep man gathered in the kick, the other ten players would surround him and the ball would be slipped to the gargantuan lineman Turk Edwards. Then all the

Boston players would run downfield, pretending to hide the ball behind their backs. The befuddled kick-coverage team didn't expect the man actually carrying the ball to be the lumbering, 260-pound tackle.

The Redskins' office became "the Teepee," and Marshall, of course, became the "Big Chief." He also signed several of Dietz's former Haskell players, including Lawrence "Chief" Johnson, a lineman, and Louis "Rabbit" Weller, a halfback.

Dietz put together a pretty good team. On October 18, 1933, his war-paint-wearing Redskins invaded New York and defeated the Giants 21–20. Eighteen thousand fans at the Polo Grounds witnessed one of the best individual performances in the NFL's young history. The Redskins' Cliff Battles ran over, around, and through the Giants' defense. Carrying the ball sixteen times and averaging better than thirteen yards a carry, he wound up with 215 yards. It was the first time any running back had gained more than 200 yards in a single game. The record held for seventeen years.

The 1933 Redskins also beat the Bears for the first time ever, 10–0. Marshall was ecstatic, but vanquishing the Monsters of the Midway turned out to be the high point. The team ended the season with another break-even record, 5-5-2, finishing third in the Eastern Division, behind the Giants and the Dodgers. Box-office sales were slightly better than those from the previous year, but nowhere close, in Marshall's estimation, to what they ought to be.

Dietz stayed on as coach for the 1934 season, but he had to endure an owner who was beginning to consider himself something of a co-coach. One example that became legendary: when the Redskins hosted the defending-champion Giants, the "Washington laundryman"—as razzing sports writers would come to call him—advised the coach to kick off if the Redskins won the toss, thereby establishing early field position if, as expected, Boston's sturdy defense held.

Having delivered his words of strategic wisdom, Marshall, his flashy coonskin coat flapping at his knees, hurried up the stairs to what he called his "vantage point," a corner of the press box where he had installed a phone line to the bench. He had trouble adjusting his earphones, which were in a tangle. Once he got himself settled, he stared down at the field and was astounded to see the burgundy and gold lined up to receive. Marshall grabbed the phone.

"Dammit, Lone Star," he shouted, "I told you to kick."

"We did, Chief," Dietz replied.

The Giants' return man had hauled in that kickoff and run it back down

Redskins' throats for a touchdown. With less than a minute gone from the game clock, Boston trailed 7–0.

Marshall paid his Redskins "employees" as little as he could get away with, and tried to wring as much out of them as he possibly could. He paid his players only for league games, so he tried to schedule as many games as possible to market his team and generate revenue, the players' physical condition be damned.

In addition to regular-season games, Marshall scheduled his team to play several semipro teams every year. In those days, the Akron Awnings, the St. Louis Gunners, and the Ironton (Ohio) Tanks drew large crowds eager to see the pro stars in action. On September 13, 1934, Marshall sent the following telegram to Michael V. DiSalle, a future Toledo mayor and Ohio governor, exploring the possibility of a game with a semipro Toledo team:

> as we already have three games scheduled for that week coach refuses to play another game stop am sorry and thank you for offer stop maybe we can get together at later date. george marshall

Marshall had attempted to coerce Dietz into playing four games in a week. It mattered little to the imperious owner that the 1934 Redskins roster consisted of twenty-four players. Most of them played both ways.

For the third straight year, the Redskins broke even, finishing the 1934 season with a 6-6-0 record, good for second place in the Eastern Division. Second place was not good enough for the increasingly impatient owner. He fired Dietz and hired a true-blue Bostonian, Eddie Casey, an Irishman who had been an all-American at Harvard in 1919 and the Crimson coach for four seasons before joining the Redskins.

For the NFL as a whole, 1934 was a very good year. Nearly a million fans witnessed the fifty-eight NFL games, and the Associated Press reported that in its annual poll, sports editors had voted pro football the fastest-growing sport in the country.

The Redskins opened the 1935 season under Casey with a 7–3 victory over the Brooklyn Dodgers, and the owner was sure he had a winner in the former all-American. Marshall sat next to Casey on the bench almost every game, offering plays he had diagrammed and strategies he had come up with himself.

Unfortunately, the luck of the Irish eluded the hapless local hero for most of the season. The team finished the year with a dismal 2-8-1 record, and attendance was equally dismal. The coach with the Harvard degree was smart enough not to wait for the Marshall tomahawk. Before the impatient owner could fire him, Casey announced that he was retiring from football to devote himself full time to working with the National Youth Administration, a New Deal agency.

TURNING THE CORNER WITH FLAHERTY

Marshall was just about ready to give Boston back to Paul Revere, but he still wasn't ready to give up on his Redskins. His patience was rewarded in 1936, a very good year for the flamboyant owner. He found a glamorous new movie-star wife (Griffith), became president of the Roosevelt Raceway, and celebrated FDR's reelection. And his Skins presented him with their first winning season.

His experience with Casey had taught him a lesson—that is, that showmanship alone wasn't enough to win games. The man who made Marshall's year was his new coach, Ray "Red" Flaherty, a man who knew what he was doing. A Gonzaga graduate, Flaherty was a former all-pro tight end for the New York Giants who knew not only football, but also how to handle men.

Flaherty had begun thinking like a coach himself even before his playing days were done. In the NFL's 1934 championship game, played on an icy field at the Polo Grounds, it was Flaherty who suggested using basketball shoes. The Giants put them on at halftime and upset the heavily favored Chicago Bears.

He served as a player-coach with the Giants in 1935 before Marshall named him head coach of the Redskins. He would prove to be one of the most successful coaches of his time, posting a 54-21-3 record.

A tough, no-nonsense kind of guy who had played for the great Giant teams under "Stout" Steve Owen, the florid, freckle-faced Irishman was determined to mold the Redskins into an image of himself. His teams would be disciplined, workmanlike, certainly not flashy. He also negotiated a clause in his contract that forbade Marshall from being on the field during games.

In the spring of '36, NFL owners voted to institute a college draft, hoping to spread the talent around and prevent the wealthier teams from cornering the market on the best players. The Redskins managed to acquire a handful of players who would form the nucleus of a championship-contending team for the next several seasons. Their first pick was Riley Smith, a dependable Alabama quarterback and kicker. They also acquired a speedy Gonzaga halfback, Ed Justice, and two fine linemen, Jim Karcher of Ohio State and

Bob McChesney of UCLA. The team's real find, though, was Wayne Millner, a future Hall of Famer.

Millner, an all-American end at Notre Dame, was known as a clutch performer, as Sam Baugh would discover in years to come. At six feet one inch, 195 pounds, he had good size and could catch anything thrown in his vicinity. He also was a fine downfield blocker and a tough defensive end.

The Redskins dropped their '36 opener against the Pittsburgh Pirates, 10–0. They beat the Eagles and Dodgers, lost to the Giants and Packers, beat the Eagles again and the Cardinals, and then lost a second time to the Packers. Although the Redskins seemed to be heading toward yet another .500 season, they still were in the thick of the division race at the halfway point.

The Bears invaded Fenway Park for the ninth game of the 1936 season. With the two bitter rivals both in contention, Marshall, the consummate showman, saw possibilities. The Boston newspapers saw it differently. They ran a couple of stories announcing that a game was to be played, nothing more. The Bears won 26–0, dealing a potential deathblow to the Redskins' hopes of finally winning a division title.

When one of the papers ran a six-column spread on the fortunes of the Radcliffe College field hockey team, Marshall threw up his hands in disgust. He gave up, not on football, but on Boston. He made no announcements, of course, but he resolved to shake the dregs of Beantown from his feet as soon as the season ended.

Pittsburgh came to town, needing only to beat third-place Boston to claim the division championship outright.

Game day, Corinne Griffith recalled, was cold, snowy, and gray. "Occasional snowflakes," she wrote, "large, gray and wet, emerged from the fog, slithered to the ground and slid against our faces, making it difficult to see across the field to the bleachers, where about twenty-five people huddled together to keep warm." Actually, fewer than 5,000 people huddled in the stands that gray day in Boston. They watched the Redskins stomp the Pirates 30–0.

The Giants also lost that weekend, which set up a December showdown with Boston at the Polo Grounds for the division championship.

On the way back to Washington, the Marshalls stopped off in New York to have dinner with famed writer Damon Runyon and his wife Patrice at 21, the celebrated restaurant and Prohibition-era speakeasy on West 52nd Street. It was Runyon's brassy Broadway women, horseplayers, bootleggers, gangsters, and high-society swells who populated his *Guys and Dolls*, along with dozens of other books and countless articles. Marshall loved him.

"Halfway up 21's homespun stairway to 21's homespun second floor,

= SLINGIN' SAM =

a southern accent, thick as molasses, stopped us," Griffith recalled in her memoir. It was another famous sportswriter, Grantland Rice, calling to them from below.

Rice declined Marshall's invitation to join the dinner party—explaining that he had important business to finish at the bar—and the Redskins' owner shouted down from the stair railing: "Then tell me what you know about a kid down in Texas named Baugh."

"Ah know plenty 'bout him," Rice answered [the southernisms are from Griffith]. "Ah think he's the greatest passer Ah've ever seen in college football. Whether he could stand the gaff of pro football is another question." And then he added: "He's the skinniest guy Ah ever laid mah eyes on . . ."

"Well, I was just wondering what you thought," Marshall said. "My scouts tell me he's great."

"Oh, he's great all right, but take mah advice," Rice advised. "If you get 'im," have his right arm insured for a million dollars, 'cause those pros'll break it off."

Marshall—and his wife—would get back to the skinny kid down in Texas a few months later. Meanwhile, the Redskins had a division championship to win. The team set up camp in Rye, New York, to prepare for the December 6 showdown against the Giants. Back in Boston, team offices were shuttered and the portable football stands at Fenway Park were dismantled.

"Coached by a great coach, Steve Owen, the Giants were with clock-like precision, powerful, weather-beaten and self-assured, the idols of the greatest city on earth," Corinne Griffith recalled, "and the Redskins, poor little Orphans of the Storm, didn't know whether they were Boston Redskins or Washington Redskins or just plain redskins on the warpath trying to win back the island of Manhattan, given away so long ago by another group of Indians—to these self-same Giants."

By game time, a drenching winter rain had been falling all morning, and the field, in the words of Arthur J. Daley of the *New York Times*, was "the stickiest, clammiest mud imaginable." The Giants had installed an innovative five-man defensive-line scheme a few days earlier, designed primarily to stop Cliff Battles. Flaherty countered by using Battles as a decoy for most of the game and relying on a newly acquired running back, Don Irwin. On defense, the Redskins teamed up with the mud and moisture, sometimes relying on a ten-man line, and stopped the Giants offense cold. At halftime, the Redskins led 7–0.

Rain continued to fall, and as the second half began, a fog rolled in. Puddles of water were forming on the field, and mud-slathered players were almost impossible to distinguish. "On nearly every play a towel was used to

||||||||||

76

wipe the ball clean of excess mud," the *Times* reported. "It probably is just as well that Owner Marshall of Boston is in the laundry business."

The gray afternoon faded to charcoal, and fans began yelling, "Lights, lights!"

As the third quarter became the fourth, the rain stopped and the lights came on, lending a magical Midas effect to the proceedings. The Redskins stopped a long Giants drive at the twenty and took over on downs. On the first play from scrimmage, Riley Smith handed the ball to the incomparable Battles, who knifed off tackle and sloshed through the Polo Grounds swamp. When he reached the New York thirty, only one man was between him and the goal line. He thought it was Tuffy Leemans of the Giants, but when he got closer and prepared to juke the defender, he saw it was a mud-covered Pug Rentner, his own man. He ran on in for an eighty-yard touchdown. And that did it. The Redskins, 14–0 victors over the Giants, were the Eastern Division champs.

The Bears' owner, George Halas, received a telegram after the game: "george stop guess what stop you get to watch us in the big game stop gpm."

CAPITALIZING

After the game, a deliriously happy Marshall announced to the New York press that the Redskins were leaving Boston. "I'm licked," he told them. "Fans in paying quantities don't seem to want us. Maybe they don't want me. Whatever it is, five years of trying and $100,000 in money is enough to spend in one place. We'll stay in, but it will be somewhere else. I don't know where, but there are two or three possibilities."

Actually, he did know where, even if he hadn't made an official decision. He would heed the advice of his wife and head home. She recalled that her husband had brought up the topic at the 21 dinner with the Runyons a few weeks earlier. He told them that his wife "has this crazy idea that I should move the team to Washington." Griffith recalled in her memoir:

> I tried to explain my viewpoint. "You see, Damon, there are so many displaced citizens in Washington, from places such as Muleshoe, Texas, Ekalaka, Montana, and even Beverly Hills, California, I know. As a matter of fact, the D.C. after Washington means: Displaced Citizen."

Those displaced citizens, she maintained, needed something to do on Sunday afternoons other than sitting in the city's beautiful parks and feeding the squirrels and pigeons. "I am convinced that if the team should move to

Washington, it would give these same D.C.'s an opportunity to expend some of their surplus energy," she told Runyon.

As Griffith recalled the conversation that night, her husband broke in as she was enumerating the reasons for moving to the nation's capital:

> "Will you tell her to leave me alone and let me run the football team? Will you tell her what you think?"
>
> "Sure I will," said Damon, "I think you should move the team to Washington."

Marshall had reasons to be reluctant. His experience with the Palace Big Five was a precursor to the Redskins' unhappiness in Boston; his D.C. basketball team had played its games in virtual secrecy. Marshall was tired of game venues that echoed with emptiness. Conventional wisdom also held that Washington wasn't a football town, that its residents didn't support the local college teams—Georgetown University and George Washington University—the way Boston backed Harvard and New York and its Connecticut suburbs supported Yale.

But as Griffith reminded her husband, he would be going home, and in Washington, he wouldn't be a foreigner. And the nation's capital was growing, she pointed out. It was beginning to outgrow its image as a sleepy southern city. She had no doubt the town was ready for professional football.

Meanwhile, the homeless Redskins, with their best-ever 7–4 record, had a championship game to play against the Green Bay Packers, who had edged the Bears for the Western Division championship.

The '35 title game had been a home game for the Western Division team, so the '36 would be a home game for the champion Redskins, although NFL rules didn't stipulate that the game had to be played at home. In a parting insult to Boston and the Boston newspapers, Marshall announced that the NFL championship game would not be played in Boston but at New York's Polo Grounds.

"We'll make much more in New York than in Boston," Marshall told reporters. "We certainly don't owe Boston much after the shabby treatment we've received. Imagine losing $20,000 [the Redskins' 1936 losses] with a championship team." NFL president Joe Carr announced that the Packers also preferred playing in New York: "Since the playoff game is largely one in which the players are rewarded for winning the division titles and their sole remuneration is from the players' pool made up from gate receipts of the playoff, it was decided that New York was the place in which the players would benefit to the greatest degree possible under existing conditions."

Arthur Daley of the *New York Times* reported that when the Redskins had met the Pittsburgh Pirates at Fenway Park a week earlier in a game that helped decide the division championship, there were only 3,715 paid spectators, who paid just $4,600. "We have to be fair to the kids who won the championship," Marshall said. "If we meet Green Bay in Boston, they wouldn't get enough out of it to buy Christmas presents. But here in New York, they may get something substantial."

Marshall was right. The game drew nearly 30,000 fans, who paid $1.10 for general admission and $2.20 for reserved seats. Although New Yorkers had no partisan interest in the outcome, most of them cheered for the Eastern Division champion Redskins. It wasn't enough. The Packers scored in the first three minutes after recovering a Riley Smith fumble, and Cliff Battles injured his leg on the Redskins' first play from scrimmage after receiving the kickoff. The Redskins never recovered. The Packers, led by the future Hall of Fame end Don Hutson, won 21–6. Corrine Griffith called it "a very dull game."

Dull perhaps, but momentous. Although her husband continued to insist he had no idea where the Redskins would be playing next season—"I rather like the idea of Newark," he told the *New York Times*—he had invited a contingent of Washingtonians to the game, including Clark Griffith (no relation to Corinne), who was owner of the Washington Senators baseball team and of Griffith Stadium. After the game, Marshall talked to Griffith about leasing the ballpark, and the two men reached a tentative agreement. A week later, the embattled owner announced that he was taking his team home to Washington. The announcement was buried at the bottom of a *Boston Globe* sports page.

In Washington, the ambitious impresario would stage a second act. The star of his show, a skinny kid still in school in far-off Fort Worth, Texas, hardly knew the Redskins existed.

1936

BAUGH'S SENIOR YEAR AT TCU

S am's senior season started slowly. In Brownwood, in the mud, TCU's mighty Horned Frogs barely scraped by lowly Howard Payne College. Late in the game, Sam engineered a ninety-eight-yard drive that he capped off with a touchdown pass with less than a minute to play. The defending national champions skulked the ninety miles back to Fort Worth hardly bragging about their 6–0 win.

In Lubbock the next week, they picked on somebody closer to their own size, and lost. Again playing in the mud, the Texas Tech Red Raiders kept the pressure on the all-American quarterback and upset the Frogs 7–0.

An even tougher opponent was coming to town the next week. According to reports out of Fayetteville, the formidable Arkansas Razorbacks had shaved their heads en masse, leaving only a row of bristles atop the crown. They resembled, of course, razorbacks, the feral hogs that inhabited the Ozarks hills and hollers.

Theatrics aside, the Razorbacks were a good football team—the best in the Southwest Conference, in fact. Dutch Meyer was glum. His vaunted spread offense had scored a grand total of six points in the first two games. The ground game was anemic. The offensive line couldn't protect Sam.

At midweek, Dutch announced that he thought he might shake up his sclerotic offense. At tailback, he might start Sam's understudy, a remarkable sophomore from Dallas named Davey O'Brien, who was all of five feet seven inches tall and weighed about 140 pounds (and who would win the Heisman Trophy his senior year). Sam would start at right halfback. The Frogs worked on the new scheme in practice, and the offense did seem to have a bit more pep.

Still, the Razorbacks, led by a stellar quarterback of their own named Jack Robbins, were the favorites.

Dutch said later he wasn't sending mixed signals into the hills of Arkansas; he had, in fact, intended to start O'Brien at tailback and Sam at halfback had the Frogs received the opening kickoff; he planned to stay with the new lineup for at least a quarter. Since TCU kicked off, Sam was already in the game at safety, and he stayed in the game—perhaps because Dutch changed his mind shortly before kickoff, when Sam came to him and said, "Just put me in there at quarterback, and I'll play you a game of football."

He was true to his word. "In fact, as the minutes wore on, some of the more dubious were beginning to wonder if Davey O'Brien weren't a myth," Flem Hall observed. "But there was nothing mythical about Baugh. He was all-American to a 'T' all the way, as he heaved the ball, slammed into those crouched red-shirts or booted the ball far down the field."

Sam was on the field the whole sixty minutes. He threw for 183 yards, and in the fourth quarter he set the red-clad Razorbacks back on their heels with a forty-yard punt that died on the Arkansas five-yard line. When TCU got the ball back, Sam threw a touchdown pass to Vic Montgomery. Arkansas scored with two minutes left to play, but TCU escaped with the win, 18–14.

Although it would be Arkansas's only loss all season, at the time it was seen mainly as a huge psychological lift for the downtrodden Horned Frogs. Meyer was so happy he rushed into the shower after the game and lifted a naked Sam Baugh off the floor in a jubilant bear hug.

Sam came out of the Razorback game with both shoulder and ankle injuries, and during the week before the Tulsa game, he caught a cold. Dutch decided to start his second unit, hoping to rest his quarterback and get him healthy in time for the Aggies the next week. But with three minutes left in the half and with TCU trailing the Golden Hurricanes 7–0, Dutch sent in Sam and the rest of the first string. The ailing passer threw for 180 yards, and put Tulsa in the hole with a punt that bounced out of bounds at the one-yard line. Halfback Montgomery threw a touchdown pass, and Walter Roach kicked a last-minute field goal for a 10–7 win.

Sam was still ailing as the Frogs prepared for A&M, a team led by a slashing running back Sam would get to know well in later years, Dick Todd from Crowell, Texas. Sam said later he went to Dutch and insisted that he go with O'Brien. "I told him I really thought Davey was ready, and I just couldn't go," Sam recalled. "Hell, I was limping around like a cripple, and Davey was getting better every week."

Sam said that what he was really worried about was his ability to play safety on defense. He knew that if Todd broke into the secondary or got open on a pass route, a gimpy safetyman, even if he were Sam Baugh, wouldn't be able to catch him. Meyer told him he would wait to see how Baugh felt just before game time before making a decision.

Sam started, and what he feared would happen did happen. "He ran right past me for two long touchdowns that day and they beat us. I couldn't have hit him with a handful of gravel," Sam recalled. The Aggies beat TCU for the first time in twelve years, 18–7. That was the only time he ever second-guessed Dutch Meyer, Sam said years later.

Still nursing injuries—he also had injured his throwing hand against the Aggies—Sam sat out the next game, a nonconference tussle with Mississippi State. The Frogs and the Bulldogs slopped to a 0–0 tie in the rain at the Cotton Bowl. Dutch wasn't pleased about the listless tug-of-war, but otherwise his strategy paid off; Sam Baugh was ready for Baylor.

The Bears came to town with their own high-profile backfield star—Lloyd Russell, known as "the crooning quarterback" for his habit of singing while he ran with the ball. Waxing rhapsodic about the Baylor star, the *Star-Telegram* wrote that his "feet seem to fly on the wings of songs he sings himself as he slashes enemy lines." Running a punt back for a touchdown against Southwestern College, "as the Southwestern tacklers grabbed futilely at Russell's flying feet, the clear, melodious notes of a tenor voice could be heard over the roar of the crowd."

Russell told reporters he had no idea why he did it. "I have a peculiar habit of singing after the ball is snapped, often when I'm tackled," he said. "Some of the opposing players have told me that just before I am tackled I start mumbling and singing. I don't willfully start singing, but I have caught myself doing it."

Alas, the Frogs left Russell with nothing to sing about. Sam threw for three touchdowns in the first twenty minutes and then retired to the sidelines. TCU shut out Russell and his Bears 28–0.

"What burned Baylor more than the defeat Saturday was the manner in which it was inflicted," Flem Hall wrote in the *Star-Telegram* the Monday after the game.

They are sick and tired of seeing TCU score on passes, and when you consider the facts it's easy to understand their feelings. In the last two games between the old rivals, the Frogs have made 56 points, crossed the goal line eight times and never yet have they carried the ball over on a running play. It has been pass, pass, pass, pass, pass, pass, pass and pass.

Hall noted that teams were so desperate to stop Sam's passing that they were resorting to rather odd defensive schemes,

but Baylor, we believe, had the most cock-eyed of all. It varied from what amounted to a four-man line to an eight-man, but most of the time it was either a five or six. The middle linebacker often huddled as close behind the left guard as he could get, and was an extremely hard gentleman for a blocker to find, much less get.

But the Frogs don't fret. They just keep passing.

"They should handicap Baugh like they do race horses," columnist Jinx Tucker of the *Waco Times-Herald* wrote. "Against Baylor for instance, he should have been forced to carry 30 pounds on his back. Defeating Baylor with those passes was like shooting quail in a cage."

Next up were the Texas Longhorns, in Fort Worth, and it promised to be a great game. Jack Chevigny's squad relied on power and deception with a quartet of big, speedy running backs. TCU, of course, had Sam and some of the finest receivers in the Southwest.

It was homecoming, and Coach Meyer took his players off campus after practice Thursday afternoon so they wouldn't get caught up in what the *Star-Telegram* called "the hip-hip and hooraying of well-wishing friends." The Longhorns worked out Friday in Dallas on a high school field.

Texas, then as now, was the team that TCU—and every other Southwest Conference school—loved to beat. That sense of satisfaction was evident not long after Sam got his hands on the ball and started passing the Longhorns crazy. TCU center Ki Aldrich ambled up to the line of scrimmage early in the game. Aldrich, only a sophomore, had grown up in Temple, two years behind Sam, and he would play with him again in Washington. "He wanted to play football more than any player I ever coached," Dutch Meyer once said.

Looking across the line at a listless bunch of Texas Longhorns, he put them on notice. "Gentlemen," he announced, "Mr. Sam Baugh is about to throw another pass. I don't know exactly where he's going to throw it, but I suggest you get yourselves ready, 'cause it's gonna be a good one."

Aldrich proved prophetic. Nineteen times Sam faded to pass; fourteen times he threw "a good one." The Frogs led by twenty at halftime and eventually racked up twenty first downs and gained 316 yards total offense. In addition to his passing and punting, Sam contributed a sixty-one-yard runback of an intercepted pass. Harold McClure, one of the Masonic Home Mighty Mites, scored four times.

Coach Chevigny also proved prophetic. "The only way Baugh can be stopped," he had told reporters earlier in the week, "is if he stops himself." He didn't. TCU beat Chevigny's Longhorns 27–6. Chevigny, the former Notre Dame star, was on his way out at Texas.

The Frogs had one more nonconference game to play, a November 14 contest against Centenary College. It was significant only because it was Sam's last game at Amon Carter Stadium.

He played only the first quarter. On the first play from scrimmage, with the ball on TCU's forty-eight, he threw an eighteen-yard completion to Walls, and on the next play found Walls wide open again. The rangy end twisted across the goal line for the score.

Three minutes later, Sam was at it again, with a twenty-three-yard touchdown pass to McClure, and then he was on the bench, much to the dismay of the home crowd.

"Coach Dutch Meyer, saving the potent Baugh for Southern Methodist and other conference rivals, removed him and most of the other first-stringers," the Associated Press reported on Sunday. "Tiny reserve quarterback Davey O'Brien, 145-pound triple-threat star being primed to step into the graduating Baugh's shoes, never let up on the disorganized Gents, and in the second half drove across two more touchdowns." The Frogs beat the Gents from Louisiana 26–0.

TCU got past Rice the next week, thanks in part to a timely interception by big Ki Aldrich. Sam completed sixteen passes for 153 yards and a touchdown in the 13–0 victory.

"By bombing the Owls into submission at Houston Saturday," Flem Hall wrote, "Sam Baugh made it a brass-bound cinch that he will be rightfully recognized as the most valuable football player in the Southwest Conference for the 1936 season." That left the Frogs, with a 4-1 conference record, tied with Arkansas for the lead and needing only a win over SMU, the team that had crushed their hopes the year before, to claim at least a share of the Southwest Conference championship.

Mustang coach Matty Bell, Dutch Meyer's close friend, began crying crocodile tears early in the week. "How can you expect a team like ours—4-4 with a three-game losing streak—to beat TCU, the way they're going, and with Sammy Baugh hot as a firecracker?" he asked reporters. "Yeah, we know what he's going to do, but that doesn't mean we can stop it."

Most experts agreed. "Comparing the results gained by each eleven thus far in the season, it is obvious that TCU boasts an overwhelming strength," the *Star-Telegram* noted, "but taking into consideration the grudge between the teams, it is possible that the final score may lean in either direction."

On Saturday, inside the handsome redbrick walls of SMU's Ownby Stadium, the Frogs and the Ponies sloshed onto a field of mud. Torrential rains made it almost impossible for Sam to get a passing game going, and he played the worst game of his career—the only game, in fact, in which he failed to complete a pass.

It seems unusual today for the finest passer in the game not to have completed a pass, but the game was much different in the 1930s. For one thing, the ball was bigger—and in the rain, heavier. It was wet every time Sam tried to throw it. For another, the passing game was much less technical in those days, the routes less precise, Sam's technique more haphazard. Although Baugh did much to change the passing game, it was still a game of chance.

As the *Star-Telegram* put it, it was "the first time since Sammy started chunking 'drug store' footballs back in the third grade that he failed to complete at least one pass." The paper noted though that he "turned in one of the most brilliant kicking performances of the year in the Methodist dead heat. He kicked, ran and tackled superbly, but none of his five passes found a catcher. And that was the story."

TCU gained 160 yards to SMU's 60, but the Frogs couldn't score. Late in the first quarter, Harold McClure got loose for fifty-three yards before being dragged down at the seven. The Frogs tried three times to punch it in and then attempted a field goal, which sailed wide right.

SMU had its chance in the second half following a fumble recovery, but Walter Roach blocked a field-goal attempt, and the game ended in a dreary 0–0 tie. Once again the Frogs had fallen short in their quest for a conference championship.

"It was more than a shame that it rained today," said the former TCU coach Francis Schmidt, who witnessed the game. "It was a tragedy."

Sam gave credit to the Mustangs for shutting him down. "I think I threw the ball too damn hard," he recalled years later. The reason he threw it so hard, he said, was because the Mustangs were jamming the middle to stop his short passes. He had to throw the ball hard to zip it past multiple defenders. (Actually Sam could have been confusing the SMU game from 1936 with the one from the year before, when his receivers dropped nine passes, but the same thing happened his senior year.)

The next weekend, the Arkansas Razorbacks got by the Texas Longhorns 6–0 and claimed their first Southwest Conference championship. The Frogs had failed yet again to win a conference championship during Sam's time wearing the purple and white.

The Frogs had one more regular-season game to play. Normally, it would be a meaningless intersectional contest out west with the University of Santa Clara. As the 1936 season wound down, though, the Broncos were the only unbeaten, untied team among the nation's major colleges. They had given up only thirteen points in seven games and had whipped Stanford 13–0 and Auburn 12–0. The Frogs, coming off a debilitating loss and with running back McClure and others injured, were decided underdogs.

Forty thousand fans packed San Francisco's Kezar Stadium, and for the third straight year, the Broncos couldn't handle Slingin' Sam and his talented Frog teammates. "Led by the greatest passer this football-mad section ever has seen—cool and courageous Sammy Baugh—Texas Christian handed University of Santa Clara its first defeat of the season today, 9–0," the Associated Press reported on December 12. "Slingin' Sammy' pitched, punted and ran the ball occasionally for 60 minutes of bitterly fought battle. He was the big gun, the powder charge and the igniting spark in the Texans' terrific attack."

TCU gained only two yards on the ground that afternoon, but Sam completed thirteen of twenty-six passes for 122 yards and a touchdown. His uncanny punts—five of them inside Santa Clara's ten-yard line, one for sixty yards, another for sixty-five—kept the Broncos penned up in their end of the field. TCU added a field goal to clinch the victory, 13–0. The defeats by TCU were Santa Clara's only losses in the 1936 and '37 seasons.

"Baugh did it almost single-handedly," one West Coast writer observed. "Baugh gave one of the finest exhibitions of offensive and defensive play any gridiron has seen," Grantland Rice wrote. "Santa Clara was the best team we ever played, and we beat them three years in a row," Sam recalled. "They had some good boys on that team, and we ended up beating them every year, even though we probably shouldn't have. And mainly it [was] because our passing game evened the field for us against the more talented teams."

Once again TCU used the Santa Clara game as another excuse for a merry West Coast jaunt, with Amon Carter picking up the tab. "Dutch said we were gonna stay a week, break training, whatever," L. D. Meyer recalled.

We had just knocked off the only unbeaten team in the country, and everybody was feelin' good. The town was ours.

Sam was a big celebrity—they really loved him out there. They all thought he was the greatest quarterback in the world.

Sam and his buddies may have been small-town boys, but it didn't take them long to appreciate the delights of the City by the Bay. "One night, we were sitting in this bar—me, Sam and Willie Walls—and this guy comes up and starts talking to us," L. D. Meyer told Canning.

And he says, "You see that football game with TCU? Boy that Sam Baugh has got to be the greatest passer in history."

So Willie says, "Ah, he ain't that good—I've seen better." And the guy gets really mad and starts talking real loud, telling us we don't know anything about football and that there's never been anyone better than Sam.

So finally, we said, "You want to meet him?"

He looks at us and he says, "You know Sam Baugh?" So we pointed to Sam across the table and said, "You've been talking to him for 30 minutes."

Well, the guy starts lookin' at Sam, and pretty soon he's squinting, and checking him out, and suddenly he runs out the door and comes back in with a newspaper—and there's Sam's picture. He couldn't believe it.

After that, Meyer recalled, their number-one fan showed the boys the town—clubs, floor shows, the works, "and everywhere we went he would stop the music and announce that the great Sam Baugh was with us. And he told us, 'Nobody pays but me.'"

Sam and friends finally wore him out. "We called him Good Time Charlie," Meyer said, "but he finally drank so much he kinda fell over in his seat when we were in a cab, so we had the cabbie take him home."

In 1935, inspired by the success of Pasadena's Rose Bowl, a Dallas oilman named J. Curtis Sanford decided that his hometown needed a bowl game of its own, particularly on the centennial of Texas independence and with a newly remodeled stadium available at Dallas's Fair Park. The next year he launched the Cotton Bowl Classic, so named because Dallas was a major trading market for cotton. Not until 1941 did the Cotton Bowl make an arrangement with the Southwest Conference for its champion to play in the Cotton Bowl, so in 1937 any two teams Sanford and friends thought they could entice were fair game.

The Cotton Bowl committee, on the prowl for crowd-pleasers for their inaugural contest, picked two teams with spectacular passing quarterbacks—TCU and the Golden Avalanche of Marquette University.

Sam's counterpart was Marquette's Ray "Buzz" Buivid, who had made several all-America teams and who, in the Midwest at least, was considered the equal of Sam Baugh when it came to throwing the ball. Buivid finished third in the Heisman Trophy voting, Sam fourth.

"Marquette's Golden Avalanche, just one peg away from national title consideration, vowed that Capt. Ray 'Buzz' Buivid would bomb Texas Christian clear out of the Cotton Bowl on New Year's Day," the United Press reported. "Buivid, however, lacked their certainty. The hardened pheasant hunter who pitched Marquette within a game of the national championship wanted none 'to think we're looking forward to a joyride.'" The UP also reported that "the mammoth Christian line, averaging 201 pounds, will outweigh Marquette's starting line some 19 pounds to the man."

During the week between Christmas and New Year, Dutch Meyer told reporters he was worried about Marquette's "trickery" on offense, which he feared would totally befuddle his Horned Frogs. TCU's scrubs, running the offense in practice against the regulars, were zipping up and down the field with ease, the Saturday Fox reported.

The Frogs were indeed banged up. Vic Montgomery would start in place of the oft-injured McClure at halfback, and L. D. "Little Dutch" Meyer would start at end in place of Willie Walls, who had cracked a bone in his foot. Meyer knew that he was probably playing his last football game; he would go on to play professional baseball. With Sam's help, he made his final game a memorable one.

TCU took control of the game almost from the opening kickoff, despite a sixty-yard punt return by Marquette's speedy Art Guepe, who could talk as fast as he could run. His twin brother, Al Guepe, also was on the Marquette team. "They looked like two peas in a pod," Sam recalled. "They could run like hound dogs, and all during the game, he [Art Guepe] would run by our bench, and he'd say, 'Tell Sam to kick that ball to me, and I'll run it back for a touchdown.' Dutch had seen pictures of him, and he said, 'Don't kick the damn ball to him.' He said, 'He'll run the damn thing back down your throat.' He said, 'I've seen it happen all year long.'"

Most of Sam's punts either angled away from Guepe or sailed out of bounds, but one didn't. "Danged if that little sucker didn't run it all the way back for a touchdown," Sam said.

That was the end of Marquette's scoring, though. At halftime, the Frogs led 16–6, and L. D. Meyer had scored all sixteen points—two touchdown catches from Sam, an extra-point kick, and a field goal. "They were real scrappy," L. D. Meyer recalled, "but I just don't think they had ever seen a passing attack like the one we had."

Dutch Meyer started pulling his twelve graduating seniors early in the second half, much to the consternation of the TCU fans, who realized they were seeing one of the game's great quarterbacks play for the last time. Finally, late in the fourth quarter, Meyer motioned to the young man who, more than any other player, was responsible for TCU's success. Sam Baugh ambled back onto the field.

The crowd rose, cheering, acknowledging the man who, during his tenure as TCU's starting quarterback, had led the Frogs to twenty-nine victories and a mythical national championship, had thrown for 3,471 yards and thirty-nine touchdowns, had walked onto the campus of a tiny school few beyond the bounds of the Lone Star State had ever heard of, and had put TCU on the national football map. And now he was done.

He led the nation in both punting and passing in his final two seasons at TCU, although he didn't win the Heisman Trophy. Some say his performance attracted so much attention to TCU football that he paved the way for his successor, Davey O'Brien, who won the Heisman in 1938.

Sam was through playing football at TCU, perhaps through playing anywhere. It was 1937; the Depression still held the nation in its grip. Soon, young Sam Baugh would need a job.

CHAPTER

8

....

1937

On an April afternoon in 1836, General Sam Houston's ragtag army of Texians took Mexican general Antonio López de Santa Anna by surprise and in eighteen minutes annihilated the vastly superior forces Santa Anna had led northward to put down a bothersome Texas rebellion. The Battle of San Jacinto severed Texas from Mexico and led in a few short years to the Republic's annexation by the United States. A hundred years later, Texans were in a mood to celebrate.

The plan was to stage the first "world's fair" to be held in the Southwest. Three Texas cities—Dallas, Houston, and San Antonio—competed to host the central exposition.

San Antonio would seem to have been the obvious choice. The old Spanish settlement was, of course, home to the Alamo, the cradle of Texas liberty, where a motley gathering of fewer than two hundred men, including Colonel William Barrett Travis, Colonel James Bowie, and Davy Crockett with his buckskin-clad Tennesseans, held out for eleven days against Santa Anna and his army of six thousand. The new San Antonio, with a population of 232,000, had become a bustling center of commerce and home to a number of large military bases.

Houston would seem to have been the next logical choice. After all, the site close to where Buffalo Bayou meets the San Jacinto River, where Sam

Houston and his men yelled "Remember the Alamo!" was just outside what would become the state's largest city. The hero of San Jacinto, the man whose name the city proudly bore, was elected the first president of the Republic of Texas.

Both cities were passed over though. The state's official centennial commission picked Dallas, a city that had not existed during the early days of Texas and had no connection whatsoever to the state's founding fathers. Dallas won the prize the same way it had wrested the railroad from its neighbors some decades earlier—by being brash, confident, and organized. The North Texas metropolis came up with the largest cash commitment ($7,791,000); it already had the State Fair of Texas facility with plans for expansion; and it relied on unified urban leadership headed by prominent bankers and civic honchos Nathan Adams, Fred F. Florence, and Robert L. Thornton. Once the decision was made, the state legislature and the federal government each appropriated $3 million for the project.

The official $25 million exposition, occupying fifty buildings on the grounds of Dallas's Fair Park, opened on June 6, 1936. It featured a dual theme: history and progress. The "Cavalcade of Texas," a historical pageant depicting four centuries of Texas history, became one of the exposition's most popular attractions. "Visitors to the Centennial will find in Dallas a rich, up-and-coming city of 260,000," *Time* magazine reported, "filled with tall, white buildings, smart shops, good restaurants, fine homes, sophisticated citizens."

All the favorable attention visited upon Dallas galled "Mr. Fort Worth," Amon G. Carter. The newspaper publisher, developer, and philanthropist took it upon himself to organize a rival celebration. The competing non-official Fort Worth Frontier Centennial Exposition opened on July 18 and featured the entertainment genius of the Broadway showman Billy Rose. As the producer of Fort Worth's Casa Mañana show, Rose himself explained the difference: "Go to Dallas for education; come to Fort Worth for entertainment."

Both celebrations ran for about six months, and both cities were so happy with their extravaganzas that they started up again in the summer of 1937. Carter and his Fort Worth compatriots brought Rose back for a repeat performance.

As the *Washington Post* society reporter breezily put it, Rose

took in hand entertainment features of Fort Worth's frontier fiesta and transported a bit of Broadway out to where the West begins in a manner that strongly appealed to natives of the State where men are men and a woman was once Governor. Billy Rose's shows—Casa Manana, Pioneer Palace, Firefly Garden and Melody Lane—are still thrilling thousands of Texans at each performance. Casa Manana, the spectacular revue featured at the fiesta, reduces the plots of four best-sellers to 15 minutes of dance, song and pantomime that breathes Broadway with every lilting tune.

Dallas called its second-act celebration the Greater Texas and Pan-American Exposition and hired its own "Billy Rose"—one George Preston Marshall, who, in the words of the *Post*, "turned into a $1,000-a-day producer almost overnight." Until they left for Malibu, the *Post* reported, Marshall and his wife, Corinne, "could be spotted almost any evening at the 2,000-seat blue and chromium auditorium known as the Casino, where thousands nightly see a smash-hit revue that would do honor to Broadway."

Rose's productions were still drawing thousands—never mind the Depression—but Dallasites were quite proud of their own hired showman, who was being paid $100,000 for his services, the *Post* reported. "His first-rate entertainment has set a new high in the show world, and his top-flight salary for producing it gives exposition-goers plenty to talk about."

From balcony to stage, the Casino was terraced with tiers of tables to accommodate the crowds who packed two shows nightly. Handsome George Marshall and his glamorous movie-star wife, a child of Texas herself, were in the audience each time the show changed, through June and into July. Sometimes they watched the revue from a close-up table for two, but more often they were in the company of friends. They entertained a number of guests, including Mrs. James Farley, who returned to New York shortly afterward to join her husband, the postmaster general.

"The list of stars who have appeared and will appear on the stage reads like the blue book of the American show world," the *Post* reported. "Settings and scenes were designed by the 36-year-old Paris-born artist, Joe Mielziner, and lighting effects were worked out by George Gebhardt. With costumes by famed Constance DePinna, stage production by Chester Hale and musical numbers arranged by Ray Kavanaugh, it's no wonder Texans have a real show this summer."

In her memoir, Corinne Griffith recalled how her husband had landed his Dallas gig. He had signed on to stage a series of Pan-American athletic contests for the Dallas event, and was attending a conference of Dallas bankers who were backing their city's extravaganza.

His wife recalled the conversation he had with the bankers, ardent city boosters to a man:

"How about a show, too—one that will close up Billy Rose's Fort Worth show?" asked one of the bankers at the conference. He was in shirtsleeves, his head thrown back, thumbs hitched in his suspenders. His bank had just announced their deposits over a hundred million. Mr. Nate Adams' bank had one hundred and twenty million on deposit. With the combined amounts of the other banks represented by their presidents, there was over a cool half billion dollars talking in that one room, but their chief concern seemed to be that Fort Worth was enjoying a very successful show backed by Amon Carter and produced by Billy Rose.

Marshall told the bankers he was interested but felt he ought to call Carter first.

"Amon Carter!" screamed the banker in shirtsleeves, "why, them's fighting words over here in Dallas." He was so mad he could spit—and did.

Marshall, according to Griffith, called Carter anyway.

"Go ahead," Amon said. "If you can close us up, that's all right with me, but don't expect me to help you much."

With Amon's encouragement and the soft persuasion of a cool half billion dollars, George gave them a very warm "yes."

Back in New York, Marshall arranged for his wife to meet with Leon Leonidoff, a producer of the Radio City Music Hall spectaculars from the day the hall opened in 1932 until his retirement forty-two years later. "I discussed the show with him. We broke it down into working form, whereupon I left saying I would return the next day," Corinne Griffith recalled.

She drove out to Roosevelt Raceway, the harness-racing track at Westbury on Long Island, where she found her husband in his office. "Everything has worked out beautifully," she told her husband. She tapped her handbag. "I have the whole show right here under my arm.'"

Her husband shushed her. He was calling London. Cupping his hand over the mouthpiece, he told her, "It won't be necessary for you to do the show. Hassard Short is going to do it—and for only $15,000.00. Isn't that wonderful?"

Griffith agreed it was wonderful that one of Broadway's greatest directors and lighting designers had agreed to stage a show in Dallas. "Of course, my show would have been $15,000 cheaper since you weren't paying me anything," she reminded her husband.

The next day she was on the phone with Leonidoff, telling him the deal was off, when her husband burst in with the news that Short had reneged. He had wanted an extra $10,000 for the famed dancer and choreographer Albertina Rasch, and Marshall refused to pay. Leonidoff was "sweet and understanding," Griffith recalled. He agreed to do the Texas show.

Griffith met with him after lunch the next day.

> I picked a number I had seen at the [Radio City] Music Hall, Ravel's "Bolero" for the final number of the show. I wanted an all white number, with 36 girls in white dresses, white wigs and large, white ostrich fans. He thought that would be good. George wanted a blue number for the Texas state flower, Blue Bonnet. Then we decided on a colorful Gaucho number for a male chorus for the opening that would tie up the Pan-American idea.

One morning in May a few weeks later, hundreds of people hurrying through New York's Grand Central Station on the way to and from their trains were startled to see twenty-four Lynn Murray singers stomping down the steps, the syncopated sound echoing through the vast main hall. They wore cowboy boots and hats and were followed by thirty-six girls in sombreros and boots, also stomping and all singing "The Eyes of Texas."

"They stomped and sang all the way to our special train, which was loaded and waiting on the platform below," Griffith recalled. "They were crammed into the observation car and onto the rear platform, where a round, red disk of light spelled 'Dallas Exposition.'"

The troupe pulled into Dallas's Union Station at midnight, where a happy crowd welcomed them to Big D. Once they were checked into the downtown Adolphus Hotel, Dallas's best, they rehearsed until two in the morning.

Opening night was a huge success, Corinne Griffith recalled. "Billy Rose and Amon Carter came as our guests. 'The Eyes of Texas' was played at the opening of the show and at the opening and closing of each show thereafter—twice a night and four times on Saturday and Sunday. It is the National Anthem to Texans and they stand each time it is played."

Between standing up and sitting down, she and the audience listened to the sounds of jazz bands and twenty-four male singers, plus the crooner Rudy Vallee, and watched thirty-six precision dancers dance. The Argentine and Brazilian ambassadors were the Marshalls' special guests, as were

Jack Benny and Mary Livingston, who were broadcasting the show. Also at their table was a young man George Marshall had invited at the last moment.

"I was asleep at 11 a.m., May 10, 1937," Griffith recalled.

We had rehearsed until two that morning. The show was to open that night. From Fort Worth, Amon Carter had sent some prize steer beef, and Nellie [her assistant] had kept the steak especially for that day. She said we should have it for breakfast-lunch. It was going to be a long day, last-minute rehearsals, with no time for dinner. I was awakened by George fumbling in the top dresser drawer.

"What are you doing?"

"Oh, nothing—just some money. Tell you later."

He disappeared into the living room, which was across the hall. I heard voices, then he returned.

"That was a kid I'm trying to sign up for the Redskins," he explained. "He's going to the opening tonight. His name is Sammy Baugh, and I want you to look out for him—he's such a shy kid. Didn't have a dinner coat, so I sent him to buy one."

"But maybe he can't afford a thing as expensive as a dinner coat."

"Oh, that's all taken care of," said George. "I just gave him sixty dollars."

Nellie the assistant—if Griffith is to be believed—fed Sam the prized Carter steak. George told Corinne:

"Nellie said he looked so thin and hungry while he was waiting for us to wake up, that she cooked that steak for him—the one Amon sent us." But even before I could complain he gave me a most winning smile. "Promise me you'll look out for Sammy tonight, won't you?—he's such a shy kid."

"Oh, yes," I replied, "I'll look out for Sammy all right, but who'll look out for me? If he's shy, I'm the Queen of France."

In a photograph taken the night of the opening, Sam is seated next to a bejeweled Griffith at a table in the crowded Casino. Wearing a white dinner jacket with a black bow tie, sitting up straight and tall, his dark hair neatly combed and a smile on his lean face, he stares at Griffith as she converses with a man and woman who have stopped by the table. The caption reads: "Resplendent in his first dinner jacket and black tie, Sammy Baugh is agape and agleam with interest as Corinne Griffith chats with friends at the opening of the Casino at Dallas' Pan-American Exposition." "It was a great night for Sammy," Griffith recalled. "He wore his first dinner coat and black tie. He saw his first New York show and because of a law in Texas against serving hard liquor, Sammy had his first Champagne cocktail."

She was probably right about the cocktail. Apart from an occasional beer with the boys or on a hot day, Sam didn't drink, perhaps because he didn't like the taste of liquor or maybe because of memories of his father.

Griffith's account of her introduction to Sam Baugh partook of a bit of literary license. Her husband had been following his football exploits for at least a year, probably longer. His scouts had kept an eye on the lanky youngster during his two all-American years at TCU. Robert L. Humphrey, a Dallas public affairs executive who was director of sports and entertainment for the Pan-American Exposition, made sure that Marshall heard about Slingin' Sam. Humphrey himself also had talked to Sam about the Redskins. Humphrey was so proud of his matchmaking role that when he died in 1976, the headline on his *Washington Post* obituary didn't mention his career as a public relations executive or as publisher of a trade journal for the oil industry. It read, "Robert L. Humphrey Dies; Scouted Sammy Baugh."

On December 12, 1936, the NFL held its annual meeting and considered franchise applications from Cleveland, Los Angeles, and Buffalo, but action was deferred until February. Meanwhile, owners and coaches selected ten college players for each club's "negotiation list." Newspapers made note of the draft, but barely.

"The players will be offered contracts with the club that selected them for the list getting first call on their services," the Associated Press reported on December 13. "As in the baseball 'draft,' the club finishing lowest in the standing was given first choice as the lists were made up in 'round robin' fashion."

Unless the selection process was rigged, Marshall was holding his breath as Philadelphia led off by picking Sam Francis of Nebraska. The game's greatest showman knew what he could do with a spectacular West Texas quarterback known as "Slingin' Sammy," not to mention what Slingin' Sam could do for the Redskins in their inaugural season in the nation's capital. He also knew he would have to be lucky for another team not to pick the best-known passing quarterback in America.

The team most interested in Sam was none other than George Halas's Chicago Bears. Although the Monsters of the Midway had finished higher in the standings than the Redskins, they had acquired higher draft rights through a trade. Marshall learned, however, that his bitter rival also was interested in Buzz Buivid, the great Marquette halfback. So the laundryman from D.C. let it leak out that he meant to take Buivid in the first round. Halas heard the rumor, wagered that the Marquette star would be a bigger draw in the Midwest than the kid from Texas, and promptly passed on Sam. Marshall was as happy as B'rer Rabbit in the briar patch.

The Brooklyn Dodgers picked Ed Goddard of Washington State. Marshall's dream stayed alive. The Chicago Cardinals picked Gaynell Tinsley, a star end for the LSU Tigers, the team that had fallen to Baugh's Horned Frogs in the Sugar Bowl eleven months earlier. The Giants chose Ed Widseth of Minnesota.

When Pittsburgh picked hometown boy Mike Basrak, Duquesne's center, it began to dawn on the Redskins' owner and his head coach that other teams were afraid to take a chance on the slender young passer from Texas. He may have been the best passer and the best punter in the nation, but they feared he was too frail to survive the pounding he would take in the NFL. Marshall himself had no such concerns. Letting out a sigh of relief, he smiled as Flaherty called out the name of the man who would make the franchise—Slingin' Sammy Baugh of TCU.

Coach Flaherty told reporters toward the end of the '37 season that he was shocked Sam was still available by the seventh pick.

I didn't have any idea we'd land him. Six other clubs had choices of the college crop before it was the Redskins' turn. I'd have bet they all would put in for Baugh. . . . By the time three or four clubs passed Baugh up, I began to hope, but I still didn't think it was possible. Then five clubs passed Baugh up. Then they asked Steve Owen of the Giants what player he wanted. He said, Widseth, of Minnesota. Then it was my turn to pick. With Baugh not yet drafted, I thought I was dreaming. Anyway the league president said "Flaherty, who is the Redskins' choice?" Well, by gawd, I think I bellowed Baugh so loud that it must have been heard downtown, and we had him.

Sam was not holding his breath. In fact, he had no idea a draft had been held, and he knew little if anything about the Redskins and the NFL. He enjoyed playing football, but the Depression still held the nation in its grip. He needed a job, and playing football for pay might be an option, but it wasn't necessarily any more lucrative than other jobs. In fact, most players expected to work in the off-season because they couldn't live on their football salaries. Meanwhile, he was preparing for the Cotton Bowl, getting ready for his final semester at TCU, and playing basketball for the Frogs.

THE GRIDIRON OR THE DIAMOND?

He also was looking for work when he graduated in the spring. He had a line on a job with a lumber company, plus the possibility of a high-school coaching job in Phoenix, Arizona. On January 31, 1937, the Associated Press reported that Sam had agreed to become the head football coach at Phoenix Union High School. A photo showed him with the coach he would replace, R. R. Robinson. Just before Sam signed a contract, talks broke off and he was again in the job hunt.

Sweetwater had lost its football coach to Tyler, Texas, and the locals were interested in their hometown hero coming back to coach, but nothing came of the informal discussions. In March, he accepted a job as TCU's freshman coach. Signing a contract in the office of L. C. "Pete" Wright, the business manager for TCU athletics, he agreed to coach football, basketball, and baseball for slightly less than $5,000.

"Pro football was not something that was really on a lot of people's minds. Hell, at that time I couldn't have named any of the pro teams for you—and I had no idea how many there were, exactly," he recalled. "The Washington Redskins' hopes of signing 'Slingin' Sam' Baugh for 1937 are fading, what with Baugh ready to accept an offer as assistant coach at Texas Christian University," the *Post*'s Shirley Povich reported on January 13, 1937.

Marshall the showman swung into action. He called Sam in Fort Worth and told him an airplane ticket to Washington was waiting for him. On February 6, 1937, Sam played in a basketball game against Texas A&M; the Frogs lost in two overtimes, 39–38. The next morning, he hitched a ride to the Fort Worth airport east of town and boarded a plane to Washington. It was his first plane ride, and as the plane circled over the wide Potomac, Sam looked down at the sparkling white Jefferson Memorial and the soaring Washington Monument just across the river from Washington Airport. The twenty-two-year-old kid from Sweetwater wondered what was in store.

Marshall had instructed him to buy a few duds before he boarded the plane—mainly, a pair of hand-stitched cowboy boots, a wide-brimmed Stetson, and a western-style suit.

"What size do you wear?" Sam asked the Redskins' owner.

"They're not for me, son, they're for you," Marshall said.

Sam owned a pair of boots and a hat—what West Texan didn't?—although he didn't tell Marshall. As a town boy, he didn't wear them all that often. He good-naturedly acquiesced in Marshall's plan, which is how it came to be that on a cold February morning, an American Airlines DC-3 rolled to a stop in front of Washington-Hoover Airport's terminal building. The last passenger off was, from all appearances, a genuine Texas cowboy who had to bend almost double to get his ten-gallon hat through the airplane's door. He stumbled a bit as the toe of his boot caught at the top of the stairs.

A gaggle of reporters, photographers and newsreel men were on hand to record the scene. "This young Mr. Baugh, as you know, is a Texan, and if you didn't know it, you knew it after taking one quick gander at him," Povich wrote in the *Post* on February 7. "If the map of Texas can be humanized or personified, then Mr. Baugh is it. Gaunt, I guess, is the best way to describe him, his 185 pounds spread over 6 feet 2 inches of frame, his feet clad in high-heeled cowboy boots and his head bedecked with a sombrero that smacked of the ranchos."

Marshall, hand outstretched, strode onto the tarmac to meet the tall Texan. "How are you, Sam?" he said.

"Mah feet hurt," Sam told him. Those were the first words he uttered in Washington.

After a news conference, he and Marshall boarded a train in nearby Alexandria for a ten-minute ride into Washington's majestic Union Station, then made their way over to the Occidental Hotel dining room for Sam's welcome-to-Washington luncheon. In confidential asides, Sam admitted to reporters that he was the phoniest cowboy ever to visit Washington, Povich later recalled, but Marshall was paying his expenses both ways and giving him a $500 bonus for signing, so Sam claimed, "Ah guess Ah gotta dress to suit him, not me." Marshall, ever the booster, introduced Sam as not only the greatest quarterback in Texas but also the state's lasso champion.

Marshall and Baugh did not sign a contract: NFL rules forbade a college athlete from signing until he had graduated, and the rustic young Texan proved to be a better businessman than Marshall expected. Sam returned to Fort Worth after having missed only a day of class.

He was committed to playing for the Redskins if he played professional football at all. Baseball was still in his blood, and if he were to become a professional athlete, baseball probably paid better and could guarantee him a longer career than football. He had had a good year for the Frogs, playing third base and pitching occasionally, and scouts were coming around.

After he took his last exam at TCU, he didn't wait around for his diploma. He headed north to Pampa, in the Texas Panhandle, where he had a job with a lumber company that also sponsored a semipro baseball team, the Pampa Roadrunners. Although he had played third base his whole life, the

Roadrunners' manager moved him to shortstop to make room for a major-league third baseman who had been cut by the Washington Senators and was trying to make it back to the Big Show.

Years later, Sam recalled what happened when the Roadrunners traveled to Denver for an annual semipro tournament that attracted teams from around the country. It was a single elimination tournament: lose one game and you go home. "As soon as I saw this one team from the East, I knew we weren't going to win that tournament," Sam recalled. "It was a team from the Negro League. Turns out they had won that tournament every year."

Sam and his Pampa teammates were in awe of the Negro-league players. They had never seen anybody run the way Cool Papa Bell, the fastest man in baseball, could scamper around the bases. They had never seen anybody hit with power like Josh Gibson, the Negro leagues' Babe Ruth. And they had never seen anybody craftier than the great pitcher Satchel Paige, who would make it to the major leagues in his forties after Jackie Robinson broke the color barrier a decade later. The black stars played the game with passion and panache, with confidence bordering on arrogance.

Sam usually went down swinging to Paige on the few occasions he faced the crafty right-hander. "I hit one off him," he said. "I got a kick out of just watching him."

"We won our first two games, and then we played the Negro League all-stars," Sam recalled.

During that game, Cool Papa Bell hit a line drive to left-center field. He was so damn fast. He rounded first and headed for second, but when the ball bounced high and the center fielder knocked it down, Cool Papa took off for third. The ball and Cool Papa arrived at third base at the same time. He went in with his spikes up and hit that sumbitch right in the face. [Sam, of course, was playing shortstop, not his usual third base; the third-basemen was Sammy West, a future major leaguer.] The third basemen rolled backward a few feet and was out cold. Blood was gushing out of his face like oil.

Both teams charged out of their dugouts armed with bats. They were swinging at heads. "Hell, I don't mind telling you I've never been so damn scared in my life," Sam said.

I'd never seen anything like that. Guys without bats would throw up their arms to keep from getting hit in the face and their arms and fingers would be broken. I've never seen a bloodier bunch of people than I saw that day. There were only four or five policemen, and they couldn't stop it.

The biggest guy on the Negro league team, a six-foot-six-inch pitcher, went after the biggest guy on the Pampa team, the six-foot-two-inch shortstop. Sam recalled:

> I thought, "What the hell am I going to do?" When he got to me, he grabbed my jersey. I grabbed his jersey. We just held on to each other and watched the fight in front of us. When we took a step, it would be backward.

When the cops finally got the fight stopped, so many players were hurt that the game was called. Tournament officials, perhaps fearing a race riot, cancelled the rest of the games. Sam went home to Sweetwater.

On June 5, 1937, the *Washington Post* reported that Marshall, in Dallas at the Pan-American Exposition, had sent a telegram back to Washington reporting that Sam had signed to play for the Redskins. "Marshall, an astute businessman, is believe to have offered him an option of $350 per game or a flat salary of $6,000 for the season," the *Post* reported. "At the firm's local office, it was said that Baugh would be one of the league's highest paid performers."

The *Post* got it wrong, or Marshall was blowing smoke, or Sam reneged, because Sam still wasn't signed—with the Redskins, that is.

Rogers Hornsby, one of baseball's all-time greats and the manager of the St. Louis Browns, had been aware of Sam throughout his TCU career. When the Browns fired Hornsby during the '37 season, he touted Sam to Branch Rickey, the St. Louis Cardinals' owner. Both of the old baseball men thought Sam showed promise. They had never seen a better arm on an infielder. Hornsby told Sam that the Cardinals were ready to sign him to a contract, but that he would have to go to Greenville, South Carolina, and sign with Rickey himself. "So I did," Sam said. "But I told Mr. Rickey that I was going to play football first, and he agreed."

On August 29, the *Post* reported that Slingin' Sammy Baugh, "who was supposed to chuck footballs for George P. Marshall's Washington Redskins, may chuck the football business." Sam was in Evanston, Illinois, north of Chicago, back to playing football again. He was working out with the college all-stars, preparing for the annual battle between the collegiate best and the NFL champion, in 1937 the mighty Green Bay Packers. "The tall Texan, who, as Texas Christian University's quarterback for the past three seasons stamped himself the greatest forward passer in modern football history, denied that he had already signed a contract with the Redskins," the *Post* reported. Quoting the young quarterback, the *Post*, as newspapers would do throughout his career, made him sound like a character out of Uncle Remus:

"Ah don't quite know how come they said ah was signed. Ah never did sign any papers."

He revealed for the first time that he had been talking to the Cardinal baseball organization. Whether it was a canny bargaining ploy on the part of the young quarterback or whether he really was keeping all options open is impossible to know. Sam never said, although in those days, playing baseball for the St. Louis Cardinals was more prestigious than playing for any NFL franchise.

"Their scouts gave me a pretty swell report after watching me play shortstop and third base for TCU for two years and Ah've had two talks with Mr. Branch Rickey," Sam told reporters.

> They've drawn up a contract with me and I'm supposed to hear from them Monday—that's tomorrow.
>
> If they put in the right salary figures, Ah guess Ah'm through with football. Ah don't think Mr. Marshall will pay me what Ah think Ah deserve anyway. Those offers he's already given me don't suit and Ah've told him.

Povich reported that Marshall began to realize during the summer that he might not sign the game's premier passer, whose salary demands would make him the highest-paid member of the team. The owner, who could be chintzy, was reluctant to pay an unproven rookie that much money, no matter how heralded he was.

"To combat the possibility that he would not be able to sign Baugh, Marshall prevailed upon Dixie Howell, Alabama's famed Rose Bowl star, to join up with the Redskins," Povich reported in a *Post* column on August 29, 1937.

> Howell, nearly as famed a passer as Baugh, would bolster the team's aerial attack and thus it is likely that Marshall may not feel inclined to meet Baugh's wage demands.

Povich, who would have much to do with crafting the "Slingin' Sam" legend over the years, seemed a bit peeved.

> Big league clubs sign up hundreds of young fellows each year, Sammy, but that doesn't necessarily mean they stick. The chances are, Sammy, that unless you're some kind of a sensation, you're doomed to the minor leagues at best, and did you ever hear of the $400 monthly salary limit in most of the minor leagues? And that means only for the six months of the baseball season, which, with a bit of quick arithmetic, sounds like $2,400.

The *Post* columnist also reminded Sam that he didn't really fit the mold of the classic major-league infielder.

> I mean you have a natural handicap in those 6 feet 2 inches of yours. Big league infielders don't come that big. Guys like you are too tall. They don't bend so well for those ground-hugging balls and the chances are that your long stride wouldn't be much help. Hornsby was almost as big as you, I know, but there hasn't been another Hornsby in nigh onto 20 years.

Povich conceded that Sam might want to give baseball a fling and that he could always come back to football if his diamond dreams were dashed. "But, Sammy," he warned,

> you're ripe now to cash in on all that fame you accumulated at TCU with those forward passes of yours, and next year the football moguls might not be so anxious to hand out that heavy sugar.

Marshall's highest-paid player the year before, the superb running back Cliff Battles, earned $2,100 for the season (plus about $180 for playing in the NFL title game). Whatever the Redskins owner initially offered Sam, he kept it a well-guarded secret.

Meanwhile, Sam had a football game to play. A summer game between the defending NFL champions and a team of the best college seniors was the brainchild of the *Chicago Tribune* sports editor Arch Ward, who was more promoter than journalist. Ward also was the man behind baseball's midseason all-star game; the first one had been played in Chicago on July 6, 1933.

NFL owners at first rejected Ward's proposal to match the pros against the nation's top collegians as selected by the press. What if they lost to a bunch of amateurs?

George Halas and Pittsburgh owner Art Rooney finally convinced their fellow owners that the game had real promotional possibilities, since every newspaper in the country would cover the game and the NFL could count on at least 80,000 in the stands at Soldier Field. The all-stars tied the Chicago Bears 0–0 in the first game, before 79,432 fans.

In 1937, on a muggy August night in Chicago's Soldier Field, Sam took the field against the champion Packers before a crowd of 84,560. Red Flaherty was among them. Less than two weeks before the Washington Redskins' first practice, he had boarded a Chicago-bound train in Spokane. He wanted not only to see his passer of the future in action, but also to urge him to sign a contract as soon as possible. He knew about Sam's baseball flirtation, and he wanted the youngster to realize that he had a future with the Redskins.

Flaherty, a straw hat on his head and a cigarette in his hand, was pleased with what he saw. Early in the first quarter, with the ball on the Packers' forty-six, Sam backpedaled away from the grasping Packers defenders and managed to find LSU's Tinsley, who would be catching passes for the Chicago Cardinals in a few weeks. Tinsley caught the bullet on the run at the twenty-eight, raced past the Packers safetyman, and scored the all-star's only touchdown.

The Packers made seventeen first downs to eight for the all-stars, and gained 343 yards of total offense to 185 for the collegians. Final score: all-stars 7, Packers 0.

"Tonight's game was rated as the most thrilling and the best played of the series," the Associated Press reported. "Baugh and Tinsley matched the marvelous passing of the professional, Arnie Herber, and the catching of Don Hutson. Baugh not only passed his team to victory but intercepted two throws and punted beautifully."

On September 3, a few days after the game, Povich was back to singing Sam's praises in the *Post*. He quoted Gus Dorais, the Detroit Lions' coach, who designed the college all-stars offense. As Notre Dame's quarterback in 1913, Dorais had surprised Army with a new offensive weapon, the forward pass. Knute Rockne had been his primary receiver. "He'll do until some supernatural passer comes along," Dorais said, speaking of Sam.

> He showed me something last night. He showed me that he's all the Texas people claimed him to be. It didn't make any difference to Baugh whether he was on the spot or not. Those pros knew he was back there to pass, but that didn't stop him. That ball he threw to Tinsley for the touchdown was floating so lightly through the air that a babe could have plucked it.
>
> Baugh took plenty of time back there. He wasn't long discovering that he didn't have to hurry with Vernon Huffman, of Indiana, back there blocking for him. He took full advantage of Huffman's blocking and didn't let that ball go until we shook somebody loose. And then when he did throw it, it was a thing of beauty. If anybody could thread a needle at 30 yards with a football, Baugh can do it.
>
> Course he's got a bit of an edge out there when he's in the tailback position. He doesn't have to throw that ball. He can romp with it and the smart team

won't rush him too fast and get sucked in. They've got to be wary about it, and that gives Baugh time to look the field over.

He's an exception, that Baugh. Usually when a coach picks up one of these passing babies and sticks him in there to throw, he sacrifices something in the running attack or the blocking or on the defense. But Baugh is no drawback in any way. He can do his share of the blocking and he's big enough to take a beating. And he will run that ball for you, if you like.

But I'd say that outside of his passing, his best point is his defensive play. He's a dream guy as a safetyman. Cagey, smart and fast and they stay tackled when Sammy hits 'em. You notice he was always the safetyman when he was in there last night. I had a lot of fellows among those 65 on the team who came to me with reputations as safetymen, but Baugh was tops.

George Marshall has got something there.

If Povich was using his *Post* column to get Sam into the Redskins corral, Marshall was using the press to backtrack and play down his value. Maybe Sam wasn't all he was cracked up to be. Certainly he was unproven as a pro. Maybe he wasn't the best passer the world had ever seen (and he certainly wasn't the Texas state lasso champion). It just might be that the Redskins could get along without him. As Marshall told reporters:

I wouldn't say that Baugh proved himself out there at Chicago the other night when he threw that pass to Tinsley to beat the Packers. That might have looked good, but it wasn't a fair test. The game didn't prove anything in my book.

Marshall's excuses were laughable.

Baugh and those college guys were playing against a bunch of pros who had only two weeks' training. That's not enough. I know the collegians only had two weeks' practice, too, but they're all young guys and easier to get in shape. These pros average four or five years older, perhaps more, and they need to stay in shape. The All Stars were playing a bunch of tired guys.

And if I were president of the Pro League, I'd have something to say about the size of two squads. It isn't quite fair to give the collegians a squad of 65 players to throw in there against the pros' 25. Especially at that time of the season when neither club has a game under its belt. That makes it tough on those pros.

Marshall reminded the scribes that Baugh was unproven and that other NFL teams had passed him by before the Redskins drafted him:

So I wouldn't say Baugh was red-hot. Five [six, actually] other clubs passed him up. That ought to make him come down in his demands. He isn't that good.

Povich noticed that it was difficult for Marshall to take himself seriously. His pride in drafting Sam and his anticipation at seeing him in a Redskin uniform were hard for the old stage actor to hide: "Even at the expense of tipping his hand, Marshall found himself saying nice things about the big Texan who is balking now at the terms of the contract he signed." Povich quoted Marshall: "Ya know, neither Coach Flaherty nor myself ever saw Baugh play when we signed him and offered him one of the highest figures any pro star in the league is getting. But if he was half as good as our scouts said he was, he must have been something down there with TCU. All I want to see is that guy with a football in his hands throwing it to some of our guys who can really catch passes. We'll be hot."

Marshall told Povich he didn't know what he would do if Sam absolutely refused to join up with the Redskins. The only thing he knew, he said, is that he would take legal action to prevent him from playing with any other football team, and he might even go so far as to enjoin him from taking a coaching job. Marshall asked: "But where would Baugh get a coaching job that would pay him anywhere near what he could get from the Redskins? Hell, what we're offering him is more than his own coach got paid down at Texas Christian University. The TCU coach gets $4,500, which is better than an average coaching salary. Anyway, whoever told Baugh he is a coach? We know he can play football. He'd better stick to playing."

In early September, the St. Louis Cardinals chipped away at Sam's bargaining power when Branch Rickey told him that the Cardinals expected him to live up to his Redskin contract. Marshall sent a telegram to Sam, who was in Dallas practicing with a second group of college all-stars, this one set to take on the Chicago Bears:

Through Joe Carr, president of the National Football League, Branch Rickey of the St. Louis Cardinals makes the following statement: "The St. Louis Cardinals expect Baugh to live up to his contract with the Washington Redskins just the same as they expect him to live up to his contract with baseball. They have no objection to his playing professional football. The St. Louis Cardinals do not attempt to violate contracts or interfere in other contracts made by other parties."

Any statement other than this issued to the press is untrue. Expect you here Tuesday afternoon.

Marshall told reporters he was confident the Cardinals' statement would bring Sam into the Redskins fold. He said Sam still had his permission to play in the Dallas all-star game on Monday night, but if he refused to report within a reasonable time, he would be put on the NFL's suspended list.

Years later, Sam told *Sports Illustrated* that he hadn't been sure he wanted to play pro football until he joined the college all-stars in Evanston. "I talked with the rest of the boys on the All-Star squad and found that a bunch of them were going to play pro football," he recalled. "I found that most of them were just like me—that they hadn't been out of the country too often themselves—and that I could play ball better than 99 percent of them. So I became more confident. As it turned out, we beat Green Bay, and then Mr. Marshall got after me pretty hot."

With the season only days away, Sam turned to his old mentor, Dutch Meyer. "I didn't have any money, and I didn't expect any," Sam said years later. "But when I was talking contract with Marshall, he called me, and I wouldn't tell him yea or nay but said I'd go talk to Dutch and told Marshall to call me the next night. So I'd go talk to Dutch. The first contract they offered me was for $5,000."

It was an offer worth considering, he realized. Nevertheless, he already had a job, and jobs were not something you took lightly. Sam had seen too many breadlines, too many men following the wheat harvest, riding freight trains looking for work. Plus, he knew next to nothing about professional football, how solid the league was, or whether the Redskins were a reputable outfit.

I talked to Dutch and Dutch told me, he said, "Well, you know that's pretty good. There's no coach here making $5,000."

I hadn't thought about it that way, and I told him, I said, "Well, I'm satisfied with that, but I feel like I'd like to see if I can get him to go up just a little bit." And Dutch said, "Well, you can do that. Maybe you could give him a figure that you wanted to split the difference." So I told him, "Well, I think that I would like to ask him for $8,000. I don't know whether he can go that high, and maybe he'll split the difference with me." So Dutch said, "That'll be fine."

So Marshall called me the next time, and I told him, "What would you think about $8,000?" He thought a minute, and he said, "All right. Are you ready to sign?" I said, "Yes." He said, "All right. It'll be $8,000." Hell, I got more money than I was thinking he'd give me. To me that looked like a million bucks.

"Slingin' Sammy Baugh tore off a long gain for the telephone company yesterday when he haggled over salary terms for 20 minutes before accepting the Washington Redskins' final offer," the *Post* reported on September 8.

> George P. Marshall, owner of the Redskins, reached Baugh by long-distance phone at Fort Worth, Tex., and convinced the forward-passing ace it would be to his benefit to sign.
>
> Marshall announced that a satisfactory adjustment of Baugh's contract had been made and that the Texan had agreed to report to the Redskins today after boarding a plane at Fort Worth. Marshall received a wire last night which stated that Baugh would arrive at 6:30 p.m.
>
> Coach Ray Flaherty expects to put Baugh into scrimmage tomorrow. "It won't hurt him. He ought to be in shape after those two All-Star games, and it's high time he's started to learn some of our plays," Flaherty said last night.

Corinne Griffith wrote in her memoir that her husband also relied on the persuasive skills of Amon Carter to corral the tall Texan. She said that Marshall called Carter, who managed to track down Sam.

> At three o'clock in the morning, George talked to 'Slingin' Sammy Baugh, and the Washington Redskins and the Washington Redskins fans will always owe a deep debt of gratitude to one Amon Carter of Fort Worth, Texas—"Out Where the West Begins."

Griffith offered one other observation:

> The general impression is that . . . Baugh signed with George. That impression is entirely erroneous. The truth is that George signed with Sammy. Sammy was just too shy to agree to anything less than the highest salary ever paid a player in the National Professional Football League—and at that moment Baugh's standing was that of amateur.

....

THE 1937 SEASON

BAUGH AND THE REDSKINS
DEBUT IN WASHINGTON

On the morning of September 9, 1937, Sam Baugh stepped off an Eastern Airlines plane at Washington-Hoover Airport and proceeded to the team hotel in downtown Washington. "Slingin' Sam's in Town," the *Washington Post* proclaimed above a photo of the "wiry Westerner," this time outfitted in a somber double-breasted suit, a fedora in his left hand. Coach Ray Flaherty, Shirley Povich reported, would throw Sam into "the thick of a serious scrimmage" later in the day.

Both Flaherty and Marshall were on hand to shake the talented right hand of the young Texan. Many years later, a sculpted version of that hand would occupy a place on Marshall's desk and later in the Pro Football Hall of Fame.

"It's about time that fellow arrived," Flaherty had grumbled the night before. "If he's going to play football with us, he'd better show up in a hurry, or there won't be any place for him." Sam had missed nearly a month of preseason practice with his new team. The Redskins' first game—against the New York Giants—was, indeed, just a week away, and when Sam finally arrived at the practice field, Flaherty asked him sarcastically, "Do you want to participate?" "Sure do," Sam said. "Ah'm in shape for most anything. Got two games under my belt already, that's more than any of your fellahs can say. Ah'll be in there ready to work. You don't have to worry about me."

(Whether those were Sam's words or Povich's, or some amalgamation, is impossible to determine, although Sam was indeed in playing shape after his two all-star games.)

Flaherty would come to learn that Sam hated losing, and like all world-class athletes, the young passer knew that practice was the best insurance against that possibility. When the rookie stayed after practice until he had completed 100 consecutive passes—he was likely to start over if he missed one—Flaherty may have thought Sam was making up for lost time. He would come to realize that was Sam's regimen—and would be throughout his career.

In the week before the first game, Flaherty had to whittle down his team to meet the roster limit of twenty-five, which accounted for the bruising scrimmages the Redskins had held so far, each player battling to make the cut. The day before Sam arrived, Coach Dutch Bergman of Catholic University had declined Flaherty's invitation to let his squad scrimmage against the Redskins. "Thanks, Ray, but I'd rather not let my kids work out with your club," Bergman said. "Those fellows on your squad are too tough for us. I wouldn't mind scrimmaging against your regular team, but putting my kids in there against a bunch of guys who are trying to win professional football jobs would be suicide. Thanks, just the same."

The Redskins trained at Fairlawn Playground in Anacostia, across the river from downtown Washington. When Sam ambled onto the practice field on the hot September afternoon, he found more fans lining the practice field to greet him than had showed up at some of the Redskins' games in Boston. Marshall sat on the sidelines, and Flaherty took calisthenics with his players. Povich reported on the scene:

> Baugh put on a show for the 3,000 and Coach Ray Flaherty and Owner George P. Marshall and his new Redskin playmates by rifling dozens of forward passes into the arms of his colleagues—long ones, short ones, flat ones, high ones—and any time the ball wasn't caught, it wasn't Sammy's fault.
>
> He was throwing a light ball that his ends could pluck out of the air with the ease of picking grapes off a vine and he was throwing a heavy ball that ker-plunked into their stomachs when the need was for a fast, short pass over the center of the line. He was a passer with a change of pace.

He had a unique way of gripping the ball in his big right hand. Instead of holding the ball with his fingers on the laces, like most passers, he had his thumb on the laces and his fingers on the smooth side of the ball near its nose. "All that matters is how it feels in your hand," he explained to a reporter years later. "To tell you the truth, the reason I did it was because when you're finessing a ball, when you've got to get it up and let it drop over a [defensive] man or something like that, I could get more feel from that first seam than I could from the laces. If I was gonna throw long all the time, I probably would have gripped the seams."

Flaherty kept his defense from rushing Sam too hard, but still it was obvious the young passer was the real thing. A proud George Marshall paced the sideline in shirtsleeves, sporting a new pair of burgundy and gold suspenders and watching with a smile. He was pleased not only with his new tailback but also with other acquisitions, including halfback Don Irwin from Colgate and fullback Max Krause, a 198-pounder who was, in the words of Povich, "built along the lines of a pagoda." With Sam at tailback in a single-wing backfield that included Battles at halfback, Irwin at fullback, and 200-pound Riley Smith at quarterback, Marshall was confident the Redskins would field the most potent backfield in the league.

Sam was not the Redskins' quarterback until his fourth season with the team. Before that, he was the tailback in Flaherty's single-wing offense. Smith, positioned toward the flank as a blocker, called all the signals. That was how single- and double-wing offenses were meant to be played. The quarterback didn't become the focal point of the offense until the early 1940s, when the T formation gradually replaced the single wing, requiring the quarterback to initiate the play from under center.

At one point during the afternoon scrimmage—or so the story goes—Flaherty pulled his rookie tailback aside and said:

> "Look, Sammy, Wayne Millner here is going to run a buttonhook, and I want you to hit him in the eye with that football. Right in the eye, understand?"
>
> "Yessir," Sam said, his Texas drawl slower than usual, "but one question, Coach."
>
> "Yeah?"
>
> "Which eye?"

The anecdote may be apocryphal—although Flaherty himself was known to tell the story—but the reason it has lingered down through the decades is because it is completely in character. Sam was always confident in his abilities from the beginning, and he never took himself too seriously. He enjoyed himself.

The minimum pay of Redskin players was $125 per game, Povich reported, "but the envelope of Slingin' Sammy Baugh contains $450 every Friday," adding, "Cliff Battles is the No. 2 man on George P. Marshall's payroll." Povich also noted that when Babe Ruth was drawing his $80,000 annual salary from the Yankees in 1928, he was being paid $519 per game—for 154 games. Despite the salary difference, the Redskins accepted Sam from the beginning. "They liked the way he forgot his college fame and got down to work like the veriest rookie trying to make good," Povich wrote. "And they appreciated, too, his forward passing. The guy could throw that ball, there was no doubt of that."

Meanwhile, Marshall had been working on other showbiz aspects of his Redskins' D.C. premiere. Corinne Griffith recalled getting a call earlier in the summer from Barnet "Barnee" Breeskin, the leader of the Shoreham Hotel orchestra, the big hotel on Rock Creek Park that often hosted Washington's upper crust for dining and dancing. On Saturday nights in the fall, Breeskin staged a musical football show at the Shoreham, announcing the scores of the day's big games while playing the school songs of the teams involved. Breeskin told Griffith that since the Redskins were going to be in Washington, the team should have a song, and he had written one he couldn't wait for the Marshalls to hear.

"I wrote it in just about five minutes," Breeskin recalled. "For the first and last parts of the song, to get a Southern flavor, I used the basic chords of 'Dixie,' and interpolated a different melody. For the chorus I wanted a Redskin, or Indian theme, so I gave it the tom-tom effect, which conjures up a picture of an Indian war dance."

Once Marshall heard the song—called "The Washington Redskins March" before it became "Hail to the Redskins"—he loved it, and he sent the music to Buddy DeSylva, who was the lyricist for such popular tunes as "A Kiss in the Dark," "When Day is Done," and "You're a Sweetheart." DeSylva told Marshall that a rousing team song was beyond his abilities, so the owner turned to his wife to write the lyrics. Here's what she came up with:

> *Hail to the Redskins.*
> *Hail Victory!*
> *Braves on the warpath*
> *Fight for old D.C.*
> *Scalp 'um, swamp 'um, we will*
> *Take 'um big score.*

Read 'um. Weep 'um, touchdown,
We want heap more.
Fight on, fight on, 'til you have won,
Sons of Wash-ing-ton.
Rah! Rah! Rah!

Hail to the Redskins.
Hail Victory!
Braves on the warpath
Fight for old D.C.

"We had a team; we had a song; so we had to have a band," Griffith recalled. Her husband found one in a group organized under the auspices of a local dairy. The band members agreed to play for nothing in exchange for free admission to the games.

On a hot night in the middle of August, the fledgling Redskins band invited the Marshalls to attend a rehearsal at an old firehouse in Mt. Rainier, Maryland, a small town just over the District line. As Griffith recalled, her husband marked the occasion by making an introductory speech about one of his obsessions—congressional representation for the District of Columbia (ignoring the fact that the rehearsal was taking place in Maryland): "We were told how we of the District of Columbia were burdened with 'taxation without representation'; how we who resided in the greatest Capital on earth were deprived of our constitutional rights and how we taxpaying citizens of the greatest Democracy in the whole wide world were not allowed to vote."

After his speech, Marshall told the band members that a great song had been written for the team, and he directed his wife to sit down at the piano and plunk out the tune. Marshall felt the dairy band boys were insufficiently impressed, so he climbed atop a chair and in a quavering falsetto sang an entire chorus of "Hail to the Redskins."

"It is a lasting tribute to Barnee Breskin's musicianship that 'Hail to the Redskins!' survived that performance to become the rousing opus whose first few bars can set an entire stadium to roaring," Griffith wrote.

BAUGH TAKES THE FIELD AS A REDSKIN

On September 16, 1937, a warm Thursday night, nearly twenty-five thousand spectators rode streetcars, taxis, and Model A Fords to Griffith Stadium, at Georgia and Florida Avenues in northwest Washington, a few blocks north of the Capitol. The stadium was normally home to the Washington Senators baseball team of the American League, which had lost to the Detroit Tigers before a small crowd that afternoon. Clark Griffith, the owner of both the perennially underachieving Senators and the stadium, had agreed to add removable steel seats that would accommodate an additional ten thousand spectators. He also installed a modern lighting system, a new public-address system, and a tarpaulin that would cover the entire playing field and keep it dry.

Griffith Stadium was a homey little place, with a tree just outside the center-field fence. It grew in the backyard of a property owner who had refused to sell to Griffith when the stadium was built. Sam would always say that the Griffith Stadium playing surface was one of the worst in the league—uneven, and frequently puddled after a rain—but on that warm fall night, neither the Redskins nor their new fans were concerned about such things. The fans came ready to roar.

The size of the crowd filled not only the stadium but also Marshall's heart. Advance ticket sales had been slow, and he was afraid he would face a repeat of his Boston nightmare. For the Redskins' inaugural season in Washington, tickets sold for $1.50 a game or $9 for a season ticket, a price that attracted only 916 season-ticket holders. Marshall had pleaded for support from Washington sports editors. "With what I'm paying Baugh, I need 12,000 fans in the park every game to break even," he said.

As Corinne Griffith put it:

> The great night arrived. The night we were to know whether Washington would take the Redskins into its heart or give them the Boston brush-off. The night we were to take "take the wrappings off 'Slingin' Sam,'" the famous forward passer of TCU.

In the cramped Griffith Stadium dressing room, Coach Flaherty gathered his team around. "All right, you guys. You've got a football game out there," the no-nonsense coach told his men.

> What are you going to do about it? You're gonna kick hell out of those Giants, that's what. You've got to. You've moved into a new town, you and me and all of us. And the future of pro football in Washington depends on this game tonight, here. And me, too. And we want to keep those jobs. And that means we've got to win this ball game. Not only that, but there's a hell of a crowd out there tonight. They've come out to see what pro football is like. Well, show 'em.

I want 60 minutes of the best that's in you. I won't take anything less. Sixty minutes of 100 percent effort. Those Giants are going to be tough tonight. You know how they hate us. And I'll tell you something, I've found out that they're out to get Erny Pinckert. I want you guys to give Erny plenty of protection. I don't want anybody standing around when they start to give Erny the works. You've got hands, use 'em. You're as big as they are. And I think you're tougher, understand?

Pacing back and forth, the red-faced young coach glanced at the young tail-back from TCU.

For three years now, you guys who've been with the Redskins have been com-plaining that you haven't had a passer. Well, we've gone out and got you one. And I want plenty of protection for Sammy Baugh. You know damn well those Giants will be out to cut Sammy down the first chance they get and try to get him out of there. Well, what are you going to do about that? You know damn well what I want you to do. I don't want to see a Giant get to Sammy. Don't let 'em get to Sammy, understand?

Before the Redskins could get after the Giants, they had to endure pre-game festivities that Redskin fans would come to associate with the team's razzmatazz owner. He had each player introduced individually, and as a burgundy-jerseyed Redskin trotted from the dugout onto the field, a spot-light picked him up and followed him to midfield. The brand-new Redskin band played "The Star-Spangled Banner," and an American flag was raised from behind the grandstand. As it reached the top of its white flagpole, the banner caught the breeze and unfurled against a purple sky.

Captains Turk Edwards of the Redskins and Mel Hein of the Giants trot-ted over to the box where Jesse Jones, the Texan who headed FDR's Recon-struction Finance Corporation, was waiting to throw out the first ball. Jones, substituting for a president who wasn't particularly interested in sports, held up the white ceremonial football in his right hand while pho-tographers captured the historic moment.

"We ascended the long ramp to the upper tier of seats," Corinne Griffith recalled. "The glare of floodlights gave off an unnatural fuzzy, blue haze. I caught a glimpse of the crowd. It was like a dream come true. Into the white circle of light were packed 23,000 people waiting to welcome the Washing-ton Redskins in their opening game against the New York Giants."

The Giants were preseason favorites to win the NFL's Eastern Division.

They relied on one of the best rushers in the game in fullback Alphonse Emil "Tuffy" Leemans, popular in Washington because he had starred as a halfback for George Washington University a couple of years earlier.

The Giants kicked off, and the Redskins' deep man, none other than Sam Baugh himself, gathered the ball in on his own six-yard line. With the Giants' kickoff team bearing down on him, the long-legged Texan managed to thread his way up the field thirty yards before being brought down. On the first play from scrimmage—the first offensive play of his Redskin career— Sam completed a pass to Erny Pinckert for a five-yard gain. After Hein, playing safety, knocked down a pass intended for right end Charlie Malone, Sam punted to Leemans, who was downed on the Giants' twenty-eight after a seven-yard return.

After a Giant punt, the Redskins took over on their own twenty. Don "The Bull" Irwin, behind Pinckert's blocking, sliced through right tackle for a fourteen-yard gain. Sam, on a counter play, picked up another eleven yards around left end. Irwin picked up fourteen more, although a backfield-in-motion penalty cost the Redskins five yards.

On the next play, Sam picked up eight yards over right tackle, and on second down Irwin gained three more. The Giants, fearing Sam's arm, were lined up in a 6-2-2-1 defense, which allowed the Redskins to make yards on the ground. On first down at the Giants' twenty-eight, the defense stiffened, stopping Sam on two running plays at the line of scrimmage. On third down, he ducked under the grasp of Giants left tackle Ed Widseth and rifled a pass in the flat to Malone, who picked up thirteen yards and a first down at the Giants' fifteen.

The Giants held, and Riley Smith lined up to kick a field goal from the sixteen-yard line, with Sam holding. Smith kicked the ball straight through the uprights for the first points ever scored by the Washington Redskins.

Washington's 3–0 lead held up until the third quarter, when the Giants' Tilly Manton kicked a field goal from the fourteen to tie the score.

After Irwin returned the Giants' kickoff thirty yards to the Redskins' twenty-five, Sam took over. He banged over right tackle for a nine-yard gain. After Irwin got the first down, Sam faked a pass and then ran for ten yards. He rifled a pass to Malone for a twelve-yard gain, and then hit him again for twenty yards, although the Redskins end fumbled the ball away to the Giants.

The Giants gave the ball back on a quick kick that slithered off Ed Danowski's foot, going out of bounds on the Redskins' forty-three. The third quarter ended with the score still tied.

Sam picked up where he had left off the previous offensive series. He hit Krause for a sixteen-yard gain, to the Giants' twenty-eight. Then he found Malone open in the middle of the field for a fourteen-yard gain, to the Giants' fourteen. Next he hit Bob McChesney, who was wide open, but the receiver dropped the ball. After another pass went incomplete, Smith kicked another field goal to give the Redskins a 6–3 lead.

The Giants returned Smith's kickoff to their own thirty-four, but on third down, Ed Justice intercepted a Danowski pass at the Giants' forty-four. Sam ran over right tackle for five yards, and then completed a thirteen-yard pass to McChesney for a first down. He threw to Justice for a seven-yard gain that put the ball on the Giants' nineteen. Rushed by right end Pete Walls, from TCU, Sam was thrown for a twenty-three-yard loss. He gained eighteen back when he found Malone open on the next play, but the Redskins stalled.

With time running down, Smith intercepted a long pass on the run at the Redskins' forty-yard line, streaked down the sidelines behind a quartet of blockers, and crossed the goal line standing up. He also kicked the extra point.

The Giants weren't finished. They put together a drive that ended on the Redskins' one-yard line, where the Redskin defense held. "Right there from the 1-yard line that solid wall of Redskins climbed into the hearts of 23,000 fans," Corinne Griffith recalled. "And that's how the Washington Redskins were born."

Final score that first and fateful night: Riley Smith 13, New York Giants 3.

Although Smith was the hero, the *Post*'s Povich and the team's new fans also liked what they saw of the heralded young passer from the wilds of West Texas. "If there was any doubt about Baugh's passing ability in the professional league, it was dissipated that night," Povich wrote later in the season. "He threw 16 passes against the Giants and completed 11 of 'em. The Redskins were falling back to protect their new star as if he were something sacred."

"As for the near 25,000 crowd," sportswriter Bill Dismer Jr. of the *Washington Evening Star* observed, "methinks the patrons were more than satisfied with professional football's debut and believe that the pros, like the talkies, are here to stay."

Here to stay they were, but for a few weeks after the opening-night victory, the Redskins played as if they had left their A game in Boston. On a Friday night at home—Sundays worried Marshall, given the empty seats he had seen in Boston—Washington's new team lost its first game, falling to the lowly Chicago Cardinals when rookie end Gaynell Tinsley, from LSU, scored three times on sixty-yard-plus pass plays. Final score: Cardinals 21, Redskins 14.

The first Redskins schedule featured five home games. As the leaves turned burgundy and gold in Rock Creek Park, the Brooklyn Dodgers visited Griffith Stadium on a Sunday afternoon with an opportunity to take over undisputed possession of first place in the Eastern Division of the NFL. On a cold drizzly day, Sam's passing and a tough Redskins defense banished the Dodgers into fourth place. "Throughout the first half Brooklyn more or less was always in trouble," the *New York Times* reported. "Before the game was three minutes old, Baugh sent a long quick kick to the Dodgers' 22-yard mark and thereafter, except for one brief respite midway in the initial quarter, the invaders were trying to crawl out of unfavorable situations."

With rain falling, Sam threw a touchdown pass to Wayne Millner late in the first half, and Riley Smith kicked a thirty-five-yard field goal in the third. In the fourth quarter, Turk Edwards blocked an attempted punt by Reno Nori on the Dodgers' goal line, and the ball rolled out of the end zone for an automatic safety. The Dodgers scored late in the game after recovering a Redskin fumble, but Washington escaped with the victory, 11–7. Sam was ten of fourteen for 137 yards.

A week later, the Redskins couldn't score a point against the cellar-dwelling Philadelphia Eagles. Bill Hewitt, the Eagles' superb end who played without a helmet, scored on two pass plays, and the 14–0 victory was one of only two the team managed all season. At that point in the season, the Redskins seemed to be reverting to their old .500 form, and Marshall must have been wondering about the wisdom of his investment in the man they called Slingin' Sam. Despite showing flashes of brilliance, the young passer was inconsistent.

But then things began to click. Against Pittsburgh, which had changed its name from the Pirates to the Steelers, Cliff Battles ran wild. He intercepted a pass and took it sixty-five yards for one touchdown, then reeled off sixty- and seventy-one-yard touchdown runs. Final score: Redskins 34, Steelers 20.

In a rematch the following week with the Eagles, Sam threw a fifty-nine-yard touchdown pass to Charlie Malone for one touchdown, and then completed several passes in the closing moments to put Riley Smith within field goal range. Smith kicked the ball through the uprights with twenty-five seconds left on the clock, and the Redskins managed a 10–7 victory.

Invading Brooklyn's Ebbets Field for their seventh game of the season, the Redskins held the Dodgers scoreless while the Baugh-Battles duo accounted for three touchdowns. The 21–0 victory vaulted the Redskins into a first place tie with the Giants, who lost to Chicago, 3–0.

The Redskins traveled south to Richmond, where they defeated the semipro Richmond Arrows 30–0, and then lost a close one to the Steelers the next weekend, 21–13. It was the last time they would lose a game that year.

The Redskins bounced back against the Cleveland Rams in a blizzard. Slogging through ankle-high snow, Battles starred again in a 16–7 victory.

With the Redskins running neck and neck with the Giants for the Eastern Division title, the world champion Green Bay Packers paid a visit to the nation's capital. The Packers featured the magnificent Don Hutson, a swift, acrobatic receiver from Alabama whose collegiate career had ended with a two-touchdown performance against Stanford in the 1935 Rose Bowl, a game the Crimson Tide won 29–13.

Hutson thought his football career was over after that game. He and a former teammate named Paul "Bear" Bryant were all set to go into the laundry business when he got a telegram from the Packers' owner, Curly Lambeau. Hutson, a skinny kid who could spring up and grab the goalpost crossbar with one hand and catch a football with the other, signed with the Packers and became an instant star.

Thirty thousand Washingtonians packed Griffith Stadium—the largest crowd yet—and kept up a steady roar the whole game. The Redskins, particularly those who had experienced the dark days in Boston, had never heard or seen anything like it.

The fans were treated to a magnificent defensive battle from start to finish. The only score of the first half came when Hutson, the "Alabama Antelope," took a pass from tailback Arnie Herber and left the Redskins' secondary, including Sam, clutching at air as he glided into the end zone. The half ended with the Packers leading 6–0.

The Redskins shut down the Packers in the second half. When the Redskins had the ball, the Packers braced for the expected Baugh barrage. Instead, they got Battles, who rode the blocks of Erny Pinckert, Don Irwin, and Baugh to march steadily down the field. Battles smashed into the end zone, Riley Smith made the crucial extra point, and the Redskins led 7–6.

As the game moved into the fourth quarter, the Skins' defense remained unyielding, and the offense kept the ball on the ground. With the ball inside the ten, Battles, as expected, got the ball and was buried at the line of scrimmage. The Packers again keyed on the splendid running back and buried him under a pile of forest green jerseys at the line of scrimmage, but Battles didn't have the ball. It was still in the long-fingered hands of Slingin' Sammy

Baugh, who rifled a pass to Malone in the end zone. The Washington fans nearly shouted the stadium down, and when the stadium clock read 00:00, they refused to go home.

"I just can't get over them fans," tackle Turk Edwards told reporters. "They're the greatest I ever saw."

"I think just about everyone on the team felt that way," Wayne Millner later recalled. "Boston was a funny town. They never did take to us there. But from the moment we came to Washington, things were very different. I felt that I had found a home."

"This was the exact moment when Washington football fans took their newly acquired football team to their hearts and bosoms," the sportswriter Morris A. Bealle wrote years later. "It was the exact moment George Marshall's Redskins became a civic institution in the Nation's capital. It was the exact moment they made themselves a home after their sour experience in Boston."

The Redskins' 14–6 victory over the defending champions set the stage for a crucial rematch against the league-leading Giants, who, with a 6-2-2 record, had lost only one game since the opener at Griffith Stadium. They led the Redskins, who had a 7-3 record, by a half game. It would be winner-take-all at the Polo Grounds on December 5.

In just three short months, the Redskins had become the toast of Washington. Battles was the league's leading rusher, and the tall rookie from TCU was the league's leading passer.

"Slingin' Sam is the hottest thing professional football has known since Red Grange, the erstwhile Wheaton iceman, came to town and drew 70,000 customers, including two Chinese who were misled by the association of tongs with his name," wrote the *New York Times* columnist Allison Danzig. "It isn't just a coincidence that professional football has enjoyed its biggest season." Danzig speculated that if Marshall had endured one more season in Boston, the city would have warmed to the Redskins just as Washington did; Slingin' Sam would have won them over. As it was, Boston had cast them out, Danzig noted, just as the city had surrendered Babe Ruth to New York back in 1919.

On a cold December morning, fifteen thousand raucous fans, most of them with burgundy-colored feathers stuck in their hatbands, gathered at Washington's Union Station, across from the broad expanse of the

Capitol grounds. They crowded onto fifteen extra trains that Pennsylvania Railroad officials had managed to scrounge together from their yards for the three-hour ride northward. The first train pulled away from the station at six in the morning, its cars draped with signs hanging from windows that read "Sammy Baugh Club," "Cliff Battles Club," and others.

Many passengers, flasks raised frequently in triumph, started celebrating as early as Baltimore, forty miles to the north. They kept celebrating as the train rattled across rural Maryland, past the sparkling waters of the Chesapeake and through Delaware. Ignoring a stern William Penn looking out from atop Philadelphia's stately city hall, they kept celebrating up the spine of New Jersey. When the train pulled into New York's Penn Station, more than a few burgundy-befeathered passengers staggered onto the platform, trying to recall where they were and why.

The Washington Redskins Band was on board too. Resplendent in their burgundy and gold uniforms and tall white-feathered Indian headdresses—Marshall had gotten them from a Hollywood costumer he knew—band members formed up in front of the station and marched up Seventh Avenue to the sound of "Hail to the Redskins." Bright sunlight bounced off their white-feathered finery. The leader and two drum majors wore chief's warbonnets, streamers of white feathers dangling down their backs to the ground.

A gaggle of noisy fans straggled along behind, creating a procession several blocks long. Sunday traffic was light, so New York's finest declined to interfere as the manic mob surged all the way to Columbus Circle, twenty-five blocks away.

The jubilant Redskin owner, resplendent in his coonskin coat, stepped down off the train and proclaimed, "The Indians have come to reclaim Manhattan Island." Marshall, of course, led the parade. Bill Corum of the *New York Journal* put it this way on December 5: "At the head of a 150-piece brass band and 10,000 fans, George Preston Marshall slipped unobtrusively into New York today."

Washington's fans were coming to appreciate the owner's showmanship. Two weeks earlier, he had arranged for Santa Claus to parachute into Griffith Stadium, although children in the stands were disappointed when a gust of wind snatched St. Nick's chute and he drifted over the right-field wall and landed on Florida Avenue.

The fans' appreciation was reciprocated. Only a year earlier, the team had been homeless, Corinne Griffith recalled. "Now they had a home and a large family and ten thousand of the family were there to prove their loyalty. In fact they were simply full of loyalty and red feathers and other things."

As the crowd of Washingtonians streamed into the cavernous Polo Grounds a little after noon on a glorious winter day, Marshall watched—and wept, no doubt thinking of the Boston misadventure. He told his wife: "I can't believe it—my home town—what a wonderful group of people." Griffith was stunned.

> I didn't know what to do. It wasn't that I hadn't seen a man cry before, but this was different. After all, I had never had one six feet two weep into a brand new raccoon coat in front of sixty thousand people. So I wiped his eyes and blew his nose.

Earlier in the week, Giant coach Steve Owen had made the mistake of providing the Redskins with just the sort of motivational fodder he no doubt warned his players to avoid: "I don't think the Redskins are in the same league with us now," he told reporters. The Giants' "great line," plus a new 5-4-2 defense installed just for the championship game, would render Slingin' Sam and friends helpless.

Owen also told reporters that he had failed to include a single Redskin player on his all-pro ballot. He apparently wasn't impressed by the fact that Sam led the league in pass completions (81) and yards gained passing (1,127), or that Battles had rushed for the most yards in the league (874) and scored the most touchdowns rushing (5). Baugh and Battles did make the all-pro team, despite Owen's slight, as did Charlie Malone, the league's third-ranked receiver, and Turk Edwards, the dominant lineman in the league.

The Washington papers played the Owen story big. The Giants coach and his team trotted onto their home field to a thunderous chorus of boos.

The original Polo Grounds, built in 1883, was on the northern edge of Central Park. Its successor was built in 1911 in the Bronx, between Coogan's Bluff and the Harlem River, and was shared for a number of years by the baseball Yankees and the Giants, football and baseball. Its spacious outfield was enclosed by a towering double-deck grandstand.

The Polo Grounds was a roaring cauldron as the Giants' kickoff tumbled into the tree-trunk arms of Turk Edwards, all 270 pounds of him. The giant left tackle lumbered twenty yards upfield before a gaggle of Giants managed to gang-tackle him. On the first play from scrimmage, Battles fumbled the snap from center, and the Giants recovered but were unable to do any damage.

On the next series, it was all Battles. He carried five straight times on runs of two, sixteen, nine, six, and four yards, scoring on the fifth carry.

The next time the Redskins got the ball, the Giants were keying on Battles, so Sam took charge. A series of bullet passes to Battles, Millner, and Malone made the score 14–0. The Redskins scored again before the half ended, making it 21–0.

The Giants scored twice in the third quarter, to make it 21–14, but just when it seemed they were back in the game, Sam began threading deadly passes through their befuddled secondary. In ten short minutes, he completed eleven of fifteen passes for 128 yards, including a perfect pass he dropped into the lap of long, lean Ed Justice, who had gotten five yards behind the nearest defender. Justice scored easily, and the rout was on.

A few plays later, Battles took the ball on his own twenty-seven-yard line and headed around right end. Cut off, he reversed his field all the way to the left sideline, reversed it again, and continued zigzagging his way into the end zone. The splendid West Virginian's seventy-three-yard romp covered an estimated 200 yards. Late in the game, he intercepted a pass and took it seventy-six yards for another touchdown.

With the clock ticking down and the scoreboard showing "Visitors 49, Home 14," crazed Redskins fans rushed the field. (Those who could, rushed; others staggered.) They tore down both goalposts and made happy fools of themselves before making their way back downtown to Penn Station. The next day, Stanley Woodward of the *New York Herald Tribune* would write: "The Giants used a 5-3-2-1 defense. They should have used a 12-7-5-4."

I n the dark of night four hours later, rain was falling on Washington, but the moisture did nothing to dampen the glee of some 5,000 fans at Union Station, eager to welcome home the Eastern Division champs. As the special trains disgorged the giddy, raucous mobs, they blocked traffic, shouted themselves hoarse, and held impromptu pep rallies until long past midnight.

Corinne Griffith recalled sitting in the Marshalls' limousine with their driver, Welles, the car parked on a side street away from the excitement. It was a little before midnight. The rain had stopped, and she could see the ghostly white Capitol dome through the shadowy outline of trees, with the Washington Monument in the distance. She also saw an old police patrol wagon parked not far away, with three or four policemen standing in a semicircle nearby. They were arguing, it appeared, with a tall man in a raccoon coat. Behind him were dozens of Washington Redskins Band members.

Suddenly she saw her husband begin to beat his chest.

I waited for the wild jungle call of Tarzan, but instead one hundred and fifty white head-dresses were lifted high in the air and one hundred and fifty voices shouted.

"Hoorah!" The head-dresses lowered, then raised again, and another.

"Hoorah!" Then lowering of the head-dresses and a third!

"Hurrah!"

What was happening, Welles found out, was that the cops were determined to arrest the 150 band members because they wanted to parade up Pennsylvania Avenue without a permit. Marshall was insisting that they arrest him instead. "That explained the chest beating," Griffith wrote. "I can imagine it was one of those, 'Do with me what you will, but touch not one feather of those old, white head-dresses.'"

Marshall climbed into the limousine and instructed Welles to drive up Pennsylvania Avenue. At a certain cross street, Welles pulled over to the curb and waited for the band and a good-sized group of fans to catch up with them. Marshall and the band had concocted a plan. Having ditched the cops, the musicians would march just one block to one chorus of "Hail to the Redskins" and everybody would be happy.

Almost everybody, that is. Suddenly, another patrol car pulled up, and a police sergeant strode over to the Marshalls' limousine. After much discussion with Marshall and members of the band, the sergeant—who told Marshall he wasn't a football fan and cared not a whit what had happened in New York—arrested the drum major, who was bundled into the backseat of the police car, warbonnet and all.

"Follow that patrol car," Marshall instructed Welles, who drove the limousine to the Precinct No. 1 station house. Marshall jumped out, ran up the steps of the building, and yelled over his shoulder to Welles to bring whatever money he had on him. Griffith waited in the car.

Her husband came out a few minutes later and asked her whether she had $5. Marshall and his driver together could only raise $20 toward the $25 bail. Griffith dug through her purse. Fortune shone on the drum major—and on the Washington Redskins. She found $5 exactly.

CHAPTER

10

....

THE 1937 NFL CHAMPIONSHIP

> **SLAYING THE MONSTERS OF THE MIDWAY**

T
he two Georges—Halas and Marshall—first got acquainted in the 1920s when they owned teams in the fledgling American Basketball League. In fact, the Halas-Marshall rivalry started on the basketball court.

During that first season, Marshall's Washington team, the Palace Big Five, was playing Halas's Chicago team, and Halas was the official timer. Marshall, ever suspicious, found a stopwatch and sat beside Halas as the associate timer. With the Big Five holding a single-point lead and the final seconds ticking away on both watches, Marshall's timepiece showed the game was over, but Halas refused to blow the whistle. Only after a Chicago player hit the game-winning basket did Halas declare that time had run out. A red-faced Marshall was furious. He slammed his stopwatch to the floor and stomped on it. Halas laughed—and so did Marshall, eventually. It wouldn't be the last time the two men would almost come to blows over an athletic contest.

Years later they were still battling. The hated Bears invaded Boston in November 1936 and quickly built a lead against the Redskins. From his box seat high above the playing field, it looked to Marshall as if his boys were not only having to battle the Bears, but the officials as well. The zebras seemed to be intimidated by Papa Bear himself. Finally, the Redskins' owner could stand it no longer. He stood up, marched down the aisle, and clambered over a railing onto the field, where he flew into a spitting rage against the guys in striped shirts.

When Halas saw what was happening, he raced across the field and got in Marshall's face, jabbing him in the chest with his right index finger. All eyes in the stadium were on the two men; the crowd was going crazy.

"Get off the field, you sonofabitch," Halas yelled.

"George!" Marshall yelled. "This is my field and my town! I can do as I please!"

At that moment, Marshall's own coach, Ray Flaherty, inserted himself between the two bloviating bulls. In a firm voice, he reminded his boss about a certain item in his contract: owner confines himself to the stands, hands-off the team during games.

Marshall tried to argue with his no-nonsense coach. "Halas needs to shut his damn mouth," he said.

"Go back to your seat," Flaherty muttered. "Or find yourself another coach."

For once in his life, the imperious owner did as he was told. As he walked back up the aisle—while an official walked off fifteen yards against his team—a fan threw a beer at him, the odoriferous brew splattering down his raccoon coat. Marshall glanced down at the sopping fur, then decked the fan with a left jab to the jaw and a right to the solar plexus.

Waiting for Marshall to return to his seat was Corinne Griffith. She was outraged by the whole scene, by her husband's impetuousness but also by Halas's language, by the way he had treated her husband. When she began to berate the Bears' owner, her husband stopped her in midsentence: "Don't you *dare* say anything against Halas," he said, shaking his finger under her nose. "He's my best friend!"

For the first time, the two "friends" would play for the NFL championship. Halas's mighty Bears, already legitimate Monsters of the Midway, had gone 8-1-1 to clinch the division title for the third year in a row.

Halas was smart enough not to make the same mistake the Giants' Steve Owen did. When reporters asked him which of the Redskins would be on his all-pro team, he named a Redskin to every position. "Please see that these selections get into the paper before Sunday," he said.

Three seasons earlier, playing in the Polo Grounds for the 1934 NFL championship game, the Bears had the Giants on the ropes when the wet field began to freeze as the afternoon sun sank behind the stands. With the thermometer plunging into single digits, the field became an ice rink. The Bears led 10–3 at halftime.

At the start of the second half, the Giants, to the surprise of the Bears, trotted onto the field wearing white gym shoes. By the fourth quarter, many of the Bears were so frustrated by the icy conditions that they had stripped off their useless cleated shoes and were playing in their socks, their frozen feet bloodied by the ice. The team many considered the greatest in NFL history lost 30–13 to the tennis-shoe-shod Giants. Halas vowed he would never be unprepared again.

Reading in the Chicago papers about Sam's aerial exploits against the Giants in the division-championship game, the Bears' owner could almost pray for snow and ice. If his prayers went unanswered, Halas thought he had another plan for controlling the slender young passer from Texas. He would injure him, knock him out of the game.

It would be perfectly legal. In those days, the rules allowed the defense to stay after the quarterback until the play ended and the whistle blew. Even if he had thrown a pass thirty yards down the field and the action had shifted with the ball, a burly defender could continue hammering the passer until his receiver was either brought down or had crossed the goal line. Quarterbacks literally had to run for their lives until the play ended.

"A passer had to learn to throw and move," Sam recalled. "You would never see him just throw and stand there looking. You had to throw and start protecting yourself, because those linemen were going to lay you flatter than the ground every time."

As the Redskins' tailback, Sam also ran the ball several times a game, which meant he often ended up on the bottom of a punishing pileup, where a knee could be twisted, a strong right arm bent at the elbow, maybe a thumb bent back toward the wrist. And when Sam wasn't running or throwing, he often was assigned to block the defensive end, invariably a guy bigger than he was. He knew the Bears would try to hurt him every chance they got. Since nobody wore a face mask in those days, it was easy to gouge an eye or throw a grinding punch to the nose.

Teams carried only twenty-two or twenty-three men on a squad, and most were playing both ways, so, in Sam's words, "if you lost two good ones, you were dead."

Halas, like most other coaches, intended to use the rules to his benefit. He coached by intimidation, and he expected his men to play angry. Cheap shots were perfectly respectable as long as they didn't cost the team penalty yardage. Sam would be a marked man on Sunday.

"I want you to hit that sonofabitch until blood is coming out of his ears,"

Halas told the Bears when they gathered for practice on Tuesday morning before Sunday's game.

If the Bears defense couldn't get him, the offense would. The Bears' bounty hunter, and Sam's chief nemesis, was the toughest man in football, the legendary Bronko Nagurski. The all-American fullback from Minnesota didn't just run over people; he ran through them. If the 235-pound Nagurski broke through into the Redskins' secondary, as he invariably would, he would be on the lookout for the Redskins' safetyman, a 180-pound rookie from TCU. "The only way to stop Nagurski is to shoot the sonofabitch before he leaves the dressing room," the Giants' Steve Owen remarked before the NFL championship game in 1932.

The blue-collar Bronk played linebacker on defense, and with his lateral speed and his nose for the ball, he was lethal. When he exploded into a runner's chest and drove him to the ground, the man with the ball often stayed there.

The *Chicago Tribune* described his approach to the game as "smashing, driving and forever fighting." Playing against the Chicago Cardinals on an October afternoon in 1931, the Bronk ran out of bounds and collided at full speed with a mounted Chicago policeman. When his left shoulder slammed into the horse's girth, all four hooves lifted off the ground and, as a news photo showed, the cop flew about two feet above the saddle. Neither man nor beast was hurt, but Nagurski apologized to both.

Although he was a mild-mannered sort off the field—except when he was wrestling professionally in the off-season—opposing players were afraid of him. Even his teammate the great Red Grange dreaded having to tackle him in midweek scrimmages. "When the Bronk hits you, it's like getting an electric shock," Grange told reporters. "Better not hit above the ankles. He'll kill you."

On the Friday afternoon before the last regular-season game, a storm hit Chicago, two days before the Bears were to meet their crosstown rivals, the Cardinals, in Comiskey Park. By game time, the playing field was as slippery as oiled glass. Most of the fans who ventured out to watch the fourth-place Cardinals take on the division champs packed a flask. Whiskey-fueled, they broke up the wooden bleacher seats and started bonfires. Halas got into a fight with the Cardinals' coach, Milan Creighton, and threw a punch that missed Creighton but decked the referee. Meanwhile, the game turned into an offensive circus that lasted so long the final few minutes were played in the dark. The Bears won 49–21.

Three days before the championship game at Wrigley Field, Halas got the snow- and ice storm he wanted. "The beautiful white snow turned gray from the dirt of Chicago, and some of it turned blue, just from being so cold," Corinne Griffith recalled. "Ice formed everywhere, on the sidewalks and on the sides of the street where the snow had been shoveled. On the edge of the lake, great blocks of ice, some five or six feet long, had broken and piled up in frozen defiance."

With the mercury falling toward zero at night, flat surfaces, including football fields, became miniature glaciers. On Saturday, the Bears' organization brought in road-construction asphalt burners to thaw the ice, and had its crews spread hay over the field to soak up the water. Workers then covered the entire playing surface with a tarpaulin. By Sunday, the field was in relatively good shape, with only scattered patches of ice.

By game time, the temperature was fifteen degrees above zero, and the wind whistled through Wrigley Field at about twelve miles an hour, creating a wind chill factor of about six degrees below zero. Only 15,000 hardy souls were huddled inside 25,000-seat Wrigley Field. Many were cloaked in blankets and long woolen coats. Most of them huddled beneath the steel awning along the third-base line. "It was colder than nine miles in an iceberg, slippery as a Vaselined eel and wetter than a duck's spats," columnist Robert Ruark wrote.

Three thousand of the fans were Washingtonians who had made the trip by special train. As during the Cardinal game a week earlier, fans built bonfires in the stands, although the flames did little, if anything, to ward off the punishing cold. Those who braved frostbite and chilblains saw a game they would never forget.

Fans could be forgiven for staying home by their radios—and not just because of the weather. Even though the Redskins had gone 8-3 and had decisively whipped the Giants a week earlier, the Monsters of the Midway were of a different order. They were 9-1-1, they were big and punishing and fast, and they had a slew of players who would have been dubbed superstars had they played decades later. They had two other punishing runners, Ray Nolting and Jack Manders, in addition to Nagurski. They also had Hall of Fame linemen Joe Stydahar and Danny Fortmann.

The Redskins would receive the kickoff at the north end of the field, near the outfield wall. Surveying that end of the field, Sam noticed there was more ice than at the south end. His receivers would be able to avoid slippery patches; backpedaling defenders might not.

The Bears' Manders kicked a line drive that skittered along the diamond-hard field and off the cold fingers of Cliff Battles. It slid through the legs of

Erny Pinckert before Max Krause managed to scoop it up at his own one-yard line. Krause immediately disappeared under an avalanche of rampaging Bears.

On the first play from scrimmage, Riley Smith smashed his chin into the knee of one of the Bears and lost a tooth. Shortly afterward, the Bears' Bernie Masterson kneed Pinckert and sent him to the sidelines for the rest of the game. These were the Bears, after all.

The first time Sam got his cold hands on the ball, he started slingin'. As tailback, he took the snap from center and initiated the play, but he didn't call the plays. That job belonged to quarterback Riley Smith, who functioned primarily as a blocking back. But as the season had progressed, Sam more and more offered his opinion in the huddle or occasionally took over calling the plays himself.

Backed up against his own goal line, Sam looked around the huddle, ten men snorting steam in the punishing cold. "We're gonna trick 'em," he said. "I'm dropping into punt formation. But I ain't punting. Cliff, see that chunk of ice right over there? Run straight to it, cut to the sideline and look for the ball."

The Redskins broke their huddle and lined up in punt formation, as the Bears expected, since punting on first down was standard strategy in those days when a team was bottled up in its own end of the field. The Bears knew that Sam was one of the best punters in the game—possibly the best, but the NFL did not keep punting statistics in those early years.

Sam waited for the snap about two yards inside the goal line, but instead of stepping into the ball with his strong right leg, he began running to his right toward the goalposts, which were still at the front of the end zone in those days. An unblocked defensive end had an angle on him, but just before he was enveloped in a punishing Bear hug for a safety, Sam spotted Battles, who had carefully set his pivot foot and cut in front of safetyman Gene Ronzani at about the seven-yard line. As Ronzani slipped on the ice, the Redskin halfback gathered in Baugh's toss over his right shoulder and motored up the sideline past pursuing Bears and patches of ice for a forty-two-yard gain. (The *Times* found it notable that Ronzani wore gloves during the game; just before he was ready to receive a punt, he would yank them off and tuck them in his pants.)

Although the Bears held shortly afterward, the pass from the end zone delivered a message: the Redskins' brilliant young passer wasn't going to allow the elements to dictate strategy. Neither the weather nor the Bears scared him.

Chicago bogged down on its first possession. When the Redskins took over, they moved methodically downfield on the strength of four straight Baugh passes. From the Chicago ten, Battles took the handoff from Sam, broke off left tackle, and literally dived into the end zone.

The Bears, lined up in T formation, responded in character, with Nagurski bulling his way into the Redskins' secondary on six straight carries. With the ball at the Washington forty, Nagurski took the ball again and roared through a large hole opened up by 260-pound George "Moose" Musso. One man stood in his way, a slender safetyman wearing number 33. Nagurski lowered his shoulder and hit Sam like a runaway train.

The Redskins' trainer had to help Sam off the field. Trying to clear his head, he managed to remark, "That sonofabitch ran plumb over me." For the rest of the game, Sam merely tried to hang on to the Bears' monster back when he rampaged into the secondary, praying all the while that help would arrive.

Sam's "bodyguards" did their best to keep the rampaging Bears off their man. Play after play, Big Turk Edwards would trot up to the line and warn them not to try to get dirty with the passer. On one play, he was so obsessed with protecting Sam that he backed into him and knocked him down for a fifteen-yard loss.

The Bears finally got to him in the second quarter when he took off running through the middle of their defense. After a ten-yard gain, he hit the frozen turf with four beefy Bears on top of him. He was limping when he got up out of the pile, and the back of his throwing hand dripped blood.

Years later, Sam remembered the blood. The field had been muddy before the ice storm arrived, and clods of dirt gouged out during a high-school playoff game a week earlier had frozen as well. "Every time you hit that icy field, you'd slide and everybody was bleeding. You'd hit those little pebbles that were frozen, and they'd just slice you. When we got in the dressing room and undressed, everybody was bleeding." Edwards and his fellow linemen were slipping and sliding all over the field, and yet the weather was just what Papa Bear—and the Bear offense—had ordered. Quick-opening power plays, straight-ahead running by Nagurski behind a big, mobile line—the Bears were hampered by the slippery conditions, but not nearly as much as an offense built around precision passing.

With Sam on the bench, the Bears' Masterson connected with Edgar "Eggs" Manske on a sixty-yard pass play. With the ball on the Redskins nineteen, Nagurski charged nine yards around left end and Manders, the NFL's leading scorer, dashed through a hole up the middle for ten yards and the touchdown. Manders then kicked the extra point, tying the game.

On the Redskins' next possession, the rookie tailback, still a bit woozy, threw an interception to Bears end George Wilson at the Redskins forty-nine. With the Redskins keying on Nagurski, Masterson found Manders open over the middle at the Redskins twenty, and a block by Wilson on Battles—who claimed he was clipped—allowed the running back to score standing up. The extra point made it 14–7, Bears. Sam twisted his knee—or had it twisted for him in a pileup—and sat out much of the second quarter.

Corinne Griffith wrote that at half time "the score was Chicago 14, Washington 7, Thermometer 0."

The two teams hurried to the blessed warmth of the dressing room, where Flaherty talked strategy and Sam tried to treat his various injuries. Dreading the dangerous cold, both teams hated going out again, but they had no choice.

Halftime was a lifesaver for Sam, and early in the third quarter, he limped back onto the frozen field and began to connect. After Don Irwin made a first down on the Bears' forty-five, Millner dropped a Baugh pass. On the next play, though, the former Notre Dame all-American cut sharply across from the opposite end of the field, despite the ice, and took a pass from Sam that, as one observer described it, "virtually hung on a peg." In a foot race with Masterson across the icy tundra, Millner scored on a thirty-five-yard run. Reliable Riley Smith added the extra point to tie the game at 14.

The Bears came back. Starting at their own twenty-three, they marched methodically down the field, relying primarily on Nagurski's mad-bull thrusts. With the ball at the Redskins' four-yard line, Masterson faked a handoff and then lobbed a jump pass to Manske in the end zone. Chicago led 21–14 after Manders's extra point.

Sam would not allow his Redskins to fold. They had come to realize during the course of the season that as long as he had the ball in his hands, they were still in the game. He didn't have to say much. He didn't get excited.

Against the Bears, he brought them back by teaming up with Millner, known as the "money player" for his penchant for coming through in the clutch. Against Ohio State in 1935, he single-handedly won the game in the last minute for Notre Dame with a leaping one-handed grab at the back of the end zone of a pass from Bill "The Bard" Shakespeare. He also was used to playing in cold weather.

With the ball on his own twenty-two, Sam faded back, scanned the field, and fired a forty-five-yard pass to Millner, who gathered in the ball on the dead run exactly at midfield. Once more he led Nagurski and Manders on a fifty-yard chase to the end zone. Smith again kicked the extra point to tie the score.

Sam had thrown three touchdown passes within a span of ten minutes on the game clock.

"It was amazing the way Baugh worked," the *Times'* Arthur J. Daley wrote. "Without him Washington would have been buried deep in the drift of Bear touchdowns. For this was weather and these were conditions that were hand-tailored for Chicago." Chicago used five defensive linemen, one less than normal in those days, and tried to cover Sam's receivers with six people. They couldn't stop him.

Late in the third quarter, Sam drove the Redskins deep into Bear territory, relying on short passes to Millner, Malone, and Irwin. With the quarter winding down, Sam took the ball on the snap, leaped into the air, and faked a jump pass to Millner. With his feet back on the ground, he fired a thirty-five-yard bullet to Ed "Chug" Justice, who was wide open in the left corner of the end zone. With the extra point, the Redskins led the mighty Bears 28–21.

"Baugh threw passes that had to be seen to be believed," Daley wrote the next day. "He pitched them while in full flight and hung them on a nail. He tossed them as tacklers were carrying him to the ground, but so accurate were they that a blind man could have caught them."

Grainy film footage from the game shows that Sam really did sling the ball on occasion, in part perhaps because the ball was still watermelon shaped. (In his later years, he was more likely to cock the ball at his ear, which became the standard way of throwing a football.) As Daley noted, he also threw off his back foot, threw on the run, flicked it with his wrist over the shoulders of rampaging linemen about to take him down. Invariably, however the ball was thrown, it traveled on a line to his receiver.

Throughout the punishing game, the Bears tried to send Sam to the sidelines for good. By the third quarter, he was limping from a banged-up knee and a bruised hip, and blood trickled from his nose. He stayed in the game.

When Dick Plasman caught a pass from Masterson, Sam, still in at safety, caught up with the Bears' end and bounced him out of bounds. Plasman, who played without a helmet, landed headfirst on the cold hard ground. Immediately, he bounced up and punched Sam in the face. (Daley of the *Times* called it "a gentle punch.") Sam punched back.

"They've hit Baugh!" Marshall screamed, leaping over the rail.

Unfortunately for Plasman, the Redskins' owner wasn't the only one who came after him. The six-foot-three-inch, 210-pound end happened to be standing directly in front of the Redskins' bench. Sam's teammates, eager to protect their all-star, piled on Plasman, while the Bears came roaring off their own bench and raced across the field. Fans poured out of the stands. "Riot! Riot!" people yelled.

"Coach Flaherty was the first to leap to his feet and the first to rush to the battle scene," Shirley Povich later wrote in the *Post*. "He tackled Plasman high—high around the mouth—with a set of knuckles and put an end to the battle." Here is how columnist Ruark described the melee: "The team arose as one Indian, and systematically commenced to separate Mr. Plasman from his hair, hide and tallow."

The mighty Nagurski played peacemaker. Striding into the melee, he tried to pull players off the swarming pile and stop the fight. Once Bronk and the officials had dug down to the bottom of the pile, they found the Washington trainer, Roy Baker, atop Plasman. "He had fastened himself to Plasman's pelt," Ruark wrote, "and apparently was trying to bite his initials into Dick's ear. In between bites he was belaboring Plasman's puss with both knotty little fists, and a luscious, iridescent mouse even then had appeared on Plasman's peeper."

Plasman left the field with a bloody nose, gashed eye and split lip. Sam emerged unscathed. No penalties were assessed. The crowd settled back into their cold hard seats.

The Redskins held the Bears scoreless throughout the fourth quarter. With only seconds to play, the Bears were on the move. Tailback Masterson spotted his backup end, Les McDonald, uncovered at the Redskins' thirty-two-yard line. McDonald gathered in the pass and set sail for the goal line, only to get tangled up with the back judge, Ed Cochrane, a *Chicago Tribune* sportswriter who moonlighted as an official. Cochrane, limping from a sprained knee, had slipped and fallen on the ice, and by the time McDonald got himself untangled, Sam and Cliff Battles were on hand to bring him down. The gun sounded seconds later.

Washington had waited twenty-four years for its first baseball pennant. Now, in their inaugural year in the nation's capital, George Preston Marshall's Redskins—young Sam Baugh's Redskins—were NFL champions. Sam had completed seventeen of thirty-four passes for 358 yards. At a time when the single-season passing record was a mere 1,236 yards, it was an astounding number. It also was the greatest passing performance in NFL history.

As the players left the gridiron tundra, happy Redskins fans still yelling in the background, Nagurski extended his hand to the young Texan. "You're a fine fella and a great quarterback," he said. Sam thanked him and then asked him a question: "Did you know that when you'd break through the line and head towards me, nobody ever blocked me?" Nagurski laughed. "No one was supposed to put a block on you. Hey, I was supposed to run over you and get you out of the ballgame."

Sam and his teammates, banged and bruised, their burgundy jerseys stained with blood, made their way to the warmth of the dressing room. Several hundred delirious Redskin fans mobbed their heroes at the door. They tried to get close to their exhausted idols—Cliff Battles, Turk Edwards, and the young quarterback who had changed the face of professional football with his sterling performance.

Inside the steamy clubhouse, Marshall was uncharacteristically modest. He told reporters he was particularly proud that his team had won a championship their first season in Washington.

Sam was modest as well. Saying that he planned to head home to Texas the next day, he drawled: "What the heck, anyone can do the pitching—but it takes real ball players to do the catching." Sportswriters weren't buying it. "Against Baugh [the Bears] prided themselves they had a defense," Povich wrote. "But there was no defense for the deftness of those pitches he made today and there was no defense, furthermore, for the raw, naked courage of the tall boy from Texas."

"There are a lot of other fine football players on the Washington Redskins, as New Yorkers well know from their work against the Giants," Allison Danzig of the *New York Times* observed two days after the championship game.

> But Pinckert, Smith, Battles, Irwin, Millner, Karcher, Kawal, Malone and company could never have won this one without Slingin' Sam. The giant Musso and his mates stopped Cliff Battles, as great as he was at the Polo Grounds, and they put on such pressure at the middle of the line that it seemed at times that Nagurski and Manders would never stop running. But they couldn't stop Slingin' Sam any more than could Winter's icy hand. The ayes of Texas are now unanimous. John Nance Garner and Jesse Jones will please shove down to the end of the Washington bench.

Povich agreed. "All season, the fellow was uncanny," he wrote, "and his Texas admirers were guilty of vast understatement all these years when they were saying that Slingin' Sammy could bloody your nostrils with a football at 50 yards."

Sam impressed the coaches as well. The Detroit Lions coach, Earl "Dutch" Clark, told the Associated Press that Sam "is the greatest passer I've ever seen." Ray Flaherty, Sam's own coach, called his performance "the greatest one-man show ever put on in pro football."

For their heroics on that frigid Chicago afternoon, Sam and his teammates—twenty-three players in all—each earned $234.26.

The week before Christmas found Sam back in Sweetwater, where the folks who knew him as a youngster could show him their appreciation with a "Welcome Home, Sammy" banquet arranged by the Board of City Development. Two hundred forty townspeople, former teammates, and former classmates gathered on a Monday night to honor the young man who had done more to "put Sweetwater on the map than any citizen in its history."

The master of ceremonies was Ney "Red" Sheridan, the Sweetwater football star whom TCU had tried to sign instead of Sam and who had just completed a stellar career as a Texas Longhorn. He told the crowd that what stood out most about Sam was that "all the adulation had not gone to his head." He still "has his feet on the ground" and was still "the level-headed, likable kid he was back in 1931 and 1932, when in high school."

Seated at the head table with his mother, his sister, Edmonia Smith (his high school sweetheart and now fiancée), and her parents, the twenty-two-year-old football star, cool and calm on the football field, admitted to a bit of nervousness when he spoke to the local folks. His voice quavered a bit, Flem Hall of the *Star-Telegram* noted. "It's hard to get up and say things to a crowd made up of folk who know you as well as you know yourself, and I don't mind telling you I'm a bit scared," Sam said. "If I told you this was the happiest moment of my life, I wouldn't be telling the truth, because that moment is to come when I sit down."

Sam told about life in the NFL and predicted that professional football would grow. It would probably take its place beside major league baseball, he said, but would not cut into college football.

The hometown folks had taken up a collection to buy a ring for Sam. It was solid gold in the shape of a football, with diamonds representing the ball's threads. He wore the ring for most of his life. He liked it, he said years later, because it was from the people who knew him best. "That Hall of Fame ring, I could throw it away and never miss it," he said. "I liked that ring I got from the Sweetwater people."

....

CARDINAL SAM?

BAUGH TRIES THE MAJOR LEAGUES

S am Baugh was a child of the Depression. Although he made a comfortable living as a professional football player, he knew he could take nothing for granted, particularly playing for a mercurial owner like George Preston Marshall. He enjoyed playing football, reveled in the competition and the pride of accomplishment, but he had no illusions about why he was playing: football was a business, and if he could do better for himself doing something else, he would have to consider it.

The way Marshall handled his star running back, Cliff Battles, was a reminder to Sam—if he needed one—that the owner of the Redskins could turn on him in an instant. Battles, an all-pro and arguably the best running back in the NFL, was twenty-eight years old and at the peak of his career. In his rookie season, the Redskins paid him $200 a game; six years later, he was only making about $300 a game. With small bonuses for exhibition games, he averaged about $4,000 a year.

Battles asked Marshall for $5,000. Marshall said no.

Disappointed and more than a little disgusted, Battles quit. He joined Lou Little's coaching staff at Columbia University. When he left professional football, he had gained more yards rushing than any runner in NFL history—3,622. He would be inducted into the Pro Football Hall of Fame in 1968.

Marshall not only refused the raise, but also accused Columbia of stealing his employee. Three years later, after the Chicago Bears annihilated the Redskins 73–0, Marshall accused Battles of selling Redskin plays to Chicago. The two men didn't speak to each other for years. "It wasn't just the money," Battles said years later. "It was also the fact that he [Marshall] just didn't seem to appreciate me. It hurt my feelings."

Sam, who twice during his career proposed that his own salary be reduced when he felt he didn't perform to expectations, felt bad for his friend. "Hell, if I had known about it, I would have given him the $300 myself, because after that first year I was making $12,000," he said years later.

Baugh led the league in passing during his first year as a pro, with 81 completions out of 171 attempts for 1,127 yards and 8 touchdowns. Besides being only the second back in professional football history to pass for more than a thousand yards in a season, he was the team's stellar defensive back and punter. He also earned for himself all-pro honors. Still, playing for Marshall, he could never be sure of his status.

On January 19, 1938, Sam announced that he would sign a baseball contract with the St. Louis Cardinals. Although he and Marshall had not agreed to contract terms after Sam led the Redskins to a national championship, the sensational passer said the Redskins' owner had agreed he could play baseball during the spring.

He told the Associated Press that he had conferred with Marshall, who had proposed two salary arrangements: a flat, one-year contract for between $13,000 and $14,000, or a three-year renewal at the same salary he made his rookie year, which amounted to approximately $727 per game.

"One year's football at $13,000 or $14,000 is considerable money," Sam said, "but I'm a pretty frail boy, you know, and I'm liable to go out any time.

> Suppose I signed for a one-year term; got hurt. I'd be through. Under terms of the three-year contract, I am protecting myself for that length of time—broken leg, smashed career or not.

Protecting himself was an immediate concern. Marshall had his team playing at least three exhibition games in the off-season, including two against the Bears. And he scoffed at rumors that he was holding out for a $25,000 contract.

> Me get $25,000? Whoever heard of such a thing? It's the bunk—just publicity.

Salaries just don't come that high in professional football. The amount I made in my first year was very good for a youngster. It's tough going though—having those big fellows slam you around on the tail end of every pass. Guess maybe I earned that money.

Sam added he still intended to coach some day, although not any time soon.

It doesn't hurt to keep your name before the public when you are shooting for a coaching job. I'm learning more football all the time.

And he assured everyone that he still enjoyed playing.

After that Chicago game for the title on that icy field, Sammy had enough football. But then I came on down home, rested up for a couple of weeks and now I'm ready for more.

The Redskins were still playing. In an exhibition game in Dallas, they again beat the Bears 10–0, and then faced them in Miami on February 6. Before a shirtsleeved crowd of 16,000, the Bears finally won, defeating the Redskins 16–10 in a game marked by out-and-out brawls. Eight players, four from each team, got tossed out. Sam stayed on the field but was ineffective, attempting eleven passes and completing only four. He played only briefly in the second half after receiving a slight injury to his left shoulder when he was tackled while throwing a pass. The Redskins' trainer said he had strained a ligament.

A week later—the same week Battles announced that he was leaving—Sam told reporters he would play one more year and then retire to enter the college coaching ranks. He made his announcement from Chapel Hill, North Carolina, where he was serving as backfield coach for the University of North Carolina under head coach Ray Wolf.

"The professional football racket is tougher than any professional athletics there is," Sam told the *Washington Post*. "One more year of gittin' banged around for me—and then I'm gittin' out." He said he expected to make not less than $15,000 playing for the Redskins. He said that would give him a bit of nest egg that would allow him to go into coaching with no financial worries.

In March, still unsigned by the Redskins, Sam reported to spring training with the St. Louis Cardinals in St. Petersburg, Florida. He told reporters he wouldn't sign with the Redskins unless "Marshall comes across with a considerable amount of cash," adding, "I think I'm entitled to more than Marshall offered, and I'm not going to sign until I get what I want. I'm only going to play one more year of pro ball anyhow, so I'm gonna get what's coming to me."

He said he would either be a baseball player full-time or he would coach football. If he made the grade with the Cardinals, he said, he would give up football altogether: "I realize that you can't play football without endangering your baseball career, and I'm in this thing for keeps."

He said he liked football as much as baseball but was looking at his career from a business angle. Baseball players, he pointed out, lasted longer than football players. He said he didn't expect to break into the major leagues right away: "If I can't stick with the Cards, I hope the club will find a place for me on one of its farm teams. Of course, I want to play for the Cards, but if they ship me out, I hope it will be to Houston."

The Cardinals, with Dizzy Dean and his brother, Paul "Daffy" Dean, manager Frankie Frisch, scrappy infielders Pepper Martin and Leo "The Lip" Durocher, and slugger Joe "Ducky" Medwick, were known as the Gashouse Gang, the most colorful team in all of professional sports. They were also very good.

"I had a good time with those damn boys," Sam recalled. "There was never anybody exactly like that bunch, and I enjoyed it." He roomed with Medwick, one of the best hitters in baseball. The Cards coaches told Sam and the other rookies that Medwick was the only hitter in their system who could hit any pitch a pitcher could throw. They told the youngsters to watch him in batting practice.

"One guy that really tried to help me was their third baseman, Pepper Martin," Sam remembered. "He'd played football somewhere, and he'd bring a football to practice and ask me to throw it to him. We'd throw it before practice, and he could really catch that ball."

As the Gashouse Gang gathered to work out winter's kinks, the big story was not the arrival of a championship football player, but whether Dizzy Dean, a thirty-game winner in 1934, would be back in form. The irrepressible Dean, loud, outrageous, and preternaturally talented, had become baseball's biggest attraction after Babe Ruth retired in 1934.

In 1937, the year before Sam joined the team, fans of big headlines had plenty to choose from—Amelia Earhart's disappearance, the explosion of the *Hindenburg*, the bombing of Guernica—but for baseball fans, the biggest headline of all concerned Dean's big toe.

On July 7, 1937, at Washington's Griffith Stadium, the temperature ninety-two degrees and President Franklin D. Roosevelt in attendance, Diz was on the mound for the National League all-stars. At the plate with two outs in the third inning was Earl Averill, a Cleveland Indians outfielder. Averill drove Dean's first pitch right back at him, and the line drive hit Diz on the left foot. The Cards pitcher limped from the field, and it wasn't until some time later that he found out his toe was broken. Trying to come back too soon, he altered his pitching motion because of the pain in his toe, and ended up hurting his arm.

The injury to his arm was so serious that some suggested he sit out the '38 season, but Diz would have none of it. Having taken a $7,500 pay cut without complaining, he told sportswriters his arm would "be the same ol' great soupbone."

"I believe him, I do," said the Cardinals' general manager, Branch Rickey. "The boy's got fire in his eyes. And that may mean a lot to our ball club. The Cards are a seventh-place team on paper, but the spirit Dizzy is showing may be catching."

As usual, Diz and his Gashouse Gang teammates were making news. Early in 1938, J. Edgar Hoover, the head G-man, revealed an aborted plot to kidnap Diz. Peter Anders, a former Dillinger gang member, had planned to hold him for $50,000 ransom, Hoover said, but backed out because he wasn't sure the Cards would pay.

In late March, Frisch talked to reporters about his rookie football player. "That bird with No. 21 on his back at third base. That's Sammy Baugh," he told the New York Times. "He can field," Frisch said. "He's a natural. Good thrower too. But can he hit? That's what tells the tale in this league. You've gotta get those base hits, or there's no soap."

What Frisch didn't know is that Sam was injured. After the Redskins had won the title, Marshall and Halas scheduled three exhibition games in January to make extra money. Near the end of the third game, in Miami, Sam broke his sternum.

"I've still never felt such pain," he recalled years later. "I couldn't let them operate, because I was supposed to report to spring training with the Cardinals in March. Naturally, when I got to spring training, I couldn't throw or hit because of my sternum. People said my baseball career ended after one season because I couldn't hit a curveball, but hell, who could have hit with a broken sternum?"

John Kieran of the New York Times noted: "Baugh hasn't looked like Lou Gehrig or Muscles Medwick at the plate so far in his big-league career, but the Cardinals are a long way from giving up on him in a hurry. Every morning Onkel Franz leans on the batting cage and gives Slinging Sam special instructions in hitting."

Frisch told Kieran that a half hour of instruction daily ought to bring him up to major-league par. "He's a great prospect," the manager said. "We'll keep him around for a while—let him see what the big league looks like. The rest is up to him."

Sam told Kieran that he would like to play baseball in the spring and summer and then switch to football in the fall. Kieran reminded him that if he made the Cardinals roster, he was likely to find a little stipulation in his contract that wouldn't allow him to play football. Sam said his baseball contract allowed him to play football. "That's all right for now," Kieran wrote, "because nobody knows whether or not he can hit well enough to stay in the big leagues."

Kieran suggested that if he developed as a baseball player, he would switch sports. "At the moment, Slinging Sam is a great football star coming up for a baseball trial," he wrote. "But he can certainly handle himself in the field, and if he can learn to hit there will be an opening for a good forward passer on Mr. George Preston Marshall's Washing-Done Redskins. Probably not this Fall, though. Slinging Sam, at best, for baseball purposes, looks to be a year away."

Sam was one of six third basemen in camp that spring, and he was ranked at the bottom of the six. On the Cards' early trips around Florida for exhibition games, Frisch didn't even take him along with the squad. After a few days, though, the manager realized the other five were even more inept than young, inexperienced Sam Baugh.

"I never saw a worse bunch of third basemen in my life," Frisch told Shirley Povich of the *Washington Post* after a particularly irksome workout in St. Petersburg. "We're in a bad way. I'll really show what I think of the third basemen on this club. I'll show you how bad off we really are. I'm going to put a football player out there on third base. Tomorrow it's going to be Sammy Baugh in our lineup."

So there was Sam—"the ugly duckling of the bunch," Povich called him—on the field against the Yankees next day. He met the challenge like a pro. He handled ten chances like a big leaguer, Povich noted, and on one occasion faked a throw to first and trapped a Yankee off third. He also got three hits, one of them a double. "And," Povich wrote, "he appeared to be all the Cardinals needed in the way of a third baseman."

Povich also revealed that Sam's hitting woes were the result of a football injury. He had hurt his shoulder in an exhibition game in Miami in January and couldn't follow through on his swing. Now that his shoulder was getting better, though, Frisch was getting excited. (No word about the sternum injury.) "He's a better ballplayer than I was when I came into the league," said the Cardinals manager, who had been a fixture in the New York Giants' infield from the day he left Fordham University.

That was on April 3. On April 4, Povich reported that Sam was on his way to the minor leagues. "Frisch has given me my choice—Houston or Columbus," Sam told him. "It was pretty nice of him to put it that way. I don't know yet which club I'll join. I'll figure it out in a couple of days." He didn't stick with the Cardinals, Povich reported, because he still wasn't a reliable hitter and because of his inexperience.

Sam didn't appear all that disappointed, Povich said. "I'm satisfied I made a good showing for a fellow who never played much except college baseball," Sam said. "I learned plenty here with Frisch. I'll be back with the Cardinals next spring—perhaps before that. Steady work in a fast minor league will help me more than sitting on the bench with the Cardinals."

The next day, Sam told the *Post* he had rejected the contract Marshall sent him for the '38 season. "He's offering me the same salary I received last year," he said. "What does a fellow have to do to make good in that league?"

On April 6, the *Post* reported that Sam had been optioned to the Columbus Redbirds, the Cards' AA team in the American Association, where Frisch wanted him to play shortstop.

On April 9, Sam caught a Delta Airlines plane out of Atlanta—he was still with the Cards in Florida—and flew to Dallas's Love Field. "I probably will play pro football one more year, maybe more," he told the *Dallas Morning News.* "Football pays me well, although I think baseball beats football, because you can play it longer. But I'll probably be on the gridiron again next season. After that I'll decide whether I want to play it any longer or not. I may and I may not."

He then drove to Sweetwater, where he and Edmonia Smith, his high-school sweetheart, planned their wedding. Sam told the *Fort Worth Star-Telegram* that Edmonia still hadn't decided exactly who would be at the wedding. As for the best man, Sam said he hadn't met him yet.

The young couple—Sam tall and rawboned, Edmonia petite, demure, and dark haired—married in a quiet ceremony in the Sweetwater home of the bride's parents. The United Press reported that the bride was dressed in navy blue net with a bolero jacket. Even though Sam had left the marriage license at his mother's house, Edmonia's father, Dr. Gary L. Smith, a Presbyterian minister in Sweetwater for the previous eleven years, went ahead with the ceremony. He laughed and told Sam he could pick up the license afterward.

Sam had used some of his football money to buy a little house on Sweetwater Lake with about 750 acres, some cattle, and a horse. The young couple didn't live there at first. Right after the wedding, they left for Fort Worth on their way to Columbus.

Edmonia—friends and family called her Mona—seemed less than excited about the baseball experiment, even though the *Star-Telegram* reported that she was "apparently happily resigned to her life as an 'athletic widow' for the next few years." Having never lived anywhere but West Texas, it all seemed a bit daunting to the young woman.

A reporter caught up with her in the coffee shop of Fort Worth's Blackstone Hotel the day after the wedding. "We'll be home in January and February, anyway—unless we discover we can play ice hockey," Mona said (whether with a smile or a grimace, the reporter didn't indicate). "Sure, I knew what I was in for," she said. "Football from September through December, baseball from March to September. It will be worse than a 'golf widow,' but I don't care."

She said that she and Sam were a bit embarrassed that they couldn't go anywhere in Fort Worth without being recognized, whether it was the coffee shop, the hotel lobby, or the street.

Sam said the couple didn't plan to get a house in Columbus, at least until he had a better idea of what the future held. "Frankly, I don't know how I'll do in baseball," he said. "They want me to play shortstop and it's a new position for me. The Cards have a mighty big chain, you know. If I don't go at Columbus, I may be shipped to a dozen other places. We can't plan much until we see how things come out."

Sam would always remember one of his teammates at Columbus, a tall rookie who looked like he might weigh 125 pounds, no more. He remembered how the rookie outfielder would do calisthenics between pitches, putting his glove in his back pocket, turning his back to the plate and touching his toes. The vets, players whose big-league dreams had been dashed, hated the young prima donna, but Ted Williams didn't much care.

Sam didn't have an opportunity to play very long on the same team as the man who would become one of the greatest hitters of all time. A few weeks after his marriage, Columbus optioned him to the Rochester Redwings of the International League, where his batting average was about .220 and he mostly rode the bench. "As far as his value to the Rochester club is concerned, Baugh will have no difficulty in getting permission to start football work on August 10," Povich reported.

L. D. Meyer, Sam's old TCU teammate, spent six years in the majors with the Cubs, the Tigers, and the Indians. Sam, Meyer recalled years later, "was definitely a big-league third baseman": "He had the greatest arm I ever saw, and tremendous hands. He could catch anything—and then fire those strikes to first base from behind his ear all day long."

In later years, Sam always said he gave up on baseball because of one man, Marty Marion. He realized that he would never be as good as the slick-fielding infielder, who was about seventeen at the time and who would go on to be the Cardinals' stellar shortstop for eleven seasons. "Anyway, I had problems with the curveball," he said.

In July, Marshall scoffed at press reports that Sam was unhappy with his salary. "We will pay Baugh his price," the owner said, "but it will be my price too. I will not have any trouble with Sammy Baugh. He can't keep away from football. If it came right down to it, he'd probably pay us to let him play."

On August 3, the *Post* reported, "football's greatest forward passer scrawled his prized signature on a three-year contract with the Washington Redskins."

Sam was in Baltimore to play Rochester's last game of the season when he got a call from Flaherty. After meeting with the coach and Marshall at the Annapolis Hotel, the trio drove to the Redskins' office on Ninth Street, where Marshall announced that Sam had signed over to the Redskins the rights to "all his athletic endeavors" for three years at a sum that Marshall termed "unprecedented in the history of professional football."

Marshall wouldn't reveal how much he was paying, just that it was substantially more than the $7,500 the Redskins had paid Sam the year before. He said it wasn't as much as Red Grange made for one year during his peak, but that for a three-year period it constituted a new high.

Four Redskins remained unsigned, including Sam's favorite target, Wayne Millner, "but the biggest part of my worries is over," the owner told reporters. "You can tell Washington football fans for me that this is the greatest thing that could have happened to local football. This three-year exclusive rights contract guarantees that Baugh will play with the Redskins until the end of the 1941 season. Also that he cannot accept any coaching offers or even play baseball without our permission during that period. . . . He can play down on the Texas sandlots if he wants to, but no more infielding for the St. Louis Cardinals or the International League." Sam told reporters he was more than satisfied with the new contract and was "sure glad to get it off my chest."

Whether he would ever play baseball again rested solely with Marshall, who told reporters he believed baseball helped football players stay in shape. "Look at Sammy," he said, "in condition now, a week before practice starts." The *Post* reporter, describing Sam as "a picture of sartorial elegance in a blue sports ensemble," noted that he certainly appeared to be in shape. He weighed 183, about five pounds below his playing weight, but expected to put on about ten pounds before the first regular-season game.

Also in August, Sam inaugurated a thrice-weekly column in the *Washington Post* about his career, football techniques, and the NFL. "This is my first offense as a sports writer, so kindly don't rough the passer, at least until I am squared away," he wrote.

Actually, Shirley Povich, the *Post*'s beloved sportswriter for more than four decades, ghostwrote that line and all the others attributed to Sam. Years later, Povich confessed that he not only wrote the columns but also invented many of the postgame quotes. He recalled that in the early days, he was the only *Post* reporter covering the Redskins, which meant he had to write the play-by-play, the color, the postgame comments, and his own column. "Just a night's work on the road. I did not feel abused," he wrote years later.

"Ghostwriting was not a wholly dishonorable profession, although sometimes there were extremes," he recalled. His favorite ghostwriter, he said, was a reporter named John Gilhooly of the Boston Hearst newspapers, who wrote for the morning paper under the name of Eddie Stanky, the manager of the Boston Red Sox. In the afternoon paper, under his own byline, he wrote a column second-guessing the Stanky story he had written that morning.

"Baugh couldn't be bothered with any discussion and gave me a blank check to write anything I liked, and I did," Povich revealed.

> Every Sunday with Baugh's help I would diagram a Redskin play, labeling it one that had beaten some other team. But once, when Baugh was unavailable, the team's trainer came forward with a play we could publish.
>
> "When did it ever work?" I asked. "We never really used it," he said, "but I always thought it would work."
>
> So the play was diagrammed and published, and that day the Redskins took an awful beating from the Bears. Two days later the sports editor got an

angry letter from a lady who complained, "How can the Redskins expect to win when Sammy Baugh gives away their best plays every Sunday?"

Even when the Redskins won the NFL championship in 1937, the first in Washington and team history, Povich was the sole reporter on the Redskins beat. He didn't have time to track down Sam and get exact quotes, so he invented what he expected Sam would have said, usually aw-shucks observations that made the Texan sound like a young Will Rogers—if Rogers had been a Boy Scout. The real Sam was one of the nicest guys in the league, but he was gloriously profane; Povich's Sam was straight from the pages of a Clair Bee sports novel for boys.

"Right now, I want to refute a story they've been telling about me ever since I broke into the pro league," Povich's Sam wrote in his inaugural column.

Up until this time, I've let it stand, but the thing ought to be cleared up. I don't like to be sailing under false pretenses.

The story I'm talking about is the one they tell about me and Coach Flaherty the day I reported to the Redskins last year. Flaherty was pointing out the differences between pro football and college football and he was discussing passes with me. He said the pros were particular and that pass receivers weren't in the habit of jumping all over the lot for wild passes.

According to the story, Flaherty said, "Sammy, on those short passes where the ends cut sharp to the opposite side, you've got to lay that ball right up there for 'em. Throw it right at their eye."

The story went that I told Flaherty that was all right with me, but which eye did he mean?

That isn't true. I never said that. Coach Flaherty never leaves anything to the imagination. He is plenty thorough and specific. He made it all plain in the beginning. He told me I had to throw my passes at the right end's left eye and the left end's right eye, on those cut-back plays.

....

THE 1938 AND 1939 REDSKINS

GIANT VICTIMS

S am's value to the Redskins extended beyond his slingshot arm, his strong right leg, and his winning ways. His Texas drawl and his easy-going attitude toward life made him an instant hero for the newly established Redskins fans. "In one short season, his first as a professional, he became football's greatest thrill," the NFL's president, Joe Carr, wrote not long after Sam's rookie season.

The excitement he brought to the game and the success he brought to Washington helped the Redskins build the kind of solid fan support that they had never known in Boston (and that continues to this day). "The fact that fans in the nation's capital are among the most ardently loyal in the league can be traced directly to the arrival of Slingin' Sam, cowboy hat and all, back in Washington's first season in the NFL," wrote the team's historian, Richard Whittingham.

Of course, the city was his, as it would be for any young and handsome sports hero. He couldn't go anywhere in D.C.—to a barbershop, a restaurant, or the movies—without being accosted by admiring fans. Sam liked the attention, but even as a young man, he didn't let it go to his head. He realized, even then, that although he was a talented athlete, that didn't make him any better than anyone else.

For their summer training camp in '38, the Redskins moved to a softball stadium in Ballston, Virginia, just across the Potomac from Washington. Except for Cliff Battles, the world-championship team was pretty much intact, and fans were excited.

Not only was Sam, rookie year under his belt, expected to set the league afire yet again, but the team had added several promising newcomers also. The biggest of the bunch was Wilbur "Wee Willie" Wilkin, a tackle from St. Mary's College, who would go on to have a stellar career with the Redskins even as he established himself as a real character. Also expected to play major roles on the '38 team were rookies Tilden "Tillie" Manton, a fullback from TCU; Bob Masterson, an end from the University of Miami; and Frank Filchock, a quarterback from Indiana. Andy Farkas, a halfback from the University of Detroit, was slated to step into Battles's shoes.

Two-a-day workouts began on August 10, the weather hot and humid in Washington. Thirty-six players, including eighteen rookies, answered the morning call. Sam missed the morning workout but arrived by plane shortly after lunch. A shirtsleeved crowd of about 200 watched from portable bleachers. Among the spectators was Battles.

Three weeks later, the world champion Redskins opened their exhibition season at Chicago's Soldier Field against the college all-stars. The day before the Wednesday-night game, Ray Flaherty blistered his men for their lackadaisical attitude. "You fellows are acting too much like world champions before the game," the red-haired, freckle-faced coach shouted, pacing the floor of the team locker room between benches filled with his players.

The time to act like the champions is Wednesday night. We won the league championship because we didn't underestimate the opposition. And if we lose to the college All-Stars, it will be because you fellows underrate them. That team those college coaches will put on the field will be a tougher outfit than anything we saw last year. But you fellows don't seem to think so. You're not working as hard. You're not taking this game seriously enough. You're letting me down, and you're letting down those Washington fans who supported you last season and are expecting big things from you Wednesday.

Even though the rah-rah exhortations sounded more like something that would come from the *Post*'s Povich than from Flaherty, the coach had reason to be concerned. Before nearly seventy-five thousand fans the next night, the all-stars whipped the world champions 28–16. The collegians thoroughly outplayed the defending champions, and Sam's collegiate counterpart, Cecil Isbell from Purdue, showed up the previous year's rookie sensation. Isbell's passing and running resulted in two touchdowns and set up a field goal. The spotlight going into the game had been on a Colorado running back named Byron "Whizzer" White, but the future Supreme Court justice played only sparingly.

The Redskins gave up two interceptions, but two rookies, George Karamatic and Bill Tuckey, threw them, not Sam. He had injured his foot early in the week and wasn't really a factor in the game.

Despite the loss to the youngsters, the Redskins got off to a good start in the regular season. Opening at Municipal Stadium in Philadelphia, the team rode the passing arm of their star, who was twelve of thirteen passing in the first half.

Just before the end of the half, Sam went back to pass and found Max Krause open as an avalanche of Eagles drove him to the turf. Krause scored on the forty-seven-yard pass play; Sam stayed on the ground. When he finally got up and limped off the field, twenty thousand Eagles fans gave him a standing ovation, "for he had treated them to an amazing spectacle of forward passing," wrote Povich, who was at his lyric best:

> Get the picture of a Redskin team, leaderless, reeling, with Sammy Baugh forced to the sidelines by painful injuries. Get the picture of a team stripped of its greatest attacking threat, bereft of the weapon it always had counted on and worried by the prospect of losing the first defense of its national championship.
>
> Then get this picture: That same team summoning some strange hidden force in the second half, fighting in sheer desperation, and twice finding the power to produce two Hollywood-script touchdowns to come from behind and win the game.
>
> That was how the Washington Redskins beat the Philadelphia Eagles, 26–23, in a supersensational game today before 20,000 wildly gibbering professional football fans goggle-eyed at the amazing pace.

The Redskins won on a trick play. With Bill Hartman from Georgia replacing Sam at tailback, and the ball on the Redskins' thirty-eight-yard line, Hartman dropped back to pass. His right end, Wayne Millner, dropped into the backfield just before the ball was snapped, which made a guard, Bill Young, pass eligible. The Eagles never even noticed the 245-pound lineman as he rumbled down the field. Hartman saw him, though, and flipped a pass to Young, who gathered it in on the Eagles' thirty-five-yard line. "With the ball in his grip, Young no longer lumbered," Povich wrote. "He was off with all the speed at his command and in the clear. It was 245 pounds of guard streaking it for the goal line and making it with ridiculous ease, for not an Eagle was in the vicinity."

Even with Sam on the bench for the next three games because of his shoulder separation, the Redskins were 4-0-1 when they traveled to Detroit to face the Lions.

Andy Farkas, heir apparent to Battles, was playing his first pro game in his hometown before the largest Lions crowd ever. He let his nerves get the best of him in the early going. After the Lions scored on a field goal near the end of the first quarter, Farkas fielded the kickoff inside his own ten and, mentally reverting to the college game, where the goalposts were at the back of the end zone instead of the front, assumed he had fielded the ball in the end zone for a touchback, which meant the Redskins would get the ball on the twenty. When he realized his mistake, he attempted to circle behind the goal posts and run the ball out, but the Lions were on him before he could escape the end zone. The Lions led 5–0.

The score stayed that way until shortly before the half, when the Lions lined up for a sure-thing field goal. Wee Willie Wilkin made sure it didn't happen. At the snap, he launched his 270 pounds across the line of scrimmage, swept aside the defensive end, and barged into the Lions' backfield. The deep blocker, Ace Gutowsky, moved to stop the giant rookie, but Wee Willie picked up the 200-pounder and hurled him at the Lion kicker. The ball bounced off Gutowsky's helmet; blocker, kicker, and ball scattered like bowling balls.

In the second half, Farkas redeemed himself, hauling in a number of Baugh passes and scoring the winning touchdown. The Redskins won 7–5.

Meanwhile, the Redskins were in near revolt against their owner and what they called his "chiseling tactics." Marshall arranged for the team to play a number of exhibition games before, during, and after the regular season, but he refused to pay his players for them. "We received nothing for playing the exhibition game at Louisville in September, although the Redskins front office received a sizeable guarantee for the game," an unnamed player told the *Post*. "And we have already been told that we can expect nothing from an exhibition game scheduled at Richmond in

November." That anonymous player could well have been Sam, who always called the Redskins owner "Mr. Marshall" but certainly wasn't intimidated by him. The team's superstar had quickly established himself as a leader despite his youth.

In the same article, several players told the *Post* that their contracts with Marshall called for them to be paid for exhibition games as well as league games. "Our contract says that we are to receive a 'sum to be agreed upon' for the exhibition games. We have reminded Marshall about that, but received nothing." The player quoted above noted that every other club in the league paid its players for exhibition games scheduled during the league season. "Even the Pittsburgh Pirates, who are losing money this year, are paying their players," he said.

The Redskins' discontent began in January after they had won the championship and set out on an exhibition tour to California and throughout the South. Marshall lost $6,000 on the tour, but the players believed it was his own fault. "We wanted to play the exhibition games on percentage, but he wouldn't let us," the player said. "He thought he could get a terrific gate out of a Los Angeles game, and he insisted on paying us our regular weekly salary instead of a percentage. The Los Angeles game fell through, the others didn't draw and he took the loss instead of us."

Marshall's "chiseling" was nothing new. From the beginning, he and other owners scheduled as many exhibition games as possible to market their teams and generate revenue— never mind that the players ran the risk of getting hurt and ruining their ability to play during the regular season.

For example, in 1937, Marshall attempted to schedule semipro games in cities near those with NFL franchises, as a way to cover travel expenses for league games. On August 19, the Redskins' general manager, J. K. Espy, wrote a letter to LeRoy White of Terre Haute, Indiana, that illustrates the fly-by-night nature of scheduling in the early days:

> This is to advise that the Redskins would be interested in a proposition to play in Terre Haute sometime between November 14th and November 21st.
>
> On those two dates we will be playing in Pittsburgh and Cleveland respectively and might very well be able to play some team in your city between the League games, providing, of course, that the terms are suitable.
>
> If you can schedule a team of players who are eligible in the eyes of the National Football League, of which we are a member and whose rules we must adhere to, we will be willing to play you for a guarantee of $2500.00 with an option of 50% of the gross receipts after the federal taxes and park rental have been deducted.

With the players in almost open revolt in 1938, Flaherty told the Redskins' owner the players deserved to be paid for exhibition games. "It isn't Flaherty's fault. He's for us," the anonymous player told the *Post*, "but Marshall isn't doing himself any good by chiseling on us. In fact, Marshall is ham-stringing Flaherty. That's what it amounts to. One of Ray's big jobs is to keep the players on his club contented, but he's not getting any support from Marshall. We're not kids anymore. Flaherty's pep talks can't make us forget that we're getting a raw deal." One of the Redskins, a veteran, suggested that the team's poor showing against Brooklyn—the Redskins managed only a 6–6 tie, despite being heavy favorites—was the result of the pay dispute. "The fellows just didn't have the old spirit," he said, "and I think I know why."

The dispute simmered for years. Owners, as columnist William Rhoden of the *New York Times* once observed, "were essentially feudal lords who often treated their teams like fiefdoms, their players like subjects."

Marshall was even more imperious than most, but Sam and his teammates, however much they grumbled, put up with "Mr. Marshall" and his high-handed ways. They were well aware that he owned them.

Roy Zimmerman was one of the few who stood up to him. A running back and quarterback drafted by the Redskins out of San Jose State in 1940, Zimmerman was a superb football player. He played in the Pro Bowl in 1942, was All-Pro twice, and in 1945 led the league in interceptions.

In the summer of 1943, the Redskins played the College All-Stars. When Marshall refused to pay for that game, Zimmerman refused to play in it. The Redskins owner unloaded him to the Steagles (the merged team of the Philadelphia Eagles and the Pittsburgh Steelers during World War II). Zimmerman's obstinacy, plus a lawsuit filed a few years later by Bill Radovich—a lineman who played for the Detroit Lions—would lead, eventually, to the formation of the National Football League Players Association. Sam would be out of the league by then.

Marshall may not have been eager to pay his players, but he did buy them new burgundy and gold uniforms. "Satin pants which weigh less than two pounds, feature the new regalia, while a positively foreboding Indian head decorates the jerseys," the *Post* reported. Sam was lighter as well. He weighed only 177 pounds, ten pounds less than he did his rookie year. He blamed the weight loss on his summer of baseball.

On November 13, the Redskins invaded Chicago for their first regular-season meeting since the '37 championship contest, and on a cold, windswept Wrigley Field, the Bears beat them in more ways than one. It was "a brawl game," Shirley Povich wrote, "a bruising battle of doubled fists, crushing knees and cleated anger. Tempers were short from the outset, but when the two teams settled down to football at odd moments, the Bears were superior."

The tone was set early when, on the third play of the game, Redskins running back George Karamatic hauled in a punt at his own thirty-yard line and was immediately hammered in the face by the ham-sized fist of big Joe Stydahar. Karamatic, out cold, dropped the ball, and the Bears recovered on the Redskins' thirty-six-yard line.

George Marshall was enraged. He vaulted the railing in front of his box seat, strode onto the field, and demanded that the officials penalize the Monsters of the Midway for unnecessary roughness. Bear fans went crazy as the red-faced owner argued nose-to-nose with the referee. Later in the half, three players—two from the Bears and one from the Redskins—were kicked out the game for what the *Post* called "flagrant slugging with closed fists."

Sam was ineffective for much of the day and also had a punt blocked. The Bears won 31–7.

Halas rubbed it in after the game, "apologizing" that the Bears were too tough on their visitors. "That's too bad, girlies," he told reporters. "I'm awfully sorry my boys were a little rough. What say we all go down to the corner for a double banana split and a fistful of chocolate éclairs? And get this, Gertrude—one more squeak out of you pantywaists and I'll lick the lot of you myself, and that goes for your boss too."

On the way back to Washington that evening, Marshall burst into Shirley Povich's Pullman compartment, holding a check in the air and crowing that it was the biggest check any visiting team had ever taken out of Chicago. The next day, as Povich walked through the train cars, he noticed that Marshall had moved his players from the more comfortable Pullman cars back to coaches, and that some of the injured players were lying in the baggage cars. In a column, Povich contrasted Marshall's penny-pinching with his boasting. Marshall banned the *Post* columnist from the locker room.

On a wet, cold Sunday afternoon at Griffith Stadium two weeks after the Chicago loss, the Pittsburgh Pirates kept the Redskins offense bottled up for three quarters in a game the Redskins had to win in order to stay in the title chase with the New York Giants. As Sam sat on the bench, still not 100 percent, the rookie Whizzer White ran up and down the field almost at will. "Whizzer White justified all his pregame notices," Povich reported. "The slender White, playing with a team that has won only three of its games this season, was a dazzling fellow with his shifty gallops, and for the 45 minutes he played he was a constant menace for the Redskins."

Somehow the Skins were leading 3–0 when Sam made his first appearance on the field. The more than twenty-five thousand overcoated and blanketed fans in the stands rose as one to cheer as the slender, young tailback, seemingly unconcerned about the wet, slippery ball, took the snap from center and immediately began passing. He whipped a long low pass to his buddy Wayne Millner, who had gotten behind safetyman White. The scoring play covered fifty-seven yards. Three minutes later, Sam found Bob McCheney for a fifty-six–yard touchdown pass.

Sam threw eight passes that day, completing five. His receivers dropped the other three, no doubt because of the wet ball.

With Sam hurt most of the year and without Battles in the backfield, the Skins struggled throughout the '38 season. Still, they found themselves in a familiar place at the end of it, battling for the division title with the Giants.

In New York, Richards Vidmer of the *Post* reported, "everything seems to be going along as usual."

A lot of people don't even seem to be aware of the fact that the New York Giants and the Washington Redskins are going to play in the Polo Grounds on Sunday for the Eastern championship of the National Professional League. . . . But it's different in Washington. The Capital has become a campus. Everybody seems to be aware that the Redskins are going to play the Giants in New York on Sunday, and the old college spirit is running up and down Pennsylvania Avenue like a lobbyist looking for an appropriation.

Vidmer professed to hear Washingtonians singing the Redskins' fight song as they walked along the city sidewalks.

The professionals, as a whole, don't go in for the campus spirit, but Washington is different. It's probably due to the influence of George Preston Marshall.

Vidmer noted that although Marshall had not gone to college, he was always looking for a local college team to call his own—sometimes Georgetown, sometimes George Washington, occasionally the University of Maryland, one season Catholic University.

He organized various teams to cheer about. One was a professional basketball team and there was a report that he spent one entire evening looking for a line to rhyme with "Fight for good old Palace Laundry." Finally he was forced to give up his basketball team. He couldn't find a rhyme.

Twelve thousand Redskins fans made the trek north to the Big Apple; they might as well have stayed at home. "Caught in the fury of ceaseless onslaughts by a Giant team in a passion for revenge for the Redskins' 49–14 victory of last year, the Redskins were utterly routed," Povich wrote. "Their defenses shattered, their attack a puny puerile thing today, their balance and precision lost in the face of the Giants' assaults, the Redskins were not only beaten but humiliated."

"In the middle of the fourth period the Redskin brass band marched out in a body, leaving their football players to save their lives and uniforms if possible," John Kieran of the *New York Times* reported. "The band had seen enough. So had the Giant rooters. Last year's humiliation had been royally revenged."

The Giants beat the Skins 36–0, at the time the worst loss in the club's history.

Sam completed only four of twelve passing attempts and threw three interceptions. After the game, the Texan tossed his helmet into a trunk, yanked off his flimsy shoulder pads, and peeled tape off his legs. "I'm mad and don't let anybody tell you any different," he told reporters. "Hell, they played on the same field we did, didn't they? They played with the same football, and they were the same club we slapped down last year, weren't they? But everything went wrong." The Skins ended the season with a 6-3-2 record.

S am endured something of a sophomore jinx in 1938, although at least one good thing happened that year that probably extended his career by at least a decade. Marshall was finally successful at convincing his fellow owners to change the rule that allowed defensive players to pound on a quarterback until the end of the play, even after he had gotten rid of the ball. Sam and his fellow quarterbacks were often literally running for their lives, even though the man with the ball might be twenty yards downfield.

"Passers took a terrible beating," Sam recalled. "That's one rule Mr. Marshall finally got changed. I remember he called me and asked me if it would help if he could get a rule through that would protect passers. I said, 'Heck, yes, it would probably let me play 10 years longer.'"

S am went back to Texas as soon as the season was over. When he reported back to the Redskins in the late summer of 1939, he reported not to hot, humid D.C. but to Spokane, Washington, Coach Flaherty's hometown. The team trained at Cheney Normal School, eighteen miles outside Spokane. The coach believed that the more comfortable climate—Spokane is two thousand feet above sea level—would help his guys get in shape more quickly. He blamed the loss to the Giants in the division-title game on poor physical conditioning.

On their cross-country trek back to D.C. to start the season, the Redskins won exhibition games in San Francisco and Los Angeles. The regular season started off with the Redskins' biggest rivals, the Giants, coming to Griffith Stadium. The game ended in a frustrating 0–0 tie, the only scoreless tie in Redskins history. During the following three weeks, they beat Brooklyn 14–13, the Chicago Cardinals 28–7, and Philadelphia.

The game with the Eagles before 33,258 fans in Philly's Municipal Stadium—the largest turnout in Eagles history—was billed as a duel between Slingin' Sam and little Davey O'Brien, the Heisman Trophy winner who had been Sam's understudy at TCU. It didn't turn out that way. Neither team scored through three quarters. Early in the fourth quarter, Sam threw a thirty-yard touchdown to end Charley Malone, and the Redskins won 7–0.

Next up was Pittsburgh. Sam Boyd, who had joined the Steelers that year after an outstanding career as a receiver at Baylor, recalled years later playing against Sam. (Boyd was later Baylor's head coach.)

> From the first time he stepped onto the field, Sam was the best quarterback in the league—the best there ever had been. And in all my years of playing and coaching, I still can't think of anybody I ever saw who could throw the ball like he could.

Boyd recalled that 1939 was the year that Dick Todd, a Texas A&M standout, joined the Redskins.

> I knew all about Dick, because I'd played against him for three years, but nobody else up there had ever heard of him. The first time we played Washington, I tried to tell our people we needed to watch out for the new running back. But they told me, "We don't worry about rookies." Well, early in the game we had them backed up on their four-yard line, and all of a sudden Sam takes

a snap and just straightens up and throws a quick slant to Todd, who runs 96 yards for a touchdown.

The Steelers paid a lot more attention to the rookie after that, but it didn't really matter. With Todd running and Sam passing, the Redskins beat Art Rooney's team 44–14.

The next game was with the Green Bay Packers, in Green Bay. The Packers handed the Redskins their first defeat of the season, 24–14. Washington rebounded with victories over Pittsburgh and Detroit, thus tying the Giants for the Eastern Division lead. The final game of the season was in New York, where for the third straight year, the Redskins would be facing off against the Giants for the division championship.

As usual, the exodus from the nation's capital began early on the morning of December 2. Buses, private cars, private trains, airplanes—every conveyance that could ferry fifteen thousand rabid fans to the Big Apple was jammed. As usual, Marshall and the Redskins Marching Band led thousands up Broadway toward Columbus Circle. At the Polo Grounds, thousands were turned away as a record-breaking crowd of sixty-three thousand jammed into the stadium.

The Giants kicked two field goals before Sam got his arm unlimbered. Although he completed a string of passes, the Redskins had to give up the ball on downs. For the Giants, it was three and out, and the ensuing punt ended up on the Redskins' three-yard line. The Redskins opted to punt out of trouble. Just as the ball left the foot of kicker Jimmie Johnson, a Giants player knocked him down. Although referee Bill Halloran was right on top of the play, he declined to throw his flag, and the Giants took the ball at the Redskins' thirty-yard line. The Giants settled for their third field goal of the game, making the score 9–0 going into the fourth quarter.

Early in the final quarter, Wee Willie Wilkin blocked a punt, and backup tailback Frank Filchock hit Bob Masterson for a touchdown. Masterson kicked the extra point, making the score 9–7.

The next time the Redskins got the ball, Filchock again found Masterson open, and the receiver caught the ball on the Giants' two-yard line. Thinking the sideline was the goal line, he stepped out of bounds, exultant that he had scored what was likely the game winner. The Redskins fumbled on the next play, and the Giants recovered.

Washington, still trailing by two, got the ball back with five minutes left to play. Sam drove them down the field on a sixty-five-yard march to the Giants' eight-yard line and a first down. Two plunges into the line got them to the Giants' three—three yards for a touchdown and the Eastern Division championship with a minute and a half to play. The overflow crowd was on its feet, the noise deafening. The Redskins called time out, and Bo Russell, who hadn't missed a field goal all year, trotted onto the field for a chip shot and the championship. More than sixty thousand were silent.

Filchock, the holder, took the snap. Russell stepped into the ball and sent it sailing through the uprights. Filchock and Russell hugged each other. Mel Hein and other Giants tore their helmets off in disgust. The brass band, directly behind the goalposts, began beating drums of victory. Referee Halloran, staring toward the goalposts as if transfixed, brought his hands up as high as his waist, preparing to signal that the kick was good, when suddenly he brought them down and across his knees, signaling "no good"! He claimed the kick was wide right.

The Redskins couldn't believe it. And neither could the Giants. As fans poured onto the field, fights broke out. When the game ended a few minutes later, police tried to escort a wide-eyed Halloran from the field through the milling mass of infuriated Redskin fans. As the cops struggled toward the exit, another fight broke out, and Halloran was roughed up but not seriously injured. Redskins player Ed Justice, who was in the middle of the melee, appeared to hit Halloran.

Flaherty also caught up with the referee. In the dressing room, he told reporters what he had found out: "Halloran told me he could have called it either way. He said it was like a close decision by an umpire on a ball or strike. I could argue, but it would do me no good. If that guy has got a conscience, he'll never have another good night's sleep as long as he lives."

Corinne Griffith recalled that the rain began shortly after the Redskins' entourage pulled out of Grand Central. "As we passed through the brightly lighted coach, I had my nearest view of a team unjustly defeated," she recalled. "The tragic looking faces reflected the gall in their cup of bitterness; it was heartbreaking, the more so because there was no word of comfort to offer; nothing one could say or do; just a hopeless, helpless feeling."

The Redskins arrived in Washington two hours late, but more than seven thousand fans were waiting in the rain. The stationmaster called it "the largest crowd since the troops returned from France." As Griffith recalled, there were "men, women, children, newsboys, Congressmen, Judges, fans—black and white—all of one accord—all in unity—all of one mind—all agreed on one thing: 'We was robbed!'"

The morning papers in both Washington and New York carried pictures showing the ball well inside the uprights as it sailed past the cross bar. Newsreels showed the same thing. The NFL's president, Carl Storck, insisted the pictures taken from an angle proved nothing. The National

Geographic Society offered to make a scientific survey of photos made by the Associated Press, but Storck refused the offer. Storck also ruled on the Redskins' Justice, who faced a $500 fine and a life suspension from professional football. According to Halloran, the player had not struck him, so Justice lived to play again.

The *Post*'s Povich recalled years later that he got scores of irate letters about the infamous kick. One in particular was memorable, from a fan whose fanaticism may have been a bit spirit fortified. "I was sitting on the 50-yard-line," the fan wrote Povich. "I saw two balls and two sets of goal posts, and I know damn well one of those balls went through one of those posts."

THE 1940 NFL CHAMPIONSHIP

THE MONSTERS' REVENGE

I n 1940, the Redskins headed back to Spokane, the theft of a division championship a few months earlier still rankling, and set up camp at Flaherty's (and Bing Crosby's) alma mater, Gonzaga College. Vincent X. Flaherty of the *Washington Times-Herald* described the training facility as "the most ultramodern" he'd ever seen, "with its rigging of nickeled heat lamps, violet ray contraptions, lily white cots and rubbing tables which would make a Hollywood masseur blink in admiration."

The team started strong, with exhibition wins over Green Bay, 28–20, and an outfit called the Eastern College All-Stars, 35–12. That game was played in Boston, of all places; twenty-five thousand fans showed up. Before the regular season began, they Redskins had traveled 7,229 miles by train, playing football along the way.

They opened at home against Dan Topping's Brooklyn Dodgers before a crowd of thirty-three thousand; the ice-skating star Sonja Henie threw out the first ball. Sam, completely free of injuries for the first time in three seasons, got off to a great start. Against a tough Brooklyn team, he completed eleven of fourteen passes, including a forty-one-yard touchdown pass; averaged better than fifty yards on three punts, including a crucial fifty-seven-yard quick kick; and carried the ball twice for a total of ten yards from the left halfback position. The Redskins won 24–17.

"Baugh, starting the final season of his three-year contract with the Washington club, was the cause of Coach Ray Flaherty's greatest postgame rejoicing," the *Washington Post* reported. "Even more significant for Flaherty than the victory over Brooklyn was the knowledge that Baugh is ready for a great season. 'They're a great ball club, make no mistake of that,' said Brooklyn coach Jock Sutherland, 'and in Baugh they possess one of the greatest players in football today.'"

Marshall let it be known that he wasn't so sure—for the most transparent of reasons. Sam's three-year contract would be up after the '40 season, and the niggardly owner was planning to pay him just as little as he could get away with, even as he goaded him into another great year. "I think he will get out of football if he bumps into another spotty season," Marshall told a reporter. "I think he will make a good coach. It's unfortunately true that the last two of Sammy's seasons here have been spotty." He also predicted that Sam would never be as good as he had been in 1937.

Sam was a proud man, but he also knew his owner was a blowhard. As he would do throughout his career, he went out and played as well as he was able. More often than not, that was better than anyone else in the game.

Years later, Sam would label the 1940 Redskins the best team he ever played on, despite the nightmare ending to that season.

The second game of the season was with the same team that had "stolen" the Eastern Division title the previous December. This time the Redskins won, 21–7, before 34,713 at a packed Griffith Stadium. Dick Todd, the "Crowell Cyclone," ran back a punt seventy-eight yards for a touchdown. The former Texas Aggie star played so well in several games that Sam remarked, "Dick Todd is the greatest running back I've ever seen in my life—and I'm not excepting Cliff Battles. Get Dick into the open field and nobody will catch him."

The Redskins won their first seven games before falling to the Dodgers in a rematch, 16–14. Despite the loss, Sam completed an NFL record twenty-three completions in a single game. Two were for Washington's only touchdowns.

That set up one of the two grudge games the Redskins played every year, with Halas's Chicago Bears coming to town in a game that was billed as a preview of the championship game. It turned out to be that and more.

The Redskins came into the game 7-1, the Bears 6-2. From the start of the year, the Bears had been the odds-on favorite to win the NFL title. "No one's going to beat the Bears this year," said Bert Bell, the then owner of the Eagles, in the preseason. "They're the greatest team ever assembled."

Although the Bears didn't go undefeated, they did have six future Hall of Famers in their starting lineup: quarterback Sid Luckman, the first modern T-formation quarterback; halfback George McAfee, the most dangerous broken-field runner in the league; center "Bulldog" Turner; tackle Joe Stydahar; and guards Danny Fortmann and George Musso. The team also featured several all-pros. Most opponents agreed with Jim Lawrence, a Philadelphia lineman: "It was worse when the Bear second string came in because they were breathing fire trying to prove they should be first string."

The sellout crowd of thirty-six thousand at Griffith Stadium expected a high-scoring affair from the NFL's two top offenses. Instead, they saw a defensive battle as the Bears' Hunk Anderson kept Sam running for his life most of the afternoon. The Redskins' defense kept the Bears bottled up as well—as did two booming punts from Sam that each traveled more than seventy yards. The only touchdown pass of the day was thrown not by Sam or Bears star Sid Luckman, but by the Redskins' backup, Frank Filchock. In the second quarter, the halfback was sweeping right when he suddenly pulled up and tossed an eighteen-yard pass to Todd at the back of the end zone.

The Redskins led 7–3 with forty seconds left to play when the Bears' backup quarterback, Bob Snyder, took the snap at midfield and found receiver George McAfee loose at the fifteen. McAfee, the fastest man in the NFL, appeared to have a clear route to the goal line. Todd, playing defensive halfback, gave chase and, with a diving tackle, managed to bring down McAfee at the one-yard line. On the next play, Wee Willie Wilkin burst through the line and smothered the Bears ball carrier five yards behind the line of scrimmage.

With only two seconds left on the clock, Snyder fired a pass into the right corner of the end zone, where fullback Bill Osmanski was open for a split second. Filchock came up fast and hit Osmanski just as the ball arrived. It looked as if the Redskins defender had pinioned Osmanski's arms and the Bears receiver couldn't hold on. "Interference!" the Bears screamed, and an enraged Halas raced onto the field. The referee thought otherwise, but the Bears continued to protest long after the final gun had sounded.

The Bears were devastated. Some of the players were crying as they walked down the ramp toward the locker room. Bulldog Turner came up alongside his old Sweetwater pal. "Just remember," he muttered to Sam, "we'll be seeing you bastards in three weeks. Don't forget that."

Sam knew better than to rub it in, but a graceless Marshall did not. Reporters asked him about the call, and the Redskins' owner, not surprisingly, shot from the hip. Still fuming about the Halloran incident that ended the Redskins' '39 season, he had no sympathy for "We wuz robbed" arguments. "Crybabies!" he called the Bears. "Quitters!" Marshall couldn't contain himself. "They fold up when the going gets tough," he said. "Just look at what they did today. They don't know how to win a close game."

Sam and his teammates cringed when they read Marshall's comments in the Monday-morning papers. They respected the Bears, and they knew how they would have reacted if it had been Halas making such ill-advised remarks.

"I never played against a poor Bears team," Sam recalled. "I always thought they had the toughest damn defense in the league. Day in and day out, they were the best team when I was up there. We never had any game with them that was easy. Any time we went up against them we got two or three boys hurt."

Meanwhile, the Bears breezed through the final two weeks of the season. The Redskins traveled to New York with an opportunity to wrap up the division title against the Giants. Even though the Giants weren't in contention, they managed to be a pain, beating Sam and his boys 21–7, thereby handing the Dodgers a chance to catch the division-leading Skins.

The Redskins took care of business, though, by defeating the Eagles in the regular-season finale to win their third division title in five years—their fourth in the view of the many fans who still couldn't stomach what had happened in New York the year before. Their record of 9-2-0 was the best thus far in team history. Sam, named all-pro for the second time in his four-year-old career, completed 111 passes for a league-leading 1,367 yards and 12 touchdowns.

The Bears had won the Western Division title, and the stage was set for the first world championship game ever to be played in the nation's capital. The game sold out in three hours, the quickest sellout in NFL history. "We could sell 100,000 tickets," Flaherty noted.

"Plainclothes detectives, keeping a sharp eye out for known ticket scalpers, also had instructions to keep their eyes open for 'amateurs,'" Marshall told the *Post*.

"There were more red feathers in downtown Washington last Sunday than had been seen all fall at Harvard, Cornell and Stanford put together," *Time* magazine reported. "Not since the World Series of 1924 had there been so much excitement in the nation's capital. Louisville might have its Derby, Indianapolis its auto race, but this year Washington had the show of shows: their beloved Redskins were playing the Chicago Bears for the professional football championship of the world."

Marshall kept it up. He sent a telegram to Halas that read:

congratulations. you got me in this thing and i hope i have the pleasure of beating your ears off next sunday and every year to come. justice is triumphant. we should play for the championship every year. game will be sold out by tuesday. right regards, george

The owner's glamorous wife was on top of the world. Writers were giving her credit for designing the team's burgundy and gold uniforms, for writing "Hail to the Redskins," for "becoming the most influential woman in modern sports."

And now, only three years after persuading her headstrong husband to give Washington a chance, her Redskins were once again playing for the championship. "Senators, Congressmen, Big Shots, Tough Guys, Influential Persons, college coaches, football experts, sportswriters, real sports, phony sports, begging—threatening—every man, woman and child in Washington, its suburbs, Virginia, Maryland and parts of Pennsylvania and West Virginia, seemed to want tickets for the game," she recalled.

The Bears arrived in Washington on Thursday and checked into the Mayflower Hotel on Connecticut Avenue in downtown D.C. While the team worked out at Griffith Stadium on Saturday, carpenters were busy expanding the press box to accommodate some 150 sportswriters. In addition to 115 radio stations broadcasting the game, Paramount, Metro-Goldwyn-Mayer, Fox, Universal, and Pathé planned to make newsreels. Also on Saturday, the two coaches were interviewed on the Mutual Radio Network. The Redskins' Flaherty spoke "in a very modest sort of way," Griffith recalled, "and Halas in a very self-assured one."

The Bears were a great team, *Time* observed, but Washington had "his Excellency, Slingin' Sammy Baugh" and three of the best receivers in pro football.

Only three weeks ago, the Redskins had taken the Bears 7–3. They had just averted defeat, to be sure, with a miraculous tackle on the one-yard line in the next-to-last play of the game. But the score is what counts. Thus Washington residents, from Cabinet members to White House flunkeys, mesmerized by the big talk of the Redskins' Big Chief, George Preston Marshall, trooped into Griffith Park . . . convinced that it was all over but the whoopee, and all set to drape the Washington Monument with red bunting after the game.

The Redskins were solid favorites, despite injuries to Dick Todd, Bill Young, and Wilbur Moore. The *Post* advertised that the game story would appear on Monday's front page. What the oddsmakers didn't know was that Halas, a player, coach, and owner for nearly thirty years, had his men ready to play—not only physically but also psychologically.

In 1940, Stanford coach Clark Shaughnessy, considered one of the offensive geniuses of college football, came up with the T formation. The T soon would become standard in football at all levels, with the quarterback lined up directly behind the center and the running backs four or five yards behind the quarterback. But in 1939, it was revolutionary.

Before the T formation, most teams, college and pro, ran the single wing, invented by Glenn "Pop" Warner at Carlisle in 1912. The tailback took most of the snaps from center and could either run, pass, or kick. Most single-wing offenses relied on power, not passing, because of the unbalanced line. The quarterback, also known as the blocking back, could line up behind either guard or between them, or sometimes between the strong-side guard and the tackle. Passing was rare.

The T allowed running plays to develop much quicker. Rather than wait for blockers to mobilize in front of the ball carrier, the T popped the runner through the line before the defense could get moving.

The T formation also solved the basic problem of the single wing, which is that the tailback had to be incredibly versatile. He had to be able to run with power and speed as well as to throw. The T allowed backs to specialize.

Halas, considered the NFL's great innovator, hired Shaughnessy as a consultant, and the Stanford man adapted his version of the formation to the Bears. He introduced the hand-to-hand snap, with the quarterback right up under the center. Previously, the quarterback stood a half yard to a yard behind the center, and the snap was a short toss of the ball. The hand-to-hand snap got the play moving quickly because the quarterback didn't have to wait to make sure he had control of the ball. From the T formation, he could immediately move out from under the center and hand off the ball to one of his three backs or drop back and pass.

Shaughnessy also widened the splits between the offensive linemen. When the defense adjusted, holes opened up for running backs reaching the line of scrimmage at full speed.

Although Halas had used the T in the 7–3 loss to the Redskins, who managed to contain it except on counter plays, the Bears didn't have it fully implemented. Preparing for the championship game, Halas and Shaughnessy studied films of previous Redskins-Bears games, looking for tendencies and studying the Skins' defense and the team's reaction to various features of the T-formation attack. They produced a modified T-formation offense that focused on counter plays and a number of others tailored to the Redskin defense, including a mystifying man-in-motion maneuver that left the Redskins vulnerable to quick openers up the middle.

At last it was Sunday afternoon in D.C. Fans around the country settled in to listen to the NFL title game on network radio, with the game broadcast to 120 stations over the Mutual Broadcasting System. Mutual paid $2,500 for the rights. Red Barber provided play-by-play and analysis.

Inside the stadium on Florida Avenue, on a warm and sunny December day, a sellout crowd of thirty-six thousand watched the brass section of the Redskins Marching Band step onto the field, then the chief and two drum majors strutted out, and then the trumpeters, heralding the arrival of the full 150-piece band. They played "Hail to the Redskins," interspersed with "Dixie," and the crowd went wild.

In the visitors' dressing room, with the noise of the band and the crowd filtering through the cement walls, the Bears gathered on benches or knelt on the floor around their coach. As he looked around the room, staring into eyes both determined and apprehensive, Halas pulled a newspaper clipping from his pocket and began reading a story that quoted Marshall. He read it slowly and clearly, looking up occasionally to make sure his men were listening closely: "The Bears are a team that folds under pressure in the second half against a good team. If they come down here to play us in the championship game, they'll have to win by a big score or they won't win at all." Halas let the words sink in. He folded the paper and put it in his pocket. "Gentlemen," he said, "this is what the Redskins think of you. I think you're a great football team, the greatest ever assembled. Go out on the field and prove it."

Shaughnessy, a distant man who rarely spoke to the players except in meetings, stepped to the blackboard. As he drew up the first play of the game, he said, "Men, I promise you this one will go for a touchdown. And if it doesn't work, I've got another one coming up that will." The play he diagrammed was an early version of the modern pro set, with two backs and two ends split. It worked exactly as he said it would.

Fans had barely settled into their seats after the two o'clock kickoff when, on the second play of the game, Bears halfback Bill Osmanski darted into a gap off left tackle and ran sixty-eight yards untouched for a touchdown, a crowd of grasping Redskins in his wake. "When I saw the type of blocking we were getting on that play, I knew it was only a question of the final score," Halas said later.

The Redskins ran the ensuing kickoff back to the Bears forty, and Sam, calmly directing the offense as usual, got them down to the twenty-six. From there, he took the snap from center, looked downfield, and spotted Charlie Malone, standing alone at the two. Sam and his favorite receiver connected with a sure touchdown pass. Incredibly, the ball hit Malone's hands, then his chest, and then bounced to the ground.

The pass was perfect, Arthur Daley of the *New York Times* noted, except it was thrown in the one corner of the field where the sun was in the receiver's eyes. Had the Redskins tied the game at that point, "it might have been a far different story," Daley wrote.

"What happened after that was a waking nightmare to the Washington fans," *Time* reported. "The Bears began to roll—like the German Army rolling through France. Dazed onlookers waited for the defenders to make a stand—in Belgium, at the Somme, at Dunkirk—but the juggernaut kept rolling, rolling, rolling. They chalked up 21 points in the first quarter, seven in the second. Radio fans, tuning in at half time thought they were listening to a basketball game—or an Atlantic City auction."

When the Redskins had the ball, as Griffith recalled, "McChesney playing with a broken hand dropped a pass. Wilbur Moore [playing with a cracked rib] dropped one. Sandy Sanford dropped one. Zimmerman missed Farkas with one. The Redskins became mentally petrified."

With the score 28–0, Sam went over to Flaherty and told him they might as well go for broke. They had nothing to lose. The Redskins started throwing on fourth down instead of punting; the Bears sat back and intercepted, eight times in all. "I remember saying, 'Hell, we may get beat 60–0, but we've got to try it,'" Sam recalled. "Well, we sure didn't get beat 60–0."

Angry and disgusted, Sam and the rest of the Redskins trudged into the dressing room at halftime determined to at least make the game respectable, even if victory already was out of reach. Inside the Bears' dressing room, Halas didn't say a word until right before his team was ready to hit the field again. "Well, fellows," he said, "are we a first-half team or aren't we? Go out there and show 'em."

The Bears—those "quitters" and "crybabies"—didn't let up after the half. Bear end Hampton Pool intercepted a Baugh pass and ran it in nineteen yards for a touchdown. Ray Nolting scored on a twenty-three-yard counter play. George McAfee intercepted a Roy Zimmerman pass and turned it into a thirty-four-yard touchdown. Bulldog Turner, Sam's old friend, picked off another Zimmerman pass and lumbered in from twenty-one yards out.

The score was 56–0 at the end of the third quarter, but the Bears were in no mood to show mercy. The fourth quarter opened with the Bears' Harry

Clark loping around end for forty-four yards and a touchdown. The Redskins fumbled deep in their own territory, the Bears recovered, and Gary Famiglietti scored on a two-yard plunge.

It was about then that Marshall had his public-address announcer make what the *Post* columnist Bob Considine called "the most ill-advised announcement in the history of sport." It was about the availability of season tickets for 1941. Considine also observed that "the unluckiest guy in the crowd was the five-buck bettor who took the Redskins and 70 points."

Clark scored the last Bear touchdown on a one-yard carry, making the score 73–0. It could have been worse; the Bears made only seven of eleven extra points.

With two minutes left to play, Marshall left his box to go down to the field. "I'm going down to those kids, *anything* might happen," he told his wife. As he made his way down the steps a fan sitting near Marshall's fifty-yard-line box shouted, "Get 'em out of here, you Lug. Take 'em back to Boston." "You come down *here* and say that, you Lug," Marshall responded. ("Lug," no doubt, was a euphemism used by Griffith.)

"I didn't even turn my head, just leaned on the rail and prayed," Griffith recalled. What she didn't say is that her husband had stadium attendants take the section and seat number of the heckler, who was told he would never see another Redskins game as a season-ticket holder.

The try for the extra point after the ninth touchdown exhausted the supply of footballs, which sailed into the stands, never to be seen again. The Redskins had to borrow a ball from the team mascot. After the tenth touchdown, referee Red Friesell scurried over to the Bears' bench. "George," he said to Halas, "this is the last football we have. Would you mind running or passing for the extra point?"

Halas was happy to oblige. Reserve quarterback Sollie Sherman passed to Joe Maniaci for the extra point. Following the last touchdown, Sherman tossed a pass toward Maniaci again, but this time the Redskins' Andy Farkas leaped high in the air and broke it up. A dwindling band of Redskins fans cheered.

Turner, who was playing center for the Bears that day and who grew up in Sweetwater, two years behind Sam, had his own recollection. "Well, after one of those touchdowns," he recalled,

Bob Snyder comes in from the bench and says to me, "Coach said to make a bad pass from center. He said we don't want to kick any more points because we're losing too many footballs." I think it was Snyder who was going to hold for that next extra point, but anyway, I said to him, "I'm going to put that ball right back in your hands, and if you want it, drop it. But I'm not going to make a bad pass." So I centered it back there, and he just turned it loose and it lay on the ground. I don't remember who was kicking—we had a lot of guys kicking extra points that day—but whoever it was, damn if he didn't kick it up through there and lose another ball.

Finally, mercifully, it was over. The Bears had piled up 382 yards on the ground, the Redskins 22. Ten different Bears scored eleven touchdowns. Six individual Bears each gained more yardage than the Redskins as a team.

Luckman told the *Chicago Tribune* years later that the Bears weren't trying to run up the score. Halas sat his star quarterback on the bench at the start of the second half and promised to put him back in only if the Redskins scored. He never got back in. "We were only ahead 28–0 at the half, and they had Sammy Baugh," said backup quarterback Saul Sherman.

"We were scared," said halfback George McAfee.

Marshall said afterward that when he got to the dressing room, the team was already inside. As he opened the door, one of the players was sobbing like a child. The others sat in stunned silence.

Povich said he saw several players crying. "Some of these elder players weren't sorry for themselves," he wrote. "They were ashamed of the way they let their Washington fans down. They were the fellows who lived through those lean days at Boston where they were playing under sufferance and who couldn't quite get over the friendliness and the warmth of Washington fans who tried to make big heroes of them." Years later, Povich observed: "The Bears visited on Washington the greatest carnage since the British torched the White House in 1814. At least in that affair, Dolly Madison saved the silverware."

The *Post* writer also posited the notion that the Redskins had been befuddled by the Bears' newly installed T formation. "That T-formation is really dread stuff and Coach George Halas comes pretty close to being the No. 1 offensive genius in the land," he wrote. "The Bears' ball carriers were under way at full speed before they had their hands on the ball and at the rate they were galloping when they hit something, it didn't make a difference whether there was a hole in the Redskins' front line or not."

Sam, who had thrown two interceptions, left the game early; from the bench, he watched as his two replacements threw six interceptions. He was mad—at himself, at his teammates, at Marshall. "That was the most humiliating thing I've ever gone through in my life," he told reporters as he peeled off a dirty jersey.

Decades later, he told *Sports Illustrated* that he had his own ideas about what had happened on that horrendous day. "I don't know whether they'd be right or not, but I think it starts with the fact that we had played the Bears three weeks earlier and had beat them 7–3," he said. "Boy, it hurt 'em. Leaving the field, both teams had to go down the same steps, and I remember some of the Bears were crying. Oh, they were cut to pieces. Their pride was hurt bad."

He also recalled that the week of the championship game, the weather was so bad in Chicago that the Bears had to work out inside, which meant that practices weren't as intense as usual. "In the meantime," he said, "we had beautiful weather in Washington, where the game was going to be played, and we worked like we were in training camp. We worked like dogs, I'm telling you the truth. But I think we left a lot of football on the practice field. Mentally we weren't ready."

Sam also believed that Marshall himself deserved a lion's share of the blame. "Everywhere he went, he would talk about it," he recalled years later, speaking of the 7–3 victory three weeks earlier.

> He just kept making fun of them every chance he got. It was ridiculous for anyone to say stuff like that about a team that was as powerful as they were back then. Year in and year out, they were the strongest team in pro football, and everyone knew it.
>
> Every time Marshall opened his mouth, they got madder and madder, and our morale got lower and lower. He basically destroyed his own team, but George was like that. I never knew anyone who liked him much.

Immediately after the game, Marshall sat on the edge of a trunk in the dressing room and berated his own team. "Those guys out there today quit," he told reporters.

> Filchock's quarterbacking was awful. Two of the highest-salaried backs in the league, Dick Todd and Andy Farkas, stood in that backfield and not once carried the ball. Boys, that's one on Ripley.

He said he felt sorry for the fans, and he promised changes.

> But it'll show up in next year's salaries. We've got some good rookies and we'll get some more. There'll be some changes.

Later, apparently aware that his words would not go over well with either his demoralized players or their fans, he tried to change his tune. "Maybe they didn't lack courage," he said, "but they lost their heads."

Most of the Redskins retreated to the showers, dressed quickly, and left. Sam hung around long enough to leave reporters with one classic line. Asked whether things would have been different if Charlie Malone hadn't dropped the sure touchdown pass in the first quarter, he squinted up at reporters and drawled, "Yeah, it would have been different. It wouldn't have ended 73–0. It would have been 73–7."

Redskins tackle Jim Barber heard what Sam said. "My locker was close and I thought, 'Damn good answer, Sam,' he recalled. "We stunk it up pretty bad. But then everybody in town had an excuse for us. Walking downtown, nobody said, 'Hey, you bums.' They were all for us. 'You just had a bad day.'"

Despite the debacle at the end, Sam had enjoyed another great year. He finished the season as the league's most efficient passer, with an astounding completion rate of 61.7 percent. He also led the league in punting, averaging fifty-one yards a kick, eight yards farther than the league's second-place punter.

He never forgot what happened on that December day in 1940, and reporters every now and then wanted to hear his recollections. More than a half century later, he offered another, very curious explanation. In 1999, he told a reporter that he believed some of his teammates had thrown the game, that they had tried to lose in a big way to spite Marshall. He acknowledged that he had no proof, and said he hadn't offered his opinion earlier because no one had ever asked him. David Baugh believed that the writer misunderstood his father. "I don't think he was saying they threw the game," he said. "He was just saying that they were tired and angry and disgusted, and just sort of gave up."

Clyde Shugart, a Redskins lineman who played in the game, was stunned by his old teammate's remarks. "Was he drunk when he said that?" Shugart asked. "I don't remember anything like that."

The remark didn't attract much attention, maybe because most people didn't want to believe it. Others, no doubt, wrote it off as the nattering of an old man. An NFL spokesman told the Associated Press that the league would not comment on Sam's remarks.

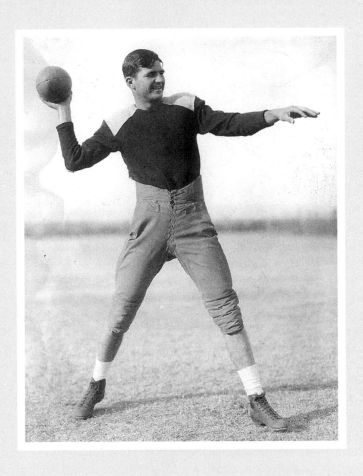

During his senior year at Sweetwater's Newman High School,
Sam may have passed occasionally, but he was primarily a
blocking back. Photo courtesy of the Baugh family.

Before he starred at TCU as the nation's premier passer, Sam considered himself a baseball player. This photo is probably from his days playing with the Mose Sims Oilers, an Abilene semipro team. Photo courtesy of the Baugh family.

Sam, shown here punting the football at TCU, worked as long and hard on his kicking as he did on his passing. Photo courtesy of the Baugh family.

Sam demonstrated his running ability in Dallas on December 15, 1936, a couple of weeks before the TCU Horned Frogs would meet Marquette University in the inaugural Cotton Bowl. Associated Press.

Washington Redskins back Cliff Battles (20) scores against the New York Giants in a playoff game at the Polo Grounds on December 5, 1937. With Battles and Baugh, the Redskins smashed the Giants, 49–14, to win the NFL eastern division championship. Associated Press.

Sam spent the spring of 1938 in the St. Louis Cardinals training camp at St. Petersburg, Florida. He fielded well at third base but had trouble hitting the curve ball. Associated Press.

Sam was injured off and on during the 1938 season, but he was ready to play on December 4 in a crucial game at the Polo Grounds against the New York Giants. Associated Press.

Sam flirted with coaching even before he signed with the Redskins. Here, he offers passing tips to fiancée, Edmonia, at the Baugh home in Sweetwater on December 21, 1937. At the time, Edmonia was a TCU sophomore. Associated Press.

When Sam and Edmonia got married in Rotan, Sam forgot to bring the marriage license. The minister, Edmonia's father, said he could bring it by later. The newlyweds posed for this photo in Columbus, Ohio, where Sam was playing baseball in the summer of 1938. Photo courtesy of the Baugh family.

Edmonia told reporters she was resigned to being a "golf widow." Photo courtesy of the Baugh family.

*Sid Luckman of the Bears brings down Washington's Jimmy Johnstone (31) in
the 73–0 NFL championship game in Washington, D.C., on December 8, 1940.
Moving in on Johnstone are Chicago's Joe Stydahar (13), Bill Osmanski (9),
Dan Fortmann (21), and George McAfee (5). Associated Press.*

Sam may not have been an Oscar-caliber actor, but he sure looked like a Western hero and he could ride a horse. His sidekick in the background in this still from 1941's King of the Texas Rangers *is Duncan Reynaldo, who would later star as TV's Cisco Kid. Photo courtesy of the Baugh family.*

From the time he stepped on the field as a rookie in 1937, Sam knew his offensive linemen would do their utmost to protect him, as in this September 13, 1942, game against the Bears in Washington. *Associated Press.*

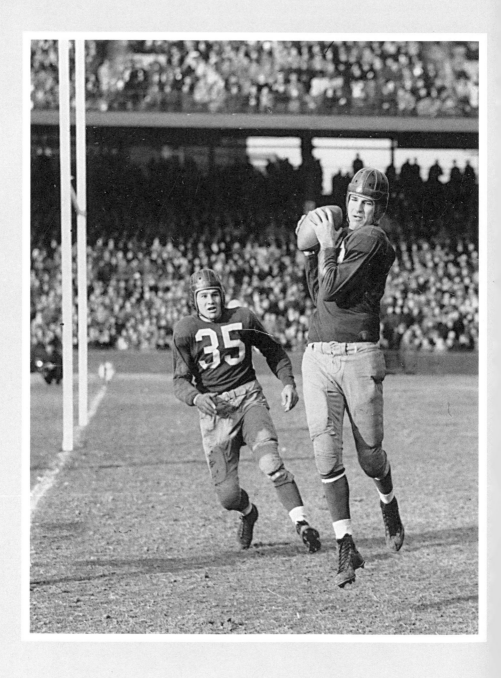

In this December 13, 1942, photo, Sam intercepts a Chicago Bears pass in his own end zone to break up a Bears scoring threat during the fourth quarter of an NFL playoff game in Washington. Coming up behind him is Chicago tackle Lee Artoe (35). Associated Press.

In this October 1, 1945, photo, the thirty-one-year-old All-Pro looks on during a Redskins workout in Washington. Associated Press.

*In this photo taken in the early 1940s, probably in Silver Spring, Maryland, young
Todd Baugh is a bit wary of the family dog. Photo courtesy of the Baugh family.*

When he wasn't throwing passes, Sam was a regular family man at the Baugh's rented home in Silver Spring. Photo courtesy of the Baugh family.

At Griffith Stadium on December 14, 1952, on Sam's last day as a Redskin,
he shook the hand of the man who helped shape his illustrious career,
Redskins owner George Preston Marshall. Associated Press.

Pulling on number 33 for the last time, Sam shows off the flimsy pair of shoulder pads he wore his whole career. Associated Press.

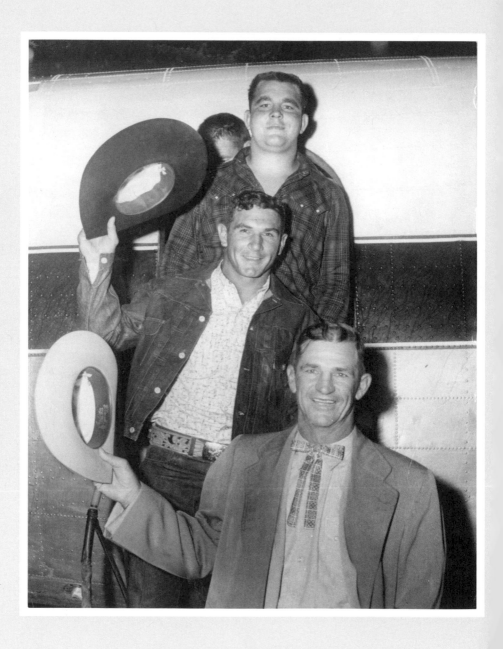

Hardin Simmons Coach Sam Baugh steps off the plane at Washington National Airport with two of his starters, tackle Burley Polk (top) and fullback Pete Hart, on October 5, 1956. The Cowboys were in town for a game with George Washington University. Photo by Jim McNamara, courtesy of the Washington Post.

Although the front office was a fiasco, New York Titans Coach Sam Baugh and his staff put together a pretty good American Football League team. Photo courtesy of the Baugh family.

Sam in about 1941 atop his beloved mare Bluebonnet. The foal in the picture is one of her half-siblings. Photo courtesy of the Baugh family.

Sam atop his mare Chubbette in about 1954.
Photo courtesy of the Baugh family.

Sam on Lucy, one of Bluebonnet's daus, in about 1968.
Photo courtesy of the Baugh family.

*Sam's athleticism, plus a good horse and hours of practice, made him a
champion roper. Photo courtesy of the Texas Sports Hall of Fame.*

*A horse-drawn wagon carries Sam's saddle-draped casket to his
burial site near Rotan, December 22, 2008. Associated Press.*

....

GO WEST,
YOUNG SAM

HOLLYWOOD CALLING

"He looks like he invented cowboy movies," one of Sam's teammates once observed of the lean, leathery Texan. George Preston Marshall, the man who had much to do with creating Sam's cowboy persona, waxed even more rhapsodic. "He looked like the personification of every cowboy star who ever straddled a bronc, only more so," the Redskins owner once said.

Hollywood agreed, despite the fact that Sam, before Marshall got hold of him, had rarely been astride a horse and had never roped a steer. He was a town boy, not a cowboy, but as far as Hollywood was concerned, he looked like what a genuine Western movie hero ought to look like. In the spring of 1941, not long after the championship-game debacle, a representative from Republic Pictures called Sam and offered to pay him $4,500 to star in a twelve-episode western serial called *King of the Texas Rangers*. That was about what he was paid, of course, to get pummeled by Giants and Bears for about half a season.

"I thought at first he was kidding," Sam recalled. "When I realized he was serious, I pointed out to him I didn't know the first thing about that sort of thing. Hell, I was a football player. He told me players like Red Grange had done okay in movies and Tom Harmon of Michigan, who had just won the Heisman Trophy, had signed to do a picture."

||||||||||

Knute Rockne: All-American had come out the year before, and fellow Texan and longtime friend John Kimbrough, the Texas A&M star from Haskell, north of Abilene, was about to sign a contract to star in Zane Grey westerns for 20th Century–Fox (*Lone Star Ranger* and *Sundown Jim*). "I guess I was the world's worst actor, unless it was John Kimbrough," Sam joked in later years.

Republic was known in those days for its quality B pictures, especially its westerns and movie serials. Hoot Gibson, John Wayne, Gene Autry, and Roy Rogers all made pictures for Republic at one time or another.

Although Sam was never materialistic, he recognized opportunity when he saw it, so he quickly signed the contract. After all, almost every player in the NFL had to work in the off-season (and were still doing so into the 1960s). Football was a part-time job that didn't pay that well to begin with. Charlie Malone sold insurance and had a vending-machine business. Turk Edwards sold cars for a dealer in D.C., while Erny Shugart worked for an ice cream company. In 1940, four Redskins quit pro football to become FBI agents. Sam himself might have found some kind of part-time coaching position or maybe wangled a job in Sweetwater.

Instead, he signed the Republic contract, got in his car, and drove to Hollywood, leaving Mona back home in Sweetwater. He didn't fly; he didn't take the train. Even though he was as famous as Joe DiMaggio and Joe Louis in those days, the bright lights of Hollywood weren't for him. During his six weeks on the West Coast, he stayed in a tourist court, rarely went out at night, and usually passed up the big parties.

"Ah, shit on celebrity," he told a magazine writer in 1999. "It didn't make sense to be showboating all over Hollywood and spending a lot of money for a steak when I could take that money back to Texas and buy a whole cow."

Sam's director was none too happy when he found out his star was not a professional actor. "Sammy Baugh? Baugh? Bah! I never heard of him," the director, Jack English, stormed (or so he said). "Why, oh why, don't they give me an actor? Even a seal. At least I could train one of them. But a football player—." Sam, according to a newspaper account, was sitting on the ground and chewing a straw while English was talking. The reporter noted: "He grinned ear to ear. A pleasant, friendly grin."

"Boy, I don't blame him," Sam said, and then got to his feet and went back to work.

"Believe me, I didn't lose any time writing Baugh's part," English continued.

I knew he couldn't handle dialogue, and I figured he'd probably have to have a side saddle.

But I'll tell you what—the guy is a natural. Yes, a natural. Of course, he hasn't learned yet how to give the right punch to a line, but he's the fastest bird I ever handled. No prima donna athlete, that fellow. He's got it in the head. He's a real find, mark what I say.

Sam, meanwhile, was emptying out his boots. Members of the crew had playfully filled them with a bucketful of sand. "This is the silliest business I ever got in," he said, while shaking out the sand. "Remember how we used to play cowboy and Indian? Well, that's all this is, except we get paid for doin' it." Still, he relished the experience. "I can truthfully say that I can recall no other six-week period that I so thoroughly enjoyed as the time I spent on that picture," he said many years later. "No way I can tell you just how great those people at Republic treated me, or just how great I thought they were."

Years later he was asked what Marshall thought about the fellow who represented nearly 90 percent of his franchise traipsing off to Hollywood and possibly breaking his neck while shooting a western.

"Lord, he was tickled to death," Sam recalled. "It was good publicity for him, the Redskins and me. In those days, pro football did good to get the game scores in the papers and anything short of going to jail that got publicity pleased everybody."

Sam had fun, but no one suggested that he quit his day job. "Baugh is no threat to Olivier, but athletically he's perfect for the role of the ever-charging lawman," John Stanley wrote in the *San Francisco Chronicle* in 1992, recalling Sam's one and only Hollywood adventure.

Sam himself realized he had a lot to learn, and fortunately his fellow actors helped him. Duncan Reynaldo, the actor who would go on to star as the Cisco Kid on television, helped more than anybody.

"The first day at the studio," Sam recalled more than three decades later, "the director handed me some paper and said it was my lines for the next day, and to study them that night. I did. And if they used those lines the next day someone else did them 'cause I never heard them. Then they gave me some more to learn that night that I haven't heard yet, either."

The next day Sam told Reynaldo he had memorized three days' worth of lines that he had never used. Reynaldo laughed and told him not to worry about memorizing lines. The director would tell him what to say on the set each day.

"I liked Sammy very much," Reynaldo once told an interviewer. "He was so green. I tried to get him to be natural and not to act. Neither [directors] Jack English or Billy Witney could do that with him; they didn't have the time nor the capacity to do that. I'm a very patient man, and I directed him really. Billy used to let me."

"One day, we couldn't film because Duncan had gone to the courthouse to be sworn in as a U.S. citizen," Sam recalled. "He was a big enough star at that time to attract a lot of media attention. When he came out of the courthouse, he stopped on the steps for a press conference. Someone asked Duncan what he had to say about becoming a U.S. citizen, and I'll never forget what he said: 'I think we should keep all the foreigners out of the country.'"

On lunch breaks, Sam never ate with the other actors.

> I always ate lunch with the technicians, because they told me some great stories. They had all the gossip. I've never understood this, but they all hated Gene Autry. I don't know why. Gene Autry was one of the biggest stars in Hollywood.
>
> It was funny because those technicians told me they knew a young guy who was going to be as big as Autry in a couple of years. They told me I'd never heard of him, but that I would because he was going to be a big star. And they were right. His name was Roy Rogers.

S am's character, Thomas King Jr., is a college football star in Texas who leaves school to join the Texas Rangers to avenge the death of his father. The elder King has been murdered by "the Fifth Column," a group of Nazi-type agents operating on the U.S.-Mexico border with nefarious plans to take control of Texas oil fields. "Fifth column" was a term that described undercover agents working inside a country on behalf of an enemy. It originated with Emilio Mola, a Nationalist commander during the Spanish Civil War, who said, "I have four columns moving against Madrid, and a fifth will rise up inside the city itself." In 1941, the year the serial came out, Nazi fifth columnists were known to be working in Mexico and throughout Latin America.

In the opening reel, Tom's Ranger father is killed at the very moment the young man is winning a football game for the Texas All Stars. Brief film clips of Sam in action on the football field establish Tom's football bona fides. Cy Feuer, the music director for Republic serials, adapted the TCU school song, "Come to the Bower," as the score for the serial.

Setting up his base of operations in a friendly little border town, the rookie Ranger uncovers a plot to sabotage nearby oil fields. Assisted by an officer of the Mexican Rurales (Reynaldo) and a winsome young female newspaper reporter, he brings his father's murderers to justice and puts an end to their sabotage activities along the border.

Each episode ends with a spectacular cliffhanger orchestrated by Howard Lydecker, the head of Republic's special-effects department. Lydecker produced a rampaging oil-field fire, an exploding dam, and, for the grand finale, Ranger King's plane plunging into a hovering dirigible and destroying the enemy agents in an exploding ball of fire. The ranger, against all odds, survives to fight again for justice and the American way.

Costars included Reynaldo, who plays a Mexican police officer named Pedro Garcia, and Sally Crane, who plays the reporter who witnessed the murder of the elder King and who, of course, falls for the tall, taciturn young Texan, resplendent in a Stetson, black western shirt and an ivory-colored bandana artfully knotted around his neck. Crane, considered a Vivian Leigh look-alike, appeared in Republic westerns with Roy Rogers and also made several Charlie Chan movies. Sam remembered her as "a very nice lady."

The serial had more than its share of gun battles—they are interminable, in fact, and hardly anyone gets hit—as well as chases on horseback and very little dialogue, a blessing in disguise for Sam. Although he may have looked the part of a western hero, he delivers his lines as if he is onstage for the junior-class play back in Sweetwater. His voice, which must have been commanding in the huddle, sounds muffled and indistinct on screen.

King of the Texas Rangers had its "world premiere," the *Sweetwater Reporter* announced, on a Sunday afternoon at the R & R Ritz Theater in Sweetwater. Also on the bill at the Ritz that fall were *Zorro* and Bud Abbott and Lou Costello in *Hold That Ghost*. The theater manager, Henry Rogers Sr., told the newspaper he tried to get Sam to make an appearance, but the star couldn't leave the Redskins' training camp on the West Coast. (It was more likely that Sam begged the Redskins not to let him go.)

The twelve-part serial popped up in movie theaters around the country for a number of years. Sam hoped, maybe even prayed, that his teammates would be too busy to see *King of the Texas Rangers*, but of course they weren't. The Washington movie house that booked it naturally had Slingin' Sam's name on the marquee, and on that first Saturday morning, a number of Redskins were in the audience—as was Sam himself, who attended under threat of physical violence from his teammates.

Every heroic feat—Sam slugging the villain, Sam vaulting into the saddle and galloping down the dusty trail—earned raucous cheers from the overgrown boys in the audience. As the gaggle of Redskins emerged from the darkened theater on that first Saturday, halfback Dick Todd looked up with adoring eyes into the face of the blushing hero. "Gosh, Sam," he murmured, "you truly were brave today." Sam took a swing at his West Texas buddy.

He was still blushing nearly a half century later. The sportswriter Dennis Tuttle, visiting Sam in the 1990s, watched an episode with the star, Sam's son, and a grandson. "He cringed, but we howled," Tuttle recalled.

In one scene, Sam throws a vase that hits one of the bad guys on the side of the head and flattens him. "The bad guy crumbles like a cracker. We are screaming at the TV, laughing like hell," Tuttle said. During a pause, Sam recalled that the vase was a prop designed to break on impact. "But this one bad guy, a stunt man, got mad during the scene and had slugged Baugh pretty hard with one of the plywood chairs," Tuttle said. "In retaliation, Baugh instantly picks up the vase and fires a rocket—I mean he really zipped him—and on frame-by-frame you can see the impact and the bad guy's head snap back."

Baugh told Tuttle the vase knocked the guy out and that he was worried he had killed him. The fellow came to seconds later with a knot on his head. Sam apologized, but the man sat up and rubbed his head. "Sammy Baugh gave me a lump on the head," he said, disbelievingly. "Wait until I show my friends!"

CHAPTER

15

....

THE NEWEST THING
UNDER HEAVEN

THE DOUBLE MOUNTAIN RANCH

Rising out of the gently rolling plains of West Texas, a few miles north of the little ranching town of Rotan, are dual promontories that resemble titanic ships adrift on the land. For untold centuries, the twin peaks served as navigational reference points for the wandering indigenous tribes that eventually would be called the Comanche. Sixteenth-century Spanish explorers and federal troops stationed in the region more than three centuries later—including a contingent led by Lieutenant Colonel Robert E. Lee—relied on the landmark, as did dreamers headed for the California goldfields, Texas Rangers, buffalo hunters, and, eventually, settlers on the sere and challenging land reaching to the far horizon.

Known as Double Mountain, it is a mountain in name only—the peaks are only 2,300 feet high—but the twin promontories thrust up from the vast prairie like solitary sentinels, their bluish tint visible as far as fifty miles away.

A branch of the Brazos River is named for Double Mountain. East of the peaks, the Double Mountain Fork, the Salt Fork, the Clear Fork, and numerous meandering creeks wind their way like veins on the back of the hand through red sandstone, shaping canyons and arroyos and rough-hewn draws. Along with the dark green stands of juniper and the indomitable mesquite, the shallow streams give character and distinctiveness to the terrain. East of the peaks, the three forks join to form the Rio de los Brazos de Dios (the River of the Arms of God). The Brazos meanders through the heart of Texas until it empties into the Gulf of Mexico at Matagorda Bay.

Double Mountain was something of a temple for the Comanche, a solitary place where the spirits gathered. A young brave would climb the rocky slopes toward the great arc of sky to receive his "medicine," his spiritual sixth sense, from the Great Spirit. Only then would he be a full warrior. Settling himself on the rimrock near one of the peaks and facing eastward, he would sing the sacred chants, smoke his pipe, and fast for four days and nights, awaiting the visitation of a beneficent spirit that would guide his life.

Long after the last Indian departed the area, white men ventured up Double Mountain in pursuit of baser rewards. They were chasing legends of gold and silver bullion, perhaps even doubloons, said to have been buried by early Spanish explorers. Although many have tried, including modern treasure hunters with earth-moving equipment, no one has ever found anything except arrowheads and marine fossils, remnants of the Permian Sea, which invaded the continent some 250 million years ago.

Near the base of Double Mountain, buffalo hunters in the 1870s set up a supply post and went on a rampage that led to the near extermination of the vast herds in West Texas and, consequently, the removal of the Plains Indians to Oklahoma. A man named Charlie Rath established Rath City, a ragtag camp that kept the hunters in salt, beans, bacon, coffee, and whiskey as they fanned out across the prairie in all directions and slaughtered the shaggy beasts by the thousands. They brought the buffalo to near extinction within a few years and then made way for those settlers hardy enough and daring enough to establish homesteads and vast ranches on the inhospitable land.

It was a way of life that always had intrigued Sam, the noncowboy. Late in the summer of 1941, he was back in Sweetwater—$4,500 richer, thanks to Republic Pictures—and he was looking to buy some land. A man named J. F. Dennis got in touch with him and told him he had some acreage for sale, so Sam looked him up.

"That's when I first saw those mountains, and the closer we got to them, the more I knew this was where I wanted to live," he recalled.

Using his movie money and a loan from a woman in Eastland, Texas, Sam bought the Double Mountain Ranch, some 7,500 acres of wild scrub and cattle country, plus a small four-room house that had been built in the winter of 1902 out of lumber brought from Sweetwater. (A black-sheep member of the Dennis family had been relegated to a dugout across the road from the ranch house at the time Sam took possession of the property.) He paid about sixteen dollars an acre for the land, which included all of what the locals call East Mountain.

The hard-packed land under a high blue sky, the ragged mesquite and prickly pear and dry, stubbled prairie grass look like "the oldest thing under heaven," a journalist once wrote—"but it smells like the newest," Sam told him.

Sam's mountain and the acreage at its base may be isolated, but the footprints of relatively recent history left their mark long before a famous football player took up residence. Robert E. Lee, chasing Comanches while stationed at Camp Cooper, camped near Double Mountain. He was impressed by its quiet majesty. A man named W. H. Kirby, a Texas Ranger and Civil War scout, camped on Double Mountain in 1859 while on an Indian hunt; a Ranger named A. C. Tackitt was the first to carve his name on top, in August 1863. In the 1870s, a Norwegian settler named Ole Nystel, kidnapped from his Bosque County home by Comanches, recalled that his captors camped on Double Mountain for three days.

Panthers found the mountain hospitable, at least until the coming of the white man. A rancher named Alex Shipp trailed two big cats to a cave on the mountain, crawled in after them, and shot both. A man named Toulas Green of the Circle Bar Ranch was trailing horses when his hounds treed a panther. Green roped the creature, dragged it down, and killed it with his pocketknife.

When Sam bought his ranch, West Mountain, with its distinctive saddleback indentation, was owned by J. D, "Uncle Jimmy" Smith, who had come to the area in 1883 to work as a straw boss on the Ten Hands Ranch. Uncle Jimmy's exploits were legendary. Once, while riding herd, he met a bear at the base of Double Mountain. He captured the animal, tied his mouth with rope, and carried him on horseback to the ranch house. The bear smothered to death en route; a visiting Englishman later took the bearskin home with him as a souvenir of his visit to the wilds of West Texas.

A few years before Sam bought the ranch, a man asked Raymond Dennis, son of the former owner, if he could dig under a particular ledge on the east peak. He told Dennis he was from Minnesota and had experienced a vision of the mountain when he was a child; he believed the bones of a giant race of people could be found there. He dug, found some bones of something, and left happy.

S am didn't care that the place was primitive—and, of course, he was away for at least half the year—but he realized that it was tough on Mona, a

Presbyterian preacher's daughter who had lived in town all of her young life. There was no electricity out on the vast prairie, so the Baughs used oil lamps for the first few years. It was so isolated that they had to go through six gates just to get to a dirt road into Rotan. The only water—for cooking, bathing, washing—came from a cistern, and if it didn't rain, there wasn't much water to be had. Mona did the washing in a big black pot over a wood fire in the yard. She and Sam bathed in a horse trough under the windmill; the trough was equipped with a wooden seat for just that purpose.

Between paying off the mortgage and trying to run cattle on the place, there was little money left over for improvements on the house. Mona had to make do. It was the kind of place he had wanted for years, but he went into a lot of debt to get it.

The economics of cattle ranching didn't always make sense either. "The first calf crop we brought in, we sold for nine cents a pound," he told Whit Canning. "By then I was learning that ranching was a little harder than it had seemed to be when I was a kid."

Paying the bills on the ranch was the main reason he stayed with the Redskins for so many years, Sam recalled years later. As the highest-paid football player in the country, he was eventually making $20,000, but what with paying off the mortgage, raising five kids, and buying more land, there never seemed enough to get ahead. He may have been a big-time football player, but for years he and Mona were in debt.

Life on the ranch was particularly hard on Mona. The first couple of years that Sam was with the Redskins, she joined him in Washington; the couple rented an apartment in Silver Spring, Maryland. After the children were born, she stayed home in Texas with them. Sam knew how hard it was for her on the ranch. He sometimes wondered why she stayed.

He knew why he stayed. Far from the roaring crowds, far from the buzz of traffic and the crowded cities, far from claustrophobia-inducing buildings and roads and trees, he had found his place on the earth. When he first moved to the ranch, a herd of antelope lived at the foot of the mountain. He was riding his horse one day when he came upon them by surprise, and when they spotted him, they did not run. "They just sort of stared at me, and I stared at them," he recalled. "They felt like they belonged there, or something, I guess. The deer that came in drove them out later, and I thought that was sort of too damn bad."

The deer stayed, and so did the jackrabbits and the wild turkeys and the roadrunners. And so did Sam. He loved the starry nights, and quiet that was almost unearthly, the stillness broken only occasionally by the soughing of doves or the howl of a coyote up on the mountain. He was a long, long way from the big city.

For the first few years, though, he was away more than he was at home. He relied on a local cowboy named Owen Brazee to take care of his cattle, brand calves, build fences, find buyers, keep the windmill in good repair, buy hay for the winter, and keep the horses in good shape. The two men met in 1941, and for nearly a decade after that Sam relied on Owen and his wife, Viola, not only for the ranch work but also to help Mona. "He didn't know much, but he learned fast," Viola Brazee recalled.

"One thing about Sam," Owen recalled, "he wasn't lazy, no way. He'd do anything."

Owen recalled the year Sam bought a bunch of roping calves. While Sam was in D.C., the cows all got sick; Owen and Mona stayed up all night tending to them. "Not many from her background would do that," the old cowboy recalled. He remembered how Mona cooked for the cowboys and helped him move cattle from one pasture to another before Sam got home from Washington, usually around Christmas.

Sam had a lot to learn—about the work, about the land. "The year we moved out here," he told Whit Canning, "one thing that really amazed us was how much it rained. We had some Hereford cattle, and the rain brought the grass up so we were really excited."

Sam happened to mention to an old-timer how much it had rained and how happy he was. The two men were sitting on the fellow's front porch. "Well, he kinda smiles and then he says, 'Son, I've been out here since '03, and I've never seen this much rain before. And you'll never see it again.'"

"Damned if he wasn't right."

....

1941

A LACKLUSTER SEASON

AND A DAY OF INFAMY

A fter the Baughs bought the Double Mountain Ranch and Mona began
staying in Texas, Sam was one of the boys, living in the Hotel Roosevelt with the other single guys on the team. Like young guys everywhere, they were determined to have fun, and their fun often involved
a particular teammate, the giant lineman Wee Willie Wilkin.

Willie was born Wilburn Byrne Wilkin but was christened Wee Willie after growing to be six feet six inches tall and weighing as much as 280
pounds during the peak of his football career. With a broad farm boy's face,
a gentle, fun-loving nature—off the field, that is—and a zany approach to life,
he was instantly likeable.

Wee Willie had played college ball at St. Mary's College in California; the
Redskins signed him in 1938. From the beginning, he was awesome on the
field and a real character off it. During his rookie year, he was fined $25 nine
times for training infractions during the eleven-week season. He wasn't
necessarily on good behavior the other two weeks; he just didn't get caught.

Don Looney, a former Horned Frog who played for the Philadelphia
Eagles, recalled staying in the same hotel with him while playing a charity game on the West Coast. One evening Willie knocked on Looney's door
and asked whether he could come in and take a shower. Looney, assum-
ing something was wrong with Willie's shower, welcomed him in. Later,

Looney stepped across the hall into Willie's room and discovered that the shower worked just fine, but Wee Willie had filled the tub to the top with iced-down beer.

Sam loved telling the story about the time Willie went missing for about a week before the Redskins were scheduled to play the college all-stars. No one had any idea where he was until he shuffled into the stadium dressing room about an hour before game time. There were rumors he had gotten back to the hotel about two thirty that morning and had gone out again about four.

His clothes a mess, his eyes bleary, the gentle giant was obviously nursing a giant hangover. Willie was in the process of pulling on his uniform when Coach Flaherty walked in and spotted him sitting on a bench, one leg of his football pants not quite pulled up to his knees, one cleated shoe on the wrong foot. An enraged Flaherty couldn't help himself; he backhanded the big man and knocked him backward off the dressing-room bench.

"You drunk son of a bitch," he growled, his face getting redder and redder, "I'm gonna start you in this ball game, and I'm gonna leave you in their 'til you die."

Willie, his pants tangled up around his knees, his legs still draped over the bench, slowly gathered himself off the floor and, with a pathetic pout on his face, looked up at the long-suffering Flaherty standing over him. "Coach, I was gonna play a helluva game for you," he burbled, "but you done broke my spirit."

Flaherty wasn't kidding. He had Willie in on every play, offense and defense, but after he started throwing up continually, the all-stars called a time-out and desperately requested that the big man be banished to the sidelines. Telling the story to friends, Sam would laugh so hard that he could hardly get through the telling.

A couple of years later, Willie was lounging around the Roosevelt lobby on a Saturday morning with Sam and several other teammates when the Redskins noticed a mink-coated society matron mince through the lobby in the company of a toy poodle. The dog was puffed and pompadoured within an inch of his life, its leash attached to a diamond-encrusted collar. Both dog and woman had their noses pointed toward the ceiling, a look of disdain on their pedigreed faces.

The Redskins got a kick out of the sight, and then Wee Willie went missing for a while; his teammates came up with all kind of wild theories about where he might have gone. They found out when the giant of a man came waltzing through the front door, his broad nose high in the air. At the end of a dirty piece of rope he had found in an alley—well rope, Sam called it—Willie was leading a scroungy stray mutt across the carpeted floor. The hotel manager was outraged; either get rid of the dog forthwith, he ordered, or all the Redskins would have to go. Sam and his friends howled.

Despite his antics, Wee Willie was a superb athlete. He was as fast as many of the backs and so strong that Flaherty once said that having him on the defensive line was like having a tank in combat. Although Marshall once complained that he spent more time bailing Wee Willie out of trouble off the field than he did enjoying his exploits on it, the giant defensive tackle made all-pro in 1940 and 1941.

During the summer of 1941, Wee Willie was joined by another character, the all-pro center Charles "Ki" Aldrich, an all-American on TCU's 1938 national championship team. Sam and Ki had lived across the street from each other in Temple. Aldrich had played two seasons with the Chicago Cardinals before the Redskins acquired him.

"I played that game for more than 20 years—in Temple, in Sweetwater, at TCU and in the pros—and in all those years I never saw anyone play football like Ki Aldrich," Sam recalled. "I never saw anyone who loved it like he did."

Sam recalled that in high school, Aldrich would come home after football practice and would spend the next hour or so banging into the garage just to toughen himself up. "He would do it again and again—just slam into those boards until they called him in for supper," Sam said.

Aldrich was an inveterate gambler who loved to play the ponies. Sitting around the Roosevelt one morning, Aldrich persuaded Sam and friends to lay down some money on a sure winner. Sam, reluctantly, bet $200. That afternoon, the Redskins gathered around a radio, most of them already counting their winnings. The race began, and the eager gamblers never heard the announcer mention Aldrich's sure-shot—until the race was over, that is. The horse finished dead last. "I never bet on another thing after that," Sam always told his friends, although his West Texas friends would remind him that ranching is a pretty good gamble all its own.

The Redskins had their fun as the '41 season began, but they were still smarting after their humiliating loss to the Bears. Coach Flaherty went home to Spokane with his dog, a majestic boxer that Marshall had given him. After the '40 championship game, Flaherty said the boxer was the only one who loved him.

Actually, even Marshall recognized that Flaherty was a superb coach, as did his players. "He had a brilliant football mind," tackle Jim Barber recalled. "He developed the screen pass. He could handle players. He knew when to kick you in the fanny and pat you on the back. Everyone respected him. Sammy had eight coaches with the Redskins, but Ray was the best by far."

Sam said the same thing.

The team opened camp in San Diego, not Spokane, since members of the Spokane Athletic Round Table, their host the year before, had spurned the Redskins for the champion Bears. The Redskins were the first NFL team to train on the West Coast, and attendance at their exhibition games persuaded league officials a few years later that California was prime expansion territory.

Marshall also liked to be close to his Hollywood pals. "He'd be in his tent having gin and tonics with them," Redskin guard Vince Promuto recalled.

All-pro lineman Turk Edwards and running back Erny Pinckert, both charter members of the Boston Redskins, retired after the '40 season. Edwards became an assistant coach. Outstanding rookies included two ends, Joe Aguirre from St. Mary's College and Ed Cifers from Tennessee, both of whom expected to be on the receiving end of many of Sam's passes.

Sam's passing and Dick Todd's running kept the Redskins in contention for much of the season, although the team faltered toward the end. One of Sam's most memorable games was on October 19 in Philadelphia's Shibe Park. Six days after the birth of the Baugh's first-born, Gary Todd, the young father threw a pair of touchdown strikes to lead the Redskins past the Eagles, 21–17.

"Young Sammy may not know it, but before senior 'Slinging' Sam' got busy today his Redskin mates were trailing that 'T' formation attack of the lowly Eagles by 14–0, and there were many anxious Washingtonians among the 19,071 in the stands who visioned a Philadelphia triumph," the *Washington Post* reported. Sam sealed the victory by intercepting an Eagle pass toward the end of the game. Immediately afterward, he flew to Sweetwater to see his new son.

On November 3, the Redskins took over sole possession of first place, temporarily at least, when they took on the Pittsburgh Steelers before more than thirty thousand Griffith Stadium fans. Sam completed twelve passes in nineteen attempts and set up the second touchdown with a fifteen-yard run through a startled Steelers defense to the two-yard line. Final score: Redskins 23, Steelers 3.

By the time the final game of the year had rolled around, the Skins were out of the title race. They would finish the season with a record of 6-5, coming in third behind the Giants and Dodgers. Sam finished with a 55 percent passing percentage and a 48.7-yard punting average.

At two on the first Sunday in December, the Redskins hosted the Philadelphia Eagles at Griffith Stadium before a crowd of 27,102. Since it was the last game of the year, the crowd included an unusually large number of governmental officials—senators and congressmen, army and navy officers, judges, Cabinet members.

Also in the stands that day was eight-year-old Lynn "Buddy" Watwood, whose family had purchased season tickets when the Redskins moved to Washington in 1937. (The family still owns them.) For the first three seasons, Buddy sat in his father's lap at all the home games; as a seven-year-old in 1940, the Redskins required that he have his own seat.

He remembered that day in December, a beautiful Sunday afternoon, temperature in the sixties. He and his dad parked in the neighborhood, about six blocks from the stadium. The fragrance of fresh-baked bread from the nearby Wonder Bread bakery wafted over the working-class houses surrounding Griffith Stadium.

In New York, the Giants, having clinched the Eastern Division title, hosted the Brooklyn Dodgers at the Polo Grounds. At Wrigley Field in Chicago, the Bears, needing a victory to tie the idle Green Bay Packers for the Western Division championship, were taking on their crosstown rivals, the Cardinals.

Before the game in Washington, there was a bit of end-of-the-season ceremony. Down on the field, Al Blozis, a tackle and shot put champion from Georgetown University, presented traveling bags to three members of the Eagles and one Redskin—all Georgetown alumni—on behalf of the school's student body.

In New York, it was "Tuffy Leemans Day." In pregame ceremonies, the Giants' veteran running back received a silver tray inscribed by his teammates and $1,500 in defense bonds. Those government securities would soon be called war bonds.

Sam was not in the starting lineup; Coach Flaherty's strategy was to feel out the opposition with his number two tailback, Frank Filchock ("Slingin' Sam" and "Flingin' Frank"). Midway through the first quarter, Flaherty nodded toward number 33 and indicated it was high time, because the Redskins, trying to break a four-game losing streak, were trailing the Eagles, 7–0.

Sam went in on defense, but as soon as the Redskins got the ball, he had them headed down the field toward the Eagles' goal line. With the ball on the Eagles' four, he threw from a spread formation and found receiver Al Krueger open in the end zone for the tying touchdown.

The first word about the catastrophe that had unfolded in the Pacific earlier that fateful day came to the sportswriters in the Washington and New York press boxes. In the first quarter, the Associated Press ticker reported a score from Chicago—Cardinals 7, Bears 0—and then the wire service interrupted its report with the words "cut football running." After a pause, the bulletins that made the football games irrelevant began to clatter across the wires.

At the Polo Grounds, the man who would direct clandestine war actions as head of the Office of Strategic Services (forerunner of the Central Intelligence Agency) was paged. "Attention please. Here is an urgent message. Will Col. William J. Donovan call operator 19 in Washington immediately."

Watwood remembered that the announcements from the public address system at Griffith Stadium began in the second half. The first, as Shirley Povich recalled years later, was for Admiral W. H. O. Bland, who was asked to report to his office at once. That announcement attracted little attention among the fans, few of whom knew that Bland was the navy's chief of ordnance. Even fewer, presumably, knew the nation faced a sudden and urgent need for the guns and ammunition under the admiral's command.

The next announcement also seemed routine: "The resident commissioner of the Philippines, Mr. Joaquin Elizade, is asked to report to his office at once."

The announcements began to avalanche—one general after another, along with admirals, colonels, ambassadors, and Cabinet members. Then the city's five newspapers began paging their personnel to come in to work. Povich recalled that by the end of the first half, the swarm of photographers working the game had been reduced to one. The others had been dispatched to the White House and to the Japanese embassy, where officials were burning documents.

Not relayed over the Griffith Stadium loudspeaker was the report of a phone call for Edward A. Tamm, an assistant to the director of the FBI, J. Edgar Hoover. Employees of the message center in the stadium knew where Tamm was sitting, so they sent a courier to bring him to the phone. Hoover, in New York for the weekend, was patched into the connection. The caller was Robert L. Shivers, the special agent in charge of the FBI's Honolulu office. Shivers reported what he knew about the attack on Pearl Harbor and then placed his phone near an open window so Hoover and Tamm could hear the sounds of explosions.

Povich, sitting in the press box next to Pat O'Brien, an Associated Press reporter, had found out about the attack eight minutes after kickoff. O'Brien had shared a message he had received over the telegraph wire from his office in the Washington Evening Star building. "Keep it short," an editor demanded. O'Brien was miffed. He sent a message to his operator: "Ask him who's giving me these orders."

The reply came quickly: "The Japs have just kicked off. Pearl Harbor bombed. War now."

"For a few moments it was our exclusive secret—Pat O'Brien's and his telegraph operator's and mine," Povich recalled. "And hard to grapple with was the stupefying news."

In Marshall's box, Jesse Jones, the Texan who headed the Reconstruction Finance Corporation, leaned over and whispered to Corinne Griffith: "I'm leaving. I've just had word the Japs have bombed Manila." "I couldn't believe it," Griffith wrote. "I was sure it was just a wild rumor. Then the telephone in our box rang and a voice from the press box said we had been attacked at Pearl Harbor."

Povich spotted the former managing editor of the *Washington Post*, his old boss, Norman Baxter, sitting in a nearby box seat. He told him the grim news. "Something's wrong," said Baxter, who was familiar with Pacific geography. "How could their bombers overlook our bases in the Philippines and fly all the way to Hawaii?" Povich had an answer from O'Brien a few minutes later: "And they've bombed the Philippines too."

Fans, long before they brought transistor radios to the game, were aware that some kind of emergency was developing, but they didn't know the details. As they watched Sam and his Redskins battle the Eagles in an unexpectedly close game, they had no idea that a sneak attack on Pearl Harbor had claimed the lives of thousands of American soldiers and sailors.

Marshall was not about to tell them. He was worried they would leave the stadium en masse—and maybe even demand their money back. For almost three hours, the Redskins owner kept them ignorant of one of the most momentous events in U.S. history.

Povich was still angry years later. "On a day when the United States was suddenly plunged into the biggest war in history, with thousands of Americans already dead or dying, Marshall ordered his staff to make no public announcement to the stadium crowd," he wrote. "Marshall's later explanation was a statement of his priorities, peculiar to himself: 'I didn't want to divert the fans' attention from the game.'"

It was a good game, to be sure. The Eagles were out in front 14–7 in the third quarter when Sam found Joe Aguirre, his big right end, open for a touchdown. As the teams lined up for the point-after attempt, Eagles right guard Bob Sufferidge, an all-American from Tennessee, burst through to block the kick, but he was offside. The teams lined up again, the Redskins center snapped the ball, and Sufferidge was again offside. He jumped four times and blocked the kick four times, but the referee refused to call the fourth one, so the score remained 14–13.

In the fourth quarter, Aguirre got open again, and Sam hit him in stride for the game-winning touchdown. Even as Redskins fans celebrated the touchdown, newsmen in the press box were asking the team's management when Marshall was going to authorize a public announcement about Pearl Harbor. Jack Espy, the team's general manager, said he had no orders from Marshall. "We don't want to contribute to any hysteria," he said.

"After all, there were still eight minutes left in the game," a caustic Povich wrote.

At the Polo Grounds, the public-address announcer at the conclusion of the Dodgers' victory over the Giants asked all members of the armed forces in the crowd to report to their duty stations.

In Washington, Corinne Griffith noticed that patches of empty seats were beginning to appear as the news slowly spread throughout the stadium and onto the field. She recalled the players being confused about what was going on.

"I guess the Redskins didn't announce it because they didn't want to cause a panic," said Clyde Shugart, a Redskins lineman who turned twenty-five that day. "We sensed that something happened, and everybody in the stands realized there was something wrong. But we didn't know what."

"We beat the Eagles, but that's not what I remember most about the game," Sam recalled years later. "What I'll never forget is how the [public address] announcer kept interrupting play by calling out people's names. We kept on playing, but that hadn't happened before, not when we had the ball. I'd be calling signals, and he'd be calling out names and saying some other stuff. Hell, I couldn't tell what it was. We talked about it on the sideline and tried to figure it out, but no one had any answers."

The game ended in almost complete silence. As the fans filed out of the stadium, they experienced what Povich called "mass shock." Newsboys shouting, "Extra! Extra!" waved papers. The headlines screamed the news that transformed the world, including the lives of everyone in the stadium that day: "U.S. AT WAR."

The Redskins' Shugart said he and several of his teammates marched on the Japanese embassy that night. "We wanted to square the account if they were looking for a fistfight," he said.

"The United States of America and the Empire of Japan are at war," the *Post* reported on Monday. "The conflict that Adolf Hitler started on September 1, 1939, has now truly become a death struggle of world-wide proportions."

Also on Monday, President Franklin D. Roosevelt addressed a joint session of Congress. His opening words: "Yesterday, December 7, 1941—a date which will live in infamy—the United States of America was suddenly and deliberately attacked by naval and air forces of the Empire of Japan."

On Monday in New York, Steve Owen, the coach of the New York Giants, talked with reporters about the NFL championship game two weeks later, but his mind seemed elsewhere. "I don't know what is going to happen," he said, and reminded reporters that the game might even be canceled. Even if the game was played as scheduled, teams might not be at full strength. He said that Jack Lummus, a rookie end from Baylor, had been called in for an interview with the navy only hours after the U.S. entered the war. "He was sent back, but there is no way of telling when they will call him again," Owen said.

The championship game wasn't canceled, although only 13,341 fans at Wrigley Field watched the Bears beat the Giants 37–9. It was the smallest crowd for a title game since 1933, when they began.

THE 1942 SEASON

AVENGING 73–0

"No sport faces a more uncertain future," a United Press reporter noted just a few days after the trauma of Pearl Harbor. "Its life blood is the constant flood of ready-made stars from the collegiate ranks to replace veterans forced into retirement by the bruising pace of five or six seasons in the National League. How many current college seniors are interested in football for 1942?"

The reporter answered his own question with the words of Bruce Smith, the 1941 Heisman Trophy winner from Minnesota: "There's a bigger game than football going on now."

The Office of Civilian Defense decreed that spectator sports were important to civilian morale, so the pros continued to play throughout the war years, although both baseball and football were deeply affected, lightly at first but more heavily as the war dragged on.

The NFL commissioner, Elmer Layden, offered the following statement: "From Aristotle's time on down we have been told, and it has been demonstrated, that sports is necessary for the relaxation of the people in times of stress and worry. The National league will strive to help meet this need with the men the government has not yet called for combat service, either because of dependents, disabilities, or the luck of the draw in the Army draft."

Several NFL teams struggled. In 1943, the Pittsburgh Steelers merged with the Philadelphia Eagles to form the Steagles; a year later, Pittsburgh pooled its players with the Chicago Cardinals. When the Cardinals-Steagles amalgamation went 0-10, sportswriters dubbed them the "Carpets." The Cleveland Rams folded.

The league managed to get by with players awaiting the draft (the army draft, that is), players too old for the draft, 4-Fs (those ineligible for the draft for various physical, mental, or moral reasons), and men who worked during the week in draft-deferred defense industries. Several teams brought back old-timers, including Bronko Nagurski with the Bears and Ken Strong with the Giants.

Although draft boards didn't begin their big push until 1943, hundreds of pro football players were caught up in "the bigger game." Baseball's Joe DiMaggio, Ted Williams, and Hank Greenburg left the playing fields.

So did George Halas, who in 1942 at age forty-seven left the Bears at midseason to join the navy. During World War I, he had enlisted as a volunteer and had asked for sea duty. Instead, he was assigned to the sports program at the Great Lakes Naval Training Station, whose football program won the 1919 Rose Bowl.

Some did not return. Al Blozis, the young man who presented the traveling bags to Georgetown alumni at Griffith Stadium on December 7, would go on to become an all-pro tackle with the Giants. Then he joined the army. On January 31, 1945, Lieutenant Al Blozis was cut down by German fire as he searched for missing members of his platoon while on patrol in the snowy Vosges Mountains of France. Jack Lummus, the Giants rookie from Baylor, was killed by an exploding hand grenade on Iwo Jima. By war's end, 638 players had served in the military; 21 lost their lives.

For the NFL draft, the Redskins and other NFL teams were scouting not just for players but also for players who would be available for the '42 season. The *Washington Post* reported that fifteen of the twenty players drafted that year were either married, had family dependents, or were unfit for army duty. "The objective of the ten league clubs was not particularly to get the big name stars first but with the war draft facing a great majority of the graduating seniors the idea was to sign up those with classifications which would allow them at least a season of pro ball," the *Post* reported.

Before the '42 season, the Redskins lost about five players, the least of any NFL team. Wayne Millner, Sam's friend and favorite receiver, departed for military service, as did Frank Filchock, Sam's backup. Players who had applied for military service were allowed to finish the season.

As a married man in his late twenties and the father of two children, and as a rancher providing beef cattle to the armed services, Sam was exempt from service. Whether he ever thought about joining up or whether his fans expected him to enlist as his patriotic duty is a mystery. His sons, Todd and David, said they never heard their father voice any regrets about not serving, and neither the *Washington Post* nor Shirley Povich in his *Post* columns ever made an issue of it.

A *Sport* magazine article in 1948 reported that Sam "drew criticism in some quarters for not volunteering. When he continued to play football, commuting by airplane each weekend, the cries grew louder." Sam told the magazine he was at a loss to understand the complaints. "As far as he is concerned, Uncle Sam didn't see fit to call him, and that was that. The draft board told him it didn't care what he did on weekends, so why shouldn't he keep on playing football?"

Maybe it was as simple as that. Despite being intensely competitive, despite being a natural leader, maybe Sam didn't give much thought to whether he ought to volunteer or whether it was his patriotic duty. He wasn't called, so he didn't go.

The Redskins were coming off their poorest season yet in D.C., a 6-5 third-place finish in the NFL East. They began the first wartime season, and what they hoped would be a comeback year, in San Diego, where the Shriners had invited the Redskins to play the Intrasquad East-West game for their Crippled Children's Fund. After three weeks of training in the cool, sunny city by the sea, the Redskins played before a packed stadium on August 20, 1942. Half of the crowd was made up of paying fans; the other half was made up of soldiers, sailors, and marines who had received free tickets to the game.

A week later, the Redskins traveled up the coast to Los Angeles to stage an exhibition game with the army all-stars, a team made up of college and professional players turned soldiers. Coaching the army team was Major Wallace Wade, who had coached Alabama in the '20s and Duke in the '30s. In Southern California, where there would be no professional football until the Rams arrived in Los Angeles in 1946, the game attracted a crowd of more than sixty thousand, including Hollywood celebrities George Raft, Ann Sheridan, King Vidor, and Linda Darnell. On the strength of Sam's passing, the Redskins won easily, 26–7, and headed back east.

The Skins opened the regular season with a 28–14 win over Pittsburgh, a game highlighted by Sam's old Texas buddy Ki Aldrich. The Redskins center knifed through the Steelers line and blocked a field-goal try, then caught the ball in midair and rumbled more than ninety yards for a touchdown.

After losing to the Giants 14–7—a game in which the Redskins made not one first down and ended up with minus yards rushing—the Redskins then reeled off six straight wins. With three games to go, special Baltimore & Ohio trains ferrying fifteen thousand fans accompanied the team to New York for a rematch. It would be the last mass exodus from Washington before travel restrictions put an end to such frivolity.

"In the first half, the Redskins fumbled nine times. . . . Fifteen thousand Redskin fans moaned and groaned; and many were driven to drink as the half ended 0 to 0," Corinne Griffith recalled.

The Giants kicked off to start the second half. Andy Farkas fielded the kick on his own goal line and then galloped 100 yards for the game's first touchdown.

Shortly after Farkas's sensational run, Sam went to work, completing four straight passes to the Giants' twenty and then finding Wilbur Moore in the end zone for a second touchdown. The Giants scored a touchdown in the fourth quarter, but the Skins managed to hang on for their first victory in the Polo Grounds since 1937. Two more victories—against Brooklyn and Detroit—made the Redskins the Eastern Division champions, with a record of 10-1. For the third time in six years, the Redskins were in the NFL title game.

The world championship the next Sunday in Griffith Stadium would be a rematch with the hated Chicago Bears, 11-0 and the winners of eighteen straight games. Theirs was the second perfect season in NFL history; the first had been a 13-0 finish by the Bears in 1934.

Five eventful years had passed since the Redskins had defeated the Bears for a championship in Chicago, two years since the awful drubbing the Bears had administered in D.C. Despite that nightmare, the Redskins had yet to experience a losing season, finishing first in the NFL twice and in third place once.

Flaherty declared the team ready, "If the Bears want to get tough in the clinches," he told reporters, "we'll get tough too. You can look at the pictures and see how they use their hands and get away with other stuff that should be called by the officials. This time we're going along with them and play their way. If there's some rough stuff, we're going to be in on it."

Flaherty had taken his one assistant coach, former tackle Turk Edwards, on a trip to Chicago to scout the Bears in their last game of the season, against the Chicago Cardinals. He left Sam and Wee Willie to run practice. While in Chicago, he happened to read the following in a newspaper column: "The Bears say that Sammy Baugh is the most overrated passer in football. They point to the records which show that Sid Luckman [of the Bears] and Cecil Isbell [of the Packers] do more damage with one pass than Baugh does with five. Baugh gets his team to the 50-yard line with five short passes and Luckman and Isbell get their teams over the goal line with one."

The two coaches returned with film from the Bears 21–7 victory over the Cardinals. The *Post* reported that Flaherty would prepare his Redskins with lighter physical training than usual and rely more on "the medium of lectures and motion pictures." He remembered the worn-down Redskins team that got annihilated in 1940.

Sam, no doubt recalling Marshall's incendiary comments two years earlier, had nothing but good to say about the '42 Bears: "Ah wouldn't say they're meaner than any other team. The Bears just play harder. That's what they're supposed to do, after all. They make it look rougher because four or five of 'em hit a ball carrier at the same time. A lot of 'em get the same idea at the same time about making a tackle, and you can't condemn 'em for that."

December 6, 1942, was a cold, crisp day in the nation's capital; more than thirty-six thousand fans filled Griffith Stadium, and a record 178 radio stations broadcast the game. It was the largest crowd to attend a sporting event in Washington since the 1933 World Series. In the stands that day were the singer Al Jolson; Dan Topping, who owned Brooklyn's football Dodgers; Kentucky senator A. B. "Happy" Chandler, who later would become the commissioner of Major League Baseball, and, of course, numerous military brass and politicians.

"Curly Lambeau, sitting with George and me, predicted the Redskins would win," Griffith recalled. "I appreciated it very much, but would rather by far have been in New York with two new hats, one for each half, listening to the game over the radio, than seeing it from that upper box exposed to those Bears, and the memory of that 73 to 0 score."

Ray Flaherty made sure his Redskins remembered it too. Instead of delivering a Knute Rockne–style pregame pep talk, he slowly walked to the front of the dressing room minutes before kickoff and wrote "73–0" on the blackboard. Then he circled it.

Enraged, still embarrassed, and barely able to wait for the kickoff, Sam and his teammates lined up along the sidelines while "The Star-Spangled Banner" was sung and the flag raised, patriotic rituals that meant more to the assembled crowd than ever before. The Bears, in blue jerseys and white pants, won the toss but got nowhere against the Skins' defense. Both teams spent the first quarter feeling each other out.

In the second quarter, Dick Todd tried to snag an errant pass from center, only to have the ball bounce off his shoulder pad. Under NFL rules at the time, a defender was allowed to recover a bad pass from center but not advance the ball, whereas he could recover a fumble and run with it. When Todd couldn't control the snap, both the head linesman and the umpire ruled the ball dead. Nevertheless, Bear tackle Lee Artoe came rushing across the line of scrimmage, scooped up the ball, and raced with it sixty yards down the field. Everybody else, on both teams, stood and watched.

Artoe crossed the goal line and touched the ball to the ground, and everyone laughed—everyone but the referee, that is, who threw up his arms to signal a touchdown. He had ruled the play a fumble.

While the crowd screamed and yelled for the referee's head, Artoe attempted an extra point but missed, and then kicked off to the Redskins, who took over on their own twelve-yard line. In the stands, a wire-service photographer caught General George C. Marshall helping his wife don heavy wool socks, while Mrs. Jesse Jones pulled on a red sweater, a superstition she relied on to bring the team luck.

Redskin fans saw Sam spit on his hands, rub them together, and get down to work. Sam took the snap—and kicked. The ball traveled eighty-five yards. Corinne Griffith called that kick "the greatest play I ever saw." She expounded:

> Ninety-nine per cent of pro-football strategy is to get possession of the ball and keep it, but Sam's quick kick was a monumental piece of contempt for all football strategy. It was notice to both the Redskins and the Bears that he believed his football team could score on the Bears whenever it pleased and he was going to kick out of the danger of his own goal-line for a mere safety precaution. The fact is that the play dumbfounded the Bears and elated the Redskins, and it put the Bears back on their own 5-yard line, in far more danger of a score by the Redskins than when we had the ball.

"That kick turned out to be a big play," Sam told reporters after the game. "When I quick-kicked, I had the wind to my back, and that's why I did it. If the quarter had run out and we had to punt, we would have had to do it against the wind."

Meanwhile, Corinne Griffith's husband was doing his part to give his men every advantage. Knowing that the Bears were using a press-box phone to assist Luckman with his play calling—Halas was the first NFL coach to do so—Marshall stationed the Redskins' band close to the Chicago box. Every time assistant coach Luke Johnsos picked up the phone to call down to the field, the band would strike up a loud number.

Shortly after Sam's quick kick, the Redskins' Wilbur Moore intercepted a pass from Luckman, the only passer in the league who could hold a candle to Sam, to give the Redskins the ball on their own forty. The Redskins caught three interceptions that day, one by Sam, and outgained the Bears on interception-return yardage, 11–0.

Again Sam went to work. Standing in against a furious Bear rush, he took his time and stood tall until he found Moore at the three. Although he was well covered by three Bears, the receiver leaped high in the air for a sensational catch and fell into the end zone for a touchdown.

"The Bears were very angry," Griffith wrote, "and they were not the papa bear and the mama bear and the little baby bear—that's another story—because our Wilbur said the language they used was not the pretty language one reads in Children's Story Books."

The Redskins' Bob Masterson booted the all-important extra point, and the half ended with the Redskins leading 7–6.

After a halftime Christmas tribute to "our boys"—Redskins in the armed services, boys on the field playing their last game, and all the other "boys" fighting for their country—the two teams came out to begin the second half. The Redskins surprised the Bears with a sustained ground march led by Farkas and Sam.

After making a first down at the twenty, Farkas carried four straight times to the one. On his next effort, he fumbled as he crossed the goal line, but officials ruled that the ball had broken the plane of the goal. The Redskins led 14–6.

In the fourth quarter, Luckman threw a long pass that Sam intercepted in the end zone. With an eight-point lead and time running out, the Redskins seemed on their way to their second world championship, but with a little less than three minutes to play, the Bears' Joe O'Rourke threw a long pass to Bob Nowaskey. Again Sam was there for the interception, but he couldn't quite pull the ball in; he only knocked it high in the air. It fell into Nowaskey's hands and stayed there. With Sam on the ground, no one was near the Bear receiver, but somehow big Ed Justice of the Redskins caught up with him and brought him down on the one-yard line.

With first and goal from the one, and the crowd in a frenzy, the Bears tried to punch it in, but the Redskins held. That made it second and goal from the two. The Bears were penalized for having a man in motion, which made it second and goal from the seven. On a running play into the line, the Bears gained four yards.

On third down and goal at the three, with thirty-seven thousand crazed fans on their feet, the Redskins held. On fourth down and goal from the three, Luckman faded, but Redskins swarmed him. He threw a desperation pass that fell incomplete. The final seconds ticked off, the 73–0 shame faded away, and once again Sam's Redskins were world champions.

"People went crazy," Buddy Watwood recalled. He was nine years old that long-ago Sunday, sitting with his father along what was normally the third-base line of Griffith Stadium. As Watwood remembered, Redskin fans spilled onto the field, tore down the wooden goalposts, and swamped Sam and his teammates. For a nine-year-old, it was a glorious day.

"By way of supplying a final madhouse touch to a football season that was noted for its lunacies and upsets, the Redskins soundly trounced the supposedly invincible Bears before an incredulous and deliriously happy gathering of 36,036 spectators in Griffith Stadium today to win the world professional championship," the *New York Times* columnist Arthur Daley wrote. "This was a team that was so much an underdog that the gamblers stopped giving 7-1 odds and handed out as much as 22 points. This also was largely the team that had been beaten 73–0 in the playoff two years ago. Yet it cracked into the mighty Bears with disregard of the Chicagoans' reputation and handled them as easily as if the Monsters were only P.S. 9."

For Sam, the victory was bittersweet. It was the last game he would play for Coach Flaherty, who joined the navy immediately after the game. Sam always called him one of the better coaches he ever played for. "Everyone respected him as a coach," he said.

Immediately after the game, the victorious Redskins posed for a team picture. Flaherty sat in front of the team, his loyal boxer at his knee. He would never coach another game for the Redskins.

During the last week of the year, Grantland Rice took his sportswriter colleagues to task for overlooking Sam when they voted for the nation's "Top Male Athlete of 1942." Those who garnered votes included Heisman Trophy winner Frank Sinkwich, Ted Williams, Don Hutson, Johnny Beazley, Gunder Haegg, Sugar Ray Robinson, Mort Cooper, Cornelius Warmerdam, Ben Hogan, Joe Louis, and Willie Pep, but not Sam. Sinkwich, a University of Georgia halfback and the first player from the South to win the Heisman, was voted the year's top male athlete; Williams, the Boston Red Sox triple-crown winner, was runner-up.

"Those are all keen, earnest fellows," Rice wrote.

They all did a fine job. But where's the fellow called Sammy Baugh, the Washington Redskins' halfback, who happens to be the 1942 standout? Apparently they haven't heard of Sammy this season. But Sammy happens to be just about the most valuable football player of all time, according to most pro coaches I've talked to. He's the lean, grim, dark, wiry Texan who took a good, but average, football team to the pro championship, rough-riding over the Chicago Bears in the climax game.

Sam was the top male athlete of 1942, Rice insisted, even though he failed to get a single vote.

He's the game's greatest passer, finest kicker and greatest competitor when it comes to the main test, as he did against the Bears this year.

Greatest ever, maybe, but Sam found himself in a bit of trouble as the year came to an end. Marshall had arranged for his team to play a team of professional all-stars in Philadelphia on December 27, 1942. Sam failed to show up.

Commissioner Layden called for a full investigation. He cleared the Redskins star after learning that Sam had missed plane connections in Dallas and after hearing his teammates swear that Sam had never even hinted that he wasn't intending to play. Layden's official report exonerated Sam, but chided him for his carelessness.

CHAPTER

18

....

THE 1943 SEASON

A BAUGH TRIFECTA AND

ANOTHER CHAMPIONSHIP LOST

T he Redskins weren't sure where they would be training in 1943. At the
last moment, the Office of Defense Transportation ruled that it would
be a boost to military morale for the team to head back to San Diego,
where they could entertain military personnel for six weeks or so.

They also weren't sure who would be wearing the burgundy and gold. Of
the thirty-two men who had played on the 1942 world championship team,
only fourteen remained. The rest were wearing a different kind of uniform,
including Coach Flaherty, who was a navy physical training instructor
in Idaho.

Around the league, four hundred pro football players or coaches were in
military uniform as the season opened. A number of college teams, including Harvard, Stanford, Princeton, and Alabama, dropped football for the
duration, and several NFL owners, including Halas, favored a hiatus as well.

Marshall wanted to keep playing, and his wife seconded his opinion.
"My training had been 'the show must go on'—the more tragic the event, the
more important to keep up the morale," she recalled. Several other owners—
Freddy Mandel (Detroit Lions), Tim Mara (New York Giants), and Curly
Lambeau (Green Bay Packers)—backed Marshall. They would play each
other home-and-home if it came to that.

At the league meeting where the owners decided the NFL would stay in business, they also made the wearing of helmets mandatory. Sam always had worn a helmet, although his headgear didn't have a face mask.

Years later, he recalled another form of protection that occasionally came in handy: "We were playing somebody—I don't know who it was—and they had an end. He was a really fine football player, but he'd come in and he'd hit me in the face. He'd make like he was hitting at the ball and swing down, and he had my face bleeding on both sides. Our linemen, they got pissed off, and they wanted to run what was called a 'bootsie play.'"

In a bootsie play, he explained, nobody blocks the "son of a bitch playing dirtier than hell." When he came roaring into the backfield, Sam would rifle a pass right between the guy's eyes.

On the particular occasion he recalled, Sam hit the rampaging lineman so hard that he stood straight up, then fell facedown like a statue. "It scared the living hell out of me," Sam recalled. "I thought I'd broken his damn neck or something and it had killed him. Shit, he got up, and they didn't even take him out of the ball game. He came just as hard, just the same damn way."

For the most part, Sam didn't seem to worry much about self-protection. He provided his own shoulder pads and used the same pair throughout his professional career. Regular pads hampered his throwing motion, so his not only were lightweight, but also had the straps cut off. "I didn't like something pulling on me," he recalled. Even though he also played defense and made countless tackles wearing the same old flimsy pads, he never thought about sturdier protection.

Helmets, maybe even shoulder pads, would have come in handy for two of the owners—the notorious Georges. At the league meeting, Marshall told the forty-seven-year-old Halas that he had no business joining the navy, that he was too old to fight. In a fit of temper, Halas clambered over the table and hit Marshall atop his head with his fist. The Bears' owner was not about to leave the fighting to somebody else.

An embittered Corinne Griffith recalled:

The 4-Fs carried on through the ridicule of two isolated sportswriters, with plenty of space and printer's ink with which to explain their own exemptions; through gambling accusations, dropped as quickly as created—and they carried the National Professional Football League to the biggest money-making season of its history. The war workers, the men in service and the men overseas wanted to see and hear the games.

The boys in Guadalcanal, North Africa, the mosquito-infested, fever-ridden, far-flung outposts of the world, battle-weary and homesick for something as typically American as American football, again heard an excited voice proclaim, ". . . and there he goes folks, right through the middle, and he's *o*-ver for a *touch*-down!"

Unlike those boys, Sam was fortunate. He could continue playing the game he loved—for pay. He could attend to his beloved ranch, unlike many Americans slogging through the jungles of the South Pacific or braving the withering fire of German guns. "If we are lucky, we can pay for the land and the house this year," he wrote Mona in a September 10 letter from Birmingham, Alabama, where the Redskins were playing an exhibition game. "I am getting $15,000 from the Redskins, and we have the cattle in Colorado—also some calves at home to sell."

Arthur J. "Dutch" Bergman took over for Flaherty in '43. A former coach at Catholic University in D.C., he had been chief scout for the Redskins in '42. A lively, humorous fellow, Bergman had been a star running back at Notre Dame, where his roommate was the legendary George Gipp. In 1936, he took Catholic University to its one and only Orange Bowl appearance.

Bergman picked up where Flaherty left off, with the Redskins defeating Brooklyn 27–0 before 35,450 fans at Griffith Stadium. In a return match in Brooklyn, Sam played sixty minutes and threw six touchdown passes.

Sam and his boys were unbeaten through their first seven games, with a tie against the Philadelphia-Pittsburgh team their only setback. Later in the season, the lowly "Steagles" beat the Redskins 27–14.

On November 15, the *Washington Post* reported on "another of Sammy Baugh's untouchable one-man shows, a truly great individual performance in which the torrid Texan smashed two more National Football League records." Here is what the writer had in mind: in the Redskins' 42–20 defeat of the Detroit Lions, Sam became the first NFL player to intercept four passes in one game, all of them thrown by the Heisman Trophy winner Frankie Sinkwich. He got off an eighty-one-yard punt and completed eighteen of thirty passes for four touchdowns. He also punted on three consecutive first downs, for fifty-four, forty-six, and sixty-six yards. "He's something out of a book," Sinkwich told Shirley Povich.

Sam would agree with folks who labeled him one of the best passers of all time and possibly the best punter. He was more modest about his defensive exploits. "I was passable," he told a television interviewer decades later. "I knew what I was doin' back there. But I was the weakest one, so they worked on me, and that gave me an opportunity to intercept passes."

Povich vociferously disagreed with his old friend. "If Baugh wasn't the Babe Ruth of football, no one was," he recalled. "Like Ruth, who pitched before he became a home run hitter, Baugh excelled at every phase of his game."

By December, the Redskins were two games ahead of the Giants, their nearest rivals for the Eastern Division championship. They had two games left to play, both with the Giants.

For the first one, the Redskins journeyed to New York, unaccompanied this time by their usual entourage of a marching band and special-train fans. Wartime restrictions prevented unnecessary travel. Three key Redskins—Wilbur Moore, Bob Seymour, and Wee Willie Wilkin—went out with injuries, and the Giants won 14–10.

The loss trimmed the Redskins' lead to one slim game, with the Giants coming to town the next Sunday. Should the Giants win, the two teams would meet in a playoff game. Commissioner Layden was in Washington in case a coin toss was needed to determine where the game would be held.

Meanwhile, the Redskins encountered a foe more formidable than the Giants as they prepared for the final game of the regular season. As Corinne Griffith recalled, she was reading the afternoon paper on the evening of December 7 when the phone rang. It was her husband, who was bringing Gabe Murphy, the Georgetown University athletic director, home for dinner. After dinner, the three were having coffee in front of the fire when Murphy told Marshall, "I think you'd better tell her."

"Tell me what?" Griffith wanted to know.

"Oh, nothing, nothing important," Marshall said.

"She'll read it in the morning paper," Murphy said.

"Yes, I know," Marshall said.

Finally Marshall revealed that a newspaper story the next day would claim that several Redskins were mixed up with gamblers and had been paid to throw the game against the Steagles the Sunday before. If it was true, he told her, the team and its owner would be ruined for life, just as the Chicago White Sox baseball team had been destroyed a couple of decades earlier by the notorious Black Sox scandal.

"Oh, that isn't true!" Griffith protested.

"Of course, it isn't true," Marshall said. "You know it isn't true; Gabe knows it isn't true and I know it isn't true, but the [Washington] *Times-Herald* is printing a story *insinuating* it just the same. It's probably rolling off the press at this very moment."

Griffith urged her husband to do something.

"What can I do?" he said. "I've spent the whole day pleading with them not to print the story. I've offered $5,000.00 to anybody who can prove that any member of the team has gambled."

"And have they any proof?" Griffith asked.

"No, all they have are some records."

"Records? What do you mean, records?"

"They've had Dictaphones placed in the bedrooms of certain Redskins."

"How awful!"

Still, investigators had no proof, Marshall insisted. "And even if they did, it couldn't be *all* the Redskins. That's what's so unfair about a blanket accusation."

Griffith suggested to her husband that he call Sam. "If he's heard anything, he'll tell you," she said.

Marshall got the Texan on the phone. Sam said he had heard nothing, although he was hot about the Dictaphone scheme. He asked Marshall to take him down to the newspaper office so that he could confront anyone who had accused him of consorting with gamblers. Marshall refused, although his wife told him it wasn't a bad idea.

On December 8, 1943, readers of the *Washington Times-Herald* woke to a front-page story headlined "Probe Reports of Pro Football Gambling." According to the story that followed, Commissioner Layden and league officials had been looking into rumors that several players were closely associated with known gamblers and that a number of Redskins were under investigation after the team's 14–14 tie with the Steagles on November 7. The Redskins had been favored to win that game by as many as twelve points.

The paper went on to report that the Redskins' November 21 game with the Bears had aroused suspicion because Sam was out with a knee injury, the Bears were 4-to-1 favorites, and yet the crippled Redskins won 21–7.

The Redskins also came under suspicion because of the outcome of the second Steagles game. Although Washington was a 4-to-1 favorite, the lowly Steagles won 27–14. Sam had a rare bad day, Willie Wilkin and Clyde Shugart got tossed out of the game, and the team looked as though it wasn't trying.

Authorities were also suspicious of the game the previous Sunday, when the Redskins had been 5-to-1 favorites to defeat the New York Giants, but lost 14–10.

"Reports that a betting coup had been effected, headed by Washington's three biggest gamblers, spread through the ranks of the underworld in New York, Chicago, Philadelphia and other major cities from coast to coast, following the second Washington-Phil-Pitt Steagle game," the *Times-Herald* reported.

All betting on National Professional League football games now has been cur-
tailed and under no circumstances will bookmakers accept a bet.

After the [November 21] game with the Bears and the second contest
a week later with the Steagles, one Washington gambler [later revealed to
be the convicted bookmaker Pete Gianaris] is reported to have won over
$150,000.

The *Times-Herald* has learned that Owner Marshall's appeal to Major
[Edward] Kelly [the superintendent of Washington police] that he investi-
gate was based not entirely upon suspicion of gambling, but that Marshall
told Kelly he suspected some of his players of visiting night clubs, taverns and
other places in the city where they should not be.

The *Washington Evening Star* asked Dutch Bergman for a statement.
"The whole thing is a gross libel on a hard-working bunch of kids," the coach
said. "It is scurrilous, and unless it can be proved it should not be discussed."

At noon on the day the story broke, Marshall called the *Times-Herald*
editor and asked whether he would gather other editors and reporters in his
office. "I'd like to bring some of the players over," he said.

That afternoon, Marshall strode into the editor's office, followed by
Coach Bergman, Sam Baugh, and twenty-four of his teammates. As many
of the Redskins as possible crowded into the office; the others jammed the
open door. Marshall faced the newspapermen. "Now gentlemen, here is the
team," he said. "You have accused some of these boys of throwing a football
game. That's a pretty serious charge. I want you to point out the guilty ones."

As Corinne Griffith told the story, none of the editors in the room and
none of their reporters could name any of the Redskins as having consorted
with gamblers. Vincent X. Flaherty, who cowrote the story, said some gamblers had told him that some of the Redskins were involved, but none of
them would sign an affidavit. "And you wrote the story on hearsay?" Marshall said. "You printed it with a banner line on the front page on hearsay? Now I demand to know what you have to substantiate it." As Griffith
recalled, none of them responded. "Their answer," she wrote, "was cow-
ardly, grim silence."

Sam recalled the incident in 1948: "Some sportswriters said back in 1943
that the whole Washington team must be betting on games. That was the
year we lost three straight games at the end of the season, when a victory in
any one of them would have given us the Eastern title."

As it turned out, the Redskins and Giants had to meet each other in a
playoff game to determine the division champion. "We fellows on the team
didn't get any extra money for that playoff game, and we'd rather not have

had to play it," Sam recalled. "We couldn't help it because we lost those other games. Sometimes, those things just happen in football."

On December 12, the Redskins took the field for the final game of the season. For the first time ever, they were greeted with boos from the hometown crowd.

For their water boy that game, the team had the services of Max Krause, a Redskin running back serving in the navy at nearby Anacostia. Flaherty of the *Washington Times-Herald* wrote that Krause wanted "nothing more than the chance to imparadise himself in the environment."

During a time-out, he rushed onto the field with his water bucket and warned his old teammates that the Giants were crisscrossing to get to Sam when he was punting. No one listened to the "water boy" that day, and Sam got a punt blocked. To make matters worse, the Giants won, 31–7.

Commissioner Layden, watching the game from the Marshalls' box, went down to the field to toss a coin to determine where the playoff game would take place. The Giants won the coin toss, which sent the Redskins to the Polo Grounds the next Sunday.

When Marshall arrived at his office Monday morning, he got a call from Cissy Patterson, the owner of the *Times-Herald.* "I'm so sorry you were unable to reach me on the telephone the other day," she said. "I would have stopped the story. But I would have given a million dollars if I could have seen the expressions on the faces of my editors when you walked in with the entire football team."

Back in the good graces of their fans, the Redskins journeyed to New York's Polo Grounds, where, as Dutch Bergman recalled years later, they were a cheerless, dispirited group. After all, the Giants had beaten them two Sundays in a row, and a sure-thing championship was slipping away. The Redskins' coach decided a little psychological gamesmanship was in order.

Strolling into the dressing room after pregame warm-ups, he could feel a definite "let's get it over with" atmosphere. "I just want to say," he began, speaking slowly and deliberately, "that we have some good ballplayers on this squad, and we have some yellow-bellied, gutless ones too. I know that some of you already have bought train tickets and are leaving for home right after the game." The coach paused to let his words sink in. "You're going out there, take your beating and slink home like whipped dogs. You don't want to play the Bears. You're yellow, gutless."

Bergman saw shock, then anger on the players' faces. Sam stood up, his face red, his voice tight. "Wait a minute there, you can't call me yellow," he drawled. "Nobody's gonna call me a quitter." Sam took a couple of menacing steps toward his coach, but Bergman held his ground. "All right, Sam," he said, "if you want to fight, go out and fight the Giants. I'll be here in this room after the game. I'll be waiting for you."

A chastened Sam did just that. Maybe he needed Bergman's kick in the pants. Playing before 42,800 fans, he had what *Time* magazine described as "a one-man field day." He completed sixteen passes, quick-kicked twice—once for sixty-seven yards—and intercepted two passes, one of which he ran back thirty-eight yards to set up the third touchdown. Final score: Redskins 28, Giants 0. "As he trotted off the gridiron after last fortnight's upset," *Time* reported, "Baugh was mobbed on the 50-yard-line by autograph hounds. The crowd swelled to a thousand and Sammy scribbled frantically for 30 minutes before policemen rescued him."

Buddy Watwood, who saw every home game Sam played, recalled that the Redskins star regularly stayed an hour or more after games, signing autographs for kids. Watwood recalled how he would dangle his helmet by the chinstrap over his left wrist and stand there and sign every single autograph.

Occasionally, when youngsters mobbed him on the field, he would tell them he had to go to the locker room and shower, but to wait for him after he had gotten dressed. They would be waiting for Sam when he came out. He would find a car running board to prop his foot on—often George Preston Marshall's Cadillac or a long, sleek LaSalle—and then he would sign countless autographs. Or he would tell the kids he was headed over to Marvin's Grill, a steak house on Connecticut Avenue near Calvert Street, and he would be happy to sign autographs there.

Bill Patten was a ball boy for the Redskins in the late 1930s. His job, he recalled years later, was to keep track of the footballs and warm up Sam before practice sessions and games. During games at Griffith Stadium, he sat on the end of the bench and looked after Duke and Duchess, two boxer dogs that belonged to Turk Edwards.

Patten recalled one Sunday when a youngster had sneaked into Griffith Stadium without a ticket. Normally, team officials would probably look the other way, and young Patten and his fellow ball boys never paid. They just came into the stadium with the team. This time, though, the police barred every kid without a ticket, including the ball boys. As Patten recalled, a boy who had sneaked in the Sunday before set a book of matches afire and burned himself badly. Marshall didn't want to be sued.

Young Billy Patten spotted Sam as he headed into the stadium and told him about his plight. "Wait right here," Sam told the youngster. He went to the dressing room, put on his uniform, and came back to talk to the police. He told them that if the ball boys weren't allowed in to sit on the bench and keep track of the balls and the dogs, there would be no game that Sunday. The Redskins star escorted the kids into the stadium.

Twenty-nine years old in 1943 and at the height of his career, Sam captured the NFL's first triple crown, leading the league in three statistical categories: in passing with 133 completions, in punting with an average of 45.9 yards a kick, and on defense with eleven interceptions. It is an unmatched feat of versatility, and likely to remain so.

It could be said, and some did say, that Sam's success was due to the reduced competition he faced during the war years. Nevertheless, he put up spectacular numbers for several seasons after the war.

Sam was the league's most valuable player in another area as well: from the beginning, he had been, without question, the team leader. His teammates looked up to him, believing in his ability to pull out a victory no matter the odds.

The 1943 championship game on the day after Christmas—against the Bears, of course, at Wrigley Field—was cold, windy, and sunny. The two old rivals took the field before a sold-out crowd at a time when the news from Europe and the South Pacific was disturbing enough to keep Americans awake at night. A football game on a Sunday afternoon was a welcome distraction, at least for a little while.

Although the war had crippled the NFL, the Bears and the Redskins, thanks to astute management and good coaching, had not only survived but also thrived. They would be playing in the championship game for the fourth time since 1937, with the Redskins holding a 2–1 edge.

Sam, who had almost single-handedly whipped the Bears in the '37 and '42 championship games, was uncharacteristically cocky as he talked to reporters a couple of days before the game. "I ain't as worried about the Bears as I am that danged cold weather in Chicago," he said. "We can handle the Bears. I just don't know whether we can handle that goddamned hurricane coming off Lake Michigan." All-pro fullback Andy Farkas was even brasher. "The Bears are a bunch of old men," he said. "We'll outhit them and outquick them."

Was it false bravado on the part of the Redskins? After all, they were tired and beat-up after their grueling contests with the Giants, and the Bears were confident and rested. They had ended their season with a record of 8-1-1. Their only loss was to the Redskins, 21-7, a game that featured the old Statue of Liberty, a trick play that became part of Sam's standard repertoire whenever end Wilbur Moore was in the game.

"If there was a tougher Redskin than Wilbur Moore, nobody can recall who it might be," a *Washington Post* writer observed in 1986. Al DeMao, the Redskins' center from 1945 to 1953, once counted the number of broken bones Moore reportedly had, and got to twenty-two before he stopped counting. "Reckless," DeMao said. "He'd throw his body anywhere. He'd guard [Hall of Fame receiver] Don Hutson all the time when we'd play the Packers. And do a good job." A famous newsreel film of Moore captures him at least six feet in the air as he flew over Green Bay center Charley Brock to tackle Ted Fritsch. "Wild on the field," said Riley Smith, an early-day Redskin. "Crazy, and a hitter."

For the Statue of Liberty play, Sam would cock his arm and look downfield as if to pass. From his position at end, Moore would loop behind Sam, grab the ball out of his passing hand, and run. Since defenders were hyperconscious of the pass whenever Sam had the ball, and trying to match receivers stride for stride as they raced downfield, the Statue of Liberty usually brought huge gains, as it did in the Giants game. Relying on three blockers ahead of him, Moore ran twenty yards for a touchdown.

O n game day, December 26, Halas strolled the sidelines in his seaman's cap and navy dress blues while Marshall, resplendent in his trademark raccoon coat, sat with his wife in their box. As it turned out, fans also got to see the flamboyant Marshall in action.

Shortly before the end of the first half, the owner began making his way down to the field from his box seat and, for some reason, chose a ramp that led to the Bears' bench. As he stood behind the bench and waited for the half to end, the Bears' general manager, Ralph Brizzolara, spotted him. "My god, it's Marshall," he shouted. He accused the Redskins owner of trying to steal the Bears' signals.

Brizzolara began yelling and waving his arms, trying to shoo Marshall away. He then dispatched the team trainer, Jack Goldie, to escort Marshall out of the area. Marshall, his raccoon coat flapping in the breeze, ducked into a lower box near the Wrigley Field home plate. Ushers asked him for his seat number, and when he couldn't produce a ticket, they called the cops. Two of Chicago's finest took him by the arm and walked him about a dozen steps before he was able to talk himself out of his predicament.

"I didn't want Marshall there eavesdropping . . . ," Brizzolara told reporters after the game. "A championship and a great honor were at stake. . . . That's the lowest way there can be of trying to win a game. . . . Yes, we threw him out—not invited him out." Marshall's response: "Fiddlesticks! It was a first-class bush-league trick. You can say for me that Brizzolara is not a gentleman. And I'll never speak to him again!"

On the field, Marshall's boys found themselves in trouble as well, almost from the beginning. After the Bears stopped the Redskins on third down, Sam sailed a forty-four-yard punt in a high spiral that landed in Luckman's arms at the Washington thirty. Luckman angled for the left sideline, hoping to pick up a bevy of blockers, but instead found himself one-on-one with Sam. As he moved in to bring down the stocky, hard-running ball carrier, Sam slammed his head into Luckman's knee; instantly, he was down for the count in front of the Redskins bench. When his teammates realized what had happened, they rushed Luckman, who had to be rescued by the officials and his teammate (and Sam's friend) Bulldog Turner.

Sam gradually got to his feet, and a couple of teammates escorted him on rubbery legs to the sidelines. As he sat on the bench, his face twisted in pain, tears rolling down his cheeks, the team doctor examined him. "Do you know where you are?" he asked.

"Fort Worth," Sam replied.

"Who do you play for?"

"The TCU Horned Frogs."

"What's the matter, Baugh, lost your guts?" Bear's end George Wilson jeered. Dazed, enraged, Sam sat on the bench sobbing.

Sam had completed eight of twelve passes for 123 yards and two touchdowns when he went out. Meanwhile, Luckman was passing the Redskins dizzy, eventually completing fourteen passes for 276 yards and a record five touchdowns. The Redskins, reverting in Sam's absence to a running game, scored on an eighty-yard drive early in the second quarter, but trailed 14–7 at halftime. As the Redskins trudged up the tunnel toward their locker room, Sam wondered out loud, "How the hell did we get to Chicago?"

In the locker room, the team doctor reexamined Sam and pronounced him fit to play. Although he threw two touchdown passes in the second half, his teammates couldn't stop the Bears. Luckman threw touchdown passes of thirty-six and sixty-six yards for a 28–7 Bears lead before Sam could get unlimbered. With the 41–21 victory, the Bears captured their sixth NFL title.

....

1944 AND 1945

YET ANOTHER MISSED CHAMPIONSHIP

AND THE END OF AN ERA

S am headed back to the ranch immediately after the championship game, back to Mona and the two kids. With the war still raging on both the Pacific and the European fronts, his football future was suddenly in doubt. In September 1944, just as the new season was beginning, the Sweetwater draft board decided to make an issue of his status. After a day of what the *Washington Post* called "conjecture, consternation and considerable comment," the board ruled that Sam had to either return to raising cattle full-time or, if he decided to play for the Redskins in '44, take his chances in the military draft. He was playing on "borrowed time," the *Post* reported. He had until October 1 to decide. Sam said he would "do as the Draft Board says."

As a rancher, Sam was still in a "second-class" essential occupation category. As a football player, he was 1-A (fit for service). The chairman of the Nolan County Selective Service Board, C. R. Simmons, told the *Post* that the board had given Sam permission to play three charity games, but he had to return to the ranch thereafter.

Corinne Griffith recalled a conversation Sam had with her husband in July 1944, which may or may not have been absolutely factual. Marshall asked him whether he would be able to play in the upcoming charity exhibition games. "Oh, yes sir," he said. "I'll be there for the charity games. I've

|||||||||

got the best ranch hand in all Texas taking care of the ranch for me those three weeks."

"Well, Sam," Marshall asked, "why can't you get him to take care of the ranch for the entire season?"

"Him? It ain't' a 'him,' Mr. Marshall, it's a 'her.' It's my wife."

When the Redskins opened at home on October 22 against the Brooklyn Tigers, a strong reserve team was ready to step in, the *Post* reported, in case the starters faltered. "The reserve team's name is Sammy Baugh."

With the government making heavy demands for beef, Sam became a long-distance commuter. He had to make sure that the government got its beef shipments on time.

He worked on the ranch five days a week, then drove to Forth Worth, where he boarded a plane and flew either to Washington or to wherever the Redskins were playing on game day. The draft board's ruling—that he work his ranch full-time or be subject to immediate call—did not apply to weekends. Marshall told Sam he needed him to hold for extra points; his kickers kept missing without Sam.

The Redskins' starting quarterback in 1944 was Frank Filchock—"Slingin' Sam" and "Flingin' Frank," the papers called them. Filchock was a former Indiana star who recently had received a medical discharge from the navy after nearly two years of service overseas. Although no one could replace Sam as a punter, Filchock filled in admirably as a passer. Against the Eagles early in the season, he threw thirty-three passes and completed twenty-five, five for touchdowns in a 31–31 tie. Against a new team, the Boston Yankees, in late September, he completed ten of eighteen passes in a 21–14 victory.

"His average of .673 is better than Baugh's best," the *Post* noted. "It would be almost folly to bench a red-hot Filchock for a Baugh who has not touched a football for nearly a month, despite Sam's brilliant record."

Dutch Bergman resigned before the season began, not because of any dispute with Marshall—the usual reason Redskin coaches departed—but because he wanted to go into broadcasting. To replace Bergman, Marshall signed Dudley DeGroot, a former Stanford all-American who had just completed four successful years as the University of Rochester coach. Turk Edwards continued as assistant coach.

DeGroot, at Marshall's behest, instituted a profound change in how the Redskins played the game, a change Sam hated at first, although he later conceded it probably extended his career. As a tailback in the single wing, he was usually on the move, either rolling to his left or right while looking for a receiver, or passing. He got battered time and again. In DeGroot's new offensive scheme, the T formation, he often got rid of the ball before defenders got to him.

"I figured I only could go maybe another year or two as tailback," Sam recalled. "Hell, I was getting beat up and hurt all the time, and my shoulders and knees were getting pretty bad by that time. But with the T formation I didn't take such a beating and that enabled me to play another seven or eight years."

Most of the NFL teams already had made the switch from the single wing to the T, and Marshall had considered it at least since the Bears used the formation to eviscerate his team in the 1940 championship game. When he finally decided it was time for the Redskins to make the switch, he hired Clark Shaughnessy, who had played a major role in the 73–0 rout. Throughout the spring, the "Father of the T" put DeGroot and Edwards through what Corinne Griffith called "T formation kindergarten." For some reason, Sam and his backup quarterbacks weren't involved in the sessions, although they got their fill when training camp began in July. Only one player, second-year guard Al Fiorino, had ever played in the formation.

"Coach Shaughnessy explained the T formation as based on the defensive strategy of the opponents; explained why telephones must be placed at various points high up in the stadium with spotters relaying information to the bench," Griffith wrote. "The Bears were the first to install the roof telephones, prior to that they had had to toss notes to the bench; then Shaughnessy charted a new system of play; developed the signal system, far more intricate in the T than any other formation; worked through April's spring days and nights, May's warmer days and warmer nights, June's hot days and hotter nights until July 1, when Dudley DeGroot and Turk Edwards were graduated—they thought."

Sam got a chance to work from the T in early exhibition games in Los Angeles; Ogden, Utah; and Baltimore. Although he was throwing touchdown passes, he still was feeling awkward after years of taking a long snap from center and surveying the field even before the ball got to him. Dropping back to pass from the T formation required him to turn his back to the line of scrimmage, plant his right foot, and immediately turn and scan the field for an open receiver. The whole process felt awkward, as did faking and spinning with the ball on running plays.

"When I switched from a single-wing tailback to a T-formation quarterback in '44, it was the most difficult thing I'd ever had to do in my football career," he said.

It didn't help that he had to leave the team after the exhibition season and get back to punching cows in West Texas. He played in a preseason game in Pittsburgh and then was lost to the team until the Brooklyn game a month later.

Some years later, he ridiculed the idea that he had resisted the T formation. "Why, that's the easiest position in football—quarterback in the T-formation," he told *Sport* in 1948. "If they'd had the T when Ah started playing pro ball, Ah could play until Ah was 40 years old. All you do is hand the ball off and pass."

Playing tailback in the single wing was punishing. "I had to block in the single wing, and when I went up against those big linemen my shoulders would shake afterward," Sam recalled years later.

He said he admired Shaughnessy, even though his offensive scheme was complicated. "Why, we had over 20 plays to get around one end," he recalled. "Only trouble was, we couldn't find anybody who could do it."

One result of the switch to the T did not work in Sam's favor: it all but eliminated the quick kick as an offensive weapon. Sam was the best quick-kicker in the history of the game.

"You use a rocker step," he explained to a reporter many years later. "From the single wing, as the ball's coming to you, you step back, step [forward] and then kick. You'd kick it just the same as any other kick except you'd kick it lower . . . and you'd kick it down the middle of the field. Normally when you punted the ball, you'd go for the sideline. But on the quick kick, you'd just try to get it over the safety's head."

With the quarterback under center, the quick kick wasn't possible—unless the center hiked the ball through the quarterback's legs to the fullback. The quick kick also fell out of favor as more and more offenses adopted the wide-open style of play pioneered by Sam and the Redskins. Kicking for field position became less an option when teams expected to score from anywhere on the field.

The old single wing—like the various iterations of the shotgun offense used today—was also more amenable to another Baugh weapon, the quick pass. He got his passes off quickly because his center knew to snap the ball to him in the vicinity of his right ear, where he could instantly whip a "short, safe, sure" pass to one of his receivers.

Despite the changes, or perhaps because of them, the Redskins got off to a fast start in '44. They opened with a tie and then won the next three to lead the division. Filchock, alternating with Sam, had the season of his life. With more than 1,100 yards through the air and a completion percentage of .571, he led the NFL in passing.

Sam, his time divided between the pasture and the playing field, didn't do too badly himself. He completed 82 of 146 passes for 849 yards and a passing percentage of .562. That was good for second place in the NFL, ahead of the Bears' Luckman, whose percentage was .497.

The aerial prowess of the Redskins duo wasn't enough. After their quick start, they only managed to break even in their final six games and finished 6-3-1, in third place behind the Giants and Eagles.

The Germans had surrendered by the time the 1945 NFL season opened, and the Japanese were in their final throes. Fewer men were being drafted into the military, so most of the 1944 regulars were on hand when the Redskins began preseason training on Georgetown University's new football field. Sam was again free for full-time quarterbacking.

When the Japanese surrendered on September 5, the Office of Defense Transportation removed all travel restrictions, and the owner immediately scheduled five exhibition games (for no extra pay to the players). That might be why the team looked tired and sluggish in the season opener, a 28–20 loss to the Boston Yankees, which listed the singer Kate Smith as a co-owner.

In Pittsburgh the following Sunday, the Redskins ignited a winning streak that lasted for six games. Sam threw two touchdown passes in the 14–0 shutout. He threw another touchdown pass to his fellow quarterback, Frank Filchock, but the thirty-yard toss was called back on a holding penalty.

Sam, now in his ninth season, was playing as well as he had played in years. In a 24–14 victory over Philadelphia at Griffith Stadium, he threw thirteen passes and completed ten. He had grown so comfortable in the T formation that he told a reporter, "I could play it in top hat and tails."

The next Sunday against the Giants, he completed twenty-three passes, including a touchdown pass to his old buddy Wayne Millner, back from the war. Another spectator also was back from the war. Corinne Griffith recalled the Redskins swing band suddenly breaking into a jaunty tune and the Griffith Stadium crowd rising as one in a mighty ovation. A man in khaki uniform stood up and acknowledged the ovation. General Dwight D. Eisenhower had come home.

At home the next week, Sam completed nineteen of twenty-five passes for 249 yards in a 24–21 victory over the Chicago Cardinals. The Redskins were averaging twenty-five points a game.

By November, other Redskins were drifting in from all over the world. Running back Dick Todd returned from the navy, and Ki Aldrich from the army.

Another returning veteran was Al DeMao, a big tough center from

Duquesne who had been drafted by the NFL in 1942 but had not yet played in a pro game. What he found when he joined the Redskins surprised him. As he recalled four decades later:

> I'd come from a very disciplined program in college, and here I am in my first meeting with a pro team. The coach is diagramming a play and saying to Baugh: "Sam, we'll run this."
>
> Sam says: "It won't work, so I won't call it."
>
> Then DeGroot says: "Okay, we'll use Filchock at quarterback." And Filchock looks up and says: "I won't call it either."
>
> I'm dumbfounded. The players are telling the coach what to do.

Sam, of course, had been around a lot longer than DeGroot—and probably knew the game better than his coach. And returning veterans like DeMao had taken orders from much more intimidating superiors than a head football coach—and in life-and-death situations—so it probably wasn't easy to take a demanding coach all that seriously.

Marshall—always "Mr. Marshall," as far as Sam was concerned—was another matter. He ruled by intimidation, and since he was signing the checks, he usually got the respect, or at least the obedience, he craved.

Sam led Marshall's team to two more wins before the Eagles tripped them up in Philadelphia, 16–0. The next week, the Skins were back in Griffith Stadium, where they defeated Pittsburgh 24–0. In the regular-season finale, the Redskins defeated the Giants 17–0, thus claiming the Eastern Division championship for the fifth time in nine years.

Sam, selected for the first time as an all-pro quarterback—he had previously made the team as a halfback—set an NFL record in 1945 by completing 70.3 percent of his passes. His 128 completions were the most in the league that year, and only the Bears' Luckman gained more yards passing—1,725 for Luckman, 1,669 for Sam.

The Cleveland Rams—soon to be the Los Angeles Rams—won their first Western Division championship, and with it the right to play the world championship game at home on December 17.

Sam was hurting, and four days before the game, doctors determined that he had suffered a broken rib in the Giants game. Marshall told his wife that he was keeping it a secret. "Be sure you don't even whisper it," he told her.

The next morning, she recalled, all the morning papers led with the story about the star's injury. "May I whisper it now?" Griffith asked her husband. He said yes.

S am and the Redskins left Washington's Union Station on Friday night for Cleveland. A huge crowd jammed the station, already bustling with holiday throngs trying to get home for Christmas and servicemen trying to get home for good. Leaving an hour late, the special train carried the team, coaches, sportswriters, fans, a 150-piece brass band, a huge papier-mâché Christmas tree, a Santa Claus sled, and six Santa Clauses (for the halftime extravaganza).

The train pulled into Cleveland late Saturday morning. One reporter observed that Sam looked weak and drawn, in no condition to play, "but Texas blood and guts demanded he be given the nod over the fresher Filchock who came back from the Navy in the middle of the season."

Sam never liked playing in Cleveland. "Out there," he told the *Post*'s Shirley Povich years later, "they pumped up the ball to make it round and hard to throw. The league didn't have a regulation ball when I broke in."

Horrible weather only added to his Cleveland woes. A blizzard had gripped the city for a week, and playing conditions rivaled those from the fabled game with the Bears in '37. Corrine Griffith recalled getting a wake-up call from a cheery Statler Hotel operator: "Good morning! It's nine o'clock. The weather forecast for today is clear and sunny. The temperature is Zero."

Cleveland's Municipal Stadium is situated on the shore of Lake Erie. The end of the stadium facing the lake was open, purposely so, to allow in cool breezes on summer nights when the Cleveland Indians were playing baseball. On December 16, the cool breezes felt as if they were gusting across the lake from the North Pole. By game time at 1:30 p.m, the temperature had fallen to two below zero.

Some 33,000 of the 40,000 ticket-buying fans huddled for some measure of warmth in the 80,000-seat stadium. They were wrapped in fur caps, earmuffs, sheepskin-lined parkas, corduroy pants, and heavy boots. Corrine Griffith and her husband had stuffed newspapers under their heavy coats and sweaters.

"They're peddling hot coffee in the stands, and the lucky fans are getting it spilled all over them," Shirley Povich wrote on the day of the game. "When one clumsy vendor attempted to apologize, he was told, 'Never mind, the pleasure is all mine.'"

Groundskeepers had spread $7,000 worth of hay across the field the night before, hoping to keep the ground from freezing. It didn't work, although players sitting on the bench covered their legs and feet with it. Icy gusts blew through the stadium opening; fine bits of frozen snow swirled through the air. The only color on the field came from the garish yellow jerseys and helmets the Rams wore.

After pregame warm-ups, the teams left the field and the trumpeters of the Redskins band marched in from the open end of the stadium. They held their feathered headdresses with one hand, their instruments with the other. At the goalposts, they halted, resting their trumpets on their hips. The director gave a command, and with a flourish the trumpeters lifted their instruments to their lips. Out came a few pathetic squeaks. The trumpets had frozen.

Early in the first quarter, the Redskins took over deep in their own end of the field. Sam, his ribs tightly bandaged, jogged gingerly onto the icy field. Fading to pass from his own end zone, he spotted his buddy Millner in the clear on a crossing pattern and let the ball fly.

It didn't fly very far. In those days—and for some years thereafter—the goalposts were on the actual goal line, not at the back of the end zone, and Sam's pass to Millner hit the goalpost crossbar. The ball bounced back for an automatic safety and a 2–0 lead for the Rams. (Marshall would get the safety rule changed at the next league meeting.)

"Everyone expected Sam to punt, because we were backed up to the goal line," Millner said later. "There was no one within a mile of me when I broke into the clear. But as Baugh threw the ball, the wind shifted and blew the ball into the goalpost. Instead of being ahead 7–0 on a 105-yard play, we were behind 2–0."

As Sam recalled the play years later, his injured ribs were to blame. "I couldn't throw very hard, couldn't put anything on the ball," he recalled. "We'd been better off with Filchock playing the whole game."

"Wayne would have gone the rest of the distance, no question," said Al DeMao, then a rookie. Sam, obviously in pain, retired to the bench, and Filchock came in and almost immediately threw a fifty-eight-yard scoring toss to running back Steve Bagarus.

The Rams came back and scored on a thirty-eight-yard pass play from the Rams' rookie star Bob Waterfield to Jim Benton, making the score Rams 8, Redskins 7. Waterfield came on to kick the extra point. Having trouble finding firm footing, he lofted a wobbly kick that landed atop the crossbar, balanced briefly, and then toppled over for the extra point. Rams 9, Redskins 7.

DeMao recalled what happened at halftime: "Marshall came into the locker room and told Coach DeGroot, 'Okay, Doug, let's get out the sneakers.' Doug said very meekly, 'Mr. Marshall, we made a gentleman's agreement that we wouldn't use the sneakers.' He was, in essence, fired right then and there. Marshall said, 'This is no gentleman's game. That's the last decision you'll ever make as coach of the Redskins.'"

In the second half—after Marshall's six-Santa halftime show, and his de facto firing of the coach—Waterfield passed forty-four yards for a touchdown, making it Rams 15, Redskins 7. This time, Waterfield missed the extra point. Sam, who had completed two passes in the first half—one for seven yards, the other for one yard—watched from the bench, his skinny legs draped in hay.

The Redskins scored again on a pass from Filchock to Bob Seymour. Joe Aguirre's extra point made the score 15–14.

Late in the fourth quarter, the Redskins stopped the Rams' final drive and, with minutes remaining, began to mount one of their own. They fought their way to the Rams' twenty-four before stalling. On fourth and four, with less than a minute to go, Sam walked painfully toward his teammates as they lined up for an Aguirre field-goal attempt. Drums accompanied a desperate chant from the frozen Ram faithful: "Block that kick! Block that kick!"

Like an old man, Sam knelt gingerly on the frozen turf and, while Aguirre waited, tried to scrape away the ice and snow so he could put the ball down. The wind died down, the drums went silent.

Sam blew on his fingers, wiped them across his jersey, and barked out a signal. He handled the snap cleanly and tilted the ball toward Aguirre, who sent it tumbling high in the air toward the goalposts. He had the distance, but just before the ball tumbled down between the standards, a gust of wind from the open end of the stadium caught it. The ball sailed just inches outside the upright. One minute later, the Cleveland Rams were NFL champions.

Since the Redskins had been in the championship thick of things so frequently, they and their fans assumed they would be back next year. So did Sam. As it turned out, there would be no next year—for Sam, for Marshall, for any of the '40s-era Redskins. Sam would see only one more winning season in his time as a Redskin, and it would be thirty-seven long years before Washington won another championship.

....

THE 1946 AND 1947 SEASONS

THE DISMAL YEARS BEGIN

"If you play long enough . . . you're going to play on a real good team, you're going to play on a mediocre team and you're going to play on some bad teams," Sam told an interviewer nearly a half century after he retired. "It's a lot more fun to play with a good bunch."

Sam's time with "a good bunch" pretty much came to an end with the 1945 season. For the next seven seasons, he played on teams that were, at best, mediocre. Although Sam still had some good football left in him, the Redskins during that period managed only one winning season. The bizarre blizzard matchup with Cleveland was his last championship opportunity.

The reasons for the decline were manifold. For one thing, the team experienced a spate of injuries during the postwar years, plus the veterans, including Sam, were aging. In addition, the free-substitution rule went into effect, which led to modern two-platoon football. Sam and his amazing sixty-minute cohorts faded into the past, to be replaced by specialists. Teams with depth prospered; the Redskins were thin at several positions.

The draft—the military draft, that is—also had an effect on the Redskins. With the advent of the Cold War, Uncle Sam needed men, and the Redskins lost several key players at inopportune times. Also, the newly established All-American Football Conference challenged the NFL for players. Most NFL owners responded to the challenge by raising salaries.

Not Marshall. He hated the new conference but was unwilling to spend money to hold on to his players.

Several Redskins decamped, including Joe Aguirre, Lou Rymkus, and Wee Willie Wilkin. The Redskins' coach, Dudley DeGroot, asked for his release and then almost immediately became head coach of the Los Angeles Dons.

Sam was no doubt approached, but he felt a certain sense of loyalty to "Mr. Marshall." Corinne Griffith recalled a conversation the quarterback had with the owner a few hours after the championship game in Cleveland: "I kind of figure it this way, Mr. Marshall, if a football player wants to jump the Redskins—that's just the kind of football player the Redskins don't want."

Not all the Redskins felt the same way about the hardheaded, flamboyant owner, who, after 1945, was a negative influence in another way as well. That was the year he sold his laundry business, which allowed him to devote all his time and effort to his beloved Redskins. That was fine when it came to ever more spectacular halftime shows, but not so fine for the unfortunate coach who had to endure his constant meddling.

"Marshall could promote the game, but he didn't know his ass from a hole in the ground, as far as I was concerned," said Hall of Fame running back Bill Dudley, who played in D.C. with Sam toward the tail end of the Texan's career. "He was just a big, damn fan."

Since he didn't know enough football to be the coach himself, he settled for hiring and firing incessantly. During Sam's sixteen-year career, Marshall went through Ray Flaherty, Dutch Bergman, Dudley DeGroot, Glen "Turk" Edwards, John Whelchel, Herman Ball, Dick Todd, and Curly Lambeau.

"Mr. Marshall would have loved to have been the head coach," recalled Joe Tereshinski, a Pennsylvanian who joined the team in 1947 after an all-American career at Georgia. "I always firmly believed that his life would have been complete if he could have coached the team for one season. He was always competing with George Halas, and it made Mr. Marshall jealous, because Halas would be on the field and Marshall would have to sit up in the stands. He would call his general manager, Dick McCann, who sat behind the Redskins bench, and tell him plays to give to the coach."

Tereshinski recalled the sight of the owner's long black Cadillac nosing onto one end of the practice field while the team was working out on the other. Marshall would summon his star quarterback to the car, Sam would amble over, and the doors would open wide. The two men would sit in the front seat, Sam in his workout uniform, for maybe half an hour and talk football—or, more likely, Marshall would talk and Sam would listen.

"Goddamn it, Sam, I want you to go over there and tell Ball he's through," Marshall growled. "No coach is going to wreck this team, and I want you to be the one to tell him."

Sam looked at the owner. "But Mr. Marshall," he said. "He's the coach; I'm just the quarterback."

Sam knew how his teammates felt about the high-handed owner; he knew how he himself felt. And yet, as far as anyone knows, he was never less than respectful with the man.

After the war, Marshall made no effort to bring back Flaherty. "Ray didn't let anybody dominate him, which was difficult when he was working for Marshall," Flaherty's wife told the *Washington Post* years later.

After DeGroot's departure, the reluctant recipient of Marshall's game-day missives and inordinate attention was Glen "Turk" Edwards. As it turned out, the recently retired Redskins lineman, a future member of the NFL Hall of Fame, was a better player than he was a coach. "Turk was a great football player with a great reputation, but he was probably too nice to be a head coach," Tereshinski recalled. "Having played with some of the guys on the team, it was hard for him to come down on those guys."

The Redskins, including Sam, struggled all year. Wayne Millner, his favorite receiver, retired, and Frank Filchock, his longtime understudy, was traded to the Giants. With the new coach constantly juggling the lineup, the team never developed any consistency. They wound up 5-5-1, the first non-winning season since leaving Boston.

Still, there were highlights. In a victory against Philadelphia on November 24, Sam spent most of the game on the bench with bruised ribs. Toward the end of the fourth quarter, though, he ran on the field, bruised ribs and all, and took charge of the offense.

"I've got to celebrate," he told Edwards and then proceeded to lead the Redskins' offense on a fifty-three-yard touchdown drive. With his injury, he couldn't raise his arm to throw a pass, so he engineered the whole drive on the ground. The game ended 27 to 10.

On the train back to Washington, Sam continued to celebrate. He couldn't throw a football, but he could toss cigars to teammates sitting around him. "Mrs. Samuel Adrian Baugh, 'the best ranch-hand in all Texas,' had just presented Sammy with their third baby boy—four forward passers in one family," Corinne Griffith wrote.

Sam went back to the ranch and his growing family at the end of the season. He got home earlier than usual, thanks to the Redskins' record.

The 1947 season was even less memorable than the season before. Although Sam came back stronger than ever, leading an offense that could score almost at will, the defense was as leaky as a sieve. The season opener against the Eagles at Griffith Stadium was a portent. The Redskins scored forty-two points—and lost. For the rest of the season, the Redskins gave up an average of more than thirty points a game.

With the team out of the running by November for a division title, Marshall started looking for a gimmick to entice fans into Griffith Stadium. He found one: a special day to honor the greatest quarterback in team history, arguably the greatest in the history of the game.

Sammy Baugh Day at Griffith Stadium was November 23, 1947; the Redskins' opponent was the league-leading Chicago Cardinals. Before the game, Redskin fans stood as one to greet their hero with a raucous ovation. The Touchdown Club of Washington had collected donations to purchase a magnificent Packard station wagon for Sam—Redskin burgundy with gold-colored wood paneling, white sidewall tires, D.C. license plate number 33, and an inscription on the side: "Slinging Sam—the Redskin Man."

After the car presentation, the usual keys to the city, and other assorted gifts, Joe Tereshinksi gathered his teammates around him and nodded toward Sam, who was still being feted at the middle of the field. "There's the best football player in the world," Tereshinski said, "Let's show him what we think of him. Let's see that he doesn't get any mud on his pants today."

Although Washington was 2-6-0 and merely playing out the string, Sam's teammates desperately wanted to win one for their leader, then in his eleventh season. They also realized that he was nervous that day, perhaps because of all the attention he was receiving or maybe because he was facing the best team in the league. That was a portent.

"The tip-off was the number of times he went to the john during the time he was getting dressed," fullback Jim Castiglia recalled. "If he went more than three times, we knew we were going to have a helluva day. You could book it." On Sammy Baugh Day, he seemed especially nervous. "I was Sammy's scorekeeper," Castiglia said, "because I had a locker next to the john. When he visited the toilet for the third time, we were all grinning. Just before time to go out on the field, he went one last time. I held up seven fingers. There was loud whooping. We knew we had this one won."

Castiglia's theory held up. Redskin fans finally had something to cheer about as Sam's inerrant missiles found Bones Taylor, Tereshinski, Dick Todd, and Joe Saenz. Playing against the best defensive team in the NFL that afternoon, he completed twenty-five of thirty-three passes for 355 yards. Six of them were for touchdowns as the Redskins beat the title-bound Cardinals 45–21.

"That was the easiest game I ever had," Sam recalled. "Our team played a great game. I was proud of them."

Sam was proud of his car too. His sister and brother-in-law had come down from Philadelphia for Sammy Baugh Day, and after the game, he drove them back home in the magnificent new station wagon. He had planned to spend the night in Philly, but on the way up he remembered that he was supposed to make an appearance at a school in Washington the next morning. After he dropped off his relatives, he turned around and headed south.

"At that time of the night there were hardly any cars on the highway," he recalled.

> I saw this car coming toward me. It was coming across the middle of the road a little too much, I thought. I slowed down a little bit. I thought he would straighten the car out. But he kept coming toward me, so I moved over to the right a little bit. He kept coming toward me, so I had to do something. I went on the gravel. I thought he was going to hit me head-on. When I hit that gravel, I slid right into a concrete bridge. It destroyed one side of the car. That guy didn't stop. He just kept going.

Sam's explanation sounded plausible, since he didn't drink. "He was actually a very good driver," his son David recalled. "He had to be, since he always drove too fast."

Sam got the car repaired and drove it home to Texas. David would remember how he and his brother Todd climbed all over it and scratched the finish with the buckles on their overalls.

The Redskins' '47 season was something of a car wreck as well. Despite the upset victory over the Cardinals, the team had its worst year since moving to Washington, finishing 4-8 for next-to-last place in the Eastern Division. One of those losses, a 56–20 thrashing at the hands of the Bears, prompted Shirley Povich to remark: "They are suffering from Halas-tosis."

The Associated Press noted that "the thin man from Texas was never better." He threw 354 times and completed 210 for 2,935 yards, setting two passing records in the process, both of which held up into the 1960s. Those numbers brought his lifetime record to 2,093 attempts and 1,202 completions for 15,194 yards and 128 touchdowns, all records at the time.

The numbers were even more impressive because Washington usually fell behind early and the opposition knew he was going to throw. Still, he was hard to stop.

"Sammy would still have all the passing records in football if he had the receivers they had today," his center, Al DeMao, recalled in 2006. "Sam never had that luxury. We had outstanding players, but they had to play both ways. Bones Taylor was probably the best end Sammy had to throw to. If Sam had those kind of receivers, there's no telling what kind of records he would have set."

"Is Baugh beginning to feel tired?" the AP wondered in 1947. "Well, he's outlasted a long line of stars brought in to succeed him. Roy Zimmerman, Frankie Filchock and Jack Jacobs all got tired and went away. And Jimmy Youell, the Iowa boy now understudying Baugh, hardly played enough this year to work up a sweat."

"I sure would like to have us win another championship before I quit," the AP reported Sam having told a luncheon gathering on December 15. "You know, I haven't got much longer—maybe only another year."

"But he didn't look as if he believed it," the AP noted. "And the record book so far has given no hint that Baugh ever will wear out. Like the Washington Monument, he may be here to stay."

His teammates felt the same way. "My locker was next to Sammy Baugh's for six years," Tereshinski recalled,

He was a tremendous guy. The first time I saw him, I walked into Griffith Stadium when he was punting the ball down the field to Dick Todd. Dick was 50 yards away and never had to move to field those punts, not at all. I never saw such accuracy in a punter. Then he backed Dick up five yards and hit him again, and another five yards, and maybe Dick had to move a yard either way to catch the ball. On broken pass plays in practice, when the routes weren't run correctly, Sam would punt the ball down to the players. He was a coach on the field. He would call pass patterns and tell receivers where to go, changing them right on the field.

Harry Gilmer, an all-American who would sign with the Redskins in 1948 as Sam's potential successor, had similar memories. "He could be very innovative, especially when he had [Dick] Todd around," Gilmer told the sportswriter Whit Canning years later. "Those two had been together so long they had developed that rapport where each knew instinctively what the other was thinking. Many times, Sam would throw to a spot and Todd would suddenly arrive to catch the ball—to the complete surprise of the defenders. Sam was kind of ahead of his time in many ways."

Gilmer was one of many players from Sam's era who were as awed by his abilities as were his fans—perhaps more so, because they understood the mechanics of what he could do, not to mention his dedication to perfection.

Gilmer also liked the man from Texas. "Sam pretty much adopted me right off," he recalled. "Actually, he could get along with anybody, and usually did. He was a straight-shooter—anything you asked him, he told you exactly what he thought, no matter what. But he was also one of the most entertaining people I've ever known."

During the season, Sam hung out with Todd, a fellow West Texan, and Bullet Bill Dudley, the team's best running back in the late 1940s. Young Gilmer became the fourth musketeer, and after a while, he and Sam shared an apartment in D.C, since neither had their wives with them.

"He could start telling stories, and you'd get up on the edge of your seat— and two hours later he'd still be telling stories and you'd still be sitting like that. And he and Todd together could keep a crowd going for hours," Gilmer recalled.

Sam and his teammates managed to put together a decent season in '48, finishing second in the division with a record of 7-5. In those days, the second-place team received shares for finishing second, and one of the Redskins called a team meeting to determine how to divide the money.

Gilmer recalled that some of the Redskins were in favor of cutting out several players who had gotten hurt or who hadn't played much, and then dividing the shares among themselves.

"Sam sat there and listened to this for awhile," Gilmer recalled, "then suddenly he gets up out of his chair and looks around and says, 'What the hell are we talking about here? Those guys are our teammates, and they're just as much a part of this team as any of the rest of us. They just had some bad luck, and we didn't!'" That pretty much settled it, Gilmer recalled. Everyone on the team received an equal share.

....

1948–1952

LAST YEARS WITH THE REDSKINS

Harry Gilmer was one of two quarterbacks Marshall signed for the 1948 season, the other being Charley Conerly from Ole Miss. Shortly after Sam returned to Double Mountain following the '47 season, he got a call from the owner.

"I just wanted to let you know that we're going to sign Harry Gilmer out of Alabama," Marshall said.

"Fine," Sam told him.

"And also, that because of the bonuses these kids are getting today, we're going to have to pay him more than we're paying you."

"Well," Sam said. "So?"

The conversation was typically Sam. His only concern about money had nothing to do with his ego. He was interested only in making enough to pay off the ranch.

The rookie Gilmer may have been an all-American in college, but he soon realized he had a lot to learn from the veteran. "The first thing I learned," he said, "was that I wasn't going to be the quarterback of the Washington Redskins anytime soon."

The second thing he learned was that Sam was happy to impart whatever knowledge he could to the man slated to replace him in the lineup. "It was amazing just to stand around and watch him," Gilmer said. "From that time forward, I stayed in pro football a pretty long time—as a player, coach or in some capacity. I saw a lot of passers come and go, and Sam was as good as any I ever saw."

As Gilmer recalled, Sam wasn't all that fast, but he had quick feet. Standing in the pocket, looking downfield for a receiver, he could take a couple of quick steps and evade rushers bearing down on him.

"I was with the Redskins for the rest of the time that Sam was there, and I really can't remember ever seeing him sacked," Gilmer said. "I suppose he was, but I don't recall it. That was always a big important thing with him, because he felt that every time he got sacked, he let the team down. He was an expert at getting rid of the ball if he had to—but he usually got it delivered."

Gilmer never did replace Sam. He suffered a leg injury in his rookie season and never completely recovered. Conerly, the other quarterback Marshall signed to replace the Texan, was traded to the Giants, whom he led as a star quarterback for the next fourteen seasons.

Sam kept coming back for "one more year." When he was on, he was still the best in the league, but there were signs that he was wearing out, that his attention was more and more directed toward home and the ranch. A cache of letters from that time suggests that his heart was back in Texas.

On November 18, 1947, he wrote his sons Todd and David:

Mother wrote me about you bringing in wood and helping her do things around the house. I think that's awful nice of you, and I'm awful proud of you. I bet both of you boys are going to be fine cowboys sometime. I hope you will help me feed the cows this winter like you did at times last winter.

Daddy gets awful lonesome and misses his boys lots and lots. I wish I could be at home and wrestle you every nite. Maybe you are getting so big now I won't be able to throw you.

On July 14, 1948, he wrote to Mona from the Harrington Motel on Hollywood's Sunset Strip. Some of the Redskins had bit parts in *Triple Threat*, a Columbia Pictures production:

We are working on the picture, but I don't have much to do with it. I'm glad because I may get home earlier than I planned.

I don't think I am going to enjoy football at all this year. I'm going to miss being home more than ever. It's nice to get away from the boys if you are with them all the time as you are, but I am really going to get homesick. . . .

Give Todd, David and Bruce a hug for me. It's not good to be away from a family you love.

Be sweet,

Sam

"Honey, I wish we were together," he wrote to Mona from Washington's Hotel Roosevelt in September 1948. "You tell the boys I think of them every day, and I wish I could be home with them." He added a postscript: "Honey I want you to fix the house even though it costs more than you intended to spend on it. I'm glad Owen got enough pipe to reach the new tower. I hope the water is softer than the other well."

Meanwhile, Sam had a job in Washington. A scouting report that Joe Tereshinski saved from an Eagles-Redskins game on October 17, 1948, included a rundown on each Eagle starter, offense and defense, plays the Redskins would be counting on against the Eagles' defense, and a pep talk introduction:

HEADS UP REDSKINS!!!!

The Philadelphia Eagles—Eastern Championship Winners of 1947, and picked to repeat in 1948—are coming to Washington Sunday, flying high and wide. They have always been a tough team for the Redskins to beat. We have not beaten them in Washington for the last four years. Let's make this our year!! we can't afford to lose this one—Our fans, and the coaches feel confident that you can and will beat the Eagles. what do you say, gang, let's be ready!!

The Eagles have several outstanding men—great competitors and stars in their own right. Men like Steve Van Buren who for the past 3 or 4 years has broken all ground gaining records. His specialty is off tackle and end runs. He must be shoulder-tackled and will cut back at every opportunity. We must be on him at every minute. Pritchard is very fast and is particularly dangerous on punt returns and kick-offs, and at present is their leading ground-gainer. He likes to run the ends and 48 turn. He is also a good pass receiver. We agree that they are great ball players. "The Cardinals stopped them—the Rams stopped them—so can the redskins". Thompson is a steady field general and if not rushed is an excellent passer. go get him "j's"!!! Pihos is a very good pro end, and does everything well. They like to pass to both him and Armstrong #80 who is their favorite pass receiver on long passes.

The Eagles have a fast well-balanced ball club. They should have beaten the Cardinals, and were tied in the last seconds of the game by the Rams. Against the Giants they controlled the ball most all of the game. Their squad is in A-1 shape and will be ready to put out 100% against the Redskins. we can beat the eagles if we think!!! and make up our minds right now to hustle, block, tackle, and carry out our assignments, and play our defenses the way they are set up.

sunday is our day!!!! let's go now!!!

The Eagles, who would go on to win the NFL championship, beat the Redskins 48–0.

Two weeks later, Dan Sandifer became the second Washington Redskin to intercept four passes in a game, returning two for touchdowns in a victory over the Boston Yankees. The *Washington Post* didn't mention the interception record in its game story and didn't get to Sandifer at all until the sixth paragraph. The reason could be that the Redskins scored a team-record fifty-nine points that day as Sam threw four touchdown passes and amassed a then-NFL-record 446 passing yards. The *Post* led off its story of the game with: "The Boston Yankees lost a Baugh game yesterday at Griffith Stadium."

In late November 1948, Sam received a letter on Big Chief tablet paper, written in pencil in all capital letters:

> dear daddy
> when are you coming home? we miss you.
>> it is cold today. david and i brought in five loads of wood. we have been helping mother clean the yard.
>> come home soon.
> love,
> todd

Todd sent his dad another letter a few days later:

> dear daddy
> i miss you. the cows are fine. the barn is full of hay.
> todd

The Redskins finished the '48 season with a record of 7-5, good for second place in the division. By the time the next season rolled around, Sam was getting tired of the grind. The glamour—and the riches—that would come to characterize the game were still decades away, as illustrated by a letter Sam wrote from training camp at Occidental College on August 10, 1949:

I am homesick now and I know it will be worse after a few weeks. I'm going to miss you boys an awful lot. Still, I guess it's worth $15,000. We can certainly use the dough later. I hope we can get some money saved up because this will probably be my last playing season.

Still at Occidental five days later, the homesickness hadn't lessened:

I miss you darling, and I miss the boys and our home. Maybe it's not very fancy, but I am perfectly happy with you, the boys and our ranch. This football is exciting but the season is too long.

Remind Owen to keep rat poison out at the barn and lots of it.

He was still concerned about the mundane in a letter to Mona the next month:

Dearest Mona,

I went down & paid Dr. Amundson $635.00 today. I presume it won't bounce

. . .

The Cardinals beat us 38–7. They really tore our line apart the 2nd half. It was 14–7 at half time, but we couldn't stop them after that. I completed 16 passes 1 for the TD, but we were never in the game after the 1st half.

I looked at some Pontiac Station Wagons today—they are awful nice. I can buy one for list price, but we'd have to sell our car at home. I'd like to trade ours in on a new one but I don't know what it would bring. They tell me I'd probably get more for it at home.

Like most aging players, Sam was hobbled by injuries and an inability to bounce back quickly. In early September, he wrote Mona that he probably wouldn't be able to play in the Redskins' opener:

Dearest Mona,

We have just arrived in Wash. And are getting ready to go to the annual Touchdown Luncheon welcoming the Redskins back to Wash . . .

The weather is cool here, and you can feel fall in the air. I hope it stays cool

. . .

I hurt my ribs in the game but there's nothing serious, just painful. I don't think I can play next Sunday against Green Bay.

In a letter to Mona dated October 5, 1949, from his usual room at the Hotel Roosevelt, Sam confided to his wife that his career was winding down:

Dearest Mona,

I have been laying in bed listening to the first game of the world series. It was a good game, but I had a difficult time keeping my eyes open.

The Redskins won Mon. nite but we received lots of injuries—some of them quite serious. I hope some of the boys recover in time for the Giant game Sunday. "Turk" was relieved of being line coach—he was replaced by Herman Ball. It was quite a popular move as far as the boys were concerned. They like Herman, but detest Turk.

I am getting awful tired and old for football—seems I can't get rested. I suppose it's for young men, and you couldn't exactly call me a freshman at this time. . . .

Be sweet and remember I love you. Tell the boys I'll be awful glad to see them.

Sam

It was getting harder and harder to be away from home for such long stretches of time. "Honey, I want you to know how much I love you, but I'm not so good when it comes to writing or talking," he wrote toward the end of November. "I guess Thanksgiving is a good time to check up and see how many things we have to be thankful for. We have many things, but you are the best—I am glad you're my wife and I want to tell you I've enjoyed every year we've had together. I have loved you so much, but I love you now more than I ever have."

He also mentioned in his Thanksgiving-week letter that he would be attending a Press Club father-daughter banquet at which President Truman and his daughter, Margaret Truman, would be the special guests. "Mr. Marshall made me promise to accept so I guess I'll be there," he wrote Mona. "Kinda like to see a President anyway."

As a family man approaching middle age, Sam probably was tired of being treated like a juvenile as well. A mimeographed letter that Redskins general manager Richard McCann sent to players near the end of Sam's career included a list of what to bring to training camp at Occidental College:

Two suits, or one suit and a sport coat with slacks;
One pair of old slacks, or dungarees, and sweater or jacket;
One pair of dress shoes;
One pair of old shores [shoes] or loafers;
Four dress or convertible sports shirts;
A necktie or two;
Six changes of underwear;

Toilet articles;

Pajamas, robe and slippers if you desire.

The ridiculously patronizing letter continues:

> The club has strict rules about wearing suit coats and ties while in pub-
> lic places such as hotel lobbies, railroad stations, airport terminals, and so
> forth. But around the training camp you may dress for comfort and most of
> the player [*sic*] wear a regulation Redskins' T-shirt, which will be issued to
> you, and old slacks. Sam Baugh, for instance, wears a T-shirt, dungarees and
> loafers in camp . . .
>
> Throughout your stay in California (about 40 days), you will have few
> occasions to dress up. These will be: dinner given by the *Los Angeles Times*
> for players participating in their great charity game; dinner given by Eagle
> Rock and Highland Park citizens. . . . And, of course, six Sundays if you are a
> church-goer.
>
> Traveling on trains, the Redskins use private cars and you may dress for
> comfort once aboard the train. However, in hotels I once again remind you
> of the club's strict rules on coats and ties. The day of the turtle-neck is past.
> You're in the big leagues . . .

The second page of the letter included a list of answers to frequently asked
questions:

> Clothes:
>
> When boarding or leaving trains or buses, or while in hotel lobbies and
> dining rooms, your wearing apparel must include a necktie and a suit jacket
> or sport coat . . .
>
> Meals:
>
> Special menus are prepared for group meals by the Redskins' dietician.
> There are no substitutes, and no seconds, for your stomach's sake.
>
> Laundry:
>
> You may charge your laundry but you will be billed for it at the end of the
> trip and the charges deducted from your first pay envelope.
>
> Phones at Occidental:
>
> OUTGOING CALLS: They are to be made on pay phones available in the
> basement of Swan Hall.
>
> INCOMING CALLS: They will be received at the phone booth in the patio
> of the Student Union Building. If you expect a call, stand by there. No personal
> calls may be received over phones in Swan Hall, or the dressing room.

Smoking:

The club has strict rules about smoking in or around the dressing room or practice field . . .

Ash-trays are plentiful in your rooms. Be sure to use them . . . not the floor.

Remember: It's somebody's mother or wife who has to clean up.

Maybe Sam was trying to escape the strict regimen when, toward the end of his career, he moved into Washington's Shoreham Hotel. The Shoreham, right off Connecticut Avenue and overlooking Rock Creek Park, was a swank place, although when Sam took up occupancy, it left a bit to be desired.

"I was a rookie in Sammy Baugh's last season in football," defensive back Dick Alban recalled.

When we got back to Washington after training camp and after playing the exhibition games across the country on the way back from the West Coast, I didn't have any place to stay. I had one suitcase full of stuff and that was it.

Sam invited the rookie to stay with him at the Shoreham until Alban's wife arrived and the couple could find an apartment. As Alban remembered:

We went to the Shoreham and went in the back entrance. I wondered why we didn't go in the front door. We walked up two flights of stairs, down the hall, and into a suite of rooms that was huge. There had to be seven or eight rooms in that suite. Outside, in the front of the building, there was a big sign that said "Condemned."

The hotel was closed. But Sammy still stayed there. He was friends with the manager of the hotel. You wouldn't think that a veteran and a star like that would help a rookie. But that was Sammy.

It wasn't getting any easier for the aging veteran. "I'm so sore from Sunday's game," he wrote after playing the Eagles. "I don't think I'll ever loosen up again."

Sammy was still in there pitching in 1949, although the results were less than spectacular. Despite a midseason coaching change, the Redskins finished the season at 4-7-1, topping only the New York Bulldogs, who were playing their one and only season in the NFL.

As a new decade debuted, the four-year-old All-America Conference folded. Over George Marshall's vociferous objection, the NFL picked up three teams from the defunct league—the Cleveland Browns, the San Francisco 49ers, and the Baltimore Colts.

Shortly after the '49 season ended, Sam flirted with becoming the head football coach at Baylor University. He was considered the top candidate among three contenders for the job, which opened up when Bob Woodruff resigned the $12,000-a-year position to take a $17,000-a-year job as athletic director and head football coach at the University of Florida. "It would be a good job and be very nice," Sam told the Associated Press, "but I believe I should stay with Washington." George Preston Marshall said Sam told him he wanted to play as long as he could.

The 1950 Redskins drafted a pint-sized quarterback from the College of the Pacific, Eddie LeBaron, as another potential replacement for their aging quarterback. LeBaron showed promise in a couple of exhibition games, but as a reserve officer in the Marine Corps, he was called to active duty when the Korean conflict exploded into full-scale war.

In a letter dated August 14, 1950, Sam recounted a busy Saturday at the Occidental training camp. After a morning workout, the team toured Paramount Studios. "We saw Bob Hope and had a few pictures taken with him," Sam wrote. "He was working on a picture called 'The Lemon-Drop Kid.' He told me his oil wells in Scurry County was making him rich—as though he hasn't been rich for years."

He wrote home a few days later:

Well I'm still sore and stiff—guess I'll stay that way. We haven't had any rough stuff yet. Have our first scrimmage Saturday. I am rooming with Nick Sebek, a qb from Indiana U.

Honey, we are going to stay at the Stoneleigh Hotel in Dallas. Don't know where it is. Never heard of it.

How are you and the boys doing? I know it's awful early to start complaining, but I wouldn't care if they cut me—if we couldn't use the money so easily . . .

Has Owen gotten someone to plough the fields? Did we ever get any rain from the cloudy weather after I left? I was hoping we would get a good soaking rain before it was over.

When the season opened, Sam and center DeMao were the only veterans left from the 1945 championship team. Although Washington fans weren't expecting much from the inexperienced team, Marshall and his new coach,

Herman Ball, were heartened when the Redskins won all five of their exhibition games. Sam, meanwhile, had received some news from Mona, and he responded in a letter dated September 16:

Dearest Mona,

Well I guess we are going to have a little girl to go with our 4 boys. I know you are disappointed—not that I can blame you—it will be an awful lot of work for you to have another baby. Still, I think a girl would be wonderful—or another little boy would be ok by me.

It's really getting to be quite a rainy country around Rotan—I am glad—I hope it rains all winter. It will be fine for the grass.

Honey, I moved to the Roosevelt Hotel today. The Annapolis was too noisy for a guy who has lived in the country for 10 years . . .

We have all our land leased for oil. I wish we didn't. I'm sure we could get more for a lease now than we did at the time we leased. . . .

I am going to buy a Pontiac station wagon. It is all steel—no wood on it at all. 3 seats. The back ones are removable.

The next day the Redskins won their first regular-season game. "This brand-new edition of the Redskins still relies mightily on the good right arm of Sammy Baugh," the *Washington Post* reported. "It was the ageless Mr. Baugh who pitched three of the five touchdowns as the Redskins crushed the Baltimore Colts, 38–14, in the National Football League home opener for both in Memorial Stadium before an estimated crowd of 26,000."

Sam was not so impressed:

Dearest Mona,

We won the game yesterday, but we didn't look very good. I hope we start clicking again next week. Our running attack was not up to par.

Honey, tell Owen to get the oats planted soon, so they will have time to root down before winter. I certainly hope the wet weather lasts. We need lots of moisture to make up for the dry years when the grass didn't grow.

Mr. Marshall was telling Gib Sandifer how nice and small you looked in Dallas. He thinks you have done a wonderful job with the boys—and didn't understand how a woman who has 4 sons can look so young and pretty. I agree with him to the fullest, and, of course, I could tell him of your other fine points but I'll keep that to myself.

After their opening-game victory over the Colts, Sam and the Redskins dropped the next three games in a row, giving up eighty-two points in the process. The team's inexperience was showing, and a raft of injuries compounded the problem. The defense couldn't stop anybody, and quarterbacks Baugh and Gilmer were forced to run for their lives. At a dinner for FBI agents, Sam managed to make a joke about his sieve-like offensive line. "Gentlemen," he said, "this is the most protection I've had all year."

Sam was getting discouraged, as evidenced by an October 2 letter on stationery from the Hotel Edison in New York:

Dearest Mona,

I am in New York today for a TV show. It is the Joe DiMaggio Show and I got $250.00 plus expenses. I will be back in Washington tonight.

We lost to Pittsburgh yesterday, 26 to 7. Our line has looked bad the last three games and there is no explanation for it. I got my arm hurt yesterday and I don't know how long I will be out. It's quite painful when I bend the elbow. I'm afraid there are some pieces of chip bone to be removed, maybe not.

Honey, I think it is a good idea to have a garage built. You have my vote on all the improvements to the house you want. I know another baby will really put a hardship on you—it's a lot of work. I hope you will be able to take care of things gracefully. I don't know of any other person, including my mother and yours, who has, or can, be as good a mother and wife as you. I'm proud of you and happy you are my wife. Someday our little boys will realize what a wonderful woman their mother is . . .

The fifth game of the '50 season was at Griffith Stadium against the Cardinals, who weren't going anywhere either. The local papers noted that the Redskins might be able to halt their skid against the Cards, something Marshall was desperate to see happen. The Redskins had lost two straight at home, and he knew attendance would begin to dwindle if the team kept losing. He also wanted to impress some 5,000 fans from North Carolina who would be making the trip north to see their Tarheel hero, Charlie "Choo Choo" Justice, an all-American and Heisman Trophy runner-up who had broken every record on the books at North Carolina. Given that the Redskins were the southern team in the NFL, Marshall wanted to hold on to his growing fan base below the Mason-Dixon Line. (This was also the reason he continued refusing to sign black players.)

The roof caved in early on the Redskins. Injuries decimated the secondary, forcing Coach Ball to use Pete Stout, a 200-pound linebacker, as a defensive back. The Cardinals picked on him immediately, with their fastest receiver running wild. The score at halftime was 28–0, Cardinals.

The Redskins, angry and frustrated, shuffled into the locker room.

Marshall, his raccoon coat flying, charged in right behind then and immediately began yelling at Stout, accusing him of dogging it and cursing him. As soon as the owner uttered the obscenity, the tough linebacker from Texas, who also had played at TCU, leaped to his feet and grabbed Marshall by the throat with one hand. Glaring into Marshall's eyes, he reminded the man that he was playing out of position and that he was doing the best he could.

The locker room was deathly silent; no one could believe what he was seeing. Neither Sam nor any other Redskin, including coaches, came to Marshall's defense. Finally, Stout released his grip.

The owner was completely unruffled. Acting as though he had planned the whole incident—and the old thespian might have—he stepped up on a footlocker and made a speech. "That's the kind of fight I expect of you, all of you," he shouted, staring into the eyes of the befuddled players around the room. "Now let's go out there in the second half and fight like you do in the locker room!"

They almost did, scoring four touchdowns. Unfortunately, the Cardinals added a touchdown and a field goal to take the game, 38–28. (Stout, by the way, was released at the end of the season.)

Over the next four Sundays, Sam and the Redskins lost to the Eagles, the Giants, the Eagles again, and the Browns, surrendering an average of twenty-eight points a game. That made eight consecutive defeats, a record for the Redskins. The next Sunday, they defeated the hapless Colts.

Sam already was looking toward season's end. He wrote to Mona on November 28:

Dearest Mona,
There are only two more games then I'll be leaving here . . .
I received a letter from a Mr. M. T. McLaughlin, concerning the Texas Tech coaching position. I couldn't give him any answer at that time. I don't know what Mr. Marshall intends to do—he wants me to play and coach the backfield next year. He said I wouldn't have to play but very little—in case Harry got hurt. I don't know what would be best for me to do—but I do know $13,000.00 would be very useful next year. I can't make that coaching unless I leave the ranch 12 months out of the year. If I stay here it will only take up my time during the playing season.
Honey, I'll be happy to get home again. I miss those boys a lot, and I think I'll try to be a better father to them. I fuss at them too much. I hope you are feeling ok—and have shaken off sniffles . . . Be sweet darling. I'll see you soon.
Love you,
Sam

The Redskins managed to beat the Steelers 24–7, and then met the Browns in a Washington snowstorm for their season finale. Some thirty thousand fans showed up despite the snow, in part because it was the day of Marshall's annual Santa Claus extravaganza, in part because the Browns were still in the running for the American Conference title.

Santa may have been a hit, but Sam and the Redskins were not. The Browns shellacked them 45–21, and the Redskins, with a record of 3-9, finished dead last in the conference. It was the worst season ever for a Washington team.

Herman Ball came back as the Redskins coach in 1951. Dick Todd was an assistant. He had retired from the Redskins two years earlier and had been a backfield coach at Texas A&M, his alma mater. Sam came back as well; he decided not to pursue the Texas Tech possibility.

The Redskins' train left Washington on July 15, a full month earlier than usual, and picked up team members as it made its way westward across the country. The reason for the early start was an exhibition schedule of seven games instead of the usual five or six. After two preseason contests on the West Coast, the team would swing through Amarillo, Birmingham, Shreveport, and Kansas City en route to the season opener in Detroit.

The players grumbled. They cursed Marshall. It wasn't so much the long train rides—they rode first-class in sleeper cars and dined well—but they hated not being paid to play. And they didn't like all the incidental expenses they incurred on the road. But though they weren't getting paid, they knew as well as Marshall did that it was important to win exhibition games. How well they performed in the six preseason games would determine how many season tickets the Redskins sold.

At Occidental, the squad held a team meeting and nominated Sam, Al DeMao, and Bill Dudley to present the team's grievances to Marshall. The players wanted just twenty-five dollars a game. The trio trooped into Marshall's Occidental office and found the owner and general manager going over some papers. Sam, the elder statesman, had been elected spokesman. He cleared his throat.

"Mr. Marshall," he said, "we're here as a players' committee to talk to you about . . ." That was as far as he got.

"Committees! Unions!" he erupted. "I don't know them! I don't recognize them! He stormed out of the office.

The players looked at each other. "Now there's a gentleman for you," Sam muttered. "Won't even listen to what we have to say."

Sam turned to McCann. "Hang tight," the general manager said. He went looking for Marshall.

He came back a few minutes later with a glowering owner, who agreed to at least hear them out. Sam went through the team's list of grievances. If not exhibition-game pay, he concluded, maybe they would settle for a little "chawin' tabacca money."

Marshall didn't hesitate. "We're not going to give you a thing," he replied quietly. The emissaries trooped out of his presence.

After practice that day, Marshall drove his Cadillac onto the field, stepped out, and asked his players to gather around.

"I understand you've been doing a lot of complaining," he said. "You think the Bears and the Lions are getting exhibition pay. I tell you they are not. And you're not going to get it either. And you're not going to get any expense money.

"If any of you don't like it"—he paused dramatically and pointed toward the stadium gate—"that's the way out of here."

With that, he stepped into his car and was driven away, leaving behind an angry, sullen group of young men.

"I don't know what he would have done if we didn't go on with practice," DeMao recalled. "But no one made a move to leave, and we started practicing, and we were back to where we had been."

The Redskins played their first two exhibition games on the West Coast, losing both by large margins, and then headed to Amarillo and Birmingham. Coincidentally, each of the three emissaries had arranged with Marshall to skip the Amarillo game and rejoin the team in Birmingham. When the rest of the team discovered the three were missing, they jumped to the conclusion that their esteemed teammates had sold out in exchange for the week off. When Baugh, DeMao, and Dudley reported to the Vulcan Motel in Birmingham, they were greeted with a sheet-sized sign draped over the balcony: "Welcome Back, Committee."

It took pretty much the whole exhibition season for the three committeemen to convince their teammates that they had not sold out, that each had independently arranged the week off before signing his contract.

Harmony was restored before the season opener, but harmony didn't guarantee victory, as Coach Ball had suspected in August. "The team so far appears to me to be a disappointment," he wrote the home office. "I had hoped we would have a fair one, but it looks like we have a rinky-dink set of backs to play defense with. So you had better light all the candles . . . and 'enjoy the lull before the storm.'"

The storm blew in as soon as the regular season began. Detroit devastated the Skins 35–17. The Giants beat them 35–14. The team traveled to Cleveland, where they were humiliated by the Browns 45–0. That was enough for Marshall. He fired Ball and replaced him with the backfield coach and fan favorite Dick Todd. Under Todd, the Redskins won five games and lost four; their overall record of 5–7 left them six full games behind the conference champion, Cleveland.

I n 1952, the Redskins were finally ready to make a change at quarterback. The last time someone other than the tall Texan had held the starting job for an entire season, the franchise had been located in Boston. At TCU, five-foot-seven-inch Davey O'Brien, an eventual Heisman Trophy winner, had replaced Sam; in Washington, five-foot-seven-inch Eddie LeBaron was set to take the reins. The Californian would go on to have a stellar career with the Redskins, despite playing on mediocre teams.

Todd was back as head coach, but not for long. He had been a great athlete, but he didn't know how to handle people. Defensive back Billy Cox recalled him ripping into his players in the dressing room before a game with the Chicago Cardinals. Finishing his rant, he started to walk toward the door, ready to lead his team onto the field. Suddenly, he noticed that none of his players were following. He turned back around. "What do you guys think you're doing?" he yelled.

"I don't know if we've got any energy left," Sam told his old friend and former teammate. "You worked us all week like it was the first week of camp, we're all tired and you're giving us a hard time." (That's how Cox remembered the quote for publication; knowing Sam, it was no doubt saltier than that.)

The coach and his quarterback stared at each other. Todd was so angry he could hardly speak. "Do you guys intend to play or what?" he finally said.

Nobody said anything. Sam looked into the faces of his teammates. "Guys, you want to play?" he drawled.

Realizing that Sam himself intended to play, they stood up and followed their leader onto the field.

After two preseason losses to the Rams and 49ers, it was Todd who walked out—in the middle of a game—and headed back to West Texas.

"He just got upset about something, but he never said anything to us," LeBaron recalled. "Just sent us out to the field for the second half, and then went home. And he never came back."

None of the Redskins minded, although they wondered what Marshall was thinking when he quickly hired Earl Louis "Curly" Lambeau, an NFL legend. A Green Bay native, Lambeau had founded, played for, and coached the Packers. In fact, he had controlled the Packers from 1919, two years before the team joined the NFL, until 1950, when he lost control of the team and was forced to resign. Before joining the Redskins, he had been head coach of the Chicago Cardinals for two years, finishing fifth in the American Conference in 1950 and last in 1951.

He had coached in the NFL for thirty-one consecutive seasons, longer even than George Halas, and had won six world championships, and yet fans and sportswriters wondered why Marshall ever imagined he and the Green Bay legend could get along. If there was anyone in the NFL as arrogant and temperamental as the Redskins' owner, it was the Packers' founder. He was known as a tough disciplinarian, the type of coach most players preferred, but he also could be abusive and unreasonable.

Lambeau expected LeBaron to take over from Sam, but not just yet. LeBaron was in no hurry. He realized he had the privilege of understudying a legend.

"The guy was in his sixteenth NFL season," he recalled, "and he was amazing. He was the best thrower I ever saw. He was very fluid, and he could throw overhand, sidearm, off balance, and hit a guy on the run wherever he wanted to. It was incredible—here was this guy winding down at the end of his career, and he was phenomenal."

Despite injuries to key players during the exhibition season—including Charlie Justice—and the loss of three starters to the military draft, the Redskins got off to a good start in their season opener with the Cardinals in Chicago.

At one point in the first half, Sam completed eleven straight passes, despite blitzes time and again by the frustrated Cardinals. Just as they got to the Redskin quarterback, he would get the ball off. They would pound him into the ground, but then all they could do was turn and watch the ball settle into the arms of a receiver downfield. It was uncanny—and for the Cardinals, infuriating.

Don Joyce, Chicago's 250-pound tackle, couldn't take it anymore. On the tenth pass, he barreled into Sam and slammed the skinny quarterback into the turf. The venerable Sam got up slowly.

On the eleventh pass, Joyce hit him again—a little late, Sam believed. The veteran quarterback got to his feet, and then, for the first time in his career, threw a punch. It landed squarely on the big tackle's nose. Joyce moved in and started swinging, but officials separated the two men before additional punches landed. Both were ejected. It was the first and only time in Sam's long career that he was ever thrown out of a game.

The Redskins went on to defeat the Cards 23–7, but the opening victory, unfortunately, was one of the few high points of Sam's last season. He spent more time coaching than playing throughout the year as Gilmer and LeBaron took over quarterbacking duties in loss after loss.

Dropping eight of their next nine games, the Redskins were disorganized and depressed. Morale was low. Lambeau didn't help the situation when he berated players in the dressing room, accusing several of dogging it. Once he blasted LeBaron in front of the whole team, blaming the gritty little quarterback for a miscall that cost the Redskins a close game.

Marshall, too, was angry and frustrated. One Sunday afternoon after yet another close loss, the team sat on the locker room benches, not saying much as they stripped off their soggy equipment and shuffled to the showers. One of the Redskins cracked a joke, and those sitting around him laughed—just as the owner strode into the room.

"What's so funny?" he snarled. "I didn't see anything funny today. If I catch anyone so much as smirking after a bad game, it'll be a $50 fine." He started to walk out and then had a second thought. "For you, Baugh," he said, "it'll be a hundred."

"Next to an explanation of why the Redskins fold in the fourth quarter, the biggest mystery concerning the local pros this year has been sparing use of Sammy Baugh," Jack Walsh of the *Washington Post* wrote toward the end of November. Walsh noted that after Sam's spectacular start against the Cardinals, he hurt his hand and played sparingly for the next few games, but even when the hand was healed, he stayed on the bench, "seeing full-time action only as backfield coach and classroom tutor to Eddie LeBaron, heir apparent."

Walsh couldn't get a straight answer from the Redskins. "I have no objection to Baugh playing," Marshall told him. "The fact that he hasn't been has been through no design of mine. The decision is up to Curly Lambeau." "You can't order a 38-year-old man to get out there and play," Lambeau said, "If Sam feels that he's ready, all he has to do is tell me." Sam said he was ready to go—"but I just can't walk on the field on my own."

In one game toward the end of the long losing streak, Marshall rang up running back Andy Davis, who was handling the sideline phone while out with an injury. "Give me Sam," the owner demanded. Davis handed the phone to player-coach Baugh.

"Put Brito in as defensive end," Marshall commanded. Sam tapped Brito and sent him in. When Lambeau saw number 80 running onto the field, he wheeled and strode to the bench.

"Who put him in?" he demanded to know.

"I did," Sam said. "Mr. Marshall's on the line and he . . ."

"Marshall's not running this team. I am," Lambeau muttered and ripped the phone lines loose. The veteran coach would hang on to his job for one more season.

The Redskins finally won again in their eleventh game. LeBaron threw four touchdown passes to Bones Taylor as Washington topped the Giants 27–17.

A nd then it was over. The last game of the season was meaningless as far as the standings were concerned, but it was a big game nevertheless. It was George Marshall's Santa Claus Day and, more importantly, the last time Slingin' Sammy Baugh would ever appear in a Redskins uniform. Some 22,000 fans trooped into Griffith Stadium to bid farewell to the greatest Redskin of them all.

"The Redskins aren't just losing a player today," the *Post*'s Walsh noted. "Sammy Baugh is an institution—in Washington and in football. . . . Aside from Babe Ruth, it's doubtful if another athlete of Baugh's stature ever won so much genuine personal popularity."

Walsh talked to Wayne Millner, the outstanding receiver who caught crucial passes in the '37 championship game. "Baugh was the greatest passer of them all," he said. "All you had to do with Sam pitching was make your fake, take two steps and the ball was always right there." Millner talked about his friend's punting, his defensive prowess.

> I remember that title game in 1937 for one thing above all—Baugh stopping Bronko Nagurski. A few times Bronko got in the clear and Sam was the only man between him and our goal. But Sammy made the tackles.
>
> I was just looking at some movies of a 1945 game with the Giants. Even after eight seasons, my boy Baugh was still looking good as a pass intercepter. He grabbed one near our goal and ran 80 yards or so before he finally was brought down. And at midfield he pulled a fake that made Mel Hein look silly.

He talked about how Sam never criticized his teammates when they made a mistake.

> I recall one vital Bears game when I was all alone in the end zone but dropped a perfect pass from Sam. When we got back in the huddle, Baugh said, "Forget that one, Wayne. Anybody can drop one." Two plays later, he threw me

another and that time it meant six points. Sam was always that way with a guy who missed a tackle or block. "Get 'im next time," was all he'd ever say.

LeBaron told the *Post* the same thing: "He's been wonderful to me. More than just teaching me the tricks of the trade, many a time Sammy picked me up when I felt low. Remember that third-down pass call in the 49er game when my throw was intercepted and we lost our one-point lead and the ball game? Baugh just told me to forget it, he once did the same thing himself."

Shirley Povich, the *Post* sportswriter whose illustrious career had evolved in tandem with Sam's, noted that in his sixteen years with the Redskins, the tall Texan "had never learned how to act like a big shot." He also recalled Sam's definition of a forward passer's greatest asset: "two big, fast ends, each with a nice pair of hands."

"Without a doubt, Baugh is the most popular man in football," fullback George Buksar told the *Post*. "Guess the only exception is Don Joyce, that clown from the Chicago Cards who took the poke at Sammy in our opening game."

According to Walsh, Sam was the only player who ever asked to have his salary cut. He did it twice. "After all Baugh did for the Redskins and for pro football, Marshall never would have cut him voluntarily," Walsh wrote. "But Sam is the kind of guy who felt that he was getting more for his past reputation than his current performance. He didn't approve of that."

Marshall told the *Post* reporter he wasn't surprised. "Baugh not only has been a great athlete," the owner said. "His approach to professional sport always has been intelligent. He never was gouging. Sam seemed to sense that what was good for the business office was good for him in the long run."

Sam may have had other ideas about his dealings with Marshall and the front office, but, as the owner noted, the two never had any serious difficulties over salary or anything else.

His biggest problem with his star quarterback, Marshall told Walsh, was getting him to cart off all the trophies, plaques, and other awards he had accumulated through the years. "Finally I had to have a serious talk with him and sort it out, making him save the things he really should save," Marshall said. "About the only way I could do it was to impress upon him that he owed it to those children of his. . . . They should have tangible evidence of the greatness of their father—particularly those four boys of his. Yes, and the baby girl, too. Baugh's name will live forever in football."

Walsh calculated that the Redskins had paid Sam more than $200,000 during his sixteen years with the team. "From movie and personal appearances, advertising testimonials and sale of sporting goods with his name, he may have equaled that amount." ("Half went to Texas, half to taxes," Sam liked to say.) "With all the fame and wealth he has acquired," Walsh concluded, "Sammy Baugh hasn't changed a bit. That's why, even if all his football records are broken, another one like Baugh may never come along."

A *Post* photograph that ran on game day shows a smiling Sam at his locker about to don the burgundy-colored number 33 jersey for the last time. He was still a slender guy, still dark haired, his long arms lacking the striated musculature of modern athletes.

Those arms are perhaps a clue to his popularity. Despite his immense athletic talents and his record-setting accomplishments, Sam was an average guy who happened to do things uncommonly well. Fans knew and didn't begrudge the fact that he made a decent salary; they also knew that, like most professional athletes of his era, he was a workingman who breathed the same air as everyone else. Long before the distorting effect of immense money and acclaim in professional sports, Sam was accessible, approachable. As Joe Tereshinski remarked, "You'd never know he was Sammy Baugh."

Also in that photo, Sam is wearing a pair of flimsy shoulder pads that look as though they belonged to a kid playing in a Pop Warner league. He liked them because they allowed him freedom of movement to pass, but he also had to wear them on defense when he lowered his shoulder to bring down Bronko Nagurski and other punishing ball carriers who had gotten up a full head of steam by the time they got to him in the secondary.

The Redskins calculated that in his sixteen seasons with the team, Sam wore out sixty pairs of shoes, thirty pairs of pants, one hundred jerseys, and seven helmets, and yet he never changed shoulder pads. He was so familiar with the tattered remnants he draped across his shoulders Sunday after Sunday that he gave them a name. He called them Blue Jays.

His last Sunday with the Redskins was anticlimactic. Fans gave him a standing ovation when he ambled onto the field, and the Redskins Band played "Auld Lang Syne," but LeBaron started the game. Sam came on for a series of plays in the first quarter—three plays that netted six yards. With the score tied 14–14 at halftime, Santa Claus made his appearance in a Brink's truck.

Sam had thrown a total of thirty-three passes all season. When the Eagles game ended in victory for the Redskins, 27–21, he still had thrown thirty-three. Fans never got to see him sling one more trademark throw.

His last play as a Redskin was to hold the ball for George Buksar's extra-point attempt with eighteen seconds left in the game. The kick was blocked.

After the final whistle, he was mobbed by about five hundred autograph seekers and spent nearly forty minutes signing programs. Finally, a couple of husky fans hoisted him onto their shoulders and ferried him to the dressing room, where he spent another several minutes posing for photographers.

When he got to his locker, Tereshinski was waiting for him. "I've got the game ball. It's for you, if you want it," he told Sam. Sam seemed embarrassed. "Well, you got it, it's yours," he told Tereshinski, who insisted that Sam take it. "I'd be very happy to have it—and I sure appreciate it," he said.

After a shower and some handshaking among teammates, Sam and Bones Taylor climbed into Sam's station wagon and headed for home. "It was dark then," the *Post*'s Jack Walsh reported.

When it was over, Samuel Adrian Baugh held thirteen NFL records at three positions—quarterback, punter, and defensive back. More than half a century later, his career punting average of 45.1 yards would still rank second all-time in NFL history. He would rank second in NFL history in season completion percentage (70.3), most seasons (four) leading the league in yards gained passing, and most seasons (seven) leading the league in completion percentage.

Sam had gained more than 23,000 yards with his passes, more than thirteen miles. Twice he had thrown six touchdown passes in a game. Against the Giants in 1948, he threw for 446 yards. During six seasons—1937, 1940, 1943, 1945, 1947, and 1949—he was the top passer in the NFL.

"Well, we had somehow got into the habit of associating Mr. Sammy Baugh with the various bronze warriors posted along our diagonal thoroughfares, and with those Vikings—or whatever they are—that stand guard over the interior archways in Union Station," the *Post* editorialized on December 18.

That is to say, Mr. Baugh seemed one of the few fixed points of reference amid the unceasing flux that constitutes the life of this great Capital. . . . He seemed to us both ageless and indestructible, and we took for granted that he would still be here when the children of our children's children were taken out to the stadium to see for themselves how far and how surely a pass could be thrown.

But now Mr. Baugh has gone permanently home to Texas. If we see him again, it will be as one of the nameless who cannot stay with us even for the brief time required in this hot-house climate for the making or remaking of a celebrity. We are thus sadly reminded that Mr. Baugh, for all his amazing durability, is but human and mortal like the rest of us; that though he might longer resist the inexorable march of years, even he could not resist forever . . .

Let us be careful, of course, not to turn our lament for his passing into an elegy. In that less strenuous world into which Mr. Baugh has now transferred himself, he will, despite the 16 years he has given us, be counted a young man, ahead of whom a long and useful life lies waiting. Still, this does not change the fact that we shall never again have opportunity to see one of those wonderful passes; and for that reason Washington—especially in the autumn months—will seem a duller and sadder place.

A RANCHER
COACHING COWBOYS

BAUGH AT HARDIN-SIMMONS UNIVERSITY

For the first dozen or so years of Sam's life as a Texas rancher, he and his fellow stockmen faced a plague almost biblical in its intensity and its consequences. They were in a constant fight for the lives of their animals and for the economic life of their ranching operations. Their tiny and torturous foe was called the screwworm.

Screwworms aren't worms at all. They are fly larvae that take hold in the open wounds of livestock and other animals. They feed on live flesh and weaken the animal until it dies. They can destroy whole herds, drive stockmen out of business. "We'd have to ride the pastures all the time looking for wormies," recalled Sam's neighbor, E. B. "Sonny" Nichols.

Sam and Sonny and their fellow ranchers finally got some relief in the early 1950s when agricultural researchers developed a screwworm-eradication program that brought the scourge under control. But the end of one Job-like vexation only made way for another.

When Sam got back to the ranch for good in the spring of 1953, he faced a foe even more relentless than screwworms, a foe more implacable than the Chicago Bears' defensive line. It was Mother Nature. She had decided that Texas west of the ninety-eighth meridian no longer needed rain.

"Each new generation tends to forget—until it confronts the sobering reality—that dryness has always been the normal condition in the western half of the state," Elmer Kelton, an acclaimed western novelist from San Angelo, once wrote. "Wet years have been the exception."

For seven years in the 1950s, Mother Nature reverted to form. For many West Texans, it was the longest drought in memory, and it left its mark upon their lives and the local culture almost as deeply as the Great Depression had done two decades earlier.

During prolonged dry spells in earlier decades, livestock would literally starve, but by the time Sam started ranching, better roads meant that stockmen could haul in feed or ship their livestock off to market. Still, a number of ranchers went under in the 1950s—largely because, as Sonny Nichols pointed out, "it cost more to haul a cow off than you could get out of it."

For Sam, for West Texas stockmen, and for dryland farmers in general, it was hard to make a living. What made it even harder for Sam was that the Baugh family had grown during the period when he spent six months of each year with the Redskins, away from home. Gary was twelve in 1953; David, ten; and Bruce, seven. The youngest son, Stephen, was four, and the baby of the family, Frances, was two.

Sam's mother, who was divorced, and Mona's mother, a widow, also lived on the ranch, which was the main reason that Mona had to oversee an expansion of the house in the late 1940s—a dormitory-style bedroom for the children and rooms in the original part of the house for the two older women. Both, by the way, were a great help to Mona, particularly while Sam was away, and both had their specialties. As David Baugh recalled, Sam's mother (Mom) tended a garden and did much of the cooking, while Mona's mother (Momo) washed dishes, sewed the children's clothes, and "tried to instill values in us kids."

There were Bible lessons at home, and the family went to church on Sunday. There was no Presbyterian church, so Mona's mother and Mona went to the Methodist church in Rotan, while Sam's mother attended the Baptist church. The two churches were close to each other, and with the windows open in the summer, David recalled, each Sunday-morning service was a battle of the choirs. Sam would go from time to time.

Mona, with Owen Brazee's help, managed the ranch and raised the kids while Sam was away. David remembered his mother's warnings while his father was back East: "If you boys don't quit doing what you're doing, I'm gonna tell your daddy, and he's coming home pretty quick."

"Course, he didn't want to come home and start beating our butts," David said.

Although by every indication the Baugh marriage was a good one, Sam's career and Mona's ranching duties tested the relationship. Toward the end of her life, she told a daughter-in-law: "I had two good years of marriage out of all the years Sam and I have been together." She had in mind those years before the children came along and before Sam bought the ranch.

"Mona was the buffer between Sam and the real world," the daughter-in-law said. Sam lived in a world of games and celebrity; Mona built additions to the ranch house as the family continued to grow. She cooked for the cowboys, helped Owen Brazee with the cattle. And as the children got older, she was the one who hauled them into town for their football and basketball games or other activities, three or four time a week.

Sam coming home when the season was over was a relief for Mona, but it also required a bit of getting used to. He disrupted the routine that Mona and the children had established. The children were used to their mother being both manager and disciplinarian, and "Buddy," as his niece Ellen Stevenson recalled, was naturally easygoing. When Sam came home, his daughter, Frances, recalled, Mona would have the children go to him whenever they wanted something. His response was invariably, "Well, what does your mother say?"

He also was partial to his little girl. Once, when two of the boys were roughhousing and bothering Sam, he told them, "If Frances had come along before you two little farts, you wouldn't even be here."

"He was pretty conservative with his money," recalled Sonny Nichols who first met Sam in the 1940s. "Everything he bought, he paid for."

Still, times were hard during the drought years, and that was the main reason Sam still had his eye on coaching. He didn't want to move away from the ranch and from his family, not even during football season. Nor did he want to give up ranching, despite the hard times, but he needed extra income.

The ideal situation presented itself in the spring of '52, while he was still with the Redskins. Murray Evans, the coach at Hardin-Simmons University, a small Southern Baptist school in Abilene, seventy miles south of the ranch, invited Sam to be an associate coach during spring training, which lasted about twenty days. He was to work with the quarterbacks.

"I won't be on salary," he told the Associated Press. "Hardin Simmons is near my home. It's a West Texas school, and I like that." He added: "I'm with the Redskins. That's my primary obligation."

Evans called him again in the spring of '53, after Sam had retired. "I got to thinking about it, and I realized I really wasn't ready to get out of football—and I had always kind of thought about coaching anyway," he told Whit Canning. "So they hired me as an assistant coach."

Not only did he enjoy coaching, but also he had an inventive football mind. "I called plays in college and all the time in pro ball," he told the sports columnist Frank Luksa. "The quarterback did in those days. We didn't get much help from the sideline. When someone asks me what's the best thing I got out of football, the most satisfying thing was beating the defense. I enjoyed that part of it."

He would need all the inventiveness he could muster while coaching at Hardin-Simmons. In 1955, the school—enrollment 1,400—decided it wanted to play with the big boys, and its president and its athletic director approached Sam. On February 2, 1955, "the gangling guy from Sweetwater," as the Associated Press called him, signed a five-year contract to coach the Cowboys, "an aggregation sometimes strong and always colorful."

> HSU officials said they thought it was Baugh's great love of football, not any financial gain, that brought about his decision to take the job. Only pressure from the athletic committee persuaded him, Baugh said, adding that he had been offered better salaried coaching jobs in the past.

The fact that he could spend most of his time at the ranch was probably the deciding factor. "It was a pretty good deal, really," Sam recalled. "It was only an hour and 10 minutes from the ranch, so I could be the head coach and still commute, and I could keep an eye on things at the ranch."

He hired his old Redskins buddy Wayne Millner as an assistant coach. The two men shared an apartment in Abilene during football season, and Sam headed home to the ranch whenever he could.

Shortly after Sam was hired, Hardin-Simmons president Evan Reiff called him in and explained that the athletic program was running a deficit. One way to fix that problem, Reiff explained, was for Sam to schedule nonconference games with Southwest Conference schools and with football powerhouses around the country, schools that would pay large sums of money for Hardin-Simmons to play them. They would all be away games for the Cowboys, who could expect to win about as often as the Washington Generals beat the Harlem Globetrotters.

Sam did as he was instructed. He scheduled Baylor, Tulsa, and Cincinnati the first year. The next year, he scheduled Southwest Conference powerhouse Arkansas, as well as Wichita State, George Washington University, and the College of the Pacific. In 1958, he scheduled seven away games and only three home games. Opponents included Baylor, Tulsa, Ole Miss, and LSU, the eventual national champion.

One of three small denominational schools in Abilene—along with the Church of Christ–run Abilene Christian College (now Abilene Christian University) and the Methodist-sponsored McMurry College (now McMurry University)—Hardin-Simmons at the time was a member of the Border Conference. Competing against Arizona State, Arizona, New Mexico, New Mexico A&M (now New Mexico State), Texas Western (now the University of Texas–El Paso), and their archrival, Texas Tech, the Cowboys more than held their own. They won several conference championships, and the Southwest Conference considered inviting them to join. In 1956, the year Texas Tech became a member of the Southwest Conference, the Cowboys beat the Red Raiders 41–14 in the last game of the year. Still, the jump from small-college powerhouse to matching up with the likes of LSU and Ole Miss was a formidable challenge—for a rookie coach or anyone else.

Almost every Saturday during the fall, Sam and his Cowboys would pile onto a chartered bus or climb aboard a Braniff Airways plane and head off to a distant stadium, where, for the money, they were expected to be sacrificial lambs for bigger, stronger football powers. "The money may have been great, but the won-loss records suffered," said Jimmie Keeling, who coached the Cowboys decades later.

In Sam's head-coaching debut, the Cowboys lost 35–7 to a good Baylor team that would eventually defeat second-ranked Tennessee in the Sugar Bowl. They lost the next game to the Tulsa Golden Hurricane 41–7 before finally winning a game, defeating New Mexico A&M 39–0. They beat North Texas State Teachers College 30–19 and West Texas State Teachers College before losing badly to Arizona State, 60–14. They beat Texas Western 23–21, lost to Cincinnati 55–20, and beat Trinity 14–0.

In the final game of the season, against Texas Tech, Sam and his players were well aware of the 61–19 mauling the Red Raiders had administered the year before. Although the Cowboys came into the game with a losing record, they still were in contention for the Border Conference championship; they had to defeat the Red Raiders to stay in the running.

It didn't happen. Trailing 16–14 late in the fourth quarter, Cowboys backup quarterback John Lyle tossed a screen pass to fullback K. Y. Owens, who rumbled fifty-three yards for the apparent winning touchdown. Back upfield, though, a red flag rested atop the grass. The Cowboys were offside, the referee ruled, thus nullifying the play.

The Cowboys were 5-5 in '55, and Sam's quarterback, Ken Ford, ranked sixth in the nation in passing.

Sam, not surprisingly, believed in the forward pass. "His offense was light years ahead of everybody else," recalled his son David, a football coach himself. "It was a pro attack, the same offense he had mastered under Dutch Meyer at TCU."

"We could move the ball against anybody," Pete Hart recalled. Hart, Sam's fullback, had grown up in Swenson, Texas, a West Texas town so small it was said to have "two stores, two whores and two blacksmith shops." Hart had known Sam since he was a kid. His grandfather owned a ranch near Sam's, and Pete had worked cattle with him. In later years, Sam would say that the two toughest guys he ever coached, college or pros, were Walt Garrison, the rodeo bull rider who played at Oklahoma State and later became an all-pro running back for the Dallas Cowboys, and Hart, an undersized fullback on offense and cornerback on defense.

Sam, even more than his team, was a draw on the road. People paid to see the legendary quarterback. During pregame warm-ups, he would take off his boots, his tie, and his little snap-brim hat, pull on some coaching shoes, and go out on the field and throw passes to his receivers. Before an HSU game against Ole Miss one year, Coach Johnny Vaught called his quarterback over and had him stand and watch the greatest passer who ever lived.

In 1956, he brought his Cowboys into Washington's Griffith Stadium for the team's third game of the year and put on a passing exhibition of his own before the matchup with George Washington.

"The former Mr. Redskin has delighted crowds at the Cowboys' games this season against Arkansas and Wichita with his informal passing shows," the *Washington Post* reported.

The West Texans suffered a disappointing 13–7 loss to GWU, although later in the year, the Cowboys upset the nationally ranked College of the Pacific 20–19. The final game of the '56 season, as usual, was with Texas Tech. After trailing 14–0, the Cowboys unleashed a high-flying offensive attack that scored forty-one unanswered points, and the Red Raiders departed the Border Conference for the Southwest Conference on an ignominious note. Hardin-Simmons finished the year with a record of 4-6.

In 1957, quarterback Ford, under Sam's tutelage, completed 105 of 205 passes for 1,254 yards, making him the most prolific passer in the nation. The Cowboys finished the season with a record of 4-5-1 and third place in the Border Conference.

Ford was also a punter, and he and Sam would stage punting duels after practice. Hart recalled watching them kick back and forth to each other, both of them able to kick the ball seventy yards in the air. "For Sam, it was always a perfect spiral, with the ball hitting the ground so it would roll end over end," Hart remembered.

Sam was a good coach, his former players recall, although he treated football as a game, not as a holy crusade. "He didn't have lectures and meetings at all," Hart recalled. "He did his coaching on the field. We scrimmaged a lot, and Sam loved to get in the huddle and call the plays." They called him "Sam," Hart remembered. "The boys loved him."

Before practice during the week, the players would dispatch a freshman to the field house to see whether the golf clubs Sam kept in the back of his pickup truck were missing. If the clubs weren't there, that meant practice would be starting a bit later than usual and players could lounge around the dorm a bit longer.

His players still tell stories about him, including the time chapel—the name for regular devotionals on campus—was being held on a weekday morning in Rose Field House, where the coaches had their offices.

Chapel was being held in the field house because the on-campus church building where it usually was held had burned. As Hart recalled, he was lying on his bed in his dorm room one morning and happened to look out the window and see smoke pouring from the steepled structure. He turned on KRBC-AM radio about the same time and heard a local disc jockey named Slim Willet (best known as the man who wrote the country hit "Don't Let the Stars Get in Your Eyes") announce that the chapel was burning. Hart's first thought was that he and his fellow students would no longer have to go to required chapel every Monday, Wednesday, and Friday.

That didn't happen. The college moved the services to Rose Field House, the basketball arena where all the coaches had their offices. In the middle of the chapel sermon one morning, students heard a loud voice from one of the offices exclaim, "How in the hell can you keep the goddamn double-six in your hand!" It was their gloriously profane head football coach, of course, whose outburst over a game of dominoes shocked the assembled Baptists. Chapel was dismissed. "Hey Coach," Hart and his teammates joked that afternoon, "we want you to play dominoes every day during chapel—and lose."

"He probably didn't worry about some of the things coaching that other coaches worry about," said Coach Keeling, who met Sam in the 1950s.

"You always got to have some rules," Sam told an oral historian in 1971. "I've always thought the fewer rules you had, the better off you were. But you had to have some rules." The interviewer asked him about players with long hair. "I wouldn't put in a rule I couldn't live with," he said. "I don't believe in making trouble for yourself."

Keeling, who coached the Cowboys years after the school had dropped football for decades and then revived it, remembered meeting Sam at Hardin-Simmons. "He was playing dominoes with some guys, and he had a big tape can to spit in," Keeling recalled. "He was relaxed. I remember later that day he went out and started throwing and catching with some guys. He was just Sam. Sam was country."

Years later, Sam called his stint at Hardin-Simmons "the best goddamn job I ever had."

Sam's most memorable game was in 1958 when the Cowboys boarded a plane and flew to Baton Rouge, Louisiana, where, outmanned and out-weighed, they were slated to be raw meat for the LSU Tigers, who would go on to be national champions that year. The Cowboys, who had lost to Baylor the week before, 14–7, were nineteen-point underdogs. About the only similarity between the two teams were their school colors: both wore purple and gold.

Tiger Stadium was one of the toughest places in the nation for visiting teams to play because of the ceaseless roar raised by howling Tigers fans. Hart recalled coming out of the dressing room and having to jog past a circus trailer, and inside that trailer was a fearsome Bengal tiger. "It was a beautiful night for football," he recalled more than a half century later. "We stayed right with 'em."

As Sam recalled, about the only advantage the Cowboys had on that steamy evening in Baton Rouge was that the defending national champions wouldn't be all that worried about "little ol' Hardin-Simmons."

"We knew they were going to run over us," Sam said in an interview years later, recalling that LSU boasted two of the best running backs in the nation, Billy Cannon and Johnny Robinson, "so we prepared to keep from losing, to keep the ball away from them." To do this, "the scheme was to pass for eight yards on first down, then try to run twice for a first down against a fearsome defense known as the 'Chinese Bandits.'"

The Cowboys couldn't throw shorter passes on first down, Sam recalled, because his offense usually couldn't gain the couple of yards needed on second and third downs.

The scheme worked pretty well once the Cowboys got the ball. Unfortunately, the Tigers had it first. On LSU's first series, quarterback Warren Rabb—whose father had died after a long illness that morning—ran in a quarterback keeper for a touchdown from the two after a sixty-five-yard drive. The next time the Tigers got the ball, backup quarterback Durel Matherne scored from the four.

After the kickoff, the Cowboys took over on their own five. Relying on the pass, they put together a ninety-five-yard scoring drive, the longest of the year against the vaunted "Chinese Bandits." The Cowboys missed the extra point.

With less than two minutes to play before the half, Hardin-Simmons punted, but the play was called back because the Cowboys' upback, according to the rules of the time, was too close to the line of scrimmage. On the do-over, the Cowboys' center snapped the ball over the head of the punter, and the Tigers recovered on the Cowboys eleven. On the next play, Cannon powered his way into the end zone.

The 20–6 halftime score was in jeopardy throughout the second half as the Cowboys controlled the ball and stayed in Tigers territory for most of the thirty minutes. Once, the Cowboys drove to the two. Hart, exhausted, came out for a breather, and his replacement lost a fumble. On the next Cowboys series, Hardin-Simmons advanced to the Tigers eleven before a fourth-down pass fell incomplete.

Even though the game ended 20–6, the big bad Tigers knew they had been in a war. The Cowboys ran eighty-six plays, compared to fifty-nine for LSU. Cowboys quarterbacks completed nineteen passes in thirty-four attempts for 201 yards. LSU coach Paul Dietzel noted that the Cowboys outgained his Tigers 328 yards to 292. "I'm not sure we ever did stop them," he said.

Years later, Sam recalled that during the off-season, he got a call from one of the LSU assistants. "I just thought you'd like to know we've been looking at the film from last year's games, and you controlled the ball on us better than anyone else we played," the coach said. "I thought you ought to tell your boys."

"I was never prouder," Sam said.

Despite the LSU loss, 1958 turned out to be a good year for Sam and his Cowboys. Playing not only LSU, but also Baylor, Ole Miss, and nationally ranked Arkansas, Hardin-Simmons compiled a 6-4 regular-season record and won the Border Conference championship. In the 1959 Sun Bowl, the Cowboys lost to the Cowboys of the University of Wyoming 14–6.

Sam coached the Cowboys for one more year, posting the worst record of his tenure at the Abilene school. "Sam was one of the finest persons I've ever known," Hart said. "The only thing I'll ever criticize him for is I think he knew he was leaving that last year and he wasn't much into recruiting."

The Cowboys were 3-7 in 1959 and finished in next-to-last place in the Border Conference. Sam resigned at the end of the year to take a position in one of the unlikeliest places imaginable for a country boy from West Texas.

BACK TO THE PROS

COACHING THE TITANS AND THE OILERS

"I stayed in that Manhattan hotel right in the middle of New York, and I was miserable the whole time," Sam once told an oral historian. "That's just not a life, as far as I'm concerned."

The reason Sam was in New York in 1960 and not home on the West Texas range was because of a telephone call he received after the 1959 season from the man who had been the Redskins' radio announcer during Sam's playing days and who also owned 25 percent of the team.

Harry Wismer, a native of Port Huron, Michigan, was short, volatile, and fast talking, the opposite of Sam in almost every way. He had been a multisport star in high school and had played football at both the University of Florida and Michigan State University before severely injuring a knee in a game against the University of Michigan. He then began broadcasting Michigan State sports on the school radio station, and in 1934 was hired as the public-address announcer for the Detroit Lions. He also owned stock in the Lions, thanks to his first wife, a daughter of the Ford family. (He later was married to the widow of Abner "Longie" Zwillman, an early Prohibition gangster who was known as the "Al Capone of New Jersey.")

Wismer was a go-getter, whatever his other faults. In the late 1940s, he was the announcer for a number of 16 mm college football films. He would add the commentary a day or so after the games were over, spicing up the faux play-by-play with crowd noise, referee whistles, and other sound effects.

After George Preston Marshall discovered Wismer doing a radio sports show in Detroit, he hired him to broadcast Redskins games.

"Wismer took considerable license with his job as the Redskins announcer, often criticizing the team's head coach, as well as any players whose play made Wismer, the part owner, unhappy," the former *Washington Post* reporter Morris Siegel wrote in *Regardie's Magazine*. "To this day, I am sure that he helped cost several coaches—whom he harshly rebuked on the air—their jobs.

"About the lone exception to his free advice," Siegel recalled, "was legendary quarterback Sammy Baugh, who was error-proof as far as Wismer was concerned. It was never Baugh's fault when he was intercepted. (Remember, these were the days before television, and Wismer's word was gospel.) Baugh's receivers either ran the wrong route or dropped a perfect pass, he would tell his listeners."

Siegel recalled that Wismer also broadcast Notre Dame games on Saturdays, and was involved in an early effort to expand football into prime-time network television. ABC would broadcast a replay on Sunday nights of the previous day's Notre Dame games, which were cut down to seventy-five minutes by editing out time between plays, halftime, and uneventful plays. Seventeen years later, ABC's *Monday Night Football* took Wismer's idea and made it work.

"Between the Irish and the Redskins, he must have set some kind of world record for name-dropping," Siegel wrote.

A slightly paraphrased imitation of Wismer's penchant for introducing every celebrity, near-celebrity and friend of his at the game goes like this: "Baugh fades to pass, he looks—and sitting there in his box watching the Redskins game is General So-and-So, along with Vice Admiral and Mrs. Whatchacallem. Also in their box is Paul Cadillac and his lovely wife. Paul is the chairman of the board of General Motors."

Only after Wismer had finished rattling off the names would he allow Baugh to complete his pass. Coincidentally, most of the people whom Wismer would introduce, whether they happened to be in the ballpark that day or not, were associated with firms that sponsored Redskins games.

Although he was a vice president of the Redskins and a 25 percent owner, Wismer eventually ran afoul of Marshall. The loud-mouthed announcer got a little too free with his advice about how the team ought to be run, which irritated the Redskins' potentate, particularly after Wismer began criticizing him for not signing black players. Marshall bought him out.

After more than twenty years as a broadcaster and publicist, Wismer hooked up with Lamar Hunt, the fabulously wealthy Dallas oilman who had been rebuffed by the NFL when he sought a franchise for his hometown. In 1959, Hunt responded by forming the American Football League, which competed directly with the NFL for players and fans.

Wismer became president of the New York Titans, one of the six original AFL franchises. The league began play in 1960, with the Titans, Boston, Buffalo, and Houston in the East Division, and Dallas, Denver, Los Angeles, and Oakland in the West.

Whereas Sam had respected "Mr. Marshall" without necessarily liking him, he found Wismer almost unbearable. "Harry was one of those guys who seemed to go out of his way to be his own worst enemy," Sam recalled.

> Frequently, you'd see Harry doing things an ordinary man doesn't need to be doing.
>
> He was always big-doggin' it. He was the kind of guy who would walk into a restaurant and yell at somebody on the other side of the room, just so everyone would turn around and look at him.

Striving to be known as a convivial man about town, he invariably greeted friends and strangers alike with a hearty "congratulations!" "I always say congratulations," he told the *New York Times*. "It makes people feel good. Congratulations can mean anything. It rings a note. It's wonderful, and it's a great opening line. Congratulations."

No doubt that was his first word when he called Sam, who was raising cattle, rearing kids, and roping calves at small-town rodeos throughout West Texas when he got Wismer's call from the Big Apple.

He was calling to offer Sam $28,000 a year to come to New York and coach his new team. Sam was agreeable to the offer, mainly because the money sounded good, but he also knew Wismer. The West Texan insisted that he get his money up front. The Titans' owner agreed.

Despite the money, Sam knew almost from the beginning that taking the job was a mistake. The day Wismer introduced his new coach to the media, he had a three-piece western swing band play "The Yellow Rose of Texas" while Sam, no doubt recalling an earlier egomaniacal owner, stood off to the side in a cowboy hat and bandana. "Going up to New York," he said in later years, "was the dumbest thing I ever did."

Wismer squabbled with everyone, eventually failed to meet his payroll, and got to where he would deal with his coach only through intermediaries. "That was one of those things that was just a bad deal from the start," Sam told Whit Canning. "In the beginning we all thought Harry owned the team, but actually he had no one backing him up. We started losing money fast, and he couldn't cover it."

The Titans played in the Polo Grounds, by then a rat-infested dump. "It was two steps down to the dressing room at the Polo Grounds . . . and the water on the floor was up to the top step after one of those games," recalled a reporter who covered the Titans. "The Polo Grounds had been closed for two years since the New York Giants baseball team went west, and goodness knows what was in that water."

Don Maynard, who had played at Yankee Stadium when he was with the Giants, compared playing in the Polo Grounds to "going from the Taj Mahal to the Kings Inn Motel in Paris, Texas—and if you've ever been there, then you know, it's not good."

In one of the first Titans games, Sam led his team into the locker room and encountered two young men making a powerful racket beating on trash-can lids. "What the hell are y'all doing?" he asked. One of the guys told him: "Mr. Wismer came down here and told us to beat on these lids to scare the rats out."

Wismer would announce a paid attendance at games of thirty thousand; maybe ten thousand, at best, would be rattling around in the huge former home of the dearly departed New York Giants. A reporter named Warren Pack wrote that half the fans who attended the Titans' first game came "disguised as empty seats."

A reporter asked Sam about not having playbooks for the team. "If you're gonna have a playbook, the first thing you gotta have is paper," Sam told him.

Wismer was insufferable. "He was always coming into the dressing room trying to give us a pep talk that nobody ever listened to," Sam recalled. "It was embarrassing just to be around him, and before long a lot of people started hating him."

Despite the hardships, Sam gave the challenge his best shot. "We're going to have a real team," he told the *New York Times* in the spring of 1960. "We'll start training up in New Hampshire with about 70 boys, none of whose names, probably, are known to the general public. But what's in a name?

Give me boys like we have signed, most of them 200 pounds and over and most of them quick, and I'll have a football team."

The first player to sign a contract was Don Maynard, a rail-thin Texan from Colorado City who had played for the Giants and then spent a year in the Canadian Football League. Sam had seen the free-agent flanker play at Texas Western, had coached him in the Senior Bowl in Mobile, and was impressed with his speed and pass-catching ability.

Maynard, who wore long sideburns and boots and who would go on to be an all-pro with the New York Jets, the successor team to the Titans, was almost as colorful as his coach. "When the AFL was founded, I was the first player signed by the Titans," he recalled. "I remember Sammy saying, 'I know who I want to sign. He beat me three years in college.' I was excited to play for Sammy, because I knew he wanted to throw the ball."

Maynard recalled Hardin-Simmons beating Texas Western in 1955, and the Miners turning the tables the next year. During his third year, Maynard and the Miners played the Cowboys in Abilene and were leading 21–20 late in the game. "Then they line up to kick a field goal," he recalled forty-four years later, "and the kick hits the left tackle in the butt, goes up in the air, lands on the crossbar and falls over and they win, 23–21."

Maynard was thrilled to play for Sam. Even if the Giants had called him back, he said, he would have stayed with the Titans because of Sam. "As far as I'm concerned, Baugh isn't just one of the greatest quarterbacks to ever play the game, he's also one of the greatest coaches," Maynard said years later. "It's like my Titans teammate Larry Granthan once said about him: he could draw up better plays in the dirt than most coaches could on a blackboard. Both on and off the field, he was one of the fairest people in the world, and I consider it a great thrill and honor to be able to say that I played for him, from Alabama to New York City."

Maynard and the Titans had the makings of a pretty good team. "I don't mean to give the impression that the Titans, in their first year, will be the greatest football team ever organized," Sam told the *Times*. "We'll have to build and experiment and change. But we'll have a football team at the start that'll be worth watching."

Ten weeks later, twenty-six young men arrived on the campus of the University of New Hampshire in Durham, New Hampshire, after a seven-and-a-half-hour bus ride from New York City. They were the first of 103 players the new team had invited to training camp. Only thirty-three would make the team.

"It's better this way," said Sam, who also rode the bus north. "Some of these boys will be eating dirt from the first day, but they won't quit. Then you have to tell them, and some go away and cry." The upstart Titans got no respect, Maynard recalled. "To reporters, the Titans were a joke, Wismer was just a drunk, Sammy was just a faded star and I was still just the world's greatest fumbler," he recalled. "Well, we'd see about that."

Sam's Titans made their debut at the Polo Grounds on September 11, 1960. They beat Buffalo in the rain, 27–3, before a crowd of 10,250 (5,727 paid).

The team was moderately successful that maiden year, playing what Maynard described as "runnin', gunnin', and high-flyin' football, the likes of which you couldn't find anywhere else." It was, of course, Sam Baugh's kind of football.

Quarterback Al Dorow turned out to be a real find—although he was Wismer's find, not Sam's, who wanted to go with his former Hardin-Simmons passing wizard, Ken "Model T" Ford. Wismer insisted that Sam play Dorow, who had starred at Wismer's alma mater, Michigan State. Dorow threw for a league-high twenty-six touchdowns.

Sam also had two superb receivers in Maynard and Art Powell, both of whom would have fine careers in the NFL. Powell, a tight end out of San Jose State, had been released by the Eagles after he refused to play an exhibition game in the segregated South.

"Sammy Baugh didn't care about any of that nonsense," Maynard recalled. "He intended to give Art Powell a fair shake. For one, Sammy was the kind of guy who would buy the whole bar a round, who judged a player only by what he could do in that space between the two sidelines. What did any of that other stuff matter? It might have mattered to some blue-blood owner up in the nation's capital, but it didn't matter to Vince Lombardi, and it sure as heck didn't matter to Sammy Baugh."

Sam and Maynard were cut from the same cloth—the same southwestern cloth, that is—and the two men remained lifelong friends. "Coach and I both shared what some New Yorkers might call 'a cowboy image'—not the most popular look in Manhattan in 1960," Maynard recalled. "I never thought about shopping for new clothes on Fifth Avenue, and I'm sure Coach Baugh didn't either. Sammy had worn cowboy boots and Levi's way back when he was a Redskins player. I had dressed the way I had since middle school, before I even knew who Sammy Baugh was."

The team finished the season with a record of 7-7, but the crowds never got better. On Thanksgiving Day, for example, the Titans defeated the Dallas Texans 41–35 in a wild offensive battle that featured Dorow—Dick Young of the *New York Daily News* labeled him "the hairless wower"—completing twenty-one of thirty-five passes for 301 yards and Maynard catching ten of them for 179 yards. A crowd of 14,344 watched the "piping-hot Turkey Day football feast, stuffed with 76 juicy points" (Young again).

Sam was able to joke about the team's dismal box-office situation. When a reporter asked him about disgruntled fans after a loss, he said, "I'm not worried about them. I think we've got 'em outnumbered."

"They didn't introduce us before the game," Sam's linebacker, Larry Grantham, once joked. "They just let us wander through the stands until we had met everyone."

Another time, the team bus was making its way through New York City traffic on its way to the Polo Grounds when a grocery sack full of garbage came flying through an open window. Sam laughed. "Well," he said, "it coulda been shit."

Just when Sam and his Titans thought things couldn't get any worse, they did. Paychecks began to bounce. On payday, one of Wismer's factotums would hand out checks at practice. Immediately, the players would rush off the field, climb into their cars and, still in football gear, race to the bank. Only one branch of a bank called Irving Trust would cash the Titans checks, and only one teller at that branch. She would check off each transaction until the money ran out, so the last players in line often trudged out the front door with their pockets empty.

For press releases, someone would go to stores that sold mimeograph machines, ask to test the equipment, and run off the releases—without buying, of course. After one game, players had to dry themselves off with their jerseys, because the laundryman hadn't been paid.

Grantham, an all-pro after the Titans became the Jets, recalled the players delivering an ultimatum to Wismer before a game against Buffalo: either we get paid or we don't practice.

"He told us we could practice on our own, but if we did, the coaches wouldn't coach," Grantham recalled. "So I coached the defense, and guard Bob Mischak coached the offense. We went up to Buffalo on our own, so did the coaches, and we won. The next week, Lamar Hunt showed up, sat at a table in our locker room, asked each guy how much his paycheck was and wrote a personal check for the amount. That's how much he knew the AFL needed a New York team."

With morale abysmal toward the end of the season, the Wismer Bonus Rule went into effect. As Sam recalled, Wismer walked into the dressing room one day after practice and announced that if the Titans won the last three games on the schedule, he would reward every player with a $2,000 bonus. Since many of them hadn't been paid in weeks, the announcement got their attention.

"Well, we won the first two," Sam recalled,

and then went out and played the [San Diego] Chargers in the last game of the year. We could both score, and it got to be one of those real see-saw games—we'd score, and then they'd score. Harry was pacing up and down the sideline looking more worried every minute.

And all through the game, people were joking with each other on the bench—pointing at Harry and saying, "Look—we got him scared to death!"

Finally, they beat us [50–43]—and you never saw an owner so relieved his team had lost.

Things got only worse in '61, and as the season wore on, Sam found it increasingly difficult to hide his frustration with Wismer's shoddy operation. When the AFL owners were about to meet late in the 1961 season to determine whether Wismer should be relieved of his franchise, the coach's sentiments were obvious. "I wish I had a vote," he told reporters.

With a week to go in the season—the Titans would again finish 7-7—the feud between owner and coach flared into public view. Charging that Sam had violated the "loyalty clause" in his contract, Wismer announced he intended to demote him to assistant backfield coach for the 1962 season. "He's rapping me publicly all the time," Wismer said. "I'm paying him $28,000 to be disloyal; that's a fine situation, isn't it?"

With a year to go on his three-year contract, Sam told reporters he hoped Wismer would fire him, but he would not quit. Dick Young of the *New York Daily News* told him of Wismer's plan. "Well, that would be just wonderful," he said. "I'd like to be an assistant at these prices. I'm not being disloyal; all I'm doing is telling the truth. I told him we couldn't win any championship without signing some draft choices." Young asked him again whether he was going to quit. "I've never quit a job in my life," he said, "and I'm not going to quit now."

The two men had been feuding all fall, but it flared up anew when Sam heard Wismer claim he intended to offer the Syracuse all-American Ernie Davis a $25,000 bonus and a three-year contract for $100,000 if Davis would sign with the Titans. Although the Buffalo Bills had the rights to Davis in the AFL draft, Wismer claimed the Bills had given him permission to negotiate with the star halfback. The Bills denied it.

"Sure, I'd like to have Davis," Sam said.

He's a great ballplayer. But while they're fooling around with Davis, 20 other boys who can help us are getting away. A bunch we wanted to sign already have been signed by somebody else.

I'm a little tired of all this Davis talk, especially since we don't even own the rights to him anyway.

Ironically, George Preston Marshall, pressured by the Kennedy administration to sign a black player, drafted Davis, the 1961 Heisman Trophy winner, as the overall number one pick and then traded him to the Cleveland Browns for running back Bobby Mitchell and the Browns' first pick. Mitchell thus became the Redskins' first black player, while Davis was expected to team with fearsome running back Jim Brown to give the Browns the most explosive backfield in the history of the NFL. Tragically, Davis died of leukemia at age twenty-three.

Meanwhile, Wismer kept telling reporters that he and general manager Steve Sebo "have been working night and day for 10 days" trying to sign Titan draft choices.

Sam wasn't through voicing his frustrations. He told reporters that Wismer had overestimated the Titans from the start of the season. "Two weeks before we went to camp," he said,

all the coaches got a letter from Wismer telling us of all the great boys he had signed and telling the coaches that we should be able to win the championship with them. We could tell, within 30 days at camp, that we had been lied to right there. He hadn't helped us on offense at all and on defense he had got us only one good boy—Danard Paulson. He even made the statement that we could beat the Giants by three touchdowns. That turned my stomach. The Giants would run us right off the field.

Sam was gone before the end of the year, replaced by his old pal Clyde "Bulldog" Turner. Since his three-year contract still had a year to run, Wismer agreed to keep him on as a "kicking consultant" for the same salary he received as coach. Turner said he had "the greatest respect" for his predecessor and would be happy to have him on his staff. "I don't know how he'd feel about that though," he added.

In the fall of 1962, Wismer was unable to meet his payroll, so the AFL assumed the costs of running the Titans until the end of the season. The next spring, a five-man syndicate headed by David A. "Sonny" Werblin purchased the franchise for $1 million, renamed the team the "Jets," and hired a new coach and general manager, Weeb Ewbank. Two years later, the team signed a young quarterback from the University of Alabama named Joe Namath—for an unprecedented $427,000—and on January 12, 1969, "Broadway Joe" led the Jets to a stunning Super Bowl victory over the Baltimore Colts. (In later years, Sam said Namath was the best passer he had ever seen.)

That victory was the catalyst in the merger of the NFL and the upstart AFL, and Wismer, for all his shortcomings, had been a prime mover. He didn't live to savor the success.

Sam recalled the last time he saw the man. In 1964, he was head coach of the Houston Oilers, who were in New York to play the Jets. Wismer called him to ask whether he could sit on the bench with the Oilers. Sam said sure and got him a pass.

Burdened by his financial losses and legal entanglements, Wismer seemed like a different person, friends told the *New York Times*. "He was still a familiar figure in midtown restaurants and hotels, but his reverses seemed to many to have taken a great zest from him."

"So he came down and sat with us, and it seemed like it really meant something to him," Sam told Whit Canning. "But at halftime, he went up to the press box to go visit some people. About the middle of the third quarter he came back down, and he had blood all over his mouth and running down his shirt. He went up there big-doggin' it again, and somebody cold-cocked him. There were just so many people who disliked Harry, and I really felt sorry for him."

Wismer died in 1967 at age fifty-six. He still owed Sam $10,000.

Sam, at least, got to go home to Texas. "I was always glad to get out of a city," he often said. "I never did stay a damn day longer than I had to."

David Baugh remembered the last Titan game his father coached. They were playing the Dallas Texans, in Dallas, and the plan was for David and his older brother Todd to drive in from West Texas, pick up their dad, and bring him home. That was how it worked out, although what David remembers from his vantage point on the Titans' bench was one particular play. The Texans punted to the Titans, and the Titans deep man let the ball hit the ground and roll. As a gaggle of Texans gathered around the ball, waiting for it to stop rolling, a giant Titan barreled into the unsuspecting players and knocked them to the ground like bowling pins. Benches emptied immediately, with players cussing, throwing punches, and grappling with each other.

David remembered his dad yelling, "You crazy bastard!" at the lineman who had ignited the riot, and wading into the melee trying to get his Titans back to the bench. Somehow, it seemed a fitting end to what had been a misadventure from the beginning.

On September 7, 1963, Sam was inducted into the Professional Football Hall of Fame in Canton, Ohio, one of seventeen charter members, a group that included George Halas, Bronko Nagurski, Red Grange, Jim Thorpe, Curly Lambeau, and others. Only Halas and Sam were elected unanimously.

His Hall of Fame profile described him as a "premier passer" who transformed the way the game was played. "Obviously, such a change could not be totally brought about by one individual. But Baugh was the catalyst that changed the game. No one had seen a passer who could throw with such accuracy."

Sam, with great reluctance, left the ranch and flew to Canton, where, during induction ceremonies at Fawcett Stadium, Harry Stuhldreher described him as "the originator, the founder of the flying circus found in the Southwestern part of the United States at Texas Christian University." Stuhldreher also noted that of Sam's many records, the one of which he was most proud was his interceptions as a defensive back.

Sam, looking dapper in a suit and striped tie, told the stadium crowd that those who should be honored were "the owners who stayed with it back in those days when they weren't making money, losing money with pro teams. They still loved the game and thought enough of it to stay there and lose their money until the game became what it is today."

He also paid his respects to George Preston Marshall, "one of the finest men I've ever been in contact with." Marshall was in Georgetown Hospital in Washington, D.C., that day, and Sam wished him a full recovery.

Flying back home to Texas, Sam may well have thought that his football days were over. Calves and rain and rodeoing were on his mind, not to mention the fortunes of his five kids, a couple of whom were grown. Not long afterward, though, he got a call from Bud Adams, the Houston oilman who owned the Houston Oilers of the AFL, offering him a job as an assistant coach. With kids in college and ranching perennially precarious, Sam said yes. A year later, head coach Pop Ivy quit shortly before the season began, and Sam took over, although he said later he didn't really want the job.

Sam coached the Oilers for the '64 season, and that was it. That season was the last year he had to leave the ranch, had to deal with nosy reporters, had to fly around the country in airplanes he didn't trust to begin with. Flying through a storm one night after an Oilers game, this most irreligious of men told the Lord that if he got down out of the lightning-splintered sky, he would never fly again. And he never did.

Meanwhile, it was an inauspicious year for a team that had won the first three AFL title games. Maybe Ivy had known something, but Sam fell into a quarterback controversy that sparked rumblings of dissension the whole year.

After the '63 season, the Oilers had drafted Don Trull, a superb passer from Baylor, and Adams wanted him in the lineup immediately. Sam considered Trull the team's quarterback of the future. His starter, meanwhile, was the ageless George Blanda, who was not only one of the best quarterbacks in pro football but also, at forty-seven, still productive on the field.

He recalled Blanda leading the Oilers to what looked like sure victory one Sunday afternoon against the Denver Broncos, and then the Oilers' punter decided to run with the ball late in the game instead of kicking it. He was tackled behind the line of scrimmage, and the Broncos managed to push him close enough to kick the game-winning field goal.

"The newspapers jumped all over Blanda, even though it wasn't his fault, and I think Mr. Adams may have instigated it because he wanted Trull in there," Sam told Whit Canning.

The next Sunday against the Kansas City Chiefs, Sam started the rookie, who could get nothing going. With the Oilers trailing 21–0, Blanda took over in the second half and threw five touchdown passes.

Although the Oilers won that game, they finished the season 4 10, and Sam was done as head coach. A head coaching job, he told reporters, demanded his full-time attention, which he could not afford to give and still operate his first love, his 6,335-acre ranch. He said the team's poor record had nothing to do with his decision and that he would be happy to stay on the staff as long as he could spend more time on his ranch.

And that is exactly what he did. He came back in '65 as an assistant to his old Redskins buddy Bones Taylor, who had served for three years as Sam's assistant. "A lot of people may think I came to Houston (from San Diego) to cut Sam's throat," Taylor told the *Washington Post*. "They couldn't be more wrong. I've learned a lot from Sam. What he wants to be is an assistant coach. I had to be sure of this before I took the job." The *Post* had caught up with both Sam and Taylor at the Touchdown Club in Washington. The Oilers were in town for an exhibition game in nearby Alexandria, Virginia, with the New York Jets.

While people said a lot of nice things about him, "Baugh squirmed in his seat, bit at the end of his cigar, occasionally surveyed the smoke curling upward toward the ceiling, but, always, he smiled," Bill Gildea of the *Post* observed. "The legend wore a seersucker jacket that hung loosely on his lean frame. At 178, he is still near his playing weight. Only his hair is thinner on top, and there are touches of gray at the sides."

Sam stayed on as Taylor's assistant for a year, did some part-time coaching with the University of Tulsa and Oklahoma State, and helped his old friend Harry Gilmer with the Detroit Lions. By the end of the 1960s, Sam was done with the game. He settled on the ranch for good.

RANCHING, RODEOING, AND GOLFING

SAM IN RETIREMENT

t is a Sunday afternoon on the outskirts of a small West Texas town. Cars, pickups, and horse trailers are parked in the dry dirt around a ramshackle outdoor rodeo arena, where a few spectators lounge atop weathered bleachers watching cowboys compete in rudimentary rodeo events. Others have backed their pickups near the arena fence and set up lawn chairs in the truck beds. The spectators—kids, wives and girlfriends, old cowboys—are eating hot dogs, drinking Cokes. Others have cans of beer on ice in Styrofoam coolers. Some are wearing shorts and T-shirts; others are dressed like the cowboys themselves.

The contestants are real cowboys, everyday wranglers on ranches in the area. Several of them, in sweat-stained hats and battered boots, perch atop the fence and watch the action, shouting out encouragement now and then to their buddies. The sun is high overhead in the bright blue sky.

At one end of the small arena, a Jersey calf darts out of a roping chute, pursued by a cowboy atop a galloping quarter horse. The rider leans over the horse's neck, one hand on the reins, the other twirling a lariat as he homes in on the calf. Within seconds, the loop flies out and settles around the calf's neck, tightening as the frightened animal continues to run a few more steps. The horse stops as soon as the cowboy throws the loop, the rope between the saddle horn and the calf snaps taut, and the animal slams to the dirt.

The cowboy bounds out of the saddle and runs toward the calf while moving hand over hand down the rope. The horse, eyes focused on the action in front of him, takes a step or two backward to keep the rope clothesline tight.

When the cowboy ducks under the rope and gets to the calf, he reaches under the animal, lifts it up, and drops it on his back, a maneuver the cowboys call flanking. Crouching beside the animal, he wraps a short length of rope called a pigging string around three of the calf's legs and cinches it with a half hitch. He then springs to his feet, hands held high to show a judge on horseback that he is done. The judge dips a small flag as a signal to a timer to stop his watch.

A good roper in Sam's time got it done in ten seconds or less. "It all looks pretty easy on TV, but it's really damn difficult to do," said David Baugh, a high school football coach who became a full-time rancher when he retired. "You have to practice a thousand times."

He should know. From the early 1940s until the late 1950s, one of the best ropers in West Texas was David Baugh's father. As David recalled, Sam didn't know anything about ranching, much less about rodeoing, when he first moved to the Double Mountain Ranch. After helping out with the branding one year, he decided he wanted to be able to drag calves with the best of them. He built himself an arena near the house, and by the next branding, he could.

Felix McKnight of the *Fort Worth Star-Telegram* wrote that Sam made his rodeo debut in 1940 at Floydada. According to McKnight, Sam "met up with an unruly calf and used up 19 seconds, which was slightly out of the money." "Shucks, out here on the ranch I've cut that time in half," Sam told McKnight. "But it was different in that arena." Sam said he would enter the rodeo at Spur in June and then the famed Stamford Rodeo during the July 4 weekend.

Owen Brazee, the cowboy who managed the ranch when Sam was in D.C., went along with him to his first few rodeos, showing him how to enter, how to take care of his horse, how to take advantage of little tricks of the trade. It wasn't long before he was competing with the best.

By then, George Preston Marshall's faux cowboy was the real McCoy. Back straight, shoulders squared, he looked as if he had been born on a horse. He loved riding, his friend Bob O'Day recalled. Some mornings, on days he didn't have much ranch work to do, he would head out on horseback, ride all morning, come back in for lunch, and then head out again.

The *Star-Telegram's* McKnight reported that Sam had hooked up with a fellow Sweetwater resident, Larrupin' Lew Jenkins, a ranch boy who had quit riding herd to become a boxer. He and Sam were thinking about raising thoroughbreds together. Larrupin' Lew, by the way, whose impressive reti-nue of nicknames included "Lashing Lew," the "Sweet Swatter from Sweet-water," the "Sweetwater Socker," and "Sweetwater Lew," became light-weight champion of the world in July 1940. Sam was among the guests when the Sweetwater Chamber of Commerce sponsored a welcome-home banquet for yet another hometown sports hero.

The Redskins knew Sam was rodeoing. Marshall hated it, fearing that he would lose his most valuable player to injury, but he never demanded that Sam stop. Although rodeoing helped him stay in shape during the off-sea-son, Sam himself got scared one year when he hurt his knee at a small-town rodeo while he was still playing football. He stayed away from roping for a while, but he enjoyed it too much to give it up completely.

"To offset the remote possibility that Mr. George (Wet Wash) Marshall, the rather easily excited owner of the Washington football club, should become alarmed over Sam's innocent hobby of wrestling with bawling calves," McKnight wrote, "the Slinger insists that he will not branch out into other rodeo pastimes—such as bulldogging steers, mounting unbroken broncs and riding wild steers with a surcingle."

He enjoyed the competition—competition with others and with him-self to be the best he could. Just as in football and baseball—and later, golf—he learned everything he could about the sport, worked at it and practiced incessantly. Sitting around his apartment in Washington with his Redskin buddies, he would have a lariat dangling between the fingers of his right hand, and while he talked and told yarns, he roped the back of a nearby chair. Back on the ranch, he would go to "ropin's" almost every weekend, where he and other cowboys practiced for upcoming rodeos. "He loved any kind of competition," David Baugh said. "He loved the cowboy life."

His ability to focus on the task at hand, whether kicking a football or roping a calf, was key to his success, but it could get wearisome to those around him. Mona would want him to pay attention to something around the house or maybe take a vacation, but Sam would be wrapped up in his lat-est obsession.

During his roping days, Sonny Nichols, before he joined the Marines at eighteen in 1945, traipsed all over West Texas with Sam, following the rodeo to Pampa, Clarendon, Seymour, Snyder, Stamford, Aspermont, all the way to Amarillo. Fourteen years younger, Nichols looked up to Sam. They would load up Bluebonnet, Sam's favorite roping mare, in the back of a pickup with sideboards, and off they would go almost every weekend. "He didn't talk much football," Nichols recalled. "Mainly we talked about ranching and rodeoing and horses."

David Baugh and his brothers traveled with their dad too. The most memorable trip for David was one to a rodeo at Spur in the early 1950s. They rode with their dad in the cab of a pickup, Bluebonnet in a trailer behind them. She was called Bluebonnet because she had a bluish-gray tinge at birth and gradually turned white as she got older. "That ol' mare, I mean you could rope on her, you could ride her," Brazee recalled. "She sure was a good horse."

At Spur that night, Sam and the boys slept in the back of the pickup. They had two old army mattresses and an old canvas tarp with a hole in the center for the broomstick that held it up. "There's a storm comin'," so do not knock this stick down," Sam warned the youngsters.

"Well, all we heard was, 'knock this stick down,'" David recalled, laughing. "We got to scuffling and wrestling, and we knocked the stick down. The water poured in, got the mattresses sopping wet."

Sam won his share of belt buckles, trophies, and prize money. One year he won the calf-roping contest at the Fourth of July rodeo in nearby Stamford, and the next year the rodeo honchos wouldn't let him compete; the rationale for their ruling was that he was a professional athlete. He was, indeed, an athlete, and the raw skills that made him a success on the baseball diamond and the gridiron translated to the rodeo arena.

Sam rodeoed throughout the 1950s until his battered knees began to give out and he couldn't get out of the saddle as fast as he needed to. After a while, he had to give up riding altogether.

By the late 1960s, when the only seasons that mattered were the growing season and the calving season, Sam had been ranching for almost three decades. By then, he had become part of the land he loved and respected, harsh and unyielding as it was. He loved the work: watching over a new batch of calves every winter (Herefords for the first several years and then Brangus), branding, cutting herds, keeping the fences up, checking the windmill, and finally hauling his cattle to market.

"You get a piece of land and you try to improve it," he once said.

> What you want to do is leave it better than you find it. It hurts you when you see that damn grass on your land die out and go to nothing. It tears you up . . .
>
> We know we're not going to have a good year every year—maybe one good year in five. But we're doing something we like, and that's what by God counts.

He also discovered that he had a knack for training horses—horses to ride, to rope off of, to herd cattle. "He did it for the pure joy of it," David Baugh said. "It was sort of like coaching."

He loved ranch people, their strength of will, their independence and self-sufficiency. "I work the cattle myself, with two other fellows about my own age," he told a *Washington Post* reporter in 1978. "You can't get help, and if you do and it's not experienced they can get hurt. We neighbors pool our labor on one another's place in the busier seasons."

His operating philosophy was, in essence, his philosophy of life. "I never want to hurt anyone," he told the reporter.

Sometimes a harsh word might. When I say something, I expect to be believed by the other fellow. When he says something, I expect to believe him.

If he agrees to pay me so much a pound for the cattle, that's good enough for me. The fellow doesn't need a contract. But if he wants one, that's all right, too.

I didn't find it that way with some people in New York and other places up that way. That's why I couldn't live there. [Perhaps he was thinking of the money Harry Wismer owed him.]

I don't care about money—although it's nice to have when you need it—if I can just earn a living and do what I wanted to do. And I do.

B y the late '60s, the Baugh children were grown and on their own. The oldest son, Todd, played football at Rice, went to law school, and then became a state district judge in Billings, Montana. David also played football, at Texas Tech, and then coached in small towns throughout West Texas. Bruce (who died in 2006) worked as a computer expert for the State of Texas, and Stephen worked for an oil company in Midland. Frances became a physical education teacher in Lubbock.

Sam and Mona stayed on the ranch, both still active, but the old competitor needed a new challenge. He got serious about golf. He never took any lessons; he learned on his own. He became an exceptional golfer, his old friend Bob O'Day recalled. "He had a great touch, a good short game," O'Day said. "He was a great putter."

As Sam got older and could leave some of his ranching chores to a ranch foreman and later to David, he began making the 100-mile round trip to Snyder to play golf on the scruffy little mesquite-lined course at Western Texas College. Four or five times a week, Sam would show up in his pickup to knock a ball around the nine-hole course with O'Day, an administrator at the junior college. When he made a particularly difficult putt, he warbled "Hail to the Redskins"—"the whole thing," O'Day recalled.

Sam and O'Day often teamed up against Rick Kahlich, the course's head pro. The threesome didn't play for big money, but the losing team had to pay a price until it reversed the outcome. Sam, if he lost, had to wear a baseball cap that featured the name "Sammy Sue" in hot-pink lettering. O'Day was "Bobby Sue," and Kahlich, "Ricky Sue." "Sam hated to wear that cap," O'Day recalled, laughing.

"He did everything fast," David Baugh recalled. "He'd hit a golf ball, hop into his cart, and speed off to the next hole. Sometimes he forgot the guys he was playing with and have to circle back to pick them up."

He drove the same way. For years he drove a maroon pickup to Snyder to play golf, and then graduated to a maroon Buick. One day he was driving the Buick to Snyder with the windows up, the air conditioner on full blast, and a country-and-western station blaring on the radio. As always, he had a chaw of Levi Garrett tobacco in his mouth, but he had forgotten the Folgers Coffee tin he used for spitting. As he drove that day, he spotted an empty beer can on the shoulder. Sam stopped, backed up, and retrieved the can as a makeshift spittoon.

"He was one of the few people I ever saw who could chew tobacco, spit in a cup, listen to the radio, turn around and talk to you—and still drive," said his old friend O'Day.

The needle was probably flirting with the century mark on the odometer as Sam, running late, sped down the lonely stretch of West Texas highway. He didn't happen to notice the state trooper, who spotted not only the speeding Cadillac but also a driver with a beer can at his lips. The trooper, siren wailing and lights flashing, swung in behind Sam. Sam didn't notice. He pulled into the golf-course parking lot at Western Texas College with the trooper on his tail, who then blocked Sam in when he swung his car into a parking slot. Sam never saw him until he decided to adjust how he had parked and backed right into the patrol car.

Sam's golfing buddies were watching the whole ridiculous farce. "Throw his ass in jail!" they shouted at the patrolman. Sam was able to convince him that he wasn't drinking, that he was just late for his golf game. Eventually, the trooper shook his head, threw up his hands, and drove away.

Sam always drove too fast and often got tickets, which he promptly stashed away in the glove compartment. Once the sheriff drove out from Rotan and knocked on the front door of the ranch house. "Sam, I've come out here to arrest you," he said.

"Aw hell, what for?" Sam said, laughing. He thought the sheriff was joking. When Sam realized he was at least semiserious, he wrote out a check for his unpaid fines, and the lawman went on his way.

Sam played golf deep into his eighties and had four holes in one over his lifetime. He played regularly on the Western Texas course, but also in small towns throughout West Texas and even in Las Vegas, where he once won $10,000 at a tournament. He helped raise thousands of dollars for charity at what would come to be called the Slingin' Sammy Baugh Classic at the Sammy Baugh Golf Course in Snyder.

"You can't believe the number of things Sam signed for fund-raisers," O'Day said. He also provided college scholarships for students at Western Texas College. "There's no telling how many people Sam helped right out of his own pocket," David Baugh recalled. "He never asked for anything in return and didn't expect anything in return. As far as he was concerned, it was just a deal between himself and whoever he was helping. It wasn't anybody else's business."

Like the evening sun setting over Double Mountain, Sam's illustrious football career gradually faded into the past. Although he enjoyed watching football on television every fall weekend, he didn't spend a whole lot of time reliving old memories. In fact, he hardly talked about the past unless someone asked him.

"Goddamnit, I don't give one hot damn for this stuff about being some old football star," he told a magazine writer in 1980.

Old teammates began to pass on—Bones Taylor in 1992, Bill Millner in 1996, Andy Farkas in 2003. One day in June 1997, an official with the Pro Football Hall of Fame called to tell him that Don Hutson had died. Sam thanked him and hung up the telephone. He sat down in the recliner in his den, and for a few moments he thought about Hutson, the gazelle-like Green Bay Packers receiver who was one of the greatest players in pro football history. Then, he thought about some of the others—Grange, Thorpe, Nagurski, Halas, and Lambeau who, along with Sam, were among the original inductees.

"I had already seen on television that Hutson had died," Sam told a reporter not long afterward. "But when he said, 'You know, Sam, you're the last survivor,' I was shocked. I knew a lot of the others had died, but I sure didn't know I was the last. You know, it feels kind of strange."

When the reporter asked him how it felt to be the sole survivor, he leaned forward, slapped his thigh, and said with a laugh: "Well, in this case, last is a hell of a lot better than first."

Shirley Povich, the legendary *Washington Post* sports editor who sang Sam's praises throughout his long career, died in 1998 at age ninety-one.

The man who constructed the Slingin' Sammy legend, the imperious George Preston Marshall, had died in 1969 at age seventy-two. His flamboyant wife, Corinne Griffith, died in 1979; she may have been either eighty or eighty-one, no one knew for sure. (She and Marshall had divorced in 1962.) The author of four books, she spearheaded a national campaign in the 1960s to eliminate the federal income tax, which she called legalized thievery.

It took a long time for Marshall's Redskins to recover from Sam's departure. As Arthur Daley of the *New York Times* put it in 1961, "They swept the town like a devouring flame, the hottest thing in the Capital since the White House was set afire in the War of 1812. But when Sammy Baugh's arm cooled off, so did the appeal of the football team. It has yet to be regained."

The Redskins regularly begged Sam to come to Washington for a Sammy Baugh Day and to retire his jersey number, but he always refused. He didn't like to fly, didn't want to wander far from home.

He was content. He played dominoes with friends, puttered around the ranch, and spent a lot of time reading, particularly books about the Indians that once inhabited the Double Mountain area. His idea of eating out was lunch at the Dairy Queen in Rotan.

"You know, somebody's always asking me to come hand out a goddamn trophy here or give a speech there or wear some lousy tuxedo to a banquet," he told a reporter in 1980. "Well, I've just had enough of it. I've traveled so much all my life, I just don't give a damn about going anywhere. You just get enough of it after a while."

Fans didn't forget though. He was still getting stacks of mail every day a half century after he retired. The mail would be addressed to Slingin' Sammy Baugh, Rotan, Texas—no address, no zip code.

His daughter or one of his four daughters-in-law would spread everything on a table, and Sam would sign whatever people sent him. People always wanted him to sign "Slingin' Sammy Baugh," but instead he would scribble "Sam Baugh" because it was quicker. His helpers made sure every item was signed and returned to sender.

He never asked for money, never gave a thought to cashing in on the lucrative sports memorabilia craze that began to develop in the 1970s. He was frequently invited to card shows and was offered as much as $20,000 to sign his name for two hours in Dallas and Fort Worth, but he said no. "I wouldn't trust any sumbitch that claimed he was going to pay me that much money to sign my name," he told a reporter.

Larry Dluhy, who traded in sports memorabilia at his shop in Houston, corralled Sam for an autograph show one weekend in the late 1990s. Dluhy knew Bob Lilly, an all-American lineman at TCU in the 1960s who went on to a Hall of Fame career with the Dallas Cowboys. Lilly and Sam were friends as well.

Dluhy called Sam and told him Lilly had agreed to appear at an autograph show in Dallas. Dluhy promised Sam that he would drive the 275 miles to the ranch, drive him to Dallas, and have him back before dark.

"You know I don't do shows," Sam told him a few days before the event, "but if Lilly's doing it, I guess I will too."

Dluhy was excited—until the telephone calls started. "What if we have a flat?" Sam wanted to know. "I've got a spare," Dluhy explained patiently. Sam called back several times with similar concerns. Each time Dluhy had an answer.

He called one more time. "I just can't do it," he told Dluhy. "I'm sorry." Dluhy said he understood.

The last night he spent away from home was in 1993 when a friend drove him to Fort Worth so that TCU could retire his jersey. Over the years, he was inducted into five Halls of Fame—College Football (1951), Texas Sports (1954), Pro Football (1963), Cotton Bowl (1999), and Hardin-Simmons (2000).

He kept a few trophies in a small trophy case at the house. In 1998, when a visiting reporter asked him which were the most valuable to him, he reached into the back of the case and retrieved a framed $10 bill and a certificate for his first hole in one.

Sam never flew after his two-year coaching career with the Oilers ended following the 1965 season. "I had four bad experiences on planes," he once recalled. "The last one came my last year with the Oilers. We had a bad flight to Oakland, and I said, 'God, if you just get me through this flight, when the season's over, I'll never fly again.' And I haven't. And I hate trains almost as much as airplanes."

For more than thirty years, executives from the Pro Football Hall of Fame tried to lure Sam back to Canton for the annual induction ceremonies. They offered to bring him by plane, train, or automobile.

"Back then, it didn't seem like such a big deal," he said about his enshrinement.

It was the first year, and there was only one building. I don't remember there being a particularly big turnout. I appreciate it more now than I did then. I'd really like to go back and see it now because I've heard so much about it, but I'll never do it.

They invited me for a long time, but I think they finally gave up. I haven't been back since the year they inducted me. Shoot, I haven't even been back to Washington since my career ended. I mean, damn, why would I want to leave here?

"Am I afraid of death?" he asked, repeating a question a reporter put to him in 1980.

Oh, hell, I don't know. I never think about dying, really. Not dying. Now every so often I think about the way I'm slowing down. You know, I feel myself about a step and a half slower than I used to be. Especially in those branding pens, when I need to move fast. I guarantee you that's when I know I'm a little worse off. But the way I look at it, I don't have to move as fast now. The only game I'm playing is golf, where that son-of-a-bitching ball doesn't move until I hit it.

Ten years later, he lost his beloved Mona. She had inherited her father's bad heart, David Baugh said, and died from complications of a stroke. Sam and Mona, high school sweethearts, had been married fifty-two years.

Her death marked the beginning of the end for Sam as well, even though he would live for another eighteen years. Sam stayed by himself on the ranch after Mona's passing, but David, retired from teaching and coaching, took over running the place. He and his wife, Jean, built a house about a mile away.

Jean fixed lunch for him every day, usually a peanut-butter-and-jelly sandwich. He also watched a lot of television, regardless of what was on.

David found him one morning eating cereal in front of the TV. "Whatcha you watching, Sam?" his son asked. "Aw, I don't know," Sam said, "some kind of little blue sons-uh-bitches." Sam wasn't familiar with the Smurfs.

Sam's children worried that he allowed people to take advantage of him. Fans would show up to meet a living legend, and Sam would invite them to stay for a few days. Often they would, and when they left, Sam made them peanut-butter-and-jelly sandwiches to take with them on the road. David suspects a lot of memorabilia went with them when they left.

Others came simply to be in the presence of a legend; all they wanted was the pleasure of his company. Cowboy Lanza, who lived in McKinney, Texas, and got to be friend, remembered staying up half the night playing dominoes. The two men sat across the kitchen table from each other, slapped down dominoes, and gambled with Reese's Peanut Butter Cups.

Every so often, treasure hunters, professional and amateur, stopped by the ranch house and told him they were sure there was gold and silver on Double Mountain. They asked for permission to dig in his mountain. "All I tell them is that if they strike it rich, I get a cut," he said in 1998. "If there's four of them, I get a fifth. If there's five of them, I get a sixth. I get a kick out of them. You know what? I don't think there's any damn gold or silver in those mountains. The only sumbitch getting rich is the guy who makes the maps."

People asked him why he didn't move into town. "Well, why would I want to move into town?" he asked. "I can walk out any door of my house, step off the porch and pee any damn place I want to. I couldn't do that in town."

His companion was his old dog PeeWee, a mutt who once cost Sam hundreds of dollars when he got hold of Sam's money clip and chewed through several hundred-dollar bills. Sam laughed—and kept on buying an extra hamburger to go whenever he ate lunch at the Dairy Queen in Rotan. A burger for PeeWee.

As the century approached its end, memories of a glorious career and a life well lived began to fade. Alzheimer's disease and dementia began to ravage his once-agile mind. Age and a broken hip robbed him of his remaining mobility.

In 2005, the Baugh children moved their father into the Kent County Nursing Home and Health Clinic in the small town of Jayton, about thirty miles away. Toward the end of his life, visitors were likely to find him sleeping in his room, a gaunt and gray old man with a burgundy and gold Redskin blanket draped across his knees.

Samuel Adrian Baugh, the greatest quarterback who ever lived, died December 17, 2008. He was ninety-four.

Newspapers across the nation marked his passing. Many noted that he was the last surviving member of the Pro Football Hall of Fame's inaugural class. The *Chicago Tribune* quoted the Bears' founder, George Halas. "Sammy Baugh said Sid [Luckman] was the greatest passer of all time. 'No,' replied Sid. 'Sammy was the greatest.'"

"He was one of the greatest ever to play the game of football and one of the greatest the Redskins ever had," said the Redskins' owner, Daniel Snyder.

"To this day Baugh remains, even in Washington, that purest of legends, the player who exists only in the retelling of his deeds from parents to children," wrote Tom Boswell of the *Washington Post*. "We may not know his face when we see it in a photo: ears and nose prominent, cheeks slightly sunken, deep lines in his face before 40 and a middle-distance gaze in his dark eyes as focused as any hawk," Boswell wrote. "But, as long as people know the Redskins, they will know Sammy Baugh. He's the Texan who branded them."

"New York had Joe DiMaggio. Boston had Ted Williams. And Washington, D.C. Well, we had Sammy Baugh, the greatest football player ever to pull on a jersey," wrote the political commentator Pat Buchanan, who grew up in the Washington area.

In a conversation with Michael Wilbon of the *Washington Post*, Steve Sabol, the president of NFL Films, recalled the first NFL game he attended:

> I was 9 years old and my father [Ed Sabol, the founder of NFL Films] took me to Shibe Park in Philadelphia to see the Eagles play the Redskins. It was 1951. My dad said: "See the man wearing Number 33? That's Sammy Baugh." That's all he said.
>
> It was like pointing out the Empire State Building, the Washington Monument or Niagara Falls. "That's Sammy Baugh." That's all that needed to be said to anyone who followed pro football in the 1940s and early 1950s.

"None of that mattered all that much to Sam," David Baugh said. "He told me once that he'd like to be remembered as 'a pretty good cowboy.'"

The Baugh family held Sam's funeral at the First Baptist Church of Rotan, where a saddle and chaps were draped over his coffin. Those who came to remember Sam watched a highlight video at the start of the service; a number of football luminaries attended.

On a cold, windy West Texas morning, a hearse took his body to the cemetery entrance. In a nearby pasture, about a dozen Brangus cattle stood at the fence, almost as if they had come to bid farewell. Two of Sam's friends, one wearing a referee's uniform and the other dressed as a cowboy, stood with hats doffed and heads bowed.

Pallbearers loaded the coffin onto a wagon drawn by two horses. Walking slowly, they carried him the rest of the way to the grave site. They laid Sam to rest beside Edmonia.

NOTES

INTRODUCTION

1   *He was our idol*: Canning, *Sam Baugh*, 28.
1   *He was our leader*: Joe Tereshinksi, interview by the author, 2008.
1   *I loved Sam Baugh*: Bob O'Day, interview by the author, 2009.
2   *He was never obscene*. Ellen Stevenson, telephone interview by the author, 2009.
2   *Sam's son David recalled*: David Baugh, interview by the author, Aug. 22, 2008.
4   *He really had a rifle*: Dan Jenkins, telephone interview by the author, 2006.
6   *Who is this man Sammy Baugh*: David Broder, "Little Lord Landrys," *Washington Post*, Dec. 19, 1979.
7   *He was so much fun*: Jeanne McNeill, interview by the author, 2007.
9   *Dear Sammy*: Warren Buffett to Sam Baugh, 2007 (used with permission).

CHAPTER 1

10   *He had two great days*: Tips, *Football—Texas Style*, 232.
11   The Baugh family tree was compiled by Sam Baugh's grandson, William Baugh.
11   *A profile of William Baugh*: "The History of Gwinnett County Georgia" is cited in a Baugh family history compiled by Brant A. Baugh, Lubbock, Texas, 2002.
12   *I wouldn't put in a rule*: Sammy Baugh, oral-history interview, Aug. 16, 1998, Southwest Collection, Texas Tech University.
13   *A local historian described*: Hazel Potter, "William Baugh Family History" (unpublished family history), cited in the family history compiled by Brant A. Baugh.

13   *We had a few dairy cows*: Canning, *Sam Baugh*, 19.

13   *Everything you could gamble on*: Kevin Sherrington, "Sammy Baugh, 1914–2008; Baugh Dies at 94; Rancher Puts His stamp on NFL History with His Arm," *Dallas Morning News*, Dec. 18, 2008.

14   *If he had a dollar*: Nell Baugh Kendrick, interview by the author, 2009.

14   *But I remember dragging*: Baugh oral history, Texas Tech.

15   *I just played by myself*: Ibid.

15   *I've often tried to think*: Ibid.

15   *The coach, after the season*: Ibid.

16   *A lot of times*: Ibid.

16   *the sorriest team Temple*: Ibid.

16   *He called me in his office*: Ibid.

17   *Didn't make a damn bit*: Frank Luksa, "Slingin' Sammy Last Link."

17   *I don't recall what happened*: Charles Burton, *Dallas Morning News*, Feb. 19, 1961.

17   *Bill was a hell of*: Baugh oral history, Texas Tech.

17   *My daddy got bumped*: Canning, *Sam Baugh*, 21.

18   *I could understand the baseball*: Baugh oral history, Texas Tech.

19   *I grew up knowing*: Burton, *Dallas Morning News*, Feb. 19, 1961.

19   *Do you know who that is*: Ellen Kendrick, interview by the author, 2009.

19   *He was just as friendly*: David Baugh, interview by the author, 2011.

20   *There's been some stuff*: Canning, *Sam Baugh*, 21.

20   *the finest running back*: *Sweetwater Reporter*, Dec. 13, 1932.

20   *Our big game that year*: Canning, *Sam Baugh*, 21.

21   *Twenty-four husky Sweetwater lads*: *Sweetwater Reporter*, Nov. 24, 1932.

21   *The way those boys fought*: *Sweetwater Reporter*, Dec. 13, 1932.

21   *I had played baseball*: Cope, "Life for Two Tough Texans."

22   *Boys, I found y'all*: O'Day interview.

22   *I told him I didn't have*: Baugh oral history, Texas Tech.

22   *So I went back and told*: Tips, *Football—Texas Style*, 232.

22   *He was a character*: John Knowles, interview by the author, 2011.

23   *I was going to TCU*: Ray Glass, "Ranch Replaces Gridiron as Baugh's Playing Field," *Lubbock Avalanche-Journal*, May 3, 1981.

23   *But when I asked Uncle Billy*: Ibid.

23   *I finally decided*: Ibid.

CHAPTER 2

24   *I think he was one*: Baugh oral history, Texas Tech.

24   *You could relate to him*: Knowles interview.

25   *bitten by the Football bug*: Moore, *TCU*, 22.

26   *It was a delightful*: Ibid.

26   *Abstain from all intoxicants*: Ibid., 23.

26   *I hunted them up*: Cohane, "The Saturday Fox," in *Great College Football Coaches*, 140.

NOTES TO PAGES 26–42

26   *I've been at TCU many years*: Ibid., 138.
27   *Dutch was dressed*: Cashion, *Pigskin Pulpit*, 97.
27   *He had perfect control*: Frank X. Tolbert, "How Dutch Got Cigarette Habit,"
     Dallas Morning News, May 15, 1956.
27   *he resembled a cat*: Cohane, *Great College Football Coaches*, 139.
27   *Stop that drop-the-handkerchief*: Ibid.
28   *After one victory*: Ibid.
28   *There was no air conditioning*: Cashion, *Pigskin Pulpit*, 98.
28   *Undoubtedly he can throw a football*: Fort Worth Star-Telegram.
29   *By that time, all the coaches*: Ibid.
29   *Anybody can throw a forward pass*: Shirley Povich, *Washington Post*, Sept. 5, 1938.
29   *He was like hundreds*: Ibid.
30   *They said I had my ends*: Cohane, *Great College Football Coaches*, 139.
31   *Short. Safe. Sure*: Dan Daly, "Unfathomable; Others Have Redefined Professional
     Football, but Baugh's Impact on the Games Evolution Is Something Very Few Can
     Appreciate," *Washington Times*, Dec. 19, 2008.
31   *Back in those days*: Canning, *Sam Baugh*, 24.
32   *I could kick it*: Baugh oral history, Texas Tech.
33   *Many of TCU's students*: Works Progress Administration, *WPA Guide to Texas*,
     259.
33   *Boasting itself the Southwest's No. 1*: "National Affairs: Superlative Century,"
     Time, June 8, 1936.
33   *one of the state's most hospitable*: Works Progress Administration, *WPA Guide to
     Texas*, 259.
33   *Nobody had any money*: Holst, *Famous Football Players*, 24.
34   *What they'd do, they'd let you*: Baugh oral history, Texas Tech.
34   *It seemed to me*: Holst, *Famous Football Players*, 25.
34   *He put up his hand*: Knowles interview.
34   *Despite those tough times*: Ibid.
35   *class entertainments in which quartets*: Moore, *TCU*, 115.
35   *The problem was*: Ibid., 106.
35   *TCU has won the conference*: Ibid., 98.

CHAPTER 3

40   *It would be hard to exaggerate*: Gary Cartwright, "0:00 to Go; Time Has Run
     Out on the Southwest Conference, but What a Time It Was," *Sports Illustrated*,
     Oct. 30, 1995.
40   *the largest crowd*: Canning, *Sam Baugh*, 30.
40   *I knew what he could do*: Tips, *Football—Texas Style*, 233.
41   *So here he had cost us*: Canning, *Sam Baugh*, 32.
41   *He was kind of a quiet guy*: Knowles interview.
42   *When we took the ball*: Ibid.
42   *Joe was a great guy*: Ibid., 34.

CHAPTER 4

44   *a lizard-legged little bundle*: Bill Cunningham, *Boston Post*, quoted in Canning, *Sam Baugh*, 37.

44   *SMU's broken-field kid*: Tips, *Football—Texas Style*, 51.

45   *Night football*: Flem Hall, *Fort Worth Star-Telegram*, Oct. 15, 1935.

46   *The next Saturday*: Hall, *Fort Worth Star-Telegram*, Nov. 13, 1935.

46   *Everybody wanted to beat Texas*: Baugh oral history, Texas Tech.

46   *Baugh was standing on*: Hall, *Fort Worth Star-Telegram*, Nov. 17, 1935.

46   *I am interested in*: Hall, *Fort Worth Star-Telegram*, Nov. 23, 1935.

46   *the flaming and furious Frogs*: Hall, *Fort Worth Star-Telegram*, Nov. 18, 1935.

46   *There never was a doubt*: Associated Press, Nov. 23, 1935.

47   *Sam wasn't merely a thrower*: Ibid.

47   *in the grip of a football frenzy*: "Rose Bowl Bid, Conference Title at Stake in T.C.U.-S.M.U. Game," *New York Times*, Nov. 30, 1935.

48   *John Knowles recalled many years later*: Knowles interview.

48   *Nearly three-quarters of a century*: Billy Sansing, interview by the author, July 9, 2009.

48   *Halfback Wilson recalled years later*: Bill Sullivan, "Legends of the SWC; A Tribute to the Southwest Conference Game of the Century," *Houston Chronicle*, July 30, 1995.

48   *Wayne Connor was a kid*: Tom Dodge, telephone interview by the author, July 15, 2009.

49   *took in hand entertainment features*: Hope Ridings Miller, "Washingtonian Gathers Fame, Fortune in Texas," *Washington Post*, Aug. 11, 1937.

49   *It was Wilson's day*: "So. Methodist Sets Back T.C.U. with Late Aerial," *New York Times*, Dec. 1, 1935.

50   *At halftime, the TCU band*: Canning, *Sam Baugh*, 41.

50   *In the SMU locker room*: Sullivan, "Legends of the SWC."

50   *Knowles remembered that he had been*: Knowles interview.

50   *Now while that long ball*: Tips, *Football—Texas Style*, 71.

51   *The two guys closest to me*: Canning, *Sam Baugh*, 41.

51   *He said he had one regret*: Sullivan, "Legends of the SWC."

51   *What I really remember*: Ibid.

52   *He merely lifted his arm*: Quoted in Canning, *Sam Baugh*, 37.

52   *The football writer Wilton Hazard*: Sullivan, *Pro Football's All-Time Greats*.

52   *He was throwing those balls*: Canning, *Sam Baugh*, 71.

52   *I think the real problem*: Ibid., 43.

52   *I learned a good coaching lesson*: Jenkins, *Texas Christian University Football Vault*, 58.

52   *The thing that galled us*: Canning, *Sam Baugh*, 43.

53   *TCU had headed west*: Ibid., 37.

53   *On Saturday, the TCU Horned Frogs*: Hall, *Fort Worth Star-Telegram*, Dec. 7, 1935.

54   *a thrill-a-minute display*: Quoted in Canning, *Sam Baugh*, 45.

54 *It must have been fun*: Greatest Moments, 9.

54 *Frog boosters collected*: Canning, Sam Baugh, 45.

54 *The whole thing was just amazing*: Ibid.

55 *The Fort Worth Star-Telegram ran a photo*: Hall, "Horned Frogs Arrive in Crescent City," Forth Worth Star-Telegram, Dec. 30, 1935.

55 *The New Orleans Picayune reported*: New Orleans Picayune, Dec. 30, 1935.

55 *I've never seen a rain like that*: Knowles interview.

55 *There was standing water*: Canning, Sam Baugh, 46.

56 *An old friend also gave him*: New Orleans Morning Tribune, Jan. 2, 1936.

56 *Sam played a good part*: Hall, Fort Worth Star-Telegram, Jan. 2, 1936.

56 *I'll never forget that*: Canning, Sam Baugh, 46.

57 *Boy! Boy! Give me five*: Tips, Football—Texas Style, 234.

57 *Texas may run dry of oil*: New Orleans Item, Jan. 2, 1936.

57 *Back then, Sam recalled*: Carlton Stowers.

57 *A Fort Worth sports writer*: David Ramsey, "Baugh Just Another Big Country Rancher," Abilene Reporter-News, Feb. 21, 1983.

58 He is a junior: *New Orleans Morning Tribune*, Jan. 2, 1936.

CHAPTER 5

59 *Whether having a shampoo*: Jack Walsh, Washington Post, quoted in Whittingham, Hail Redskins, 20.

59 *with a trick back seat*: Associated Press, Aug. 8, 1935.

61 *It was at the Walker Theater*: Whittingham, Hail Redskins, 21.

61 *apply theatrical principles to advertising*: Haggerty, "Hail to the Redskins," 9.

66 *Big League Football*: Loverro, Hail Victory, 9.

67 *not only a treat*: Whittingham, Hail Redskins, 10.

CHAPTER 6

68 *I wouldn't marry George*: Griffith, Life with the Redskins, 1.

69 *George was a delegate*: Ibid., 6–7.

69 *The whole thing was so overdone*: Bob Curran, Pro Football's Rag Days (1969), quoted in Richman, "Cliff Battles."

69 *Gentlemen, you know far more*: WashingtonPost.com, The Redskins Book, 15.

70 *They are bad for business*: Dent, Monster of the Midway, 109.

70 *In later years*: WashingtonPost.com, Redskins Book, 17.

71 *Marshall was a loud*: Quoted in Loverro, Hail Victory, 15.

71 *The remarkable William Henry*: Jackson, "Wicarhpi Isnala 'Lone Star.'"

73 *as we already*: Qureshi and Grissom, "Secret Letters of the Washington Redskins," 10.

74 *The man who made Marshall's year*: William Gildea, "In the Beginning," in The Redskins Book, 7.

75 *Occasional snowflakes*: Griffith, Life with the Redskins, 17.

75 *Halfway up 21's homespun stairway*: Ibid., 18.
76 *Coached by a great coach*: Ibid., 21.
76 *the stickiest, clammiest mud*: Arthur J. Daley, "Boston Conquers Giants in Rain, Fog and Mud to Win Eastern Title," *New York Times*, Dec. 7, 1936.
76 *On nearly every play*: Ibid.
77 *george stop guess what*: Dent, *Monster of the Midway*, 195.
77 *I'm licked, he told them*: Haggerty, *"Hail to the Redskins,"* 28.
77 *has this crazy idea*: Griffith, *Life with the Redskins*, 19.
78 *Will you tell her*: Ibid., 20.
78 *We'll make much more*: Loverro, *Hail Victory*, 13.
79 *Arthur Daley of the New York Times*: Daley, *New York Times*, Dec. 8, 1936.
79 *a very dull game*: Griffith, *Life with the Redskins*, 23.
79 *I rather like the idea of Newark*: Arthur J. Daley, "National Football League's Title Match Will Be Played at the Polo Grounds," *New York Times*, Dec. 8, 1936.

CHAPTER 7

81 *Just put me in there*: Ed Prell, "Frog Bombers Triumph over Porkers," *Fort Worth Star-Telegram*, Oct. 3, 1936.
81 *In fact, as the minutes wore on*: Hall, *Fort Worth Star-Telegram*, Oct. 3, 1936.
81 *Although it would be Arkansas's only loss*: Canning, *Sam Baugh*, 50.
82 *I told him I really thought*: Ibid.
82 *He ran right past me*: Ibid.
82 *feet seem to fly*: Hall, *Fort Worth Star-Telegram*, Sept. 26, 1936.
82 *I have a peculiar habit*: Ibid.
82 *What burned Baylor more*: Hall, *Fort Worth Star-Telegram*, Nov. 3, 1936.
83 *They should handicap Baugh*: Jinx Tucker, *Waco Times-Herald*, quoted by Hall, *Fort Worth Star-Telegram*, Nov. 3, 1936.
83 *the hip-hip and hooraying*: Flem Hall, *Fort Worth Star-Telegram*, Nov. 7, 1936.
83 *He wanted to play football*: Canning, *Sam Baugh*, 21.
83 *Gentlemen, he announced*: Rives, "Slingin' Sam vs. Father Time," 92.
84 *The only way Baugh*: Canning, *Sam Baugh*, 53.
84 *Coach Dutch Meyer*: Associated Press, "Texas Christian Routs Centenary," Nov. 15, 1936.
84 *By bombing the Owls*: Hall, *Fort Worth Star-Telegram*, Dec. 5, 1936.
84 *How can you expect a team*: Canning, *Sam Baugh*, 54.
85 *Comparing the results gained*: Hall, *Fort Worth Star-Telegram*, Nov. 27, 1936.
85 *the first time since Sammy*: Hall, *Fort Worth Star-Telegram*, Dec. 1, 1936.
85 *It was more than a shame*: Canning, *Sam Baugh*, 56.
86 *Baugh did it almost single-handedly*: Quoted in ibid.
86 *Santa Clara was the best team*: Baugh oral history, Texas Tech.
86 *Dutch said we were gonna*: Canning, *Sam Baugh*, 56.
87 *One night, we were sitting in this bar*: Ibid.
88 *They looked like two peas*: Baugh oral history, Texas Tech.
89 *They were real scrappy*: Canning, *Sam Baugh*, 56.

CHAPTER 8

91   *The North Texas metropolis*: *The Handbook of Texas*, s.v. "Texas Centennial."

91   *Visitors to the Centennial*: "National Affairs: Superlative Century," *Time*, June 8, 1936.

91   *Go to Dallas for education*: Hope Ridings Miller, "Washingtonian Gathers Fame, Fortune in Texas," *Washington Post*, Aug. 11, 1937.

91   *took in hand entertainment features*: Ibid.

92   *turned into a $1,000-a-day producer*: Ibid.

92   *The list of stars*: Ibid.

93   *How about a show, too*: Griffith, *Life with the Redskins*, 24–25.

93   *I discussed the show*: Ibid.

94   *Of course, my show*: Ibid., 25–26.

94   *I picked a number*: Ibid., 26.

94   *They stomped and sang all the way*: Ibid., 27–28.

94   *Billy Rose and Amon Carter*: Ibid., 35.

95   *I was asleep at 11 a.m.*: Ibid., 33–35.

95   *Resplendent in his first dinner jacket*: Ibid., 34.

96   *Humphrey was so proud*: "Robert L. Humphrey Dies; Scouted Sammy Baugh," *Washington Post*, Jan. 9, 1976.

97   *I didn't have any idea*: Povich, "Tales of Redskins Alarm Chicago," *Washington Post*, Dec. 10, 1937.

98   *Pro football was not something*: Canning, *Sam Baugh*, 65.

98   *What size do you wear*: Povich, *All Those Mornings*, 146.

99   *Ah guess Ah gotta*: Ibid.

100   *As soon as I saw*: David Ramsey, "Baugh Just Another West Texas Rancher," *Abilene Reporter-News*, Feb. 21, 1983.

100   *I hit one off him*: Ibid.

101   *Marshall, an astute businessman*: Lewis F. Atchison, "Club Owner Wires News from Texas," *Washington Post*, June 5, 1937.

101   *But I told Mr. Rickey*: Frank Luksa, "Baugh Relives Memory of Minor League Fling," *Dallas Morning News*, Mar. 17, 1998.

102   *Their scouts gave me*: Povich, "Ace Passer, Marshall in Salary Spat," *Washington Post*, Aug. 29, 1937.

102   *Big league clubs sign up*: Povich, "An Open Letter to Sammy Baugh," *Washington Post*, Aug. 29, 1937.

104   *Tonight's game was rated*: Associated Press, "85,000 See Big Battle in Chicago," Sept. 2, 1937.

104   *He'll do until some supernatural*: Povich, "Dorais Praises Baugh After Big Game," *Washington Post*, Sept. 3, 1937.

105   *I wouldn't say that Baugh*: Povich, "Who's Sammy Baugh? Asks Marshall," *Washington Post*, Sept. 4, 1937.

106   *Even at the expense of*: Ibid.

106   *But where would Baugh get*: Ibid.

106   *Through Joe Carr*: "Cards Back Marshall in Baugh Fuss," *Washington Post*, Sept 4, 1937.

107   *I talked with the rest*: Cope, "Life for Two Tough Texans."

107   *I didn't have any money*: Baugh oral history, Texas Tech.

107   *I talked to Dutch*: Ibid.

107   *Slingin' Sammy Baugh tore off*: "Baugh Due Here Today; Terms O.K.," *Washington Post*, Sept. 8, 1937.

108   *At three o'clock in the morning*: Griffith, *Life with the Redskins*, 42.

CHAPTER 9

109   *It's about time*: "Baugh Due Here Today; Terms O.K.," *Washington Post*, Sept. 8, 1937.

110   *Baugh put on a show*: Povich, "3,000 See Baugh Give Sensational Passing Exhibition in Pro Debut," *Washington Post*, Sept. 10, 1937.

111   *All that matters is how it feels*: Dan Daly, "Unfathomable," *Washington Times*, Dec. 20, 2008.

111   *Look, Sammy, Wayne Millner*: William Gildea, "I Thought It Was Fun, I Played Cause I Liked It," *Washington Post*, Sept. 18, 1977.

112   *but the envelope of Slingin' Sammy*: Povich, *Washington Post*, Dec. 16, 1937.

112   *I wrote it in just about*: Haggerty, *"Hail to the Redskins,"* 46.

112   *Hail to the Redskins*: Griffith, *Life with the Redskins*, 39.

113   *We were told how we of the District*: Griffith, *Life with the Redskins*, 45.

113   *It is a lasting tribute*: Haggerty, *"Hail to the Redskins,"* 44.

114   *With what I'm paying Baugh*: Povich, "Marshall: Impresario of the Redskins," *Washington Post*, Sept. 2, 1986.

114   *The great night arrived*: Griffith, *Life with the Redskins*, 47.

114   *All right, you guys*: WashingtonPost.com, *Redskins Book*, 12.

115   *We ascended the long ramp*: Ibid., 47–48.

116   *The Giants kicked off*: Details of the game are taken from the following sources: Griffith, *Life with the Redskins*, 47–50; Haggerty, *"Hail to the Redskins,"* 44; Whittingham, *Hail Redskins*, 52; Loverro, *Hail Victory*, 18; WashingtonPost.com, *Redskins Book*, 12–13; Povich, *Washington Post*, Sept. 17, 1937.

117   *If there was any doubt*: Povich, *Washington Post*, Dec. 16, 1937.

117   *As for the near 25,000 crowd*: Bill Dismer, Jr., *Washington Evening Star*, quoted in Loverro, *Hail Victory*, 18.

118   *Throughout the first half*: Kingsley Childs, "Baugh's Brilliant Passing Aids as Redskins Top Dodgers, 11 to 7," *New York Times*, Oct. 4, 1937.

120   *I just can't get over*: Haggerty, *"Hail to the Redskins,"* 44.

120   *I think just about everyone*: Ibid., 45.

120   *This was the exact moment*: Bealle, *The Redskins*, 38.

120   *Slingin' Sam is the hottest thing*: Allison Danzig, "That Man From Texas," *New York Times*, Dec. 14, 1937.

121   *The Indians have come*: Bill Corum, *New York Journal*, quoted in Griffith, *Life with the Redskins*, 61.

121   *Now they had a home*: Griffith, *Life with the Redskins*, 61.

122   *I can't believe it*: Ibid., 62.

122 *I don't think the Redskins*: Haggerty, *"Hail to the Redskins,"* 47.

124 *I waited for the wild jungle call*: Griffith, *Life with the Redskins*, 64.

124 *Follow that patrol car*: Ibid., 67.

CHAPTER 10

126 *Get off the field*: Dent, *Monster of the Midway*, 187.

126 *Don't you dare*: Griffith, *Life with the Redskins*, 74–75.

126 *Please see that these selections*: Loverro, *Hail Victory*, 20.

127 *A passer had to learn*: Baugh oral history, Texas Tech.

127 *if you lost two good ones*: Ibid.

127 *I want you to hit*: Dent, *Monster of the Midway*, 210.

128 *The only way to stop Nagurski*: Ibid., 121.

128 *smashing, driving*: Quoted in ibid., 60.

128 *When the Bronk hits you*: Ibid., 87.

129 *The beautiful white snow*: Griffith, *Life with the Redskins*, 70.

129 *It was colder*: Robert Ruark, in WashingtonPost.com, *Redskins Book*, 24.

130 *We're gonna trick 'em*: Dent, *Monster of the Midway*, 211.

130 *The* Times *found it notable*: Arthur Daley, "Redskins Defeat Bears on Icy Chicago Gridiron to Take National Pro Title," *New York Times*, Dec. 13, 1937.

131 *That sonofabitch ran*: Dent, *Monster of the Midway*, 212.

131 *Every time you hit that icy field*: Baugh oral history, Texas Tech.

132 *the score was Chicago 14*: Griffith, *Life with the Redskins*, 71.

133 *It was amazing the way*: Daley, "Redskins Defeat Bears," *New York Times*, Dec. 13, 1937.

133 *Baugh threw passes*: Ibid.

134 *Coach Flaherty was the first*: Povich, *Washington Post*, Dec. 16, 1937.

134 *The team moved no emo*. Robert Ruark, in WashingtonPost.com, *Redskins Book*, 24.

134 *He had fastened himself*: Ibid.

134 *You're a fine fella*: Baugh oral history, Texas Tech.

135 *What the heck, anyone*: Povich, *Washington Post*, Dec. 13, 1937, 15.

135 *There are a lot of other*: Allison Danzig, "That Man from Texas," *New York Times*, Dec. 14, 1937.

135 *All season, the fellow*: Povich, *Washington Post*, Dec. 16, 1937.

135 *is the greatest passer*: Associated Press, "Visiting Fans from Washington Shower Acclaim on the Redskins," Dec. 13, 1937.

136 *put Sweetwater on the map*: *Dallas Morning News*, Dec. 21, 1937.

136 *all the adulation*: Flem Hall, "Baugh Honored by Sweetwater Fans," *Fort Worth Star-Telegram*, Dec. 21, 1937.

136 *It's hard to get up*: Ibid.

136 *That Hall of Fame ring*: Baugh oral history, Texas Tech.

CHAPTER 11

138 *It wasn't just the money*: Haggerty, *"Hail to the Redskins,"* 62.

138 *Hell, if I had known*: Canning, *Sam Baugh*, 71.

138 *One year's football at $13,000*: Associated Press, "Sammy Baugh to Sign 3-Year Contract With Redskin Eleven," Jan. 19, 1938.

139 *The professional football racket*: "Ace Passer Will Accept Coach's Job," *Washington Post*, Feb. 13, 1938.

140 *Marshall comes across with*: "Sam Baugh Reports to St. Louis Florida Camp," *Washington Post*, Mar. 8, 1938.

140 *I had a good time*: David Ramsey, "Baugh Just Another West Texas Rancher," *Abilene Reporter-News*, Feb. 21, 1983.

140 *One guy that really tried*: McClain, "The Last Gunslinger," *Houston Chronicle*, July 26, 1998.

141 *That bird with No. 21*: John Kieran, "From the Backfield to the Infield," *New York Times*, Mar. 22, 1938.

141 *I've still never felt such pain*: McClain, "The Last Gunslinger," *Houston Chronicle*, July 26, 1998.

141 *Baugh hasn't looked like Lou Gehrig*: Kieran, "From the Backfield to the Infield," *New York Times*, Mar. 22, 1938.

142 *I never saw a worse bunch*: Povich, "Baugh Might Surprise and Make Good," *Washington Post*, Apr. 3, 1938.

143 *Frisch has given me*: Povich, *Washington Post*, Apr. 4, 1938.

143 *He's offering me the same*: "Houston or Columbus! That's the Choice Baugh Has to Make," *Washington Post*, Apr. 5, 1938.

143 *I probably will play*: Charles Burton, "Sweetwater's No. 1 Citizen Weds His No. 1 Fan," *Dallas Morning News*, Apr. 10, 1938.

143 *The United Press reported*: United Press International, "Baugh Marries Edmonia Smith in Sweetwater," Apr. 10, 1938.

144 *apparently happily resigned*: *Fort Worth Star-Telegram*, Apr. 11, 1938.

144 *We'll be home in January*: *Fort Worth Star-Telegram*, Apr. 11, 1938.

145 *As far as his value*: Povich, *Washington Post*, July 10, 1938.

145 *was definitely a big-league*: Canning, *Sam Baugh*, 63.

145 *Anyway, I had problems*: Don Pierson, "Sammy Baugh: 1914–2008; NFL's 'Greatest Player,'" *Chicago Tribune*, Dec. 18, 2008.

145 *We will pay Baugh*: Povich, *Washington Post*, July 22, 1938.

145 *football's greatest forward passer*: Jack Munhall, "Passer Gets Highest Wage in Pro Grid," *Washington Post*, Aug. 3, 1938.

145 *but the biggest part of my worries*: Povich, *Washington Post*, July 22, 1938.

146 *Just a night's work*: Povich, *Washington Post*, Oct. 29, 1989.

146 *Ghostwriting was not*: Ibid.

146 *Baugh couldn't be bothered*: *Los Angeles Times*, Oct. 10, 1988.

147 *Right now, I want to refute*: Slingin' Sammy Baugh, "Nobody's Sacred in Pro League, Discovers Baugh, Told to Run," *Washington Post*, Aug. 15, 1938.

CHAPTER 12

148 *In one short season*: Quoted in Whittingham, *Hail Redskins*, 58.

148 *The fact that fans*: Ibid.

149 *You fellows are acting too much like*: Povich, "Coach Ray Flaherty Hits 'Overconfidence' in Hot Speech in Redskins' Dressing Room," *Washington Post*, Aug. 30, 1938.

150 *for he had treated them*: Povich, "Sammy May Be Out for Three Weeks," *Washington Post*, ept. 12, 1938.

151 *We received nothing for playing*: "Marshall Accused of 'Chiseling,'" *Washington Post*, Nov. 1, 1938.

152 *This is to advise that*: Qureshi and Grissom, "Secret Letters of the Washington Redskins," 10.

153 *Owners, as columnists*: "Sports of the Times; NFL's Labor Pioneer Remains Unknown," William C. Rhoden, Oct. 12, 1994.

153 *Marshall traded him*: "The Eccentric Mr. Marshall; Owners Brought Redskins to Town and Made Them a D.C. Institution," Dan Daly, *Washington Times*, Sept. 6, 2001, p. E10.

153 *Satin pants which weigh less*: *Washington Post*, Aug. 28, 1938.

154 *a bruising battle*: Povich, "Baugh Is Stopped; Fists Fly in Game," *Washington Post*, Nov. 14, 1938.

154 *That's too bad, girlies*: Quoted in WashingtonPost.com, *Redskins Book*, 28.

154 *On the way back to Washington*: Povich, *All Those Mornings*, 103.

155 *Whizzer White justified*: Povich, "Redskins Beat Pirates, 15–0, to Stay in Race," *Washington Post*, Nov. 28, 1938.

155 *everything seems to be going*: Vidmer, *Washington Post*, Dec. 2, 1938.

156 *Caught in the fury*: Povich, "Win Right to Meet Packers in Play-Off," *Washington Post*, Dec. 5, 1938.

156 *In the middle of the fourth*: Kieran, *New York Times*, Dec. 5, 1938.

156 *I'm mad and don't let anybody*: Richman, *Redskins Encyclopedia*, 16.

157 *Passers took a terrible beating*: Whittingham, *Hail Redskins*, 50.

157 *From the first time he*: Quoted in Canning, *Sam Baugh*, 70.

159 *Halloran told me he could*: Richman, *Redskins Encyclopedia*, 17.

159 *As we passed through*: Griffith, *Life with the Redskins*, 09.

160 *men, women, children, newsboys*: Ibid., 90.

160 *I was sitting on*: Povich, in WashingtonPost.com, *Redskins Book*, 18.

CHAPTER 13

161 *the most ultramodern*: Quoted in WashingtonPost.com, *Redskins Book*, 26.

162 *Baugh, starting the final*: Jack Munhall, "Performance of Baugh Elates Flaherty," *Washington Post*, Sept. 16, 1940.

162 *I think he will get out*: Quoted in WashingtonPost.com, *Redskins Book*, 26.

162 *Dick Todd is the greatest*: Quoted in ibid., 27.

162 *No one's going to beat*: Whittingham, *Hail Redskins*, 200.

163 *It was worse*: National Football League Creative Staff, *First Fifty Years*, 166.

163 *Just remember, he muttered*: Dent, *Monster of the Midway*, 227.

164 *They fold up when*: Ibid., 228.

164 *I never played against*: Quoted in WashingtonPost.com, *Redskins Book*, 28.

164 *We could sell*: Ibid.

164 *Plainclothes detectives*: Al Hailey, "Fans Failing To Get Seats Disgruntled," *Washington Post*, Dec. 3, 1940.

164 *There were more red feathers*: "Washington Massacre," *Time*, Dec. 16, 1940.

165 *congratulations*: Dent, *Monster of the Midway*, 228.

165 *Senators, Congressmen, Big Shots*: Griffith, *Life with the Redskins*, 104.

165 *in a very modest sort of way*: Ibid.

165 *Only three weeks ago*: "Washington Massacre," *Time*, Dec. 16, 1940.

166 *The* Post *advertised*: WashingtonPost.com, *Redskins Book*, 29.

167 *The Bears are a team*: Whittingham, *Hail Redskins*, 205.

167 *When I saw the type*: Quoted in WashingtonPost.com, *Redskins Book*, 29.

168 *it might have been*: Daley, *New York Times*, Dec. 8, 1940.

168 *What happened after that*: "Washington Massacre," *Time*, Dec. 16, 1940.

168 *McChesney playing with a broken hand*: Griffith, *Life with the Redskins*, 107.

168 *I remember saying*: Canning, *Sam Baugh*, 75.

168 *Well, fellows, he said*: "73–0 Rout of Redskins Is Recalled," *Washington Post*, Sept. 2, 1941.

169 *the most ill-advised announcement*: Considine, *Washington Post*, Dec. 9, 1940.

169 *I'm going down to those kids*: Griffith, *Life with the Redskins*, 107.

169 *What she didn't say*: Considine, *Washington Post*, Dec. 9, 1940.

169 *Well, after one of those*: Cope, "Life for Two Tough Texans."

170 *We were only ahead*: Don Pierson, "73–0: It's Indelibly Etched in History," *Chicago Tribune*, Dec. 9, 1990.

170 *Some of these elder players*: Povich, *All Those Mornings*, 73.

170 *The Bears visited on Washington*: Povich, *Washington Post*, Dec. 7, 1990.

170 *That T-formation is really*: Povich, *All Those Mornings*, 75.

170 *That was the most humiliating*: Merrell W. Whittlesey, "Irate in Dressing Room; Changes to Be Made, He Says," *Washington Post*, Dec. 9, 1940.

171 *I don't know whether*: Cope, "Life for Two Tough Texans."

171 *Everywhere he went*: Canning, *Sam Baugh*, 74.

171 *Those guys out there today*: Whittlesey, "Irate in Dressing Room," *Washington Post*, Dec. 9, 1940.

172 *Yeah, it would have been*: Quoted in WashingtonPost.com, *Redskins Book*, 29.

172 *My locker was close*: Quoted in ibid.

172 *In 1999, he told a reporter*: Associated Press, "Baugh Has Doubts About 73–0 Loss," Nov. 28, 1999.

172 *I don't think he was saying*: David Baugh interview, Aug. 11, 2011.

172 *Was he drunk*: Associated Press, "Baugh Has Doubts About 73–0 Loss," Nov. 28, 1999.

172 *An NFL spokesman*: Ibid.

CHAPTER 14

173 *He looks like he invented*: Bob Sterling, "For a Guy Who Never Wore Boots, Baugh Became Quite a Cowboy," United Press International, Dec. 20, 1959.

173 *I thought at first*: Carlton Stowers, "Sammy Still Slingin'," *Dallas Morning News*, Nov. 6, 1977.

174   *Ah, shit on celebrity*: Tuttle, "Better Than Sonny?"

174   *Sammy Baugh? Baugh*: Sterling, "For a Guy Who Never Wore Boots," United Press International, Dec. 20, 1959.

175   *I can truthfully say*: Elston Brooks, *Fort Worth Star-Telegram*, June 9, 1974.

175   *Lord, he was tickled*: Ibid.

175   *The first day at the studio*: McClain, "The Last Gunslinger," *Houston Chronicle*, July 13, 1998.

176   *One day, we couldn't film*: Ibid.

176   *I always ate lunch*: Ibid.

178   *Gosh, Sam, he murmured*: Sterling, "For a Guy Who Never Wore Boots," United Press International, Dec. 20, 1959.

178   *He cringed, but we howled*: Dennis Tuttle, interview by the author, 2006.

CHAPTER 15

180   *That's when I first saw*: Canning, *Sam Baugh*, 101.

181   *the oldest thing under heaven*: Skip Hollandsworth, *Westward, Dallas Times Herald*, Nov. 9, 1980.

181   *Sam's mountain and the acreage*: Historical details of the ranch are from "Sammy Baugh's Ranch Includes One of Famed Double Mountains," *Fort Worth Star-Telegram*, Apr. 3, 1949.

182   *The first calf crop we brought in*: Canning, *Sam Baugh*, 103.

182   *He may have been a big-time*: Ibid.

182   *He sometimes wondered why she*: Ibid.

182   *They just sort of stared*: Hollandsworth, *Westward, Dallas Times Herald*, Nov. 9, 1980.

183   *He didn't know much*: Viola Brazee, interview by the author, 2009.

183   *Not many from her background*: Owen Brannon, interview by the author, 2009.

183   *The year we moved out here*: Reid, "Legends of the Fall."

CHAPTER 16

184   *Wee Willie had played college ball*: Whittingham, *Hail Redskins*, 121.

184   *Don Looney, a former Horned Frog*: Canning, *Sam Baugh*, 75.

185   *You drunk son of a bitch*: Sam Baugh, ESPN interview.

185   *A couple of years later*: David Baugh, interview by the author, Aug. 3, 2010.

186   *I played that game for more*: Canning, *Sam Baugh*, 21.

186   *I never bet on another thing*: David Baugh interview.

186   *After the '40 championship game*: WashingtonPost.com, *Redskins Book*, 30.

186   *He had a brilliant football mind*: Ibid.

187   *He'd be in his tent*: Riffenburgh, *NFL Encyclopedia*, 15.

187   *Young Sammy may not know it*: *Washington Post*, Oct. 20, 1941.

188   *He remembered that day*: Lynn "Buddy" Watwood, telephone interview by the author, 2010.

188   *The first word about the catastrophe*: Richard E. Goldstein, "Football Sunday, Dec. 7, 1941: Suddenly The Games Didn't Matter," *New York Times*, Dec. 7, 1980.

189   *Attention please*: Ibid.

189   *Watwood remembered that*: Watwood interview.

189   *The first, as Shirley Povich recalled*: Povich, "At Redskins-Eagles Game, Crowd Was Kept Unaware That War Had Begun," *Washington Post*, Dec. 7, 1991.

189   *The resident commissioner*: Ibid.

189   *Then the city's five newspapers*: Ibid.

189   *Not relayed over*: Goldstein, "Football Sunday, Dec. 7, 1941," *New York Times*, Dec. 7, 1980.

190   *For a few moments*: Povich, "At Redskins-Eagles Game," *Washington Post*, Dec. 7, 1991.

190   *I'm leaving. I've just had word*: Griffith, *Life with the Redskins*, 112.

190   *Something's wrong, said Baxter*: Povich, "At Redskins-Eagles Game," *Washington Post*, Dec. 7, 1991.

190   *Povich was still angry*: Ibid.

191   *After all, there were still*: Ibid.

191   *We beat the Eagles*: McClain, "The Last Gunslinger," *Houston Chronicle*, July 26, 1998.

191   *The United States of America*: Edward T. Folliard, "Hawaii Attacked Without Warning With Heavy Loss; Philippines Are Bombed," *Washington Post*, Dec. 8, 1941.

192   *I don't know what is going*: Goldstein, "Football Sunday, Dec. 7, 1941," *New York Times*, Dec. 7, 1980.

CHAPTER 17

193   *No sport faces*: Steve Snider, "Pro Grid Draft 'Joke' As War Ends Gold Era," United Press International, Dec. 12, 1941

194   *Some did not return*: Goldstein, "Football Sunday, Dec. 7, 1941," *New York Times*, Dec. 7, 1980.

195   *drew criticism in some quarters*: Rives, "Slingin' Sam vs. Father Time," 41.

195   *A week later, the Redskins*: Whittingham, *Hail Redskins*, 160.

196   *In the first half, the Redskins*: Griffith, *Life with the Redskins*, 116.

196   *If the Bears want to get tough*: Quoted in WashingtonPost.com, *Redskins Book*, 30.

197   *The Bears say that Sammy Baugh*: Ibid.

197   *The* Post *reported that Flaherty*: Ibid., 31.

197   *Ah wouldn't say they're meaner*: Quoted in ibid.

197   *December 6, 1942, was a cold, crisp day*: Whittingham, *Hail Redskins*, 164.

197   *Curly Lambeau, sitting with George*: Griffith, *Life with the Redskins*, 117.

198   *In the stands, a wire-service photographer*: Ibid., 118, 119.

198   *the greatest play I ever saw*: Ibid., 118.

198   *Ninety-nine per cent of pro-football*: Ibid., 119.

198   *That kick turned out to be*: Loverro, *Hail Victory*, 26.

199   *Every time assistant coach Luke*: Dent, *Monster of the Midway*, 245.

199   *The Bears were very angry*: Griffith, *Life with the Redskins*, 120.

200   *People went crazy*: Watwood interview.
200   *By way of supplying a final*: Daley, *New York Times*, quoted in Whittingham, *Hail Redskins*, 25.
200   *Everyone respected him*: Loverro, *Hail Victory*, 26.
200   *Those are all keen, earnest*: Rice, "Rice Lauds Play of Sam Baugh, '42's Top Athlete," *Stars and Stripes*, Dec. 23, 1942.
201   *Commissioner Layden called for*: Ted Meier, "Layden Seeking 'Full Facts' in Sam's Case," Associated Press, Dec. 28, 1942.

CHAPTER 18

202   *My training had been*: Griffith, *Life with the Redskins*, 123.
203   *We were playing somebody*: Baugh oral history, Texas Tech.
203   *I didn't like something*: Ibid.
203   *Helmets, maybe even shoulder pads*: Dent, *Monster of the Midway*, 233.
203   *The 4-F's carried on*: Griffith, *Life with the Redskins*, 124–125.
204   *another of Sammy Baugh's untouchable*: Quoted in WashingtonPost.com, *Redskins Book*, 32.
204   *I was passable*: Sam Baugh, ESPN interview.
205   *If Baugh wasn't the Babe Ruth*: Povich, quoted in WashingtonPost.com, *Redskins Book*, 32.
205   *I think you'd better tell her*: Griffith, *Life with the Redskins*, 128–130.
206   *On December 8, 1943, readers*: Ibid., 131–134.
206   *Reports that a betting coup*: Quoted in ibid., 134.
207   *The whole thing is a gross libel*: Ibid.
207   *I'd like to bring some*: Ibid., 135.
207   *Now gentlemen, here is*: Ibid.
207   *And you wrote the story*: Ibid., 136.
207   *Some sportswriters said*: Rives, "Slingin' Sam vs. Father Time," 41.
207   *We fellows on the team*: Ibid., 92.
208   *nothing more than the chance*: Flaherty, quoted in WashingtonPost.com, *Redskins Book*, 32.
208   *I'm so sorry you were unable*: Griffith, *Life with the Redskins*, 137.
208   *I just want to say*: Whittingham, *Hail Redskins*, 209.
209   *a one-man field day*: "Sport: One-Man Air Raid," *Time*, Dec. 27, 1943.
209   *Buddy Watwood, who saw*: Watwood interview.
209   *Bill Patten was a ball boy*: Patten, interview by the author, 2010.
210   *I ain't as worried about*: Quoted in Dent, *Monster of the Midway*, 283.
210   *The Bears are a bunch*: Ibid.
211   *If there was a tougher Redskin*: Ken Denlinger, "Redskins Anthology: Numbering the Epochs," *Washington Post*, Dec. 21, 1986.
211   *My god, it's Marshall*: Whittingham, *Hail Redskins*, 209.
212   *Do you know where you are*: Quoted in WashingtonPost.com, *Redskins Book*, 33.

CHAPTER 19

213 *conjecture, consternation*: "Baugh Says He'll Follow Draft Ruling," *Washington Post*, Sept. 22, 1944.

213 *Oh, yes sir, he said*: Griffith, *Life with the Redskins*, 144–145.

214 *The reserve team's name*: Al Costello, "Baugh Here, Filchock to Start Game," *Washington Post*, Oct. 22, 1944.

214 *His average of .673*: Ibid.

215 *I figured I only could go*: Whittingham, *Hail Redskins*, 60.

215 *T formation kindergarten*: Griffith, *Life with the Redskins*, 141.

215 *Coach Shaughnessy explained*: Ibid.

215 *When I switched from*: Whittingham, *Hail Redskins*, 60.

216 *Why, that's the easiest position*: Rives, "Slingin' Sam vs. Father Time," 92.

216 *I had to block*: Dave Brady, "Sammy Baugh; Giant Figure of Redskin Lore," *Washington Post*, Sept. 20, 1978.

216 *Why, we had over 20 plays*: Rives, "Slingin' Sam vs. Father Time," 92.

216 *You use a rocker step*: Daly, "Unfathomable," *Washington Times*, Dec. 19, 2008.

217 *I could play it in top hat*: Whittingham, *Hail Redskins*, 214.

217 *General Dwight D. Eisenhower*: Griffith, *Life with the Redskins*, 160.

218 *I'd come from a very disciplined*: Denlinger, "Redskins Anthology," *Washington Post*, Dec. 21, 1986.

218 *Be sure you don't even*: Griffith, *Life with the Redskins*, 162.

219 *but Texas blood and guts*: Bealle, *The Redskins*, 84.

219 *Out there, he told the Post's*: Baugh oral history, Texas Tech.

219 *Good morning! It's nine o'clock*: Griffith, *Life with the Redskins*, 167–168.

219 *They're peddling hot coffee*: Povich, *Washington Post*, quoted in Whittingham, *Hail Redskins*, 217.

220 *Everyone expected Sam to punt*: Quoted in Luksa, "Slingin' Sammy Last Link."

220 *I couldn't throw very hard*: Baugh oral history, Texas Tech.

220 *Wayne would have gone the rest*: WashingtonPost.com, *Redskins Book*, 35.

220 *Marshall came into the locker room*: Loverro, *Hail Victory*, 29.

221 *Sam blew on his fingers*: Ibid.

CHAPTER 20

222 *If you play long enough*: Baugh oral history, Texas Tech.

223 *I kind of figure it*: Griffith, *Life with the Redskins*, 178.

223 *Marshall could promote the game*: Quoted in Riffenburgh, *NFL Encyclopedia*, 16.

223 *Mr. Marshall would have loved*: Tereshinski, quoted in Loverro, *Hail Victory*, 32.

223 *Tereshinski recalled the sight*: Tereshinski interview.

224 *Goddamn it, Sam*: Cope, "Life for Two Tough Texans."

224 *Ray didn't let anybody*: WashingtonPost.com, *Redskins Book*, 36.

224 *Turk was a great football player*: Quoted in Loverro, *Hail Victory*, 32.

224 *I've got to celebrate*: Griffith, *Life with the Redskins*, 208.

224 *Mrs. Samuel Adrian Baugh*: Ibid.

225 *The tip-off was the number of times*: Haggerty, *"Hail to the Redskins,"* 86.

226 *That was the easiest game*: Loverro, *Hail Victory*, 33.

226 *At that time of the night*: Ibid.

226 *He was actually*: David Baugh interview, Aug. 11, 2011.

226 *They are suffering from*: Povich, in WashingtonPost.com, *Redskins Book*, 36.

226 *the thin man from Texas*: Associated Press, "Redskins Broken, But Baugh Unbent," Dec. 16, 1947.

227 *Sammy would still have all*: Quoted in Loverro, *Hail Victory*, 42.

227 *Is Baugh beginning to feel tired*: Associated Press, "Redskins Broken," Dec. 16, 1947.

227 *My locker was next to Sammy Baugh's*: Quoted in Loverro, *Hail Victory*, 43.

227 *He could be very innovative*: Canning, *Sam Baugh*, 83.

228 *Sam pretty much adopted me*: Ibid., 85.

228 *He could start telling stories*: Ibid.

228 *Sam sat there and listened*: Ibid., 87.

CHAPTER 21

229 *I just wanted to let you know*: Canning, *Sam Baugh*, 83.

229 *The first thing I learned*: Ibid.

229 *It was amazing just to stand around*: Ibid.

230 *I was with the Redskins*: Ibid.

230 *Sam kept coming back*: Haggerty, *"Hail to the Redskins,"* 87.

230 *A cache of letters*: Unless otherwise noted, the letters from Sam Baugh to his wife and children are in the possession of Samu Qureshi; they are reproduced with the permission of the Baugh family.

231 *A scouting report*: Tereshinski showed me the scouting report during our interview.

234 *Two suits, or one suit*: Qureshi and Grissom, "Secret Letters of the Washington Redskins," 25.

236 *I was a rookie in*: Loverro, *Hail Victory*, 44.

237 *It would be a good job*: Associated Press, "Baugh Turns Down Post at Baylor to Remain with Redskins' Eleven," Jan. 14, 1950.

238 *This brand-new edition*: Povich, *Washington Post*, Sept. 18, 1950.

239 *Gentlemen, he said*: Haggerty, *"Hail Redskins,"* 89.

240 *That's the kind of fight*: Ibid., 90.

241 *Mr. Marshall, he said*: Loverro, *Hail Victory*, 40.

242 *I don't know what he*: Ibid., 41.

242 Welcome Back, Committee: Haggerty, *"Hail Redskins,"* 104.

242 *The team so far appears to me*: Qureshi and Grissom, "Secret Letters of the Washington Redskins."

243 *What do you guys think*: Doug Fernandes, "Friends with a Legend," *Sarasota Herald-Tribune*, Dec. 21, 2008.

243 *He just got upset about*: Canning, *Sam Baugh*, 87.

244 *The guy was in his sixteenth*: Ibid.

244 *At one point in the first half*: Haggerty, *"Hail Redskins,"* 106.

245 *What's so funny*: Ibid.
245 *Next to an explanation of*: Jack Walsh, "Why Baugh Rides Bench Still a Puzzle," *Washington Post*, Nov. 29, 1952.
245 *Give me Sam*: Haggerty, *"Hail Redskins,"* 106.
246 *The Redskins aren't just losing*: Walsh, "Lean Texan Has Been Mr. Football Around Here for 16 Years," *Washington Post*, Dec. 14, 1952.
247 *He's been wonderful to me*: Ibid.
247 *had never learned how to*: Povich, *Washington Post*, Dec. 14, 1952.
247 *Without a doubt, Baugh*: Walsh, "Lean Texan Has Been Mr. Football," *Washington Post*, Dec. 14, 1952.
247 *From movie and personal appearances*: Ibid.
248 *You'd never know*: Tereshinski interview.
249 *I've got the game ball*: Walsh, "Baugh Passes from Scene without Pass," *Washington Post*, Dec.15, 1952.
249 *It was dark then*: Ibid.
249 *Well, we had somehow got*: "Hail and Farewell," *Washington Post*, Dec. 18, 1952.

CHAPTER 22

251 *We'd have to ride*: E. B. "Sonny" Nichols, interview by author, 2009.
251 *Each new generation tends*: Kelton, *Time It Never Rained*, ix.
252 *it cost more to haul*: Nichols interview.
252 *if you boys don't quit*: David Baugh interview, July 18, 2009.
253 *I had two good years of marriage*: Judy Baugh, interview by the author, Aug. 8, 2010.
253 *Well, what does your mother*: Canning, *Sam Baugh*, 105.
253 *If Frances had come along*: David Baugh interview, Aug. 11, 2011.
253 *He was pretty conservative*: Nichols interview.
253 *I won't be on salary*: Associated Press, "Hardin-Simmons 'Hires' Baugh as Nonpaid 'Associate' Coach," Feb. 13, 1952.
253 *I got to thinking*: Canning, *Sam Baugh*, 93.
254 *I called plays in college*: Luksa, "Slingin' Sammy Last Link."
254 *the gangling guy from Sweetwater*: Associated Press, "Sammy Baugh Accepts Hardin-Simmons Grid Job," Feb. 3, 1955.
254 *It was a pretty good deal*: Canning, *Sam Baugh*, 93.
255 *The money may have been great*: Jimmie Keeling, interview by author, 2009.
255 *His offense was light-years ahead*: David Baugh interview.
256 *We could move the ball against*: Pete Hart, interview by the author, 2010.
256 *The former Mr. Redskin*: Bob Alden, "Sammy Baugh Will Throw Again in Griffith Stadium," *Washington Post*, Oct. 2, 1956.
256 *For Sam, it was always*: Hart interview.
257 *Hey Coach*: Ibid.
257 *He probably didn't worry*: Keeling interview.
257 *You always got to have*: Baugh oral history, Texas Tech.
257 *He was playing dominoes*: Keeling interview.
258 *the best goddamn job*: Baugh oral history, Texas Tech.

258 *It was a beautiful night*: Hart interview.
258 *little ol' Hardin-Simmons*: Marty Mule, "Rabb Played through Tears as LSU Marched," *Daily Alexandria (LA) Town Talk*, Sept. 26, 2008.
258 *We knew they were going to run*: Ibid.
259 *I'm not sure we ever*: Ibid.
259 *I just thought you'd like to know*: Ibid.
259 *Sam was one of the finest*: Hart interview.

CHAPTER 23

260 *I stayed in that Manhattan hotel*: Baugh oral history, Texas Tech.
261 *Wismer took considerable license*: Morris Siegel, "The Fix Is In," 85.
262 *Harry was one of those guys*: Canning, *Sam Baugh*, 97.
262 *I always say congratulations*: "Harry Wismer, 56, Promoter, Dead," *New York Times*, Dec. 5, 1967.
263 *Going up to New York*: Baugh oral history, Texas Tech.
263 *That was one of those things*: Canning, *Sam Baugh*, 97.
263 *It was two steps down*: Steve Jacobson, "Early Years of Titans Were Less Than Titanic," *Newsday*, Nov. 29, 1998.
263 *going from the Taj Mahal*: Maynard and Shepatin, *You Can't Catch Sunshine*, 125.
263 *What the hell are y'all*: David Baugh interview.
263 *disguised as empty seats*: Quoted in Jacobson, "Early Years of Titans," *Newsday*, Nov. 29, 1998.
263 *If you're gonna have a playbook*: David Baugh interview, July 18, 2009.
263 *He was always coming into*: Canning, *Sam Baugh*, 97.
263 *We're going to have a real team*: *New York Times*, Apr. 26, 1960.
264 *When the AFL was founded*: Ted Dunham, "West Texas Football Legend Remembers 1962 NFL Title Upset," Associated Press, Jan. 13, 1999.
264 *Then they line up*: Ibid.
264 *As far as I'm concerned*: Maynard and Shepatin, *You Can't Catch Sunshine*, 130.
264 *I don't mean to give the impression*: *New York Times*, Apr. 26, 1960.
264 *It's better this way*: Ibid.
265 *To reporters, the Titans*: Maynard and Shepatin, *You Can't Catch Sunshine*, 124.
265 *runnin', gunnin', and high-flyin'*: Ibid., 126.
265 *Sammy Baugh didn't care*: Ibid., 122.
265 *Coach and I both shared*: Ibid., 128.
265 *the hairless wower*: Dick Young, *New York Daily News*.
266 *Well, he said*: David Baugh interview, July 18, 2009.
266 *After one game, players had to*: *Newsday*, Oct. 29, 1998.
266 *He told us we could practice*: Dave Anderson, "Blue and Gold, Then Green and White as the Titans Became the Jets," *New York Times*, Oct. 14, 2007.
267 *Well, we won the first two*: Canning, *Sam Baugh*, 92.
267 *I wish I had a vote*: Anderson, "Blue and Gold," *New York Times*, Oct. 14, 2007.
267 *He's rapping me publicly*: Associated Press, "Wismer Will Demote Baugh," Dec. 12, 1961.

‖‖‖‖‖‖‖‖

267   *Well, that would be just wonderful*: Ibid.

267   *Sure, I'd like to have Davis*: Ibid.

268   *Two weeks before we went to camp*: Ibid.

268   *the greatest respect*: *New York Times*, Dec. 18, 1961.

269   *He was still a familiar figure*: "Harry Wismer, 56, Promoter, Dead," *New York Times*, Dec. 5, 1967.

269   *So he came down and sat*: Canning, *Sam Baugh*, 98.

269   *I was always glad*: Baugh oral history, Texas Tech.

269   *David Baugh remembered*: David Baugh interview, July 18, 2009.

270   *the originator, the founder*: "Baugh's Enshrinement Speech," available at http://www.profootballhof.com/history/release.aspx?release_id=3003.

271   *The newspapers jumped all over*: Canning, *Sam Baugh*, 98.

271   *A head-coaching job*: United Press International, "Baugh Quits Oilers for Ranch Life," Dec. 19, 1964.

271   *A lot of people may think*: William Gildea, "Step Down Gives Baugh 6 Months on the Ranch," *Washington Post*, Aug. 8, 1965.

CHAPTER 24

274   *It all looks pretty easy*: David Baugh interview, July 18, 2009.

274   *met up with an unruly calf*: Felix R. McKnight, "It's Slingin' Samuel, the Rodeo Man, These Days!" *Fort Worth Star-Telegram*, June 9, 1940.

274   *He loved riding*: O'Day interview.

275   *To offset the remote possibility*: McKnight, "It's Slingin' Samuel, *Fort Worth Star-Telegram*, June 9, 1940.

275   *He loved any kind of competition*: David Baugh interview, Aug. 22, 2008.

275   *He didn't talk much football*: Nichols interview.

276   *That ol' mare*: Owen Brazee interview.

276   *Well, all we heard*: David Baugh interview, Aug. 10, 2008.

276   *You get a piece of land*: Hollandsworth, *Westward, Dallas Times Herald*, Nov. 9, 1980.

276   *He did it for the pure joy*: David Baugh interview, Aug. 10, 2008.

277   *I work the cattle myself*: Dave Brady, "Sammy Baugh; Giant Figure of Redskin Lore," *Washington Post*, Sept. 20, 1978.

277   *He had a great touch*: O'Day interview.

278   *He did everything fast*: David Baugh interview, Aug. 22, 2008.

278   *He was one of the few people*: O'Day interview.

278   *Sam, I've come out here*: David Baugh interview, Aug. 11, 2011.

279   *You can't believe the number*: O'Day interview.

279   *There's no telling how many*: *Abilene Reporter-News*, Dec. 23, 2008.

279   *Goddamnit, I don't give*: Hollandsworth, *Westward, Dallas Times Herald*, Nov. 9, 1980.

279   *I had already seen*: McClain, "The Last Gunslinger," *Houston Chronicle*, July 26, 1998.

280 *They swept the town like*: Daley, "Historic Occasion," *New York Times,* Sept. 29, 1961.
280 *You know, somebody's always*: Hollandsworth, *Westward, Dallas Times Herald,* Nov. 9, 1980.
280 *I wouldn't trust any*: McClain, "The Last Gunslinger," *Houston Chronicle,* July 26, 1998.
280 *Larry Dluhy, who traded*: Larry Dluhy, telephone interview by the author, 2010.
281 *In 1998, when a visiting reporter*: McClain, "The Last Gunslinger," *Houston Chronicle,* July 26, 1998.
281 *I had four bad experiences*: Ibid.
281 *Back then, it didn't seem like*: Ibid.
282 *Am I afraid of death*: Hollandsworth, *Westward, Dallas Times Herald,* Nov. 9, 1980.
282 *All I tell them*: McClain, "The Last Gunslinger," *Houston Chronicle,* July 26, 1998.
283 *Well, why would I want to move*: Ibid.
283 *Sammy Baugh said Sid*. Don Pierson, "Sammy Baugh: 1914–2008; NFL's 'Greatest Player,'" *Chicago Tribune,* Dec. 18, 2008.
283 *He was one of the greatest*: Joe Holley and Bart Barnes, "The First of the Gunslingers: Quarterback Led Redskins to Two Titles, Football Into Modern Era," *Washington Post,* Dec. 18, 2008.
283 *To this day Baugh remains*: Thomas Boswell, "Rock of the Redskins, Arm of the NFL," *Washington Post,* Dec. 18, 2008.
283 *New York had Joe DiMaggio*: Patrick Buchanan, "Washington's Sammy Baugh Was Quite a Player," *Salisbury (MD) Daily Times,* Jan. 9, 2009.
284 *I was 9 years old and*: Michael Wilbon, "Getting In a Word for Slingin' Sammy," *Washington Post,* Dec. 19, 2008.
284 *None of that mattered*: David Baugh interview, July 18, 2009.

BIBLIOGRAPHY

INTERVIEWS

Baugh, David. Interviews by the author, Aug. 10, 2008; Aug. 22, 2008; July 18, 2009;
Aug. 3, 2010; Aug. 27, 2010; Aug. 11, 2011; and Aug. 18, 2011. Double Mountain Ranch,
near Rotan, Texas.

Baugh, Judy. Interviews by the author, July 17, 2009; Aug. 8, 2010; Aug. 27, 2010; and
Aug. 11, 2011.

Baugh, Sammy. Interview for an oral-history project, Southwest Collection, Texas Tech
University, Aug. 16, 1998.

Baugh, Todd. Telephone interview by author, March 28, 2010, Billings, Montana.

Brazee, Owen. Interview by the author, July 19, 2009, Clairemont, Texas.

Brazee, Viola. Interview by the author, July 19, 2009, Hobbs, Texas.

Buffett, Warren. E-mail interview by the author, Aug. 14, 2010, Omaha, Nebraska.

Campbell, Dave. Interview by the author, Jan. 17, 2006, Waco, Texas.

Cashion, Ty. Interview by the author, April 24, 2010, Austin, Texas.

Cope, Myron. "A Life for Two Tough Texans." *Sports Illustrated*, Oct. 20, 1969.

Dluhy, Larry. Telephone interview by the author, Sept. 5, 2010, Houston, Texas.

Dodge, Tom. Telephone interview by the author, July 15, 2009, Midlothian, Texas.

Duvall, Robert. Interview by the author, June 17, 2006, The Plains, Virginia.

Gildea, Bill. Interview by the author, Feb. 4, 2009, Chevy Chase, Maryland.

Hart, Bill. Telephone interview by author, June 14, 2009, Baird, Texas.

Hart, Pete. Telephone interview by the author, Aug. 7, 2010, Abilene, Texas.

Holst, Don. Telephone interview by the author, Sept. 17, 2009, Chadron, Nebraska.

Jenkins, Dan. Telephone interview by the author, Jan. 25, 2007, Forth Worth, Texas.

Keeling, Jimmie. Interview by the author, July 18, 2009, Abilene, Texas.

Kendrick, Ellen. Interview by the author, July 19, 2009, Garland, Texas.

Kendrick, Nell Baugh. Interview by the author, July 16, 2009, Garland, Texas.

Knowles, John. Interview by the author, Aug. 11, 2011. Denton, Texas.

Lane, Eddie. Telephone interview by the author, Sept. 6, 2009, Fort Worth, Texas.

McNeill, Jeanne. Interview by the author, Jan. 14, 2007, Washington, D.C.

Nichols, E. B. "Sonny." Interview by the author, July 18, 2009, Aspermont, Texas.

O'Day, Bob. Interview by the author, July 17, 2009, Snyder, Texas.

Patten, Bill. Telephone interview by the author, Apr. 17, 2010, Burke, Virginia.

Qureshi, Samu. Interview by the author, Feb. 15, 2009, Bethesda, Maryland.

Rhome, Jerry. Telephone interview by the author, July 20, 2010, Atlanta, Georgia.

Sansing, Billy. Interview by the author, July 9, 2009, San Antonio, Texas.

Stevenson, Ellen. Telephone interview by the author, July 24, 2009, Garland, Texas.

Tereshinksi, Joe. Interview by the author, Feb. 4, 2008, Chevy Chase, Maryland.

Tuttle, Dennis. Interview by the author, Mar. 3, 2006, Bethesda, Maryland.

Watwood, L. M. "Buddy." Telephone interview by the author, Feb. 7, 2010, Lakewood, Colorado.

PUBLICATIONS

Bealle, Morris A. *The Redskins, 1937–1958: A Complete and Colorful History of America's Most Colorful Sports Aggregation—the Washington Redskins.* Washington, D.C.: Columbia, 1959.

Boswell, Tom, et al. *Redskins: A History of Washington's Team.* Washington, D.C.: Washington Post Books, n.d.

Canning, Whit. *Sam Baugh: Best There Ever Was.* Indianapolis: Masters Press, 1997.

Cashion, Ty. *Pigskin Pulpit: A Social History of Texas High School Football Coaches.* Austin: Texas State Historical Association, 1998.

Cohane, Tim. "The Saturday Fox." In *Great College Coaches of the Twenties and Thirties.* New York: Arlington House, 1973.

Cope, Myron. "A Life for Two Tough Texans." *Sports Illustrated,* Oct. 20, 1969.

Dent, Jim. *Monster of the Midway: Bronko Nagurski, the 1943 Chicago Bears, and the Greatest Comeback Ever.* New York: St. Martin's, 2003.

Griffith, Corinne. *My Life with the Redskins.* New York: Barnes, 1947.

Haggerty, James J. *"Hail to the Redskins": The Story of the Washington Redskins.* Washington, D.C.: Seven Seas, 1974.

Heidenry, John. *The Gashouse Gang: How Dizzy Dean, Leo Durocher, Branch Rickey, Pepper Martin, and Their Colorful, Come-from-Behind Ball Club Won the World Series—and America's Heart—during the Great Depression.* New York: PublicAffairs, 2007.

Holst, Don. *Famous Football Players in Their Fourth Quarter.* Chadron, Nebraska: Don Holst Art and Books, 2008.

Jackson, Rob. "Wicarhpi Isnala 'Lone Star.'" *Coffin Corner* 26, no. 1 (2004).

Jenkins, Dan. *Texas Christian University Football Vault: The History of the Horned Frogs.* Atlanta: Whitman, 2008.

Kelton, Elmer. *The Time It Never Rained.* New York: Doubleday, 1973; reprint, Fort Worth: Texas Christian Univ. Press, 1984.

Loverro, Joe. *Hail Victory: An Oral History of the Washington Redskins.* Hoboken, N.J.: Wiley, 2006.

Luksa, Frank. "Slingin' Sammy Last Link to Long-Ago Pro Football Era." ESPN.com, Dec. 18, 2008. http://sports.espn.go.com/nfl/columns/story?columnist=luksa _frank&id=3776948.

Maynard, Don, and Matthew Shepatin. *You Can't Catch Sunshine.* Chicago: Triumph Books, 2010.

Moore, Jerome Aaron. *TCU: A Hundred Years of History.* Fort Worth: Texas Christian Univ. Press, 1974.

Morrow, Merlin. *Hardin-Simmons Athletics: The First Century.* Abilene, Tex.: Hardin-Simmons Univ., 1997.

Neft, David S., Richard M. Cohen, and Rick Korch. *The Football Encyclopedia: The Complete History of Professional Football from 1892 to the Present.* New York: St. Martin's, 1994.

National Football League Creative Staff. *The First Fifty Years: A Celebration of the National Football League in Its Fiftieth Season.* New York: Ridge Press/Benjamin Company, 1969.

Poole, Gary Andrew. *The Galloping Ghost: Red Grange, an American Football Legend.* New York: Houghton Mifflin, 2008.

Povich, Shirley. *All Those Mornings . . . at the "Post": The Twentieth Century in Sports from Famed "Washington Post" Columnist Shirley Povich.* Edited by Lynn Povich, Maury Povich, David Povich, and George Solomon. New York: PublicAffairs, 2005.

Qureshi, Samu, and Valerie Chissom. "The Secret Letters of the Washington Redskins." *Washington Post Magazine,* Aug. 2, 2009.

Reid, Jan. "Legends of the Fall." *Texas Monthly,* Nov. 1997.

Richman, Michael. "Cliff Battles." *Coffin Corner* 26, no. 2 (2004).

———. *The Redskins Encyclopedia.* Philadelphia: Temple Univ. Press, 2007.

Riffenburgh, Beau. *The Official NFL Encyclopedia.* New York: New American Library, 1986.

Rives, Bill. "Slingin' Sam vs. Father Time." *Sport,* Sept. 1948.

Siegel, Morris. "The Fix Is In; Past Post Gambling." *Regardie's Magazine,* June 1991.

Stratton, W. K. *Chasing the Rodeo: On Wild Rides and Big Dreams, Broken Hearts and Broken Bones, and One Man's Search for the West.* New York: Harcourt, 2005.

Sullivan, George. *Pro Football's All-Time Greats: The Immortals in Pro Football's Hall of Fame.* New York: Putnam, 1968.

Tips, Kern. *Football—Texas Style: An Illustrated History of the Southwest Conference.* New York: Doubleday, 1964.

Tuttle, Dennis. "Better Than Sonny?" *Washingtonian,* Jan. 1995.

WashingtonPost.com. *The Redskins Book.* http://www.washingtonpost.com/wp-srv /sports/redskins/longterm/book/toc.htm.

Whittingham, Richard. *Hail Redskins: A Celebration of the Greatest Players, Teams, and Coaches*. Chicago: Triumph Books, 2001.

Wills, Garry. *Reagan's America: Innocents at Home*. Garden City, N.Y.: Doubleday, 1987.

Works Progress Administration. *The WPA Guide to Texas*. 1940. Reprint, Austin: Texas Monthly Press, 1986.

INDEX

Bendix, Vincent, 65

Benton, Jim, 220

Bergman, Arthur J. "Dutch," 110, 204, 207, 208–209, 214, 223

Bible, Dana Xenophon, 23

Bierman, Bernie, 49

Big 10, 38

Bland, Admiral W. H. O., 189

Blanda, George, 271

Blozis, Al, 188, 194

bootsie play, 203

Border Conference, 255, 256, 259

Boston, and professional football, 59, 65, 120

Boston Braves, 64, 65–67, 68–79; vs. Brooklyn Dodgers, 66–67; vs. Chicago Bears, 67; vs. New York Giants, 67. See also Boston Redskins

Boston Celtics, 64

Boston Redskins, 60, 71–73; 1936 championship, 78–79; vs. the Brooklyn Dodgers, 73; vs. the Chicago Bears, 72, 73, 125–126; vs. the Green Bay Packers, 78–79; vs. the New York Giants, 72–73, 76–77; vs. the Pittsburgh Pirates, 75, 79. See also Boston Braves; Washington Redskins

Boston Yankees, 214, 217, 233

Boswell, Tom, 3, 283

Boyd, Sam, 157

Brazee, Owen, 183, 252, 253, 274

Brazee, Viola, 183

Breeskin, Barnet "Barnee," 112, 113

Brizzolara, Ralph, 211–212

Broder, David, 6

Brooklyn Dodgers, 97, 164, 187; vs. Boston Braves, 66–67; vs. Boston Redskins, 73; vs. Washington Redskins, 118–119, 161–162, 204

Brooklyn Tigers, 214

Bryant, Paul "Bear," 119

Buchanan, Pat, 283

Buffalo All-Americans, 66

Buffalo Bills, 267

Buffet, Warren E., 9

Buivid, Ray "Buzz," 88, 97

Buksar, George, 247

Campbell, Webster, 69

Canning, Whit, 1, 54, 87, 182, 183, 227, 253, 263, 269

Cannon, Billy, 258, 259

Carlisle Indian School, 71

Carr, Joe, 62, 63, 64–65, 78, 106, 148

Carter, Amon G., 35, 49, 54–55, 86, 91, 93, 94, 108

Cartwright, Gary, 39–40

Casey, Eddie, 73–74

Castiglia, Jim, 225

Centenary College Gents, vs. TCU, 84

Chandler, A. B. "Happy," 197

Chevigny, Jack, 38–39, 44, 83, 84

Chicago Bears, 5, 65, 96, 162–163; all-stars game (1936), 103; NFL championships, xv–xvii, 129–135, 164–165, 167–172, 196–200, 210–212; and T formation, 215; vs. Boston Braves, 67; vs. Boston Redskins, 72, 75, 125–126; vs. Chicago Cardinals, 128, 197; vs. New York Giants, 63–64, 126–127; vs. Washington Redskins, 129–135, 139, 153–154, 163–164, 196–200, 210–212, 226; Western Division title, 164

Chicago Bruins, 64

Chicago Cardinals, 67, 97, 104; vs. Chicago Bears, 128, 197; vs. Washington Redskins, 118, 217, 225–226, 239–240, 244

Chicago Cubs, 67

Chicago Staleys. See Chicago Bears

Chicago Tribune, 103, 128, 170, 283

Cifer, Ed, 187

Cincinnati Bengals, 5

Cisco Big Dam Lobos, 15–16

Clark, Addison, 25

Clark, Algy, 67

Clark, Earl "Dutch," 135

Clark, Harry, 168–169

Cleveland Browns, 237, 268; vs. Washington Redskins, 241, 243

Cleveland Indians, 27, 64

Cleveland Rams, 119, 218, 219

Cochrane, Ed, 134

Coleman, Joe, 40, 42

College Football Hall of Fame, 281

Columbus Panhandlers, 62

Russell, Bo, 159
Russell, Lloyd, 82–83
Ruth, Babe, 3, 63, 64, 112, 120, 140
Rymkus, Lou, 223

Sabol, Steve, 284
Saenz, Joe, 226
San Antonio, Texas, and Texas Centennial
celebration, 90
Sandifer, Dan, 232
Sanford, Curtis, 87
Sanford, Sandy, 168
San Francisco 49ers, 237
Sansing, Billy, 48
Santa Fe Railroad, 13, 17
Scarborough, Dorothy, 18
Schmidt, Francis, 22, 24, 28–29, 85
Seago, Ernie "Son," 56
Sebo, Steve, 268
Seymour, Bob, 205, 221
Shakespeare, Bill "The Bard," 132
Shaughnessy, Clark, 166–167, 215
Sheridan, Ney "Red," 20, 22, 136
Sherman, Saul "Sollie," 169, 170
Shipp, Alex, 181
Shivers, Robert L., 189
Short, Hassard, 93–94
Shuford, Hary, 44, 50
Shugart, Clyde, 172, 191, 206
Shugart, Erny, 174
Siegel, Morris, 261
Simmons, C. R., 213
Sims, Mose, 10, 21–22
single-wing formation, 111, 166–167, 215
Sinkwich, Frank, 200, 204
Sinkwich, Sam, 200
Smartt, Joe, 39
Smith, Bruce, 193, 193
Smith, Edmonia. See Baugh, Edmonia
"Mona"
Smith, J. D. "Uncle Jimmy," 181
Smith, Riley, xvii, 74, 77, 111, 116, 117, 118,
119, 130, 132, 136, 211
Snyder, Bob, 163
Snyder, Daniel, 283
Southern Methodist University (SMU), 5,

44; Rose Bowl, 51, 53; vs. TCU, 43, 47–53,
84–86; vs. UCLA, 45
Southwest Conference, 23, 26, 31, 35, 38–40,
44, 46, 48, 51, 54, 254–255, 256; and Cot-
ton Bowl, 87; 1936 championship, 84, 86
Spokane Athletic Round Table, 187
Sport, 216
Sports Illustrated, x–xi, 107, 170
sportswriters, 3–4, 7–8, 53–54. See also
specific writers
Stagg, Amos Alonso, 30, 65
Stamford Rodeo, 274, 276
Stanky, Eddie, 146
Stanley, John, 175
State Fair of Texas, 91
Statue of Liberty play, 210–212
Steagles, 153, 204; and gambling scandal,
206–207
Steen, Frank, 38
Stern, Bill, 49
Stevenson, Ellen, 2, 253
St. Louis Browns, 101
St. Louis Cardinals, 101–103, 106–107,
138–143
St. Louis Gunners, 73
Storck, Carl, 159–160
Stout, Pete, 239–240
Strong, Ken, 67, 194
Stuhldreher, Harry, 270
Stydahar, Joe, 129, 154, 163
Sufferidge, Bo, 190–191
Sugar Bowl, 54, 55–58
Super Bowl, xvi. See also NFL champion-
ship games
Sutherland, Jock, 162
Sweetwater, Texas, 18, 19–21

Tackitt, A. C., 181
Tamm, Edward A., 189
Taylor, Charley, 7
Taylor, Hugh "Bones," 226, 227, 246, 249,
271, 279
Temple High School Wildcats, 16–18
Tereshinski, Joe, 1, 223, 225, 226, 231, 249
Texas A&M, vs. TCU, 41, 82
Texas Centennial, 87; celebration, 48,

Division championship games, 122–123,
158–160, 195, 218; exhibition games,
151–154, 241–242; fans, 7–8, 119–120,
120–122; gambling scandal, 205–208;
NFL championships, xv–xvii, 129–135,
164–165, 167–172, 196–200, 207–209,
210–212, 219–221; NFL draft 1936,
96–97; salaries, 111–112, 152–153, 223;
single-wing formation, 215; song, 112–
113, 155–156; T formation, 215–216; vs.
the Baltimore Colts, 238; vs. Brooklyn
Dodgers, 118–119, 161–162, 204; vs.
Chicago Bears, xv–xvii, 129–135, 139,
154, 163–164, 196–200, 210–212; vs.
Chicago Cardinals, 118, 217, 225, 239–
240, 244; vs. Cleveland Browns, 241,
243; vs. Detroit Lions, 151, 204, 242–
243; vs. Green Bay Packers, 119–120, 158;
vs. New York Giants, 113–117, 122–123,
155–156, 157, 158–160, 196, 205, 207–
209, 217, 243; vs. Philadelphia Eagles,
118, 150–151, 157, 187, 188–191, 217, 218,
231–232, 248; vs. Pittsburgh Steelers,
118, 119, 157, 187, 195–196, 217, 241; vs.
Richmond Arrows, 119; vs. Steagles, 204.
See also Baugh, Sam, and Washington
Redskins; Boston Redskins
Washington Redskins Band, 121, 123–124,
156, 158, 167, 220
"Washington Redskins March, The," 112.
See also "Hail to the Redskins"
Washington Senators, 6, 79, 114
Washington State University, 21, 66, 71
Washington Times-Herald, and gambling
scandal, 205–208
Waterfield, Bob, 220, 221
Watwood, Lynn "Buddy," 188, 189, 200, 209
WBAP, 55
Weller, Louis "Rabbit," 72

Werblin, David A. "Sony," 268
West, Sammy, 100
Western Division, 70, 78, 164
Western Texas College, 1–2
West Virginia Wesleyan, 66
Wetzel, J. C. "Iron Man," 47–48
Whelchel, John, 223
White, Byron "Whizzer," 150, 154–155
White, George, 52
White, LeRoy, 152
Whittingham, Richard, 148
Widseth, Ed, 97, 116
Wilbon, Michael, 284
Wilkin, Wilbur Byrne "Wee Willie," 149,
151, 158, 163, 184–186, 197, 204, 206, 223
Williams, Joe, 49
Williams, Ted, 144, 194, 200, 283
Wilson, Bobby, 44, 45–46, 47, 49, 50, 51
Wilson, George, 132, 212
Wind, The (Scarborough), 18
Wisner, Harry, 260–262, 266–267, 268–
269; and Baugh, 262–263, 267–268; and
Marshall, 261–262
Witney, Billy, 176
Wolf, Bear, 55, 57
Wolf, Ray, 139
Woodruff, Bob, 237
Woodward, Stanley, 123
World Series: 1932, 66–67; 1933, 197
World War II, 153, 193–194, 202–204, 217.
See also Japan; Pearl Harbor, attack on
Wray, Ludlow, 66, 67, 71
Wright, L. C. "Pete," 98

Youell, Jimmy, 227
Young, Bill, 150–151, 166
Young, Dick, 265, 267

Zimmerman, Roy, 153, 168, 227